N\S

SEX DIFFERENCES IN BRITAIN

2ND EDITION

Sex Differences in Britain

2nd Edition

Edited by
Ivan Reid
and
Erica Stratta

Gower

Published by
Gower Publishing Company Limited
Gower House
Croft Road
Aldershot
Hants GU11 3HR
England

Gower Publishing Company
Old Post Road
Brookfield
Vermont 05036
USA

BRITISH LIBRARY CATALOGUING-IN-PUBLICATION DATA
Sex differences in Britain – 2nd ed.
    1. Great Britain. Sex roles
    I. Reid, Ivan II. Stratta, Erica.
    305.3'0941

ISBN 0 566 05595 3
       0 566 05804 9 (pbk)

Typeset by C. R. Barber & Partners (Highlands) Limited,
Fort William, Scotland
Printed and bound in Great Britain by
Biddles Limited, Guildford and King's Lynn

Contents

Acknowledgements

Erica Stratta is grateful to colleagues whose support and cooperation have made this book possible; to Leslie her husband for his advice on language and style; and to Ruth Powell, whose cooperation and secretarial skills have been essential to the production of this book.

Ivan Reid is grateful to all those who helped him, directly or indirectly in the compilation and writing of this book, and especially to: Pat, Diane and Helen for their continued and unsurpassed, familial support; Sylvia Vallance for her invaluable secretarial services; and to those colleagues, students and friends, past and present, who have provided insights into sex and gender differences and helped to sustain an environment conducive to writing.

Ivan Reid and Erica Stratta are grateful to Eileen Wormald – joint editor with Ivan Reid of *Sex Differences in Britain* (1982) – for her encouragement to us to undertake this book and for the use of some of her contributions to the original in it.

The editors, contributors and publisher are grateful to the following for permission to use data and material presented in this book: Associated Book Publishers [UK] Ltd, London for data from J. Hills 'Britain' in J. Lovenduski and J. Hills *The Politics of the Second Electorate: Women and Public Participation* (1981) and from R. Mawby 'Sex and Crime; The results of a self-reported study' in *British Journal of Sociology*, 31 (1980); Athlone Press, London, for data from E. Vallance, *Women in the House* (1979); Basil Blackwell, Oxford for data from C. Greenhalgh, 'Male/Female Wage Differentials in Great Britain' *Economic Journal*, 90 (1980); Cambridge University Press, Cambridge, for data from A. Zabalza and Z. Tzannatos *Women and Equal Pay: The Effects of Legislation on Female Employment and Wages* (1985); City of Bradford, Social Services Department, for data from *The Disabled* (1983); Commission for Racial Equality for data from M. Le Lohe 'Sex Discrimination and Under-representation of Women in Politics' in *New Community*, V.; Conservative Women's National Advisory Council for data from *Women in Politics* (1985); Croom Helm Ltd, London, for data from M. Currell, *Political Women* (1974) and M. Elston, 'Medicine: Half our Future Doctors?' in R. Silverstone and A. Ward *Careers of Professional Women* (1980); the

Managing Director of Dods, for data from *Dod's Parliamentary Companion* (annually); the Equal Opportunities Commission for data from P. Elias, 'The Changing Pattern of Employment and Earnings Among Married Couples 1968–84, in *EOC Annual Report 1980, EOC Research Bulletin 8, The Experience of Caring for Elderly and Handicapped Dependants* (1980), *Sex Discrimination in the Recruitment Process* (1987), *Women and Work: A Review*, (1975); the Fabian Society for data from C. Cockburn, *Women, Trade Unions and Political Parties* (1987); the Family Policy Studies Centre, London, for data from *One Parent Families Factsheet* (1987); the Hansard Society for data from R. Stradling, *The Political Awareness of the School Leaver* (1978); the Controller of Publishing, Her Majesty's Stationery Office, London, and the Office of Population Censuses and Surveys, for Crown Copyright material from *Annual Abstract of Statistics*, no. 122, no. 123, *British Labour Statistics Historical Abstract 1886–1968* (1971), *Civil Service Statistics* (1980), *Committee of Inquiry into the System of Remuneration of Members of Local Authorities* (1977) *Criminal Statistics for England and Wales* (1985), *Education Statistics for the United Kingdom* (1982 and 1987 editions) *Employment Gazette* 80[12], 83[12], 87[12] 88[12], 89[12], 95[1][11][12], 96[12], *English Life Tables* no. 14 (1987) *General Household Survey* (1978, 1979, 1980, 1982, 1983, 1984), C. Hakim, *Occupational Segregation* (1979), J. Haskey, 'One-Parent Families in Britain', *Population Trends*, 45; Joint Review Group on Employment, *Opportunities for Women in the Civil Service* (1983), *Health and Personal Social Services Statistics for England* (1986), *Low Income Families* (1983), *Marriage and Divorce Statistics 1985, Morbidity Statistics from General Practice 1981–1982, Mortality Statistics, 1984, 1985. New Earnings Survey 1986, 1987, OPCS Monitor GHS 86/1, Prison Statistics 1985, Public Bodies* (1986), *Social Security Statistics 1986, Social Trends* no. 5, no. 16, *Statistics of Education 1986, Report on the Work of the Prison Department* (1985), *Royal Commission on the Distribution of Income and Wealth* (1978, 1980) and J. E. Todd and L. N. Jones, *Matrimonial Property* (1972); Macmillan Ltd, London, for data from S. Jones, *Policewomen and Equality* (1986) and C. Cockburn *Two-Track Training: Sex Inequalities and the YTS* (1987); the National Union of Public Employees for data from *Equal Pay for Equal Value* (1986); the *New Statesman*, for data from A. Coote and P. Kellner, *Hear this Brother: Women Workers and Union Power* (1980) and *New Statesman*, 7th November 1980; Oxford University Press, London, for data from J. G. Francis and G. Peele, 'Reflections on Generational Analysis: Is There a Shared Political Perspective

Between Men and Women?'. *Political Studies* 26 (1978); Parliamentary Research Services, Chichester for data from F. W. S. Craig, *Britain Votes 3* (1984); Pergamon Press, London, for data from A. Heath, R. Jowell and J. Curtice, *How Britain Votes* (1985); the Public Information Office, Westminster, for data from *Factsheet No. 22* (1984) and for supplying data; Trentham Books, Stoke on Trent for data from J. Harding, 'CDT what's missing', *Studies in Design Education, Craft and Technology, 15* (1982); Universities Statistical Records, for data from *University Statistics Vol. 1 Students and Staff* (1981–82 and 1984–85) University of Dundee Election Studies, for data from T. G. Karran and H. M. Bochel, *The English County Elections, 1985* (1986); Unwin Hyman Ltd, London for data from H. Land, *Large Families in London* (1969).

1 Sex and gender differences and this book

Ivan Reid and Erica Stratta

This book presents a view of sex and gender differences in contemporary Britain using empirical evidence and data. It seeks to inform current discussion, debate and political activity concerning the differences and relationships between women and men in our society, in a particular way. Its approach raises a number of issues, mainly concerning definition, scope and limitation. This introductory chapter serves to inform readers of the parameters within which the book was written.

Sex and gender

Sex, it would appear, has always been an emotive and difficult concept. Consequently, writing about it has never been a straightforward affair. While taboos, laws and social constraints which have in the past excluded it from serious public consideration may have been swept away, we are left with controversy over the definition and implications of the term.

For some, the word sex is merely and only about physiology, the two sexes having different genitals related to separate functions in reproduction. Further physical differences might be added, such as number of ribs, body hair, height, weight and proportion of fat. All other differences between the sexes are not seen as being intrinsic to sex, but as the products of society and its way of life. In other words, they are determined, or affected, by a society's culture. The term gender is often used to refer to all differences between women and men other than the physical. Gender is therefore a valuable concept to the extent that it directs attention to the almost total role of culture in the formation, maintenance and change of what can be viewed as the separate identities, life-chances and life-styles of women and men.

The people who wrote this book are all social scientists. For them the social production of female and male gender, and of the social differences between the sexes, are obvious and transparent. They conceal no belief in the straightforward biological determinism of the aspects of social life reviewed in this volume.

Indeed, they suspect that most readers, at least on reflection, will share such views. There is certainly plenty of evidence which shows the vast variety of ways in which the social roles of women and men and the relationships and differences between them can, and do, exist in different societies and at different times. Historical and anthropological evidence very clearly indicates the ascendency of culture over biology in these fields. Sceptics will find Oakley (1972) a good general introduction, while Davidoff (1973) examines historical evidence, and Friedl (1975), La Fontaine (1978) and Reiter (1975) that from anthropology.

However, there are some fallacies in the exclusive use of sex to refer to only physical, and gender to refer to only social characteristics of female and male. In real life both aspects always coexist, so sex is never simply a difference of genitals or reproductive function but is inevitably and firmly set within a specific cultural setting. Sex, like all other human attributes, including intelligence, becomes meaningful and observable only when overtly expressed, at which point the attribute is so interrelated with culture that it is, for all intents and purposes, inseparable. At the same time, even in the physical sense, the sexes are not easily separable into two discrete entities. Both sexes have female and male chromosomes in their genetic make-up and produce both types of sex hormone. Indeed, in relatively rare cases even genital differentiation is far from clear.

Hence, our understanding, and even our recognition, of female and male comes from our culture – what we have learned as a member of society. In other words, we use what amount to generalized stereotypes, which involve inaccuracies and unwarranted assumptions. In reality, all the supposed characteristics of each sex exist in both females and males, although their display and recognition are differently encouraged or discouraged. A whole series of social forces, ranging from the law, through custom and norms, institutions and the media, to humour, affect the situation. So we can all recognize in ourselves and in others, for example, that ways of behaving, thinking and feeling are very complex and not simply divisible into two discrete categories of the sexes. At the same time we are aware of how society shapes and affects not only these, but a whole range of aspects of social life along sex lines.

Because of these considerations, the writers of this book have used both the terms sex and gender to refer to women and men as they are manifested in the culture of our present-day society. In this respect the tables presented, which compare women and men on a whole host of social variables, use sex as their major dimension, while the exposed differences are those of gender.

Sex and gender differences

That differences between women and men exist in our and all other societies is an obvious and incontrovertible fact of life. For some people this fact is sufficient for them to believe that sex and gender differences are naturally ordained and/or essential to the existence of society and the well-being of individuals. Others find them to be completely unjustified and a constant source of annoyance, concern or even dismay. The range of opinions is extremely wide, and opinions are not always mutually exclusive or used consistently. At one extreme such differences are seen as the simple and continual exploitation of women by men, while at the other they are regarded as an entirely justified and reasonable division of rights and duties that allows each sex to enjoy life to the full. Between these extremes are those views which see sex and gender differences as necessary for society to work, it being assumed they are essential to the maintenance of basic institutions, especially the family and the occupational and economic structure. The shades of opinion and variations of view which surround these positions are too numerous to recount here.

The easy recognition of sex and gender differences and the controversy surrounding their existence and persistence have much in common with other forms of social differentiation in our society. The most obvious of these are the other forms of social stratification – social class, ethnic and age groups – although regional differences can be of similar order. Some people react to social differentiation in terms of indifference or even delight, in that they see them as adding to the rich variety of life. Certainly, such differences do not in themselves necessarily present society, or its members, with a problem. All such differences might well be disregarded, or even enjoyed, if it were not for a consideration of the ideas of equality, justice and equality of opportunity – which are in themselves problematic. Perhaps few people would see the ideal world as one in which everybody was identical, while, hopefully, nearly all would reject one in which groups were denied their basic rights and the means to exist. Most are probably concerned about the fact that some groups in our society can be shown to be materially deprived through no fault of their own and others disadvantaged in terms of length of life, health and access to, and quality of, services like health and education, which are supposedly provided freely and fully for all on the basis of need.

The latter concerns have fuelled and continue to fuel much political debate and some action. However, it appears that typically efforts towards ending inequality have not so much been concerned with achieving equality in itself, but rather with changing the criteria for inequality. While those concerned with equality of opportunity have not sought access to similarity but rather the expansion of opportunity to be different. Historically, action in the direction of equality and equal opportunities has to be seen as piecemeal and incomplete. For example, equality in voting was achieved without disturbing the role of the House of Lords or male dominance at all levels of politics (see Chapter 7). The expansion of educational opportunity took place alongside the continued existence of public schools and private education together with the relationship between social class and educational achievement (see Reid, 1986 and 1989) and sustained gender differences (see Chapter 5). The National Health Service has little affected the relationship between social class and health (see Reid, 1981, 1989; Townsend and Davidson, 1982), while gender differences remain (see Chapter 3) and private medicine flourishes. Likewise, sexual equality in pay, achieved through legislation, has not taken us very far towards equality of earnings (see Chapter 6).

In each form of social differentiation there appears a clear tendency to highlight the trivial at the expense of the fundamental and to indulge in rhetoric rather than review the evidence. In the case of social class, for example, great play is made of such aspects as snobbery, political views, interests and opinions, with far less, if any, attention being paid to the underlying economic inequalities affecting life chances. A further deflection from serious consideration is the constant claim that things have changed and got better – that we no longer live in a class society, since the classes have merged or become very similar; that equality between the sexes has gone as far as necessary, or has almost been achieved. An added gloss to this sort of argument is that those who appear to be disadvantaged, be they the working class or women, either actually enjoy their situation or do not want any change, and would not welcome it or know what to do with it. Such views may sound to readers to be those of the advantaged in the situations – that is, the middle class or men, since they represent those parties' interests in the maintenance of the status quo, or its minimal change.

However, it needs to be remembered that ideas and values do not necessarily have discrete boundaries and that the disadvantaged may also hold such views. Shared, general views of social reality, apparently supporting a particular group's interests, are common, particularly in social situations where one party has control or influence over information, knowledge and ideas, or where power in its general sense is unequal between the parties. This is certainly true in respect to social class and sex, where such views continue to be supported by those who have nothing to gain and, indeed, may be losing, from their continued acceptance.

The importance of entrenched values, beliefs or ideologies is almost impossible to overestimate to the extent that they are not necessarily affected or changed through experience or exposure to facts. Hopes that people would realize the injustice or unfairness of social situations merely by being told 'the facts' have often been dashed because of resistance to their acceptance caused mainly by participants' 'understandings', based on deeply-rooted cultural assumptions. Despite these cautions, it is necessary and valuable that society should have as many facts as possible readily available, to facilitate informed discussion and to provide a basis for social policy. One of the prime motivations in writing this book was the realization that amid the very considerable discussion about the differences between the women and men in our society, there was a general lack of factual evidence informing those debates, probably owing to the lack of readily accessible sources of data and evidence.

So far we have seen that sex and gender have some similarity to other forms of social stratification. At the same time it is necessary to recognize the unusual, if not unique, features of sex and gender as social categories. Unlike other forms of social stratification, there are no real problems of definition, sex being a simple, straightforward dichotomy of society. Similarly, the two sex categories are obviously all-inclusive, involving the entire society. This straightforwardness and universality makes sex unlike social class or ethnicity, whose operationalization is, in comparison, both problematic and controversial, as well as varied.

Of much greater importance is the way in which the forms of social stratification in our society are interrelated. Clearly there are inherent limitations in using a single form of stratification as if it were in isolation. For example, overall social class patterns of behaviour, unless limited to one sex, are often an amalgam of somewhat different sex patterns within the classes (for empirical examples of this, see Reid, 1989). Differences between middle-class white women and men are demonstrably different from those differences among the black working class. Moreover, our example ignores the further differences which exist between the ethnic groups and the regions in our society.

Edwards and Roberts (1980) have clearly illustrated a sex and class educational 'pecking order' of achievement and opportunity. In terms of entry to higher education it reads, in descending order: middle-class boys–middle-class girls–working-class boys–working-class girls. Of course, such interrelationships do not detract from, or deny, the very real differences between the social classes and the sexes, in themselves. Neither, typically, does the available evidence include more than one or two of the possible variables contributing to the differences. The issue is raised here to alert readers to aspects of the complexity of the subject reviewed – a complexity fully recognized by the writers of this book. That gender stratification typically embraces aspects of social class and ethnicity is well illustrated in Chapters 2 and 6.

Just as substantive an issue is how the evidence of differences has been collected, interpreted and represented. Since we live in a society which is clearly stratified, we must expect that the identification of problems and the conduct of research into them, let alone attempts to resolve them, will display at least elements of sexist, classist, racist or other forms of cultural assumptions and imperialism. Some areas of sex differences have a long history of recording and investigation, while others have little or none. In some cases both the classification of information and indeed the very questions asked can be seen to contain sexual or sexist assumptions – predictably, male. These issues are discussed below and specific examples are illustrated in the chapters that follow (see Index).

In the last three decades there has been a developing interest in, and concern about, inequalities based on sex and gender and the apparent disadvantages of women in our society. Although it is impossible to judge with any precision the actual improvement of women's position in society, especially in comparison with that of men, the awareness and attendant political action has certainly caused some change. While it is often argued that social legislation usually follows social change, the continued controversy, and indeed tribunal cases, resulting from the Sex Discrimination Act, and equal pay legislation, together with the continued need for the work of the Equal Opportunities Commission (EOC), suggests that in this event legislation was to the forefront. The women's and feminist movements have vigorously championed the cause of female equality and rights and have received considerable, though varied, coverage by the media. Change has taken and is taking place, however limited the achievements to date may be seen by their exponents. There are, too, indications of the acceptance of the need to provide more equal opportunities for women, for example, in educational initiatives which positively encourage girls to become scientists and engineers.

Again, there are some parallels with social class, particularly with respect to the trade union movement – though the legislation in respect of the working class was never as broad or comprehensive as that for women. No real equivalent to the EOC has ever been formally set up. It is also probably true that public opposition to the working-class cause was more vociferous and protracted, though it is too early to make proper comparison or assess outcomes.

A further aspect of the context in which this book was written is the considerable and rapidly growing literature on the subject of gender, and the rights, opportunities and equality of women. Much of this has been written by women, in an attempt to raise women's, as well as society's, awareness of the area. Much of this writing is understandably and appropriately polemic, and for this as well as other reasons it is difficult to judge the extent of its readership and its effect on opinion and social life.

The purpose of this brief resumé of some aspects of sex and gender differences in our society is simply to provide something of an overview of the context within which this book was written. Some of the issues raised in it are not directly addressed in the rest of the book, which was written within a specific, confined structure and with a defined aim. It is to an explanation of these that we now turn.

About this book

Our basic aim in writing this book was to present a view of sex and gender differences in contemporary Britain based on available, empirical evidence and data. As in the case of our earlier book (Reid and Wormald, 1982) the lack of a readily available source of such information was our major motivation. Most other sources continue to lack general availability, or to have limitations – being fragmentary, dated, concerned with or including other societies, or written from a specific or biased point of view. We continue to be convinced of the need of a factual base to inform discussion, debate and political activity about the differences and relationships between women and men in our society and to contribute to what has been a neglected topic in academic courses on the social structure of modern Britain. Our approach is within a long tradition in British social science – namely social arithmetic – the strengths and weaknesses of which have been identified by Halsey (1972) and are outlined in respect to our subject in what follows.

We hope that in our presentation of evidence and data we have achieved a relative degree of objectivity. As a group we do not share any particular political, ideological or philosophical point of view. However, we and our readers will recognize our interest in, and involvement with, our subject. Inevitably, the choice of the substantive areas covered by the chapters of this book reflect the interests and expertise of its contributors. At the same time the areas dealt with – health, education, welfare, employment, politics and crime – are also fundamental to current debates on gender relations and likely indicators of social change. The contributors' own political and ideological predilections have, undoubtedly, resulted in some of the differences of emphasis and content which exist between the chapters. Hopefully our presentation will make it easy for readers to review and develop their own views in relation to the material and ideas that are discussed.

In no way should our approach be seen as a subscription to the fallacy that facts speak for themselves. Not only do we all need to be aware that facts are socially produced, but also that, for most people, their own beliefs, feelings and ways of understanding are of equal or overriding importance to such facts. It is valuable and necessary therefore to appreciate the variety of ways in which the contents of this book may be interpreted – and a start can be made with the range of views and opinions outlined in the previous section, and elsewhere in this chapter and book.

In the same way, it has to be fully understood that all evidence and data have limitations, and must therefore be viewed with these in mind. In the present case limitations arise from several sources which need identification.

First, in looking at differences, just these are emphasized, and similarities are overlooked or underemphasized. Sex and gender differences are rarely, if at all, total, since while the majority of women may differ from men in a certain respect, some women and men may well be alike. In turn this raises the question of within, rather than between, sex or gender differences – why are some women different from other women? In some instances, the first type of difference may be of the same order and interest as the second. It is useful, then, to review the data in this book along such lines, though the explanation of similarity between, and differences within, the sexes and genders is not treated in any detail. It may well be that that explanation of these may be even more complex than that in respect to differences between them.

Second, limitations arise because most of the data we present were collected for purposes other than exhibiting or exploring sex and gender differences. The implications of using available, mainly 'official' data are that some interesting areas are left unexplored and criticisms can easily be raised about the data's collection, classification and presentation. The EOC have considered the latter in depth (EOC, 1980) and commented: 'the assumptions underlying the statistical portrayal of women [as contained in official publications] are, at points, so divorced from reality as to be dangerously misleading'.

Third, and perhaps most serious, is that the data are theoretically inadequate. As Halsey (1972) argues in another context:

> A recurring problem is one which arises particularly in interpreting data relevant to social policy and the provision of welfare services. This is the difficulty of gaining from the statistics any idea of quality or adequacy. Obviously any analysis of health or welfare services or of housing should include some statement about how far the standard or amount of service supplied meets the need for it. But for the most part the figures are concerned with supply; independent measures of need which would be required to judge adequacy are virtually nonexistent.

Similarly, the data in this book often lack any clear or consistent theoretical basis. Hence they are in need of some conceptual framework of equality and/or justice, to judge and interpret them. At present they do not match Halsey's call for a measure of need in order to make evaluation. Ideally, the answer to theoretically inadequate data is for research to be explicitly related to theory. As yet such research is piecemeal and, in any case, it is by no means apparent that adequate theories for research have yet been developed. Though we are unable to bridge this clear gap, we have included a review of the current state of theorizing about sex and gender in the discipline of sociology (Chapter 2). Further, Chapters 5 and 8 provide a review of theoretical explanations in relation to their topics, and there are also, throughout the book, identified examples in which data fail to illuminate current thinking or reflect outmoded thought. However, as is apparent, particularly from Chapters 2, 5 and 8, there are ongoing debates over many basic theoretical issues and explanations. While the divorce between theory and research remains largely unresolved, it needs to be borne in mind in the examination and interpretation of the data in this book.

This does not mean that this book and our approach are atheoretical other than in the formal sense. We see sex and gender as cultural products within a societal and historical setting. Consequently, differences between them are clearly related to societal organization and capable of almost infinite form and change. Basically then the position of women in our society is constrained by, or the result of, their assumed role within the family and particularly the labour market. By implication, the different position of men, and consequently differences between them and women, arise from the same factors. Our basic assumption is that differences between women and men are caused and persist because of the differences they have in access to almost all social resources, to power positions and opportunities that, in general, are to the decided disadvantage of women.

Ideally in a book about sex and gender differences the position of both women and men would be dealt with separately, explicitly and fully, though this would be tedious and space-consuming given their obvious interrelationship in society. So while the book is explicitly about such differences, our assumptions, together with the cultural setting in which we write, led us to lay a sharp emphasis on women's penetration into the social structure of Britain. Our emphasis is particularly apparent, for example, in Chapter 7, which analyses female participation in politics – until comparatively recently an all-male preserve. But it is also clearly discernible throughout the book and informs the conclusions in the final chapter. We have underlined our focus by reversing the traditional mode of presenting data (male followed by female), so that women precede men in all our tables. At the same time, the presentation of data for both sexes allows readers an opportunity to view from 'the other side' and to evaluate and possibly reconstruct the portrayal of differences between women and men presented.

Even within the parameters outlined above, this book is not a fully comprehensive view of sex and gender differences in our society. Apart from those areas for which there are no suitable data, others have been intentionally excluded. Because of the customary assumptions about women's role being primarily within the family, and differences between women and men being mainly the result of differing childhood socialization, there is no direct treatment of either by chapter. Rather, relevant aspects of both appear in considerations of perhaps less familiar and more important topics (see Chapters 2, 4, 6 and 8). In any case, the family and socialization are those best and most fully covered in the existing literature (see, for example, Comer, 1972; Harris, 1979; Bristol Women's Study Group, 1979; Barrett and McIntosh, 1982; Beechy and Whitelegg, 1986). Further, within our chosen topics, comprehensiveness, mainly through the necessity to contain the work within a single volume, has not been sought or achieved. In particular, we have had severely to limit material which seeks to explain the observed differences of sex and gender. Again these have been reviewed within the chapters and references provided to fuller treatments. As a consequence, within the general parameters identified here, each chapter reflects the particular views and priorities of its writer.

It is also necessary to point out that categorizing knowledge in any field is problematic. The following chapters provide cogent accounts of sex and gender differences observed in particular scenarios, and it is therefore possible that an impression of separateness may be deduced. This would be totally false, of course, since differences feed into and out of the different areas and should be viewed as a single phenomenon. It is hoped that readers will appreciate these interrelationships, and that the cross-referencing in the text, the index and last chapter will assist the exploration and understanding of this important point.

The other parameters we adopted are as follows. Our concern was with only contemporary British sex and gender differences, so there is very little use, mention or even reference to material from other countries, or history. While we ourselves are sensitive to the proper meaning of the term Britain, the vagaries of research and publication in our society, together with limitations of space, have forced us in places to follow the 'tradition' of using English, or English and Welsh, data, rather than those for the whole of Britain. The data used are, wherever possible, the most up-to-date and large-scale available. Our selection was made from available sources up to mid-1987. The only unpublished data used are a very few gained from certain public bodies and commercial enterprises to fill some of the gaps in published sources. The criteria of date and scale relate directly to our overall objective for the book – a general view of contemporary Britain – and nearly all data relate to the period between 1977 and 1987.These criteria have not been entirely rigidly regarded. For example, where historical comparison was adjudged vital, brief reference is made. Where there has been significant change in situations reviewed in our earlier book this too has been noted (see Chapter 9), but we have not attempted a comprehensive analysis of change between the compilation of the two works (1981 and 1989). Similarly, where large-scale studies have not existed, or where small-scale ones have made a significant contribution to the aims of the book, small-scale research has been used or referenced. In the same way, where choice has existed, data have been selected for their utility, comprehensiveness or quality and temporal compatibility with other data used, rather than simply for their up-to-dateness.

The data have been presented in straightforward tables to assist use and interpretation. As a general rule, figures and percentages have been rounded to the nearest whole number for the sake of clarity. Similarly, wherever possible and useful, base figures for both women and men (normally sample size) have been included to facilitate comparison.

We have made no mention of statistical significance in respect to the data on sex and gender differences presented. This is because the large size of the samples, or populations, used in the research means that quite small differences are statistically significant. In any case, statistical significance does not tell one much about the importance of an observed difference in real terms. For example, very small numerical differences (which are not statistically significant) are vitally important in elections, while extremely large differences in other areas may be of very limited importance or even interest. The sex and gender differences presented in the chapters which follow vary very considerably in size, and their importance does not stem from that but from interpretation. For example, the difference in the percentage of female and male school-leavers who gained two or more 'A' level GCEs or equivalents in the UK in 1981–82, which was 0.5, is capable of being viewed as insignificant or as an example of female disadvantage in education. Readers will undoubtedly interpret differences according to their own predisposition, values and beliefs. At the same time it is again a valuable exercise to bear in mind the range of interpretations that may be used by others while viewing the data which follows and to review them in that light.

Finally, because of our aim and the limitations on space, we have not attempted a full exposition of the topics dealt with in the following chapters. Our text, with the exception of Chapter 2, is more towards a commentary on the data. We have assumed that readers will have access to other appropriate descriptive and explanatory sources; that they will pursue these by means of the considerable references we have provided; or that their immediate interest centres, like the rest of this book, on the phenomena of the measured differences between women and men in our present-day society.

2 Theorizing gender

Andrew Cooper

The aim of this chapter is to discuss the more theoretical aspects of existing accounts of the social and economic position of women in British society, within the context of the data presented in the subsequent chapters. Specifically, it focuses both on current debates about the character and dynamics of women's position (especially those located within a feminist framework) and on the central theoretical issues raised by the other chapters. Throughout is a continual concern with the general problems of analysing a gendered society; that is, one marked by divisions and disadvantages based on biological sex. Additionally, it seeks to reinforce the view that sexual divisions are profoundly interwoven into the social relations and institutions of society.

It is almost axiomatic in the social sciences that the social position of the two sexes is shaped by the structure of society, and that it is historically contingent being grounded in particular 'conditions of existence'. Pivotal in contemporary sociological accounts is the distinction which can be drawn between sex and gender (see Oakley, 1972, 1981). Sex refers to the physiological and biological differences between women and men in terms of reproductive capacities and are genetically determined. Gender, however, is a social category and can be defined as 'the social construction of sex and sexual divisions to produce, however indirectly, sex-related categorisations and classifications of people' (Hearn, 1987a).

Gender, then, is rooted in social and historical circumstances rather than nature. It can most accurately be described as the social characteristics of being a 'woman' or a 'man' in particular historical circumstances. It draws attention to the way in which the sexes experience society and occupy particular positions. Further, it is clear from the evidence assembled in this book that the social differences between women and men constitute a powerful form of inequality, which is integral to society. How gender differences are produced, reproduced and recomposed has become the most prominent theoretical question for the sociology of gender. So, there is nothing natural, inevitable or universal about the social position of women and men; rather it is created, sustained and reinforced by social processes. Socialization and social control, which would be superfluous if gender roles were biologically induced, map out the pathway to adult gender identity in which appropriate feminine and masculine behaviour for the two sexes is prescribed. The division of labour allocates the performance of unpaid domestic labour to women, and constrains them to do characteristic 'women's work.'

There is now a wealth of empirical evidence, both anthropological and historical, confirming that the social position of the two sexes is not biologically determined but is shaped by social and historical processes. It reveals that the two sexes are typically in a relation of subordination and domination, and that woman are disadvantaged in most societies (Oakley, 1981; Lerner, 1986). This emphasis contrasts radically with theorizations which point to the biological facts of reproduction as the underlying cause of differences – differences which are regarded as genetically in-built and determined by the biologies of the two sexes (Goldberg, 1974; Scruton, 1980, 1986). According to biological determinism, male physical strength and female childbearing generate a division of labour in society in which both sexes perform distinctive sex-roles related to biological function. One variation of this argument suggests that a biologically-anchored division of labour, in which women care for children, for the family and for men, and restrict their lives to the 'private' sphere, is necessary for the harmonious functioning of society (Parsons, 1951). Although these arguments have lost considerable ground within most sociological analysis, it is still important to register the criticisms which can be made of them and the issues which this raises for accounts of gender; a point further underlined by the recent invocations of the New Right which stress the naturalness of gender roles and their relevance to social harmony (see evidence discussed by Kidd; Skeggs and Webb, this volume).

First, biological determinism has difficulty explaining historical variety in the social position of the two sexes. If biological function were determining, then social roles would exhibit tenacious uniformity. While in most societies men have had more power and autonomy than women, male and female relationships nevertheless have no universal content or shape. Indeed, cultures have been discovered in which the division of labour is quite different from that division claimed by determinists to be universal and inevitable (Oakley, 1972). Secondly, biological determinism can provide no adequate theory of the impact of socialization and of dominant beliefs and values about femininity and masculinity on the two sexes.

If social roles and behaviour are rooted inexorably in biology then how could we account for the range of agencies involved in transmitting gender roles? Representations of gender and 'images and messages' about the proper role of women and men pervade the whole cultural sphere in contemporary society (Coward, 1983, 1984). In fact, the involvement of cultural processes in the formation and persistence of gender roles indicates the full extent to which these roles are socially moulded and require affirmation, as opposed to being innate or inevitable.

Does this therefore mean that biology has no influence on social behaviour at all? The cornerstone of the sociology of gender is the explicit rejection of the argument that the social position of the two sexes is natural; it seeks to deconstruct naturalism by showing that the social experience of being a woman or a man, and as a consequence having a specific position in society, is determined by, and takes its meaning and significance from, social circumstances. This does not mean, however, that biological differences merit no consideration; rather it focuses attention on the way each society makes use of biological sex as a basis for socially derived gender differences which are immensely diverse, thus underlining the fact that there is no such thing as a fixed, pre-given biological fact (Rose and Kamin, 1984; Birke, 1986).

Biological determinism has, however, enjoyed something of a revival in the guise of sociobiology (Wilson, 1975; Dawkins, 1978). This aims to provide a biological basis for the understanding of all social behaviour. Its organizing proposition is that there is a female human nature and a male human nature. Thus Weeks (1986), in a discussion of sociobiology says:

> These differences begin and end, it appears, with the evolutionary characteristics of the ova and testes. Because males have an almost infinite number of sperm (millions with each ejaculation), while woman have a very restricted supply of eggs (around 400 per lifetime), it is deduced that men have an evolutionary propulsion towards spreading their seed to ensure diversity and reproductive success, and hence towards promiscuity, while women have an equal interest in reserving energy, an instinct for conservation, and hence a leaning towards monogamy. From this can be deduced the explanation of all the other supposed fundamental differences; the greater competition between men than between women, a greater male tendency towards polygamy and jealousy whereas women are more 'malleable' and amenable, and a greater sexual will and arousal in men than in women.

Weeks' extract shows clear affinities with common sense and popular views about the naturalness of the intractability of sexual divisions in society. But it collides very much with a flourishing literature on the construction of femininity and masculinity (Coward, 1983, 1984; Metcalf and Humphries, 1985; Weeks, 1986; Chapman and Rutherford, 1988). This argues that biological differences can be exaggerated (only one gene out of 100,000 needed to constitute each person distinguishes men from women (Nicholson, 1984)), that they are assigned cultural meaning and subjected to a whole process of moulding. This shapes female and male identities, which as a consequence are flexible, dynamic and vary according to context. Two pertinent examples of how biological attributes are culturally amplified into the construction of social identities in contemporary Britain are the existence of two female identities namely the homemaker, wife-mother role, and the 'over-sexualized' identity encoded in 'Page 3' portrayals in tabloid newspapers. Both identities are constructed and manufactured on the basis of biological differences and transmitted to women (and men) who accept, modify, reject or negotiate them consciously and subconsciously (McRobbie, 1978; Winship, 1978, 1983).

Sociobiology insists on the fixity of human social identity and human sexuality; it is impervious to the findings of much social and historical explanation which show that social behaviour (and sexual behaviour as a component of this) varies enormously. Ultimately, these claims are political constructs as their effect is to justify and legitimate unequal social and economic arrangements on the grounds that they arise from an unalterable 'human nature'. Lack of space prevents discussion of the relationship between sociobiology, the emergence of the New Right, and a more conservative social and moral climate but it is clear that there are obvious affinities between sociobiology and the current political climate. As a reincarnation of biologically determinist arguments, sociobiology continues to be a significant opponent of sociological and feminist accounts of sex and gender.

Theoretical issues in the analysis of gender differences

There continues to be a distinctive gap between 'commonsense' conceptions of the positions of women and sociological theory and research. 'Commonsense' conceptions are deeply contradictory in that women's position is seen as naturally and inevitably inferior to that of men – men as the 'strong sex'; alternatively, it is argued women have a distinct but not subordinate role to men – the 'separate spheres' argument; or women are seen as being in an equal position to men, an equality produced by unbroken historical progress towards full citizenship – the 'march of history' perspective. In effect the data presented in this book take issue with 'common sense', by indicating that women in contemporary Britain experience continuing disadvantage in such areas as the labour market, education, politics and social welfare. This is illustrative of a generalized subordination reflected in and institutionalized throughout society. The evidence points to systematic inequality rather than random or individual incapacity, and to inequality that is socially, not naturally produced. Further, it underlines the existence in Britain of a gender hierarchy dominated by men, in which there are discernible patterns of structured gender-based inequality, which is widely discussed in sociological writing (Delamont, 1981; Oakley, 1981; Beechey and Whitelegg, 1986).

There is broad agreement within the sociology of gender about the nature and the parameters of women's subordination, and general acceptance that it is not a single phenomenon but has a number of different forms. Germane here is the focus on unequal access to employment and economic dependency on men; the limits on personal autonomy and low levels of participation in public politics. Additionally, there is some consensus on the nature of the mechanisms which secure this subordination, for example, on the role of social policy; dominant ideologies; male violence and the organization of domestic labour. It is also worth stressing that there is some scepticism about linking women's subordination to 'original causes' and about over-generalizing about it. Most analysis concentrates on uncovering specific forms of women's subordination in particular contexts, and on identifying the immediate determinants of that subordination rather than on producing grand theory (Smart, 1984). All in all gender differences are seen as defined in historical and social settings, produced by the interconnectedness of a number of factors. To give one example, the prevalence of 'caring' and 'servicing' work for women in the sexual division of labour within the family and in the paid labour market is reflected in a system of education and training in which certain types of work are regarded as 'women's work'. This further reinforces gender divisions within the family where some roles and some work are seen as 'naturally feminine'.

This said, some vital questions remain open to debate in the analysis of gender differences. To what extent do women experience their gender communally and uniformly? Is it qualified at all by social class, and how should women's class position be established? How are gender, class and ethnicity interlinked? Should women's position in society be grasped mainly by reference to beliefs and values, to ideologies which constrain women's lives, or is it anchored in the material conditions of production? What is the interplay between ideology and material conditions? To what extent is the social and economic order reliant upon inequality between women and men in the 'private' sphere? What are the parameters of actual or potential change as between the 'private' and 'public' realms? Is women's position still essentially located in their reproductive function? Is it important to consider the construction of masculinity – men as 'gendered subjects' – alongside that of femininity? And crucially, is the position of women changing markedly under the impact of technological innovation? Given the tendency for 'new technologies' to lead to the greater concentration of social and political power, the question of women's relation to technology becomes acute. Finally, given the success of political forces in Britain, whose stated social policies is to allocate to women specific roles, what is their likely impact on women's position? To what extent is the state implicated in the continued reproduction of gender divisions? All these questions must be seen as the outstanding issues for the sociology of gender in Britain in the 1980s.

Gender differences and feminist sociology: a conceptual revolution?

The emergence of feminist sociology has transformed the understanding of the position of women and men in society. What distinguishes a specifically feminist sociology is the insistence on theorizing gender divisions as revealing male domination and female subordination – the 'oppression of women' – and on the centrality given to gender relations as determining social relations in society and history. As class, for Marx, reveals the 'innermost secrets, the hidden basis of the entire social structure', so for feminist sociologists the focus on gender relations uncovers the nature of all social institutions and the bases of social life. Furthermore, feminist sociology is explicitly 'for women' and not just simply 'about women'. It is tied to a political project; the generation of new knowledge about women's situation as a basis for strategies for change (Smith, 1979). Thus some researchers deploy a specifically feminist methodology – using 'soft' rather than 'hard' data – qualitative, subjective information about women's experiences, feelings and perceptions rather than quantitative, objective 'facts' about structures and processes (Roberts (ed.), 1981; Stanley and Wise, 1983; Dex, 1985; Segal, 1987). Feminist sociology, though, is not homogeneous; it is rather a common vocabulary, a framework of concepts and forms of analysis which has established a body of theory and research findings, within which there are debates and disputes, and different theoretical tendencies (Jaggar, 1983; Fildes, 1987).

The emergence of feminist sociology was rooted in a critique of sociology as a male discipline; a sociology which saw social arrangements which disadvantaged women as natural or necessary, and avoided or neglected women in the analysis of social, economic and political structures. It concentrated on the 'public domain' and derogated the 'private domain' – a decisive site of women's experience (Stacey, 1981). Accordingly, feminist sociology has attempted to redraw the intellectual map of sociology by rescuing women 'hidden from history' and invisible in most analysis. Prominent here are the examination of aspects of women's experience routinely excluded: for example, housework and motherhood (Oakley, 1974, 1979, 1980) and the full range of women's unpaid and paid labour which has led to a new 'paradigm of work' and changes in stratification theory (Garnsey, 1978; West, 1982; Dex, 1985; Beechey, 1987). Equally, this reconceptualization has also involved a thoroughgoing exploration of the sources and nature of women's gender identity and of their situation in society. This has focused on, for example, the role of the state, in reinforcing women's subordination through the legal system and aspects of social policy (Wilson, 1977; Smart, 1984; Brophy and Smart, 1985; Eaton, 1986); the impact of social control and cultural conditioning (Smart and Smart, 1978; Hutter and Williams, 1981; Morley, 1987); the representation of women and female sexuality in the media and in all forms of cultural production, which draws attention to how images of gender help to structure the relations between the two sexes and secure women's inferior position (Coward, 1984; Ferguson, 1985); personal relationships between women and men as political relationships, as power structured relationships (Campbell, 1984, 1987a); and on the psyche as a way of understanding the acquisition of 'femaleness' (Mitchell, 1974; Sayers, 1985; Segal, 1987). In short, feminist sociology seeks to uncover and explain the structured social inequality which women experience in all areas of 'private' and 'public' social life, and to argue that this constitutes the chronic subordination or oppression of women. Clearly a major issue is whether it exaggerates or correctly reflects such subordination.

Generally this subordination is theorized as grounded in the material and ideological conditions prevailing in society, in 'political economy' and 'culture', respectively. Material, because women's subordination is bound up with the operation of the labour market and domestic production (women have characteristic positions as wage labour and unpaid 'domestic producers'). Ideological, because women's situation is shaped and sustained by dominant values and beliefs about how women should behave, what jobs they should do, and about what constitutes 'femininity'; values embedded in popular culture, in socialization processes, in education, and in social policy. These values and beliefs are primarily ideological because they justify and legitimate the subordinate position of women – 'women's proper place is in the home' is a deeply ideological assumption, as is the view that women are more 'naturally' equipped to perform domestic tasks. Such values are also ideological because they appear as common sense or 'neutral' when, in fact, they are not, since they represent very specific versions of gender roles. Although much feminist theory is concerned with material and ideological determinants, some theory has migrated into the field of psychoanalysis to explain the psychological roots of women's subordination and there is increased interest in the relationship between psychic conditions and processes and ideologies about 'femininity' (Segal, 1987a).

Theories of women's oppression

Within feminist sociology a number of different theoretical tendencies are discernible. They spring from contrasting philosophical premises about how society should be studied (Barrett, 1980; Oakley, 1981; Jaggar, 1983; Fildes, 1987). As it is not possible because of restrictions of space to produce a full taxonomy of feminist social theory, the two most influential traditions will be reviewed: radical feminist theory and Marxist/socialist-feminism. While two broad traditions can be identified they are not self-enclosed; much theory does not fit easily into any clear-cut paradigm, rather it takes the form of a general grammar of concepts and explanations.

Radical feminism
Radical feminism sees women's subordination as the fundamental form of domination in all societies. All existing societies are seen as patriarchal – that is, dominated by men – and the power of patriarchy theorized as anchored in the nature of human reproductive biology (Firestone, 1980), and in the greater physical strength of men (Brownmiller, 1976). The sexual division of labour in any society is seen as having a biological basis. Firestone (1980) observes that:

> The sexual-reproductive organisation always furnishes the real basis, starting from which we can alone work out the ultimate explanation of the whole superstructure of economic, juridical and political institutions as well as the religious, philosophical and other ideas of a given historical period.

The emphasis is placed firmly on the facts of procreation and what are perceived as enduring biological differences between the two sexes; radical feminism stresses the mode of reproduction as the bedrock of the division of labour and men's generalized power over women. Some versions acknowledge that biological sex differences are overladen with social practices which consolidate and reinforce fundamental male domination; for example, that housework is socially organized and sustained. However, the essential determining impact of biological differences is still retained (Daly, 1979). Radical feminism claims that women's oppression is more or less constant over time and place, and while accepting cross-cultural differences in, for instance, the form taken by marriage and household structure, it regards oppression as ubiquitous in the content of social relations between the sexes if not in their shape.

One of the theoretical implications of this is the focus on a range of institutions and practices that embody and reproduce male domination and facilitate the male exercise of power over women. Central here is the view that hierarchical power relations between men and women permeate every aspect of society so that all social relations between the sexes, including those in the 'personal' sphere, become political ones. This focus on the pervasiveness of male power draws attention to the power exercised over women in social institutions and social practices which would not commonly be thought of as implicated in the structuring of power, for example the family.

Radical feminism locates women as a sex class subordinated to, and by, patriarchy. Patriarchy refers to the hierarchy of social relations and institutions in which, and through which, men are able to dominate women. It is, however, widely regarded as problematic and its deployment has provoked considerable debate (Millett, 1969; Beechey, 1979; Rowbotham, 1979; Alexander and Taylor, 1981; Delphy, 1984; Walby, 1985; Hearn, 1987a). Thus Rowbotham (1979) argues that:

> The word 'patriarchy' implies a universal and historical [sic] form of oppression which returns us to biology ... and thus it obscures the need to recognise not only biological difference, but also the multiplicity of ways in which societies have defined gender. By focusing upon the bearing and rearing of children ... it suggests there is a single determining cause of women's subordination ... Moreover, the word leaves us with two separate systems in which a male/female split is implied. We have patriarchy oppressing women and capitalism oppressing male workers ... It does not carry any notion of how women might act to transform their situation as a sex ... 'Patriarchy'

suggests a fatalistic submission which allows no space for the complexities of women's defiance.

This criticism is a decisive one since it indicates the danger of using the concept of patriarchy in a way that neglects historical specificity. There is a tendency in radical feminism to see patriarchy as a transhistorical phenomenon grounded in invariable biology and its fixed behavioural consequences – male aggression and female submission. This needs to be corrected through recognition of the particular form assumed by relations between the sexes in specific historical circumstances, the variety displayed through gender identity, and the occurrence of resistance to gender domination. Care must be taken to avoid constructing women's subordination historically as relating to 'a one-dimensional patriarchal first cause, omnipresent and unexplained' (History Workshop editorial, 1985). Patriarchy cannot be theorized as a universal, homogeneous system of unqualified male domination and female subordination; rather male domination should be seen as operating under, and through, certain social and economic structures – and assuming a specific form according to historical context.

However, although radical feminism uses the term patriarchy to refer to biologically-based domination, the term could be used in an amended form to indicate male domination on the basis of social and economic conditions. Is Britain then a patriarchal society? And what light can be thrown on this question by the empirical evidence presented in this book? Mann (1986) argues that in Britain today patriarchy has been eroded in the direction of a modified 'neo-patriarchy':

> Do we still have what I defined as 'neo-patriarchy'? Yes, to some extent, particularly in the extension of the notions of 'domesticity' and 'femininity' into the public realms of employment and the Welfare State. Thus patriarchal values and attitudes still permeate many aspects of the culture of contemporary nation-states. But we have also gone beyond even neo-patriarchy into two distinct and even opposite forms of gendered stratification. Firstly, men and women have become in certain ways abstract, interchangeable 'persons' with equivalent rights as legal and political citizens, limited of course by the other stratification nuclei around which they might cluster ... class and nation ... ethnicity and religious affiliation. Persons have equality before the law and freedom of choice as individuals in few historic societies have done. One right that has expanded, particularly for women, is the right to choose a marriage partner, to terminate that marriage freely in divorce and to hold on to a portion of its material resources thereafter. These derivatives of liberalism, reinforced by social democracy and by feminist movements, represent fundamental

changes in gender relations – whether or not feminists regard them as significant compared to the transformations they would ideally like to see. (Mann, 1986)

However, as the data in other chapters indicate, such formal and legal equality – while representing significant historical changes – goes in hand with persisting, deep-seated inequalities in women's life-chances and access to power. Patriarchy, as the undiluted power of the individual patriarch within the family, may have been displaced by the formal, legal equality of women, but this does not secure equality of condition, and the vast majority of women face low pay, unequal access to jobs and training, hidden unemployment, financial dependence on men, and an excessive share of unpaid labour.

Furthermore,

> For single or married, childless or not, women in the home, at work, and in society as a whole are subject to a deeply entrenched and all pervasive sexist culture: one in which men's desires dominate, men occupy central positions of power, and in which social assumptions and practices keep women in positions of subordination. (Coates, 1984)

Of course, women do not experience their gender in uniform ways, both class and ethnicity interlink with gender, and white middle-class women are typically in a different position in society from black working-class women, indicating that gender is itself stratified. Nevertheless, all the empirical evidence points to generalized female subordination in contemporary Britain which, although uneven in its effect on women and manifested in a variety of ways, is a central feature of existing social and economic arrangements. It is therefore difficult to escape the concept of patriarchy although there is much debate about the precise historical form assumed by patriarchy in contemporary conditions, with some theorists preferring to employ the term 'capitalist patriarchy' to denote the specificity of male domination and female subordination in the context of one mode of production (Barrett, 1980). Patriarchy does not necessarily have to imply some absolute, unchanging system of male power nor be insensitive to changes in gender relations. It can be used fruitfully to refer to an historically-specific configuration of gender relations in which female subordination and male domination are enmeshed; or to describe practices and institutions of a male-dominated gender order, for example, patriarchal welfare policies and the patriarchal family. Vital disputes do remain though about how 'to name the system' of gender domination (Jaggar, 1983; Cockburn, 1986).

Reservations about radical feminism rest on its stress on the biological determinants of social structures and the innate features of women and men which collapse the distinction between sex and gender and unconsciously endorse traditional theories of women's 'natural' role in society, and the inevitability of women's subordination. Clearly, it is crucial to an analysis of gender relations to look at reproduction – childbearing, childrearing and sexuality – in order to determine how women's wider social position becomes socially constructed. This should not be confused, however, with the argument that reproductive function is the unproblematic basis of the sexual division of labour. Radical feminism is also weakened by the claim that there is a fixed conception of human nature in which women are seen as inherently caring and nurturing. In some feminist literature there is an attempt to locate the origins and nature of male domination in personality structures produced by what are seen as historically universal features of childbearing. Segal (1987) has widely discussed this. Women are portrayed in this context as having a distinctive 'sensibility'; there is a nurturing feminine identity which makes women more peaceful and gentle; they possess an expressive and nurturing psychology in contrast to the narrower and aggressive psychologies of men. Wider sexual subordination is thus rooted in women's identification with the prime caregiver (the mother) and this prepares them for servicing men and childcare, and caring work in general. For men, the loss of early identification with the mother leads to the assertion of a compensatory masculinity involving power over women and the development of aggressive behaviour (Chodorow, 1978; Eichenbaum and Orbach, 1982). Thus Chodorow claims: 'the very fact of being mothered by a woman generates in men conflict over masculinity, a psychology of male dominance and a need to be superior to women' (Chodorow, 1978). This line of argument has, though, been strongly criticized:

> Any feminist perspective which explains women's mothering and caring work in exclusively psychological terms obscures the possibility that there may be no such universal or straightforward nurturing femininity at all. Women's mothering capabilities, when present, may be primarily their adjustment to the social and economic arrangements which require them to do the work of caring for others. Such psychological perspectives also tend to obscure . . . that women's work in our society is often stressful, isolating and undermining of personal confidence. (Segal, 1987)

Women appear to possess 'natural' mothering instincts and capabilities because they do the work of mothering not because of any determining psychological imperative. As Segal says:

'Mothering is not determined by consciousness but consciousness by mothering, to paraphrase Marx and Engels' (ibid.).

Marxism and feminism

The desire of some feminist writers to provide a material basis for women's subordination stimulated a major interest in Marx. The mainspring of the development of Marxist-feminism has been a critique and reformulation of traditional Marxism, as a result of 'silences' about the position of women; the gender-determined character of women's work, and the systematic domination of women by men (Barrett, 1980). The contemporary capitalist system it seen as structured by male domination, which is organized by the capitalist division of labour. This constitutes 'capitalist patriarchy'; structured gender inequalities taking a particular form under the conditions of capitalist production. It is acknowledged that gender inequalities antedate capitalism, and exist in other non-capitalist contemporary societies, and cannot simply be reduced universally to the 'needs' of capitalism. A core concern is to explore the interrelations between the family and work, and between production and reproduction. The traditional Marxist emphasis on the economic foundation of society is thus recomposed to include the sphere of reproduction – the family, household organization, sexual relations. The purpose is to explore the links between socio-economic structures and those of the personal/sexual/familial sphere. The precise way in which gender inequality and the capitalist mode of production interlink is the subject of considerable debate; the context for which is a great deal of empirical work on the sexual division of labour within capitalism: for example, the sex-segregated nature of the labour market, which advantages both men and capital, and on the relation between women's domestic labour and the wider economy (Dex, 1985; Walby, 1985; Crompton and Mann, 1986; Beechey, 1987; Webb, in this volume).

Underpinning this kind of analysis is an account of the distinct history of women's subordination in the context of capitalist development. Broadly, it is argued, the period of capitalist industrialization exacerbated the existing gender divisions by the privatization of domestic labour and the eclipse of the home as a unit of production:

> What marks out capitalism is not the subjection of women as such since this predates capitalism, but the privatisation of domestic labour and the exclusion of women from social labour, which serves to reproduce the subjection of women in a specifically capitalist form. (Hunt, 1980)

What broad historical forces were at work, then, which generated a specific configuration of patriarchy and capitalism? Existing gender divisions were extended into a wage-labour system in which women performed domestic labour and paid labour in the context of male domination. According to some views, women were excluded from paid labour to some extent and male workers organized to exclude them as cheaper challenges to their skilled employment. There are however some very complex disputes about the extent of women's eviction from paid labour, the specific factors which led to women performing unpaid domestic labour and whether women's experience was class specific. Brenner and Ramas (1984) have argued that childcare and participation in capitalist production were incompatible. This generated the development of a family household structure based on a sexual division of labour, which accounts for the development in the nineteenth century of the male breadwinner and female domestic labourer. They stress that the 'economic logic' of women's exclusion from wage-labour, childbearing and childrearing were key imperatives. They argue:

> Because factory production in particular, and capitalist production in general, could not accommodate childbearing and early nurturing, married women were forced to seek more marginal lower-paying kinds of work. The family household system in the twentieth century was thus produced by a confluence of the biological facts of reproduction and capitalist production. According to this view the nature of capitalist production was an important determinant; its drive for profit resulted in privatising reproduction and forced the working class family to shoulder responsibility for its dependants. Middle class women however readily embraced a domestic role as it allowed them to create a 'proper place' for themselves in society. (Brenner and Ramas, 1984)

One theorist argues that:

> When women participated in the wage-labour market, they did so in a position that was as clearly limited by patriarchy as it was by capitalism. Men's control over women's labour was altered by the wage-labour system, but it was not eliminated. In the labour market the dominant position of men was maintained by sex-ordered job segregation. Women's jobs were lower paid, considered less skilled and often involved less exercise of authority or control. Men acted to enforce job segregation in the labour market; they utilized trade union associations and strengthened the domestic division of labour, which required women to do housework, childcare and related chores. Women's subordinate position in the labour market reinforced their subordinate position in the family, and that in turn reinforced their labour market position. (Hartmann, 1982)

Emanating from much Marxist-feminist investigation is an

emphasis on women as a reserve army of labour; as performers of unpaid domestic labour and as a large part-time labour force providing cheap labour. It culminates in the view that:

> The present status of women in the labour market and the current arrangement of sex-segregated jobs is the result of a long process of interaction between patriarchy and capitalism. I have emphasised the actions of male workers throughout this process because I believe this to be correct ... capitalists have indeed used women as unskilled, underpaid labour to undercut male workers, yet this is only a case of the chickens coming home to roost ... a case of men's co-option and support for a patriarchal society, with its hierarchy among men, being turned back on themselves with a vengeance. Capitalism grew on top of patriarchy; patriarchal capitalism is stratified society par excellence. (Hartmann, 1982)

Current historical debates about the precise way in which male domination, female subordination and capitalist production interrelated vary a good deal in theoretical character and conclusion (Barrett, 1984; Brenner and Ramas, 1984; Lewis, 1985) but overall, attention is given to the emergence of the family wage with the accompanying dependency on a male wage; the emergence of the 'wife' as an unpaid domestic labourer; the incidence of lower wages for women and the use of trade union organization by males to secure advantages over female workers; and the gradual development of the 'private' sphere as a women's realm. The most salient issues for explanation concern the different 'fates' of working-class and middle-class women; the intervention of the state to uphold the domestic economy and the configuration of ideological and material factors in defining women's position, in particular whether the gender ideology was a product of a pre-industrial age or was created by the home/workplace separation.

The view that contemporary society has been shaped – and continues to be shaped – by an interaction between patriarchy and capitalism, has been a pivot of feminist social theory and the basis of grasping the relationship between the labour market and domestic arrangements, and gender and stratification. This has constituted a major advance on the functionalism of classical Marxism, which stressed that women's subordination as required by the 'logic' of capital – for example, female domestic labour 'frees' the male worker to work longer hours for capital which increases the accumulation of profit (James and Costa, 1973). Arguably, this fails to disclose the extent to which men, and not just capital, benefit from women's subordination. More broadly it is difficult to argue – which is the tendency of traditional Marxism – that all aspects of women's position and experience are linked to capitalist production – for example, violence against women, and the general social control to which they are subjected. Within the Marxist-feminist tradition, the focus on patriarchy and capitalism, both historically and in a contemporary context, has succeeded in establishing causal links between male domination, female subordination and capitalist production (Beechey, 1987); though as Cockburn (1984) has observed, the relationship between the two is by no means as yet fully understood. In part this has stimulated a shift towards more empirically-focused research on women and the contemporary labour process, as revealing how patriarchy and capitalism intersect (Pollert, 1981; Cavendish, 1982). Overall, at the concrete level, women appear as a 'disposable' reserve army of labour, as low-paid workers and as performers of servicing and caring work (Beechey, 1986). At the theoretical level it is established that women relate to the means of production in their own right (Allen, 1982); although their position in the domestic economy needs to be given equal weighting.

Marxist-feminists see the organization of procreation as part of the economic foundation of society, so that reproduction – and the social conditions which surround it – is analysed alongside production. Family structure, and the division of labour within the 'private sphere' of marriage and personal relations, are seen as historically specific without, necessarily, any universal content or shape. This constitutes a marked departure from radical feminism.

Women's subordination is manifested in different societies according to how the organization of reproductive labour relates to the wage-labour system, and according to the overall effects of the structures of both male domination and the mode of production. The cardinal issue is always the social and economic context of women's experience and the strength of Marxist-feminist analysis continues to be its charting of the links between male domination and the dynamics of capitalist production (Cockburn, 1983; Dex, 1985; Beechey, 1986, 1987).

For Marxist-feminists, women's subordination is also located at the ideological level as well as the material one, which results in debates about how material and ideological factors combine to produce the 'oppression' of women (Barrett, 1980). Mitchell (1971) identifies four structures which shape women's position – production, reproduction, sexuality and socialization. In addition, there are the ideologies which shape gender identity through socialization and the division of labour within the family (ideas about 'women's work', 'women's natural roles', 'femininity') and those which exist in social and political practices, such as educational processes, and the assumptions about gender roles underpinning welfare provision (see Kidd, this volume). This reveals how female gender identity is constructed and how a role, such as housewife-mother, comes to be lodged in popular culture and individual consciousness. Such a role exemplifies the way in which both ideological and material factors blend together. The housewife-mother is structurally anchored in the sexual division of labour, both in the sphere of reproduction and in the paid labour market; women with 'domestic responsibilities' have part-time, low-paid jobs with little access to training, promotion and other occupations. It is also ideologically produced by prevailing ideas about who should most 'properly' perform childbearing, caring and servicing work. 'Housewife-mother' is therefore both a material and an ideological construct. In conclusion, clearly all aspects of gender relations cannot be reduced simply to an economic base. The consensus within the sociology of gender is to analyse gender in relation to both how the system of production operates as well as more general forms of gender domination – for example, the cultural stereotyping of women.

Some issues in feminist sociology
As it would be impossible here to provide a comprehensive exposition of current thinking, it is proposed to give the following representative issues special consideration namely women's class location, women's role in the family, sexuality, and the role of the state in relation to gender relations.

The class location of women and the nature of female labour
For a long while mainstream sociological analysis, especially 'stratification theory', failed to give women's position in the class structure any systematic treatment and neglected to consider gender as a distinctive dimension of social stratification. Women were seen as being 'outside' class analysis because of their family and their domestic role, and were marginal in relation to the formation and existence of classes (Dex, 1985).

Feminist expositions of female labour, which focus on the divisions between 'men's work' and 'women's work', the female experience of unpaid domestic labour and the labour market, and the reasons for the subordinate position of women in the labour market, have transformed theorization in this area. They show that because women are overwhelmingly responsible for performing unpaid domestic labour, this drastically influences the nature of their involvement in paid work. It is, for example, a crucial determinant of women's involvement in part-time and home-based work (Allen and Wolkowitz, 1986). Other categories of 'women's work' are shown to be a reflection of ideological factors; thus women's extensive participation in caring and servicing jobs is a reflection of the classification of work into 'women's work' and 'men's work'. This job segregation reflects a number of interlocking and mutually reinforcing processes; it expresses the underlying sexual division of labour, which is the backbone of job allocation, and the gender ideology of the wider society which is the cultural base of women's economic dependence upon men.

The significance of domestic labour has been an important debate within feminist sociology (see Secombe, 1974; Gardiner, 1875; Molyneux, 1979; Dex, 1985; Beechey, 1987). Major issues have revolved around the extent to which domestic labour serves to reproduce both labour power (the rearing of children, the servicing of male labour) and the social relations of production (socializing tasks and support for male labour). Thus the rate of profit, in the sphere of capitalist production, was linked to domestic labour, through the suggestion that wage costs were deflated because of the existence of unpaid domestic labour; this reduces the overall cost of labour to capital by performing caring and servicing tasks. Another way of theorizing women's domestic labour is to appeal to theories of sexual politics; to argue that men benefit in general from women's unpaid domestic labour, which is both a source of, and a condition for, male control in both the 'private' and 'public' spheres. However, it must not be forgotten that women's unpaid role in caring and servicing, seriously reduces pressure on the state to provide collective provisions, and this has consequences for expenditure on social policy. The state, however, is increasingly concerned to introduce private provision for childcare, domestic servicing and care of the elderly. This helps both to maintain a specific gender order and to facilitate the policing of the boundaries between the 'private' and the 'public'. This has implications for the surveillance of women who carry the major responsibility for the private function of domestic labour.

The characterization of women's specific position in the labour process is relatively clear-cut. Women, for example, are a major constituent of a reserve army of labour; this is drawn on in times of expansion and made redundant in periods of recession; it contributes to the process of deskilling (the routinization of clerical jobs) – which can be paid lower wages. It is a decisive component of a 'flexible' labour force. Some theorists identify a dual labour market; a primary sector in which available jobs are secure, well-paid, have promotion opportunities and are based on training and credentials, and a secondary sector in which women are preponderant and where there is insecurity, few prospects of promotion, low pay (see Barron and Norris, 1976; Webb, this volume). Women's entry to the primary sector is generally inhibited by their domestic labour and by cultural stereotyping. This underlines the gendered nature of the entire fabric of the division of labour in society, and furnishes powerful evidence of gender inequalities in the labour market. However, clearly, all women are not impeded from entering the primary sector. Entry to higher education, the acquisition of credentials, and the relative opening-up of new job opportunities through technological changes have increased female employment in this sector. However, female employment is still mainly concentrated in the secondary sector (Webb, this volume), and employment in more secure jobs requiring credentials is limited.

There is much controversy about the definition of women's class position. Some writers theorize women as housewives as a class. For example, Walby (1986) points out that 'the housewife is thus engaged in a patriarchal mode of production in which she is a member of a direct producer class and her husband is a non-producer and member of an exploiting class'. This perspective sees women who are housewives as 'dependent wage labourers' working in the house for their husbands. There are some objections to this, primarily on the grounds that, as Oakley (1981) remarks:

> If women are a separate class from the point of view of the gender structure, then there must be some similarity (either manifest or latent) in the way all women relate to all men – that is, to men in the different classes that express men's relationship to the means of production. However, it is a somewhat crucial aspect of women's position that the relations of different women in different social groups to men are rather different.

Walby's perspective contrasts with that of the established orthodoxies in stratification theory, which argues that women's class position is indicated by their husband's position (see Parkin, 1972; Goldthorpe, 1983; Lockwood, 1986). Thus Parkin (1972) argues that:

> Female status certainly carries many disadvantages compared with that of males in various areas of social life including employment opportunities, property ownership, income and so on. However, these inequalities associated with sex differences are not usefully thought of as components of stratification. This is because for the great majority of women the allocation of social and economic rewards is determined primarily by the position of their families and, in particular, that of the male head. Although women today share certain status attributes in common, simply by virtue of their sex, their claims over resources are not primarily determined by their own occupation but, more

commonly, by that of their fathers or husbands. And if the wives and daughters of unskilled labourers have some things in common with the wives and daughters of wealthy landowners, there can be no doubt that the differences – their overall situation – are far more striking and significant. Only if the disabilities attaching to female status were felt to be so great as to override differences of a class kind, would it be realistic to regard sex as an important diversion of stratification.

On the basis of empirical data drawn from his Oxford mobility study, which includes women's work histories, Goldthorpe (1983, 1986) has reaffirmed that a woman's class position is determined by the occupation of her husband, and that women's participation in the labour market is insufficiently permanent to warrant separate classification. He acknowledges widespread sexual inequality, but claims that it is precisely because women are in disadvantaged positions in most areas of social and economic life that they are dependent on their husbands, and their life-chances are determined by the husband's position. Stanworth (1984) argues that a wife's employment is not necessarily conditioned by her husband's employment, and that where women are in paid employment 'cross-class' families exist, confirming that women can be classified in their own right. Walby (1986) attacks traditional class analysis and suggests that women who are married and in paid employment have a dual class position; one from their paid work, and one as a housewife in relation to their husbands. On this view, the sexual division of labour within the family/household must be seen as giving rise to social and economic inequalities between women and men. Furthermore, Walby argues that women who are full-time housewives are a class in 'their own right'.

At base this is a debate about the relationship between class and gender, and as a consequence it spills over into some highly complicated issues about the measurement of class and class formation (Crompton and Mann, 1986). Many feminists claim that women in general are oppressed by men, and that therefore gender not class is the central axis of social differentiation. Others, however, seek to retain the concept of class, and as indicated earlier in the commentary on patriarchy and capitalism, see it in conjunction with gender and ethnicity. Class and gender qualify one another; the life-chances associated with the same occupation will vary according to whether it is a woman or a man who holds the position. Equally, although there is a certain commonality of experience between all 'housewives', those whose husbands and fathers are middle-class, will have access to material and cultural resources which differentiate their experience from those with working-class husbands and fathers. On the other hand, Leonard and Speakman (1986) argue that women do not necessarily 'inherit' such capacities and resources from their husbands and fathers; women's class location is determined by their own relationship both to the means of production and the domestic economy. In taking stock of theories of women's work it is clear that some complex issues remain unresolved; it is though well established that women occupy a very specific position in the labour market. As Scott (1986) says:

> Overall, women are excluded from occupations which involve the execution of power, scientific knowledge, control over capital or technology. Women are above all ancillary and routine workers, the executors of others' decisions and the providers of welfare and domestic services.

The family

Feminist writers have been concerned to examine women's experience in the family and the relationship between the family and the wider social and economic order (Berk, 1980; Thorne, 1982; Segal, 1983; Leonard and Speakman, 1986). Doubt has been cast on the extent to which the traditional nuclear family – of a married couple, a male breadwinner and a 'dependent' housewife, and their children, is in fact the dominant form of household in contemporary Britain (Allen, 1987). Statistical evidence (*Social Trends*, no. 17, 1987) indicates that in 1985 24 per cent of all households consisted of a married couple with one or two dependent children, 27 per cent of a married couple with no children, and 5 per cent of a married couple with three or more children. Thus, married couples with dependent children accounted for 45 per cent of people in households; in addition 12 per cent of all families were headed by a lone parent (see also Kidd and Webb, this volume). The changes which have generated modifications in the traditional family framework, have been identified as a growth in married women's employment, less childbirth, an increase in one-person households and more men becoming economically inactive (Halsey, 1987).

The implications of these changes for feminist writers (Beechey and Whitelegg, 1986) are that women can no longer be seen in exclusively traditional roles within the conventional nuclear family, rather they have to be seen in a variety of household and family arrangements; for example, lone parents and breadwinners, widows and the wives of unemployed men. This underlines the diversity of women's social and economic experience and challenges some of the prevailing stereotypes of women's role in the family. In addition, feminist work has attacked the idea of the 'dependent wife' by refuting the argument that women's employment is for 'pin-money'. The necessary contribution made by women's paid labour to a family income has been well documented (Land, 1975), and women's general 'dependency' has been dismissed as largely unfounded (Land, 1976). It is argued that women 'support' the family both emotionally and materially. This is not to infer that women are financially independent, or economically secure in general, particularly since women are a large proportion of the low paid (*New Earnings Survey*), and of those in poverty (Townsend, 1979; Scott, 1984; Glendinning and Millar, 1987). Rather, it demonstrates that women do a variety of full- and part-time work; that they themselves have dependants such as elderly relatives and children, and they are often in contexts in which they do not rely on a male breadwinner such as widows, lone parents or single persons. The prevalence of the nuclear family must therefore be regarded as problematic, but although it seems appropriate to dispose of the 'myth of the male breadwinner' to some extent, and the 'myth of female dependency', women's characteristic low pay, domestic duties and disadvantages experienced in the labour market do create forms of subordination. In general, they do not command independent economic resources and are typically constrained within the family, by the nature of their husband's occupation (Comer, 1972; Finch, 1983b). Many feminists see the main source of men's authority as rooted in their greater earning power (Comer, 1972), though it is debatable if and how this is class-specific.

In addition, feminists have questioned the idealization of the family as a caring and harmonious private haven, and its celebration in popular thought and culture as the unique site of personal fulfilment (Segal, 1983). The family is regarded as deeply ambivalent for women and a major source of women's oppression (Barrett and McIntosh, 1982). Although much sociological enquiry has stressed the growth of a more 'egalitarian' family structure (Young and Wilmott, 1973), many feminist commentators emphasize that life within the family is very different for women in comparison to men. There is evidence of dissatisfaction and frustration as a consequence of the monotonous and repetitive nature of housework, and the social isolation and low status involved in being a housewife (Gavron, 1966; Oakley, 1974a). Even when women do paid work outside the home, they remain overwhelmingly responsible for domestic labour (*Social Trends*, no. 17, 1987). Thus Halsey (1987) says: 'Women still bear the main burden of domestic management in practice, and equal sharing is more of an ideal than a reality and honoured by men more in the breach than in the observance.'

The sexual division of labour within the family remains clearly marked by women's continuing performance of household tasks and childrearing. Thus the typical family structure reinforces and creates the sexual divisions found within the wider society. Domestic labour is widely regarded as a 'natural feminine activity' and this is institutionalized in the sexual division of labour within most families. In addition, the family is also the site of female training for the performance of domestic labour and childrearing. Whilst there are reservations about whether or not it is possible to generalize about family structure, given its variation according to class, ethnicity and region, nevertheless women's preponderant role in domestic labour and childrearing is a central source of their subordination, both within the family and within the wider social and economic arrangements.

Attention has also been given to the 'dark side' of family life, to violence, rape and child abuse (Dobash and Dobash, 1980; Metcalf and Humphries, 1985; Morley, 1987). These are interpreted by feminists, not as aberrations committed by disturbed individual males, but largely as expressions of male power and male sexuality. They reflect unequal power relations within the family and in other social contexts (Campbell, 1987b). Such inequalities are revealed in the generalized cultural power that men have in dominating 'public space', in physical coercion, sexual abuse and misogynous attitudes. Power is a core area in the analysis of gender and gender relations (Connell, 1987). 'Relations of power exist within the family, as within other areas of society, and overall, women's interests come off badly' (Leonard and Speakman, 1986).

The keynote of this analysis of power is the portrayal of the family as an institution of sexual power, as a patriarchal power structure. Male power manifests itself through physical coercion or abuse within the family. Feminists see the male exercise of power (and specifically violence towards women) as part of the cultural construction of masculinity and sexuality. Thus MacLeod and Saragar (1987): 'Boys learn to experience their sexuality as a powerful uncontrollable force, to equate being masculine with feeling powerful.' On this view, violence towards women is rooted in the close bonding between the cultural construction of masculinity and the exercise of power. For Weeks (1986) the explanation lies in 'the social and psychic conditions in which masculinity is acquired . . . male sexual violence is not the product of an unproblematic biology but of complex social practices and psychic structuring.' These social and psychic factors include the expectations of male behaviour; the subordinate social and economic status of women; men's superior economic power; the cultural representation of women as 'sex objects' and the socialization of males into an 'aggressive sexuality' (Metcalf and Humphries, 1985). Finally, some feminists see women's oppression in the family as deriving from the institutions (the nuclear family) and the practices (heterosexual sexual relations) of heterosexuality itself (Barrett and McIntosh, 1982). One counter-argument here would be that these accounts overlook the existence of genuine mutual dependency and co-operation between the sexes, and exaggerate the prevalence of male aggressiveness towards women. This could be said, however, to fly in the face of considerable evidence to the contrary (Strauss, 1981; Wilson, 1983; Metcalf and Humphries, 1985).

From a feminist point of view, how then are women specifically subordinate in the family? They argue that women's responsibility for most domestic tasks and childrearing is highly constraining; men generally have superior earning power; women are often 'incorporated' into their husband's occupation which will dictate where the family live, their social contacts and standard of living; a woman's autonomy is circumscribed by expectations about how she should behave within the family; women spend much time servicing others, typically with less leisure time (Finch, 1983; Leonard and Speakman, 1986).

The problematic issues here, though, are the extent to which women's life-chances, expectations and social status are still dominated by the wife-mother role. As a consequence of the wider sexual division of labour, women tend to be reliant upon the continuation of a male wage and this constitutes the basis of continuing inequality in the family and in marriage. Thus, the interplay of gender-based disadvantages in the labour market and the domestic division of labour, undermines the possibility of permanent egalitarian relations between women and men in the family and marriage.

The family has to be seen as a social unit, in which members are linked to the broader socio-economic context in different ways. Women and men, within the same family, will articulate with the wider socio-economic structure in different ways because they have different skills, promotion and career prospects (Allen, 1982) and because the labour market is already gender-segregated and shaped. In addition, earlier discussion has pointed to the family's socialization role, a hard emphasis on the family as an 'ideological state apparatus' (Althusser, 1971), and a 'soft' emphasis on the family as a vital terrain in which masculinity and femininity are shaped by the force of wider cultural influences about appropriate gender roles and by the 'internal' organization of the domestic economy (Weitz, 1977).

Some important changes have occurred in the family – they may not be wholesale transformations but they need to be considered. The nuclear family is now less common and 'unconventional households' are more visible. Furthermore, formal marriage is rejected by a significant minority and 'voluntary childlessness' is common. Arguably the 'direct authority' of the father within the family has declined, changes in patterns of fertility have occurred, and there has been the entry of some women into the public sphere (O'Brien, 1981; Hearn, 1987). These could be interpreted as being significant changes in social practices and institutions based on sexuality; for some theorists though the family remains patriarchal (Smart, 1987b). The crux of this debate revolves around whether the domestic division of labour has been fundamentally renegotiated and women have become less subordinate. The impact of changes in practices and attitudes should not be underestimated but evidence about the labour market, the domestic economy and power relations between the sexes underlines continuing, systematic gender inequality which finds expression in how the two sexes relate to one another in the family. All in all, feminist findings challenge the idealization of the family.

Sexuality

Feminist theory has developed sophisticated accounts of the social construction of both femininity and masculinity (McRobbie, 1978; Coward, 1983; Weeks, 1986; Brod, 1987). Central to this has been the exploration of dominant assumptions about male and female sexuality. It has been shown that assumptions about male desire as active, and female desire as passive, have become deeply lodged in culture so that it is possible to denote dominant ideologies about male and female sexuality (McIntosh, 1978). Such ideologies have a pervasive influence in that, as Wolpe (1987) states: 'Sexual codes are a central pivot of the moral order and its definition of correct and appropriate behaviour.' Such ideologies underlie a double standard of sexual morality: sexual 'promiscuity' is natural in males and even encouraged, whereas it is seen as 'deviant' in females (Willis, 1977; Smart and Smart, 1978; Wilson, 1978; Cowie and Lees, 1981; Lees, 1986). Female sexuality is typically represented as best expressed in marriage – a form of control over women. Although there are alternative codes and practices, as far as female sexuality is concerned this remains the dominant strand in sexual ideology. Female sexuality is placed explicitly in the context of marriage and the family and is reflected in much socialization, and in popular thought. Wolpe (1987) observes that:

reinforcing the notion that the main goal in life for girls is as wife and mother is not unproblematic. There are a number of contradictory messages which the girls receive. Sexuality as portrayed in the media and popular culture emphasizes youth, beauty and the need for girls to be available. At the same time it is only 'bad girls who like sex'. So, for the majority, their flight into sexuality as teenagers is of a temporary, transitory and usually limited nature. This has to be discarded when they become fully responsible adult women, fulfilling their roles as wives and mothers, motherhood in particular being presented in non-erotic terms .... the control over women's sexuality through its identification with family life still continues. Nor have the women's movement, or qualitative changes in aspects of the media's presentation of female sexuality, in terms other than motherhood, significantly altered the official discourse on female sexuality.

Much work on sexuality demonstrates how definitions of 'normal' female and male sexuality and 'deviant' female and male sexuality (generally, homosexuality) derive from the cultural and political context. Thus Weeks (1981): 'Sexuality is not a given. . . . It is an historical construct that has historical conditions of existence.'

Sexuality is seen in terms of the cultural meanings assigned to it, female and male sexuality are defined, and shaped, by a whole flux of cultural and political factors. These range from media representations of women as passive recipients of an active, male sexual desire, to peer-group definitions of females on the basis of their 'sexual reputation' (Wilson, 1978). The dominant assumptions and discourses about sexuality provide the parameters within which people experience their own sexuality and relate to others sexually. These sexual relations occur within the context of patterns of domination and subordination, which structure gender relations in society, and cannot be disconnected from the cultural and economic advantages that many men enjoy. Many women enter into sexual relationships with men in which their sexuality is subjected to powerful controls; this is essentially true for teenage girls (Lees, 1986). Clearly, there is resistance to dominant views about female sexuality, and there are opportunities for women to construct rewarding sexual relations with men, but sexuality is moulded by forces of regulation and control. This should not be obscured by the fact that there is more open discussion and an apparently more 'enlightened' attitude towards sexual issues (Weeks, 1986). Thus Coward (1984) points out:

When we hear talk of freedom to choose sexual partners, we can be sure we'll also hear talk of visual appeal, the mysterious alchemy which strikes from the blue at the most awkward moments. And here's the coercion. Because women are compelled to make themselves attractive in certain ways, and those ways involve submitting to the culture's belief about appropriate sexual behaviour, women's appearances are laden down with cultural values, and women have to form their identities within these values or, with difficulty, against them.

As a general statement about power and sexuality in contemporary society, it can be said that: 'the patterns of female sexuality are inescapably a product of the historically rooted power of men to define and categorise what is necessary and desirable' (Weeks, 1986). Evidence for this would include a web of practices and influences: the language of sexual abuse, stereotyping and denigration, sexual harassment, definitions of 'good' and 'bad' women; disapproval of non-heterosexuality; definitions of what is sexually desirable; the objectification of women as 'sex objects'; the prevalence of male definitions of sexual pleasure and the shaping of women's sex lives by male domination. The conclusion here is that, generally, men exercise power over women in society 'silently', as it is built into everyday social practices and cultural beliefs.

Culture and ideology

Feminist work on ideology has examined the way in which women's subordination is secured through ideological influences which help shape female gender identity, and define 'femininity' and the 'proper place' of women in society. Such ideological influences take the guise of 'commonsense assumptions' about the 'naturalness' of women's position; the stereotyping of women and 'concealed' assumptions about women's behaviour and 'personality' and social roles. They are present in, for example, the treatment of female offenders (Webb, 1984; Stratta, this volume); the hidden curriculum and organization of knowledge in education (Deem, 1978, 1980; Stanworth 1983; Weiner 1985; Skeggs, this volume) and in social policy provision (Bennett, 1983; Fitzgerald, 1983; Ungerson, 1985; Dale and Foster, 1986; Kidd, this volume). They are also present in socialization (Oakley, 1981), clearly denoting that the prevailing culture is deeply implicated in constructing women's subordinate social positions. Coates (1984) points out:

> That culture is so persuasive, the powers of men so entrenched, and the situation of women so difficult in the main, that the vast majority of women absorb large parts of that culture as their own. They then police and reinforce their own subordination. With greater or lesser degrees of enthusiasm and identification, they accept the 'space', the 'roles' and the 'attitudes' specified for them as naturally female . . . acting to reproduce those roles and attitudes in their children and woman friends.

Thus popular culture, and social practices in a variety of institutions, constrain women and encourage them to adopt certain roles.

Alongside these notions about ideology, some feminists have developed a feminist psychoanalysis to account for the persistence of female gender identity. Thus Jaggar (1983):

> Most of the current socialist feminist accounts depend on a psychoanalytic theory of character formation, arguing – for instance – that the mother-rearing of children, in a sexist and heterosexist social context, results in psychologically passive girls wit 'soft-ego boundaries' – who are dependent on others for affection and approval, and aggressive boys with 'rigid ego-boundaries' who separate themselves sharply from others. These distinctly masculine and feminine character structures are thought to produce strong psychological reinforcement to the sexual division of labour that generated them.

Much controversy remains about a social psychology of gender identity. Clearly it is necessary to avoid a simple functionalist model in which women are malleable 'cultural dopes' who behave mechanically since this takes no account of resistance or negotiation by women. Yet conformity to dominant gender roles needs to be explained by reference to psychological disposition generated by socialization and cultural stereotyping.

The state: the central political institutions

Feminist investigation of the state has led to a growing recognition of the role played by central political institutions in securing gender relations through intervention in the areas of 'social reproduction' – family, education and welfare provision. Particularly prominent has been the analysis of welfare provision and its roles in fostering the economic dependence of women on men (Wilson, 1977; Kidd, this volume). The development of social security legislation and its contemporary effects are discussed elsewhere in this book, but this does provide a major clue about how the state intervenes in the regulation of women to the labour market. McIntosh (1978) notes that:

> In the case of women, social security has worked in a curious way, on the one hand to establish married women as dependent upon their husbands (and therefore not entirely reliant on wage labour), but on the other hand by restricting their direct eligibility for social security benefits, to make them more vulnerable to use as a cheap labour power when they do engage in wage labour.

Generally this has meant that many married women are dependent on a 'male breadwinner' and, as Coates (1984) points out, are in a 'semi-proletarianized' condition when they do enter the labour market. Historically, this dependence has been accompanied by the idealization of the home and the family as the proper preserves of women, and the source of their unique fulfilment. Increasingly, the state's 'family policy' and associated changes in welfare provision are constraining some women to be 'frontline-carers' taking on an even greater responsibility for the care of elderly relatives and the sick which further reinforces the sexual division of labour. Although the family appears to be located in a 'private' sphere outside the scope of political direction, feminist insight about the intimate connection between the 'private' and the 'public' spheres uncovers very considerable state intervention in the family (McIntosh, 1978, 1984; Dale and Foster, 1986). Thus feminist analysis has shown how family law relating to marriage and divorce has helped to reproduce patriarchal relations (Smart, 1984), exemplifying how 'public' political structures shape the 'private' sphere of 'personal experiences'.

A further area which demonstrates the state's role in sustaining gender domination is located in its non-intervention; for example, a reluctance to take seriously domestic violence and sexual harassment. It is very much the case that social policy bears the imprint of hidden agendas about appropriate gender roles, in tune with the philosophy of the dominant political forces. This is as true of the period in Britain when social democratic policies were ascendant – 1945 until the mid-1970s – as it is of the current period of 'Thatcherism' (Wilson, 1977, 1987).

Some theorists characterize the state as intrinsically patriarchal – its institutions, personnel and practices. Thus Hearn (1987) says:

> If one considers the structures of state activities in relation to men's power, a number of rather obvious observations can be made, such as: the state forms a major part of men's domination of the public sphere over the private: the state is itself dominated by men – it is characteristically patriarchal.

Obviously in many areas of social life some women do challenge continued subordination but it is a matter of much debate about how effective such challenges have been although in the view of most feminist sociologists the state continues to be an important agency in the 'articulation of patriarchal and capitalist relations' (Wilson, 1987).

An assessment of the impact of feminist theory
In assessing feminist work it is clear that the most important achievement of feminist research has been to redraw the agenda of

sociology, to take account of the experiences and position of women in society, and to conceptualize gender as a primary social axis. Feminism has generated new ways of examining how women and men relate to one another in a variety of social and economic contexts – in the family, in the labour market, in the wider culture. In relation to the construction of gender differences, single factor explanations have been rejected in favour of a configuration of factors; the organization of the domestic economy and the gender-segregated nature of the labour market, 'industrial apartheid' (Wainwright, 1978); the impact of powerful ideologies encoding representations of 'motherhood', 'feminine nature' and the 'proper role' for women in society; the influence of socialization and educational processes; the construction of feminine and masculine sexuality (Coward, 1983; Metcalf and Humphries, 1985; Weeks, 1986). At the psychological level there has been an interest in the internalization of gender identity into the unconscious structures of women's personalities (Segal, 1987); and the shaping of sexuality through cultural influences and power relations (Coward, 1983, 1984; Weeks, 1986; Mort, 1987). The latter has opened up the entire field of sexual politics.

Work on the division of labour and stratification has identified the specific experiences and positions of women, both in the 'private sphere' of the household, and the 'public world' of employment and the market. This includes issues such as the role of domestic labour; the interaction between the gender characteristics of the domestic economy and those of employment, and the effects of continuity and change (Crompton and Mann, 1986).

All this raises the problem of whether women can be viewed as a homogeneous group. In the main the conclusions are that gender is stratified, and that women will experience the general system of gender-based inequalities in varying ways, according to the nature of the paid employment they have, their specific position within a household structure, their age and their ethnicity and their access to cultural and economic resources, but this requires extensive concrete investigation (Crompton and Mann, 1986). Thus whilst systematic gender differences still exist there are also relative differences between women arising from divergent social and economic experiences (Wilson, 1987). Specifically, division and hierarchies between women as 'wage labourers' should not be overlooked.

Ideology is relevant to gender relations in two specific ways through the notions of 'femininity', 'masculinity' and 'domesticity' as 'sex roles'; and in the concealment of gender inequality. It can be argued that the power of ideology resides in its lack of visibility, and its influence is especially pronounced at 'moments' of 'moral or social' crisis. Thus, debates about child abuse and sexual morality are permeated with calls for the resurrection of the 'traditional family' and 'traditional sexual morality'. It can be shown that this ideology is not imposed upon women and men, rather it forms the general cultural climate in which gender identity is shaped; individuals actively draw upon existing notions, to form 'voluntarily' their 'own' identity (Winship, 1978). This is 'active subordination' in respect of women's acquisition of 'femininity'. Feminist theories have certainly succeeded in disclosing many of the underlying reasons for female subordination but it would be fair to say that much theory is still in a process of development.

Conclusion

Although women have formal, legal equality in British society, the evidence throughout this book demonstrates that such equality is qualified and marginalized by the operation of the socio-economic and cultural systems: women typically experience social inequality in terms of unequal access to paid employment, and economic resources; they are subjected to constraints and controls on personal autonomy, not experienced by men; they have unequal access to the controlling institutions of society and suffer general social subordination. Even women who occupy 'strategic' positions tend ultimately to be subordinate (Campbell, 1987a).

How can this be most adequately explained? It could reflect the existence of a 'patriarchal society' or 'patriarchal domination'; alternatively it could be an index of a particular 'stage' in societal development. This 'liberal' view would see current inequalities as subject to erosion by further social modernization (Turner, 1986), the contemporary position of women an advance on the preceding conditions of the nineteenth and early twentieth centuries. Another explanation could be that such inequality is the result of the intrinsic workings of patriarchy and capitalist production, which generate historically-specific constellations of gender and class relations. Finally, gender inequality could be theorized as bound up with the highly complex stratification system of an advanced industrial society, in which gender appears along with ethnicity, class and status as part of multidimensional building-blocks of interwoven differences.

While changes in gender relations and in the position of women can be exaggerated, changes can be noted in contemporary circumstances. Some expansion in employment considered to be male preserves; some relaxation in the more constraining aspects of traditional world-views about the role of women; some pressure for more equal opportunities. Such changes are partially the result of political demands (women's movement, welfare rights pressure groups, Women's Aid groups, some Labour Party and trade union activity); others are shaped by economic restructuring, the growth of the white-collar sector or the reorganization of jobs involved in 'deskilling'. But the entry of women into the labour force has not, as yet, fundamentally disturbed the demarcations between men's work and women's work. Women workers are still overwhelmingly concentrated in a narrow range of occupations, and any increase in employment occurs under continuing conditions of male supervision and privilege (Summerfield, 1984). For all the arguments about changing roles, the architecture of power in contemporary Britain remains in male hands especially in terms of the major institutions of power. Although traditional assumptions about women may not be so visible, they have receded to some extent in social security regulations, and in some areas of educational practices, the unequal production/property/cultural relations of the wider society have not been dramatically disturbed, and these underlying structures continue to set limits on the character and range of changes in gender relations. Changes which have occurred historically in the position of women – in legal status, in the nature of marriage, in the attributes of sexuality and in personal expressiveness – cannot be dismissed as superficial. But some perceived changes in gender relations are not objective changes at all but rather shifts in popular consciousness which do not match actual social and economic reality. For example, the popular view that Britain is in a 'post-feminist' stage of full emancipation for women is clearly misconceived on the basis of the evidence presented in this book. Overall, women's position is deeply ambiguous and contradictory. Significant transformations occurring in economic organizations and labour markets are now opening up new areas of employment for women, but concurrently the restructuring of public expenditure and privatization appears to be generating the 'feminization' of poverty where women are the chief casualties of accelerating inequalities (Rubery and Tarling, 1982; Walby, 1983; Scott, 1984; Coyle, 1985; Wilson, 1987; Kidd, this volume). Women's position cannot be disconnected from a broad analysis of current social and economic trends and the 'politics' which in part propels them. Gender relations should be theorized as dynamic and the complexities and subtleties of women's position needs to be recognized. However, this does not prevent grasping the typical patterns discernible in women's role in society.

3   Vital statistics

Ivan Reid

Here we are concerned with several fundamental aspects of life of women and men in our society. These aspects are often, though inappropriately, seen as simple biological and intransigent facts of life. We begin with a view of something of the demography of sexes – their sizes, age structures and distribution – leading to a consideration of sex differences in the chances of survival at birth and in childhood. There are substantial accounts of various aspects of health, of causes of death and of life expectancy. Finally, we look at sex differences in that commonly regarded vital statistic, marital status and experience.

Because of the nature of these topics and the concerns of this chapter, much use is made of governmental statistics. While the purpose and manner in which such data were collected do not always coincide with our objectives, they are comprehensive in scope and in providing both a national and an historical picture. The topics covered here are not simply matters of sex. They are clearly related to the culture and development of our society. Of particular importance are the other major forms of social stratification, namely age and social class. While reference to the interrelationships of these factors with the topics covered is made in the text, space has precluded a full treatment. Interested readers will find that the quoted references usually provide more information on age and often on social class (see also, *The Health and Lifestyle Survey*, 1987). I have reviewed social class extensively elsewhere, including data in respect of birth, health and death (Reid, 1981, 1989).

As was recognized in Chapter 1, all data have limitations and have to be viewed from within these limits. These considerations, not rehearsed here, must be borne in mind when reading the present chapter, along with some particular concerns. Most medical data come from the analyses of people seeking or receiving treatment or care and so obviously tell us nothing directly about the health of others. Left unrecorded are those health incidents and conditions that are left untreated, self-treated via the chemist, or otherwise. Self-reported levels of health and ill-health are clearly subjective and cannot be categorized in a way which would

45

allow direct comparison with medical data. The categories used in medical research are often discrete entities in which aspects of the public's health concern may be lost or disguised. For example, menstrual cycle problems and forms of back pain are not recorded in a single category and do not appear in the list of the ten most frequent reasons for females consulting a doctor. If they were treated as a single category they would be among the five most frequent reasons (Wells, 1987).

Official health statistics have been accused of being male-biased and therefore relatively uninformative about women (see, for example, Macfarlane, 1980). What is clear is that until comparatively recently many studies of health have not directly addressed sex differences. Indeed, it is perhaps surprising that medical literature does not always use social variables, such as sex. This is probably because the condition, rather than the patient, has traditionally been the centre of focus. Some of these considerations are specifically illustrated below, but what we view is a picture of vital sex differences from existing evidence.

The demography of sex

The most fundamental aspect of the demography of the sexes is the biological fact that the sex ratio at birth is imbalanced in favour of males. In Western societies there are about 105–6 male births to each 100 female births, while worldwide higher variations have been observed – for example, in Korea one of 115.3 males (Novitski, 1977). It has been suggested that at fertilization the figures could be more disproportionate, at around 60 males to 40 females (Penrose, 1973). It seems likely that implantation and all subsequent stages of gestation display a higher wastage of male than female foetuses (Teitelbaum, 1972).

Despite this fact, women are the majority sex in our society. The figures in Table 3.1 reveal that, of the estimated 49,923,500 persons in England and Wales in 1985, 51.3 per cent were females and 48.7 per cent males – the difference amounting to an extra 1,263,500 females. A female majority has been the case historically, though an interesting change has taken place during the present century. Earlier this century there were more females than males in each of the age groups, reflecting the fact that, while more boy babies were born, their chances of survival and their expectation of life were poorer than girls' (see below). By the 1931 Census, as the result of improvements in medical and health care and consequent enhanced survival at birth, there was a higher percentage of boys than girls in the age group 0–14 years in England and Wales. This change has been maintained, so that by

Table 3.1   *Percentage of each sex in age groups[a], England and Wales,
June, 1985.*

Ages	% of population	Females	Males	Difference in 000s	
All	100	51.3	48.7	1263.5	More females
0–9	12.2	48.7	51.3	160.5	More males
10–19	14.7	48.7	51.3	194.5	
20–29	15.6	49.4	50.6	96.2	
30–39	14.1	49.8	50.2	33.2	
40–49	11.7	49.7	50.3	38.9	
50–59	10.8	50.4	49.6	48.3	More females
60–69	10.1	53.3	46.7	336.0	
70–79	7.6	59.5	40.5	713.2	
80–89	2.9	70.4	29.6	583.0	
90 +	0.4	80.0	20.0	106.3	

Ages	% of population	Females	% of all Females	Males	% of all Males
Under 16	20.5	48.7	19.5	51.3	21.6
16 to 44	42.1	49.4	40.6	50.6	43.7
45 to retirement age[b]	19.1	43.2	16.1	56.8	22.3
Over retirement age[b]	18.2	66.9	23.8	33.1	12.4

a. Estimated, 1981 Census-based.
b. 60 for females, 65 for males.
Devised from Table 1, *Mortality Statistics 1985A* (1987).

1985 males were the majority in all age groups up to 40–9 years,
while the older age groups displayed female majorities increasing
in size with age (see Table 3.1). It seems unlikely, however, that in
the future males will become the majority sex in all age groups.
Current projections of the figures suggest that the male majority
will remain only up to the 50–9 years age group for the next 25
years. Whereas the ratio of women over men in the 75 year and
over age group is at present 2:1, by the year 2011 it will have
fallen to 1.6:1 (Wells, 1987). Both these predictions are subject to
changes in mortality, fertility and migration.

As the lower part of Table 3.1 displays, demographic differences,
together with differing retirement ages for the sexes, means that
almost twice the proportion of women compared to that of men
were over the age of retirement (23.8 compared with 12.4 per
cent). At the same time, 65.2 per cent of males and 60.1 per cent

of females were under the age of 45 years. There are likely to be many social implications arising from the fact that women remain a majority only in the older age groups. It is of more than passing interest to note that the heightened interest in women's rights and position, together with the emergence of women's movements, have occurred at a point in history where for the first time those women most likely to be actively involved in such concerns are a sexual minority.

There is some geographical variation in the sexual composition of our society. This is mainly due to the higher male births and longer female lives, already mentioned, together with sex-selective migration. Consequently, the proportion of males is higher in areas with high birthrates and lower in areas with high numbers of the elderly. Major contrasts are to be found only between or within individual settlements (*People in Britain*, 1980). Concentrations of men are scattered and are to be found in heavily industrialized areas, such as the West Midlands, South Yorkshire, Slough and Staines, Teeside, areas on coalfields, and some inner-city areas of the Midlands and the South. Some of these areas are likely to be affected by the presence of New Commonwealth immigrant groups, among whom men predominate. Male concentrations are also to be found in rural areas as a result of female migration out, in the face of inadequate employment opportunities. On the other hand, concentrations of women are most marked in coastal retirement areas – the coasts of Kent, Sussex, Dorset, Devon, North Wales and West Lancashire. Older urban areas, like West London, Liverpool, Newcastle and Scottish cities, also have higher proportions of women, possibly because of selective migration in by younger women and out by men, together with higher male mortality rates in deprived areas (though such concentrations are absent from cities in the Midlands).

Birth, infancy and childhood
An analysis of the 694,000 live births in Great Britain in 1983 showed that 357,000 were male and 338,000 were female: a sex ratio of 105.6 to 100 (*Annual Abstract of Statistics*, No. 122). This ratio displays some variation over time, being high at 106.7 in 1973 and low at 103.8 between 1900–2. Births in 1983 represented a crude birthrate of 12.7 per 1000 population of all ages and a general fertility rate of 59.6 per 1000 women aged 15 to 44 years. Both these rates are considerably lower than in the previous decade; for example, in 1968 they were 17.1 and 88.2 respectively.

Not only are stillbirth rates slightly higher for males but figures

*Table 3.2   Stillbirth, infant and child deaths rates, by sex England and
                  Wales, 1985*

	Girls	Boys	
Stillbirths[a]	5.2	5.9	per 1000 total births
Neonatal deaths [b]	4.8	6.0	
Postneonatal deaths [c]	3.5	4.5	per 1000 live births
All infant deaths	8.2	10.4	
Death rate per million			
1–4 years	498	408	
5–14 years	255	184	
Number of infant and child deaths	3696	4979	

a. Stillbirths are births beyond the 28th week of pregnancy at which there is no sign of life.
b. Neonatal deaths are deaths within the first month following live birth.
c. Postneonatal deaths those between 1 month and a year following live birth.
Devised from tables 13 and 16, *Mortality Statistics 1985*, B [1987], table 4, *Mortality Statistics 1985*, C [1987], and table 2.21, *Annual Abstract of Statistics No. 122* [1986].

show that infancy and childhood are safer for girls than for boys (see Table 3.2). In 1985 the number of boys' deaths in the first year following birth is more than a quarter higher than that of girls – 10.4 compared with 8.2 per 1000 live births – the largest differences being in the first week and month of life. During childhood the sex differences in death rate increases with age. At ages 1–4 years the male death rate is 22 per cent higher than that for females, while at ages 10–14 years it is 39 per cent higher. Both infant and child mortality are related to social class, displaying a rise in incidence across the social classes from Registrar General's class I to class V (for a full review, see MacFarlane and Mugford, 1984, a and b). Apart from health, childhood appears less hazardous for girls than for boys; for example, girls have lower rates of hospital admission, out-patient treatment and deaths because of accidents (MacFarlane, 1979). Finally, though fortunately the numbers are relatively low, more boys than girls start life with a malformation, the rates per 10,000 total births in 1980 being 226 for boys and 196 for girls (*Congenital Malformation Statistics*, 1983).

Health, health behaviour and health services
A number of views of the distribution of sickness, disease and other conditions of ill health – normally referred to as morbidity – which indirectly provide evidence concerning the state of health of

Table 3.3   Self-reported health and health behaviour, by sex, Great Britain[a]
(percentages)

	Females	Males
Chronic sickness	32	30
Limiting chronic sickness	19	17
Acute sickness[b]	14	11
Number of restricted activity days[c]	27	20
Consulted GP[b]	15	11
Number of GP consultations[c]	5	3
In-patient hospital stay	11	8
Reported health as:		
Good	54	64
Fairly good	32	26
Not good	15	11

a. By persons aged 16 and over.
b. In 14 days prior to interview.
c. In a 12-month reference period.
Derived from Tables 8.1, 8.2, 8.3, 8.4 and 8.9, *GHS 1984* [1986]; and Table 7.5, *GHS 1980* (1982).

our society, may be gained from a variety of governmental research. There are two aspects of health, which while related do not always coincide. The subjective – how people feel about, and react to, their health or its lack; and what might be seen as the objective – the diagnosis made, and treatment given, by doctors when consulted. Those two aspects of health are the first concerns of this section, which also includes consideration of some selective specific conditions, of the relationship of aspects of lifestyle with health, together with the use of, and sexual composition of, the health services. A further, though indirect, view of morbidity is provided in the following section on causes of death. We have neither space nor data to deal with the further important aspect of ill-health, its individual and social consequences.

Self-reported health
The General Household Survey (GHS), the research for which is continuous, contains a series of questions to elicit people's views of their health and aspects of their health behaviour. Some of the topics covered are published each year, while others feature, and are treated in greater depth, only from time to time. A distinction is made between chronic sickness – long-standing illness, disability or infirmity – and acute sickness – that occurring in the fourteen days prior to interview and which restricted normal activities. As

can be seen in Table 3.3, 32 per cent of females compared with 30 per cent of males reported chronic sickness and there was a similar percentage difference (19 and 17) who saw such sickness as limiting their activities in any way (*GHS*, 1984). Similarly, a higher percentage of females reported acute sickness and more days of restricted activity due to sickness. They were also more likely to have consulted a GP in the previous fourteen days, to have consulted one more often in the previous year and to have been a hospital inpatient, than were males.

Obviously, age is a significant factor in health and sickness and, as we have seen in Table 3.1, the age structures of the sexes are different. In childhood (0–15 years) males have higher rates of chronic and limiting sickness than females (16 and 7 per cent, compared with 13 and 5), between the ages of 16 and 64 the rates are almost identical, but females have higher rates at ages 65 or over (63 and 45, compared with 59 and 42). This difference is at least partly due to longer life-expectancy (see section below), so that elderly women are, on average, older than men in the same age group. For acute sickness the percentages are closer, except in the cases of ages 65 or over, where the figure for females is 19 and that for males 11. Women over the age of 16 report a larger average number of days of restricted activity than do men, again particularly in the eldest age group where the number of such days is 53 compared with 38. On the other hand, differences between the sexes in the use of GPs are particularly pronounced in the age group 16 to 44 years, where the women's consultation rate (over twice that of men) is partly accounted for by aspects of childbirth and family planning (which accounted for 12 per cent of consultations by this group in 1981) (*GHS*, 1981), although acute sickness is more prevalent amongst women than men. This is confirmed by the *Health and Lifestyle Survey* (1987) which asked its repondents to identify which of 13 common symptoms they had experienced in the previous month. With the exceptions of painful joints, indigestion and cold/flu at ages 18 to 44 years, and ear problems and coughs at ages 45 to 84 years, a larger percentage of women than men reported they had had each symptom. Some 28 per cent of women compared with 16 per cent of men reported having suffered from four or more of the symptoms, the biggest differences occurring at ages 40–59 years.

Persons aged 16 years and over are also asked by the *GHS* to rate their own general health. A smaller percentage of women see their health as being 'good' and a larger one as 'not good' than do men (see lower part of Table 3.3). Such self-reported health differences between the sexes are also to be found among those with, and without, chronic sickness and across all the age groupings (*GHS*, 1980). Explanation of these differences is not simply a question of the incidence of health problems and hence not straightforward. Apart from the possible variation in the seriousness of conditions, it seems probable that the variation also reflects sex differences in attitudes towards health. For example, that the sexes have different concepts of good health, that men may be less and women more, willing to admit problems, or to be concerned about them. Blaxter (1987) found that both women and men tended to identify a male when asked to 'think of someone who is really healthy', hence it could be that healthiness is less readily seen as a female characteristic. At the same time, it does appear that some common problems apply particularly to women, for example, headaches, constipation, varicose veins, menstruation and trouble with the feet.

Differences in the incidence of particular types of ill-health in the sexes are indicated in a variety of separate sources – from analyses of general practitioner consultations, of absences from work, hospital admissions and the causes of death. The first three are dealt with here and the last in the following section of this chapter.

Consulting a GP

The data in Table 3.4 are the results of the careful recording of the consultations undertaken by doctors in 43 practices in England and Wales during one year, expressed as rates per thousand persons on the practices lists, by sex and diagnosis. Overall the female rate of consultation was 18 per cent higher than that of males (see row 14). Accidents, poisoning and violence is the only case where the male rate was higher than the female. Diagnoses for which the female consultation rate was particularly high in comparison with the male were: diseases of the blood (three times higher), mental disorders (twice as high) and endocrine, nutritional and metabolic diseases. In the latter case, half the women compared with a quarter of the men consulted about obesity – reflecting the sex differences in this condition (see p. 61 below).

Consultations involving such things as inoculation, vaccination, contraceptive advice, cervical smears, medical examinations and social problems were two and a quarter times higher for females than for males. The same source reveals that female rates of referral to hospital and other institutions were higher than those for males, and marginally more consultations with females were conducted in the patient's home, rather than the surgery (probably due to age and disability differences between the sexes).

Table 3.4   Patients consulting NHS general practitioners [rate per 1000^a], by selected, main diagnosis and sex, 1981–82

	Females	Males	All
Infectious/parasitic disease	128	106	117
Cancer and other neoplasms	16	11	14
Endocrine/nutritional/ metabolic disease^b	37	20	29
Diseases of the blood/blood organs	12	4	8
Mental disorders	113	55	85
Diseases of nervous system	150	131	141
Diseases of circulatory system^c	94	75	85
Diseases of respiratory system^d	282	256	270
Diseases of digestive system^e	76	68	72
Pregnancy^f	16	–	–
Accidents/poisoning/violence	110	117	114
Symptoms/signs/ill-defined conditions	182	134	160
Supplementary classification^g	273	121	200
All diagnoses^h	766	652	712

a. Of population at risk, all ages, rates are rounded.
b. Includes diabetes and nutritional deficiencies.
c. Includes heart disease, embolisms and thrombosis.
d. Includes influenza, pneumonia, bronchitis and pneumoconiosis.
e. Includes ulcers and cirrhosis of the liver.
f. For ages 15–24 and 25–44, rates are 41 and 33 respectively.
g. Includes inoculation/vaccination, contraceptive advice, cervical smears, medical examinations and social problems.
h. Includes diagnoses not specified here.
Derived from Tables, 17 and 9, *Morbidity Statistics from General Practice 1981–1982* [1986].

Incapacity for work

Consultation with one's local doctor involves not only a very wide range of short-term and chronic conditions but also the whole range of levels of seriousness of such conditions. The first and obviously deeper level of ill-health is incapacity for one's normal activities. For our purposes a useful indicator is absence from work due to sickness or injury certified by a medical practitioner (see Table 3.5). While obvious this indicator is not absolute, since variation can be assumed in both doctors' readiness to certify, and patients' seeking absence from work. Attitudes towards sickness and work, work habits, conditions and demands are clearly involved. Some manual jobs are more hazardous and more demanding of physical fitness than most non-manual ones. The *GHS* reports higher rates of absence from work due to sickness amongst manual workers (there was a rise in the gradient of such

Table 3.5   Percentage[a] of certified incapacity for sickness benefit[b], by selected, grouped causes[c] for each sex, Great Britain, 1984–5

	Women	Men
Infective, parasitic diseases	4.5	3.0
Cancer and other neoplasms	0.6	1.3
Endocrine, nutritional, and metabolic diseases	1.2	1.2
Mental disorders	11.0	7.1
Diseases of nervous system	2.7	3.3
Diseases of circulatory system	3.9	9.9
Diseases of respiratory system	11.6	12.5
Diseases of digestive system	5.1	7.7
Diseases of genitourinary system	8.6	1.6
Diseases of pregnancy, childbirth, and puerperium	8.0	–
Diseases of musculoskeletal system	14.3	18.6
Symptoms and ill-defined conditions	14.0	8.8
Accidents, poisonings, violence	11.6	22.7
Other	2.9	2.3

a. Rounded to one decimal place.
b. Spells of more than three days commencing between 2 April 1984 and 30 March 1985.
c. For details of causes see notes to Table 3.4.
N = 1 per cent sample of claimants.
Devised from Table 3.65B, *Social Security Statistics 1986* (1986).

absence across the social classes) and among those dissatisfied with their jobs. Further, when looking at the figures in the table it should be remembered that there is considerable variation not only in the proportion of women and men at work (see Chapter 6) but also in their age structures. Women at work are, as a group, younger than men, because of differing retirement ages and breaks in, or termination of, employment associated with marriage and child-bearing. With these limitations, these data for the working population show somewhat different sex differences to those for GP consultations.. Men have a higher percentage of incapacity than women because of cancer (twice as high) diseases of the circulatory system (two and a half times) and digestive system (50 per cent higher) and because of accidents, poisoning and violence (almost twice as high). Women have five times the incapacity because of diseases of the genitourinary system, which together with those of pregnancy account for nearly 17 per cent of their incapacity. A further 14 per cent of women's incapacity, compared with 8.8 per cent of the men's, is diagnosed as symptoms and ill-defined conditions. Women also have rates of about 50 per cent higher than men for mental disorders and infective and parasitic diseases.

Hospital admission

A further general indicator of the seriousness of ill-health is admission to hospital, though again there will be a variation on a host of factors – like availability of beds, referral practice, circumstances of the would-be patient and, indeed, choice. Our view is limited to NHS hospitals, though the availability and use of private hospitals also affects the situation. Note that in Table 3.6 the rates are expressed as per 10,000 population, whereas in Table 3.4 the rate is per 1000, so direct comparisons of incidence can be made only with appropriate movement of the decimal place. Also, as has been pointed out, such comparisons are limited by the fact that the data arise from separate measures (see also below). The first section of Table 3.6 shows that female admission rates to hospital (excluding maternity) are higher than male, at 1091 compared with 1015. This difference is more than accounted for by admission rates for complications of pregnancy and childbirth. Added to which the female admission rate for diseases of the genital system and disorders of the breast is three times higher than that for males. Females also have around 40 per cent higher rates for endocrine, nutritional and metabolic diseases, together with mental disorders and marginally higher rates for symptoms and ill-defined conditions. Among the causes with higher admission rates for males are diseases of the respiratory, digestive and urinary systems, and injuries.

With respect to mental health the second section of the table reveals an interesting sex difference between mental illness and mental handicap admissions. In the first, as might be expected from its incidence in GP consultations, absence from work and non-psychiatric hospital admissions, the female rate is higher than the male (47 compared with 35 per 10,000). In contrast, admission for mental handicap is higher for males and the proportional difference between the sexes is even greater: males 8.4 per 10,000 compared to 6.5 for females.

Use of health services

As we have seen above there is clear evidence that women make greater use of health services than do men. It is also clear that a major reason for this, quite apart from the age differences between the sexes, lies with conditions surrounding, and related to reproduction. We have seen how the exclusion of pregnancy and childbirth together with associated complications removes much of

Table 3.6 *Hospital in-patient admission[a] rate per 10,000 population, by
cause; mean duration of stay[b] and average number of beds in use[c],
by sex, England, 1984*

	Female	Male
Non-psychiatric		
Infective, parasitic diseases	14	17
Cancer and other neoplasms	108	98
Endocrine, nutritional and metabolic diseases	21	15
Diseases of the blood	10	9
Mental disorders	10	7
Diseases of nervous system	22	21
Heart disease	57	83
Diseases of respiratory system	77	104
Diseases of digestive system	99	115
Diseases of urinary system	18	24
Diseases of genital organs[d]	113	37
Complications of pregnancy/childbirth/puerperium[e]	140	–
Symptoms, ill-defined conditions	149	144
Injuries[f]	60	86
All[g]	1091	1015
Mean duration of stay[b]	12	9
Average number of beds in use[c]	3766	2634
Mental health		
Mental illness hospitals/units	47	35
Mental handicap hospitals/units	6.5	8.4

a. Excluding maternity; rounded.
b. In days.
c. Used daily per million population.
d. Includes females disorders of the breast.
e. Period following childbirth, normally six weeks [population is females aged 15–44].
f. Excludes fractures/dislocations/sprains/strains.
g. Includes causes not specified here.
N = One in ten sample of patients in NHS hospitals.
Derived from Tables 9.2, 9.7 and 11.2., *Health and Personal Social Services for England* [*1986*], and Table 51, *Hospital In-patient Enquiry, 1985* [1987].

the reported sex differences. What cannot be discovered from present data is the extent to which the long-term effects of childbearing and, indeed, contraception (particularly the 'pill') affect the health of women and hence their use of health services. For a discussion of the need for a new definition of reproductive mortality (see Beral, 1979). Nor can we identify the difference between the effects of reproductive health risk of women and particular occupational health risks for men, let alone the combination of the two, which some women experience. Beral (1985) analysed the causes of death of 1.2 million women aged 45 to 74 years and found that those who had given birth were more likely to have died from diabetes, mellitus and gall bladder disease and certain circulatory diseases than those who had not. However, as yet, the available data do not allow for the identification of which aspects of pregnancy are most strongly related (Wells, 1987).

These considerations apply equally to the use of hospitals. Hospital stay rates for all causes other than maternities are highest, and markedly so, for ages 0 to 4 and 65 years and over, for both sexes. Males have higher rates than females in childhood (0–14 years), lower rates between the ages of 15 and 54, and higher rates from 55 years and upwards. The average length of stay in hospital also displays a sex difference, being nine days for males and twelve for females (*Hospital Inpatient Enquiry*, 1985). This difference is due to the combination of the factors of age, cause of admission and treatment, together with the standard of home care available to, and role demands upon, discharged patients. These latter factors are probably, in general, balanced in favour of men, though clearly varying with age and circumstance. Sex differences in length of stay are pronounced at ages 65 and over. Women's average stay rises from three days longer than men at 65–9, to eight days at 75–9 and eleven days at 85–9; with 69 per cent of female beds and 53 per cent of male beds being occupied by those over the age of 65. Length of stay is very similar for sexes among children up to age 15, while between the ages of 16 and 54 the average male stay is slightly longer than the female.

Given the differences in the use of health services by the sexes we have so far viewed, it is not surprising that the average annual cost to the NHS per female is higher than that per male – £272 compared with £234 in 1984 (*Social Trends* No. 17). This difference is almost completely accounted for by the much greater cost per female aged 75 years and over (£1159 compared to £945), since from ages 0–24 and 45–74 average male costs are higher and for ages 25–44 the female cost amounts to only £6 more.

Specific conditions

Obviously the sex differences in health outlined so far, based as they are on generalized types of diagnosis, mask further and subtle differences. Because of both the lack of literature and the scope of this chapter, our view of the finer details of sex differences in health is both selective and limited. Also at this point it is appropriate to reiterate the recognized limitations of the data viewed so far. The data are only of presented and diagnosed conditions, so that the extent to which they provide a straightforward view of the incidence of ill-health in the population is questionable. To be sure that they did would require knowledge about those not in contact with health services, any sex difference in willingness to use services, and whether there was sex bias in the diagnoses, treatment and admission.

As we have seen, women apparently suffer more from mental illness and disorders than do men. A more detailed view of sex differences in the incidence and diagnoses of mental illness is provided by Grimes (1978). By relating all first admissions to mental hospitals and units in 1975 to the estimated populations of each sex, allowing for deaths, it was calculated that about 10 per cent of the entire population would be admitted during their lifetime. The sex differences were quite stark, at roughly 1 in 12 (8.6 per cent) for men and 1 in 8 (12.4 per cent) for women. Only at ages lower than 17 years was the male probability of admission higher than the female. The only diagnostic group having a higher male than female rate was alcoholism and alcoholic psychosis – the rates being very similar for schizophrenia, drug dependency and personality disorders – while all other diagnoses including depressive and other psychosis, senile and pre-senile dementia and psychoneuroses, had higher female than male rates. However, MacFarlane (1980) has raised the question of whether there is more likelihood that a mentally sick man would be cared for at home than a woman.

Data reveal that in the course of a year one woman in every 20 compared to one in 50 men aged between 25 and 75 seeks a consultation with a GP which is diagnosed as depression or anxiety (*Morbidity Statistics From General Practice 1981–1982*, 1986). Again, MacFarlane (1980) has questioned whether women run more risk of having their problems diagnosed as mental, while Brown and Harris (1979) in a study of only women showed there was considerable depressive illness among women who had never consulted a doctor about it. Measures used in the *Health and Lifestyle Survey* (1987) showed that women displayed more psychiatric symptoms and higher levels of neuroticism than men. Similarly a larger proportion of women than men were scored highly on an index of 'malaise'; based on answers to questions about psycho-social symptoms (sleeping patterns, anxiety, boredom, concentration, etc. (Stark, 1987)). While explanations have been offered in terms of constitutional differences (biological and reproductive) current reviews of the evidence reject these in favour of differences in the social environment, social roles,

Table 3.7   Sight, hearing and teeth of women and men[a] (Percentages)

	Women	Men
Sight		
Wears glasses[b]		
still has difficulty	13	8
has no difficulty	54	49
Does not wear glasses		
has difficulty	3	4
has no difficulty	30	39
Hearing		
Wears hearing aid	2	2
Does not wear hearing aid		
but has difficulty	10	13
has no difficulty	87	85
Teeth		
No natural teeth	30	21
Regular check up with dentist[c]	56	40

a. Persons aged over 16 years.
b. Includes contact lenses.
c. Percentage of those with some natural teeth.
Derived from Table 8.36, *GHS 1982* (1984); Table 7.19, *GHS 1979* (1981) and
Tables 9.41 and 9.49, *GHS 1983* (1985).

socialization patterns and tendencies to express emotional
difficulties, of women and men (Jenkins, 1985; Jenkins and Clare,
1985).

A further example is that, like most forms of ill-health, there are no
statistics for the actual incidence of sexually transmitted diseases.
The only readily accessible data are for patients seen in hospital
clinics which reveal that hospital treatment of sexually transmitted
diseases is more prevalent among men than among women. Of all
first-time patients seen in 1984, 56 per cent were men and the male
percentages for differing types were: syphillis 79; gonorrhoea, 63 and
non-specific infections, 71, other conditions, 43. However, for new
cases of gonorrhoea amongst young people aged up to 20 years there
was a female majority of 58 per cent (calculated from Tables 11.5 and
11.6, *Health and Personal Social Services*, 1986). But such data leave
unanswered actual incidence, including those treated elsewhere and,
obviously, those untreated.

An alternative strategy is to enquire directly of the population
by survey, though necessarily this is limited to more general and
less serious aspects of health. Table 3.7 summarizes *GHS* data on
sight, hearing and dental health. Men are more likely to have
good, unaided vision than are women (39 compared to 30 per

cent), while over half of men and two-thirds of women reported wearing glasses and/or contact lenses. While women of all ages were slightly more likely to wear glasses, the most marked sex difference was among those aged 16 to 44 years (women 41 and men 29 per cent). Difficulty with sight even when wearing glasses was greater for women than men at all ages (*GHS*, 1982). Similarly, the majority (over 60 per cent) of the registered blind and partially sighted persons in our society are women. Many of the causes of these conditions are mainly prevalent among the elderly and around 60 per cent of people with them are aged 75 years and over. Hence these sex differences are explained in terms of the greater expectation of life for females. However, the majority of blind and partially sighted children (0–15 years) are boys and a male majority exists among adults up to the age group of 50–64 years (*Registered Blind and Partially Sighted Persons*, 1987).

The same proportion of women and men wear hearing-aids, though it appears that in contrast to sight, slightly more males than females have difficulty with their hearing; 13 compared to 10 per cent (*GHS*, 1979). The overall percentage of women without any natural teeth is markedly higher at 30 per cent than men at 21 per cent, though the differences are only marked at ages over 34 years (*GHS*, 1983). Less people appear to be losing all their natural teeth now than in the past, though the decline has been more marked for men than women – the figures for total tooth loss in 1968 were women 40 and men 33 per cent (Gray et al., 1970). Interestingly enough, among those with some natural teeth women were more likely to have regular dental check-ups than men (56 compared with 40 per cent). As the *GHS* remarks the reasons why those with higher rates of total tooth loss are more likely to go to the dentist are not fully known. The common view that childbearing affects women's dental condition is not generally supported by dental research and there is no evidence that women are more willing to accept dentures than are men.

Lifestyle and health
There is growing evidence that certain social habits are related to health, or are hazards to health. In other words that lifestyle may well be the key to health and morbidity patterns. Being overweight, cigarette smoking, high alcohol consumption, type of diet and lack of exercise, have been so associated and display evidence of sex variation. However, health, or its lack, is the result of the interplay of many factors, the complexity of which is not as yet fully understood, rather than a single one in isolation [see also Overview, below].

Several studies have shown that women are more likely to be overweight than men. James [1979] in a study in the south-east region of England, found 8 per cent of women aged 15–29 years and 32 per cent of those between 50–65 were 120 per cent or more than the desirable body weight (as defined in Metropolitan Life Insurance Tables), compared with 6 and 18 per cent of men of the same ages. *The Health and Lifestyle Survey* used a measure called 'body mass index' which combined weight and height to derive four categories: under/acceptable/mildly over/weight and obese, separately formulated for the sexes [Cox, 1987; see also Knight 1984]. The percentage of women aged 18 and over who were obese was almost twice that for men – 15 compared to 8. While the percentage of both sexes who were obese rose from the age group 18–29 (women 7, men 4 per cent) to ages 50–59 (women 22, men 12 per cent), the percentage of obese men over this age declined, while that for women stayed at about the same level. Interestingly enough, the study also showed that women had better eating habits than men – more fruit and salads, less fried food and chips – and that about a quarter of both sexes thought they ate too much. However, food is not the only factor in obesity.

While regular, energetic physical activity is very much a minority pursuit there is clear evidence that those who indulge have lower resting pulse rates and blood pressures, better respiration functioning and less weight problems, than those who do not [Fenner, 1987]. In addition, exercise is associated with protection from, and prevention of, a variety of forms of ill-health, including mental, and with independence in old age [Wells, 1987, Fenner, 1987]. Women are less likely than men to take part in active leisure pursuits. For example, *GHS*, 1983 found 24 per cent of women compared to 39 per cent of men had indulged in at least one outdoor activity in the four weeks prior to interview, while excluding walking the percentages were 10 and 26 respectively. However, the critical factors in exercise are its frequency, length and intensity. *The Health and Lifestyle Survey* measured these and divided the reported activity of its respondents in the two preceding weeks into three groups – none, some, a lot. Among 18–39 year olds the percentage of women in 'none' was 45, and that in 'a lot' 17, while the corresponding percentages for men were 37 and 32.

Cigarette smoking is probably the best recognized health hazard and is regularly surveyed in the *GHS*. Table 3.8 contains the results for 1984. As will be seen, women were less likely to be smokers than men (32 compared with 36 per cent), much more likely never or only occasionally to smoke, and, if smokers, to use

Table 3.8   Cigarette smoking[a] by sex (percentages)

	Women	Men
Current smokers	32	36
Heavy smokers[b]	10	16
Light smokers[c]	22	20
Ex-regular smokers	17	30
Never or only occasional smokers	51	34
Average number of cigarettes smoked per week per smoker	96	115

a. By persons aged over 16 years.
b. 20 or more cigarettes per day.
c. Less than 20 cigarettes per day.
Derived from Tables 10.1, 10.6 and 10.7, *GHS 1984* [1986].

fewer cigarettes. It is of interest to note, however, that, in the face of a general decline in smoking, the sex difference has narrowed. Between 1972 and 1985 the percentage of men who smoked fell from 52 to 36 while the percentage of women decreased from 41 to 32 – only half the proportion. During the same period average consumption of cigarettes per week of male smokers decreased from 120 to 115 and that of the female increased from 87 to 96. Women are more likely to smoke low tar cigarettes and less likely to roll their own cigarettes (*GHS*, 1984).

The Royal College of Psychiatrists [1986] has estimated that alcohol is responsible for some 4000 deaths and 5000 first admissions to psychiatric hospitals each year. While the major concern has been with men who have higher levels of consumption than women, evidence is growing which suggests that women may be at higher risk of physical harm than men to a given quantity of alcohol. Accurate data on the population's drinking are, of course, not easy to collect. The data from the *GHS* in Table 3.9 however display a wide sex variation. Women were twice as likely to report being abstainers or only occasional drinkers than were men, while the latter were ten times more likely to be heavy drinkers (2 compared with 20 per cent) and three and a half times more likely to be moderate drinkers. The definitions of levels of drinking used are very wide [see footnote to table] and reported drinking has been consistently lower than would be expected from alcohol sales figures [*GHS*, 1984, 1986a].

Medical personnel
Our picture of sex differences in health would be seriously lacking without a view of the sex structure of those who provide health

Table 3.9   Adult alcohol drinking habits, by sex, Great Britain, 1984

	Women	Men
Heavy[a]	2	20
Moderate[b]	4	14
Light[c]	61	50
Occasional[d]	20	9
Abstainer	13	7

a. Drinks 7 or more units [eg $\frac{1}{2}$ pint beer/measure of spirit/glass of wine] between once a week and most days.
b. Drinks 7 or more units once/twice a month or 5–6 units between once a week and most days.
c. Drinks 1–4 units between once a month and most days.
d. Drinks 1 or more units between once a year and twice in six months.
Note: since drinking was based on type of drink most regularly used it may underestimate drinking of those who use more than one.
Derived from Table 11.2, *GHS 1984* [1986].

services. Table 3.10 shows a large male preponderance amongst hospital medical and dental staff and among general practioners. It is clear, however, that the situation is changing. Since 1977 the proportion of female hospital medical staff has increased by a third (from 18 to 24 per cent), with similar proportions among both consultants and senior registrars. Among general practioners, the female increase was of a quarter in medicine (16 to 20 per cent) and over a half in dentistry (11 to 17 per cent). However, the current position continues to have implications. While open to speculation, it is easy to appreciate that the present imbalance of the sexes among the chief, front-line providers of health services is likely to affect sex differences with respect to rates of consulting, type of diagnosis made and treatment received. As in many other arenas reviewed in this book, the medical profession can be characterized as male in definition and operation (see also Chapters 6, 7 and 8). The extent to which this may be changed, or affected, by the changing sexual composition of the profession remains to be seen. Nursing staff display an opposite sexual imbalance, with only 14 per cent of full-time and but one per cent of part-time nurses being men. Among male nurses the proportion who were registered (SRN, RMN or RMNS) as opposed to enrolled (SEN) was much higher than for female nurses. In stark contrast to the sexual composition of medical staff specializing in gynaecology and birth, hospital midwifery staff were still exclusively female in 1985. Only among community health service staff does the balance of sexes directly reflect that in society.

Table 3.10   Medical personnel, by sex, in England, 1985[a] (percentages)

	Women	Men	Number
Hospital medical staff[b]			
All staff	24	76	35,859
Consultants	13	87	13,458
Senior registrars	25	75	3,132
Hospital dental staff[b]			
All staff	22	78	1,248
Consultants	5	95	511
Senior registrars	16	84	97
Nursing staff			
All full-time	86	14	265,131
All part-time	99	1	137,400
Registered			
Full-time	78	22	89,809
Part-time	98	2	38,967
Enrolled			
Full-time	87	13	46,488
Part-time	99	1	30,466
Midwifery staff	100	0	21,185
General medical practitioners	20	80	25,788
General dental practitioners	17	83	14,334
Community health medical staff	57	43	6,145
Community health dental staff	51	49	1,864

a. Figures for nursing, midwifery and medical GPs are for 1984.
b. Excludes hospital practitioners and para 94 and 107 appointments.
Devised from Tables 3.5, 3.12, 3.17, 3.25, 3.30, 3.32 and 3.34, *Health and Personal Social Services Statistics 1986* [1986].

Death

Here we look at sex differences in only two aspects of death: mortality rates and causes of death. As has been suggested, males have a higher mortality at all ages than females, so their survival rates and expectation of life (see next section) are both lower. Table 3.11 provides a straightforward portrayal of this dramatic difference. The number of deaths and the population of each sex at given ages have been used to compute mortality rates (average number of persons in each sex and age group to die in a year); the table shows the male rates expressed as a percentage of the female.

Table 3.11   *Male mortality rates for 1980†82, expressed as percentages (rounded) of those for females by age*

Age	Male mortality as % of female
0	129
10	133
20	266
30	169
40	149
50	163
60	187
70	193
80	162
90	123

Devised from Table II, *English Life Tables* (1987)

The excess of male over female mortality is more than 50 per cent at nearly all ages from 15 to 80, and ranges from around 30 per cent during infancy and childhood to almost 100 per cent at age 70, with a single peak of 166 per cent at age 20 (due mainly to heavier male mortality from road accidents). As the Government Actuary remarks, the mortality rates for women aged 20 to 50 were no higher than those for men four to five years younger, widened to about seven years by the age of 65 and were still five years at age 80 (*English Life Tables*, [1987]). The same source reveals considerable improvement in mortality rates at every age and for both sexes throughout this century. Dramatically, infant mortality in 1980–2 was but a tenth of what it was in 1910–12 (1 compared with 11 of each 100 babies dying before their first birthday) and was only two-thirds of what it was in 1970–2. For women similar reductions have occurred for ages up to 30 years and 50 per cent reductions to the age of 70 and beyond. For men, other than in infancy, the reductions have not been as great, though the 1980–2 rates for ages up to 50 years are less than 50 per cent of those in 1910–12. At older ages the improvements are quite different for the sexes, women's rates for those over 80 have declined by 44 per cent and those for men by only 20 per cent.

In other words, premature mortality appears to be a male problem. Men account for nearly two out of every three deaths before the age of 70 and more than 26 per cent of male deaths occur before the age of 65 years compared to less than 16 per cent of female deaths (Wells, 1987).

There are a number of ways in which sex differences in the cause of death might be presented. Space here precludes a

Table 3.12   Death rates per million from selected, grouped causes[a] by sex,
             England and Wales, 1984

	Female	Male
Infectious/parasitic diseases	43	49
Cancer and other neoplasms	2563	3008
Endocrine/nutritional/metabolic diseases	200	140
Diseases of the blood	49	35
Mental disorders	279	149
Diseases of nervous system	211	210
Diseases of circulatory system	5576	5633
Diseases of respiratory system	1028	1262
Diseases of digestive system	388	292
Injury and poisoning	299	462
All causes of death[b]	11,149	11,646

a. For detail see notes to Table 3.4.
b. Includes causes not specified here.
Derived from Table 3, *Mortality Statistics 1984* (1985).

demonstration, by sex, of the obvious relationship between age and cause of death (the basic figures, without commentary, are to be found in the annual *Mortality Statistics* and for a commentary on women see Wells, 1987), so that here simple, overall views must suffice. Table 3.12 shows the sex differences in the number of deaths by selected, grouped causes in 1984, as rates per million of the population. As would be expected from our considerations so far, the overall rate and for most causes is higher for males. However, several causes show higher rates for females: diseases of the blood and digestive system, mental disorders, and endocrine, nutritional and metabolic diseases.

While the causes shown in the table are the same as those used in Table 3.4 (for consulting a GP) and Table 3.6 (inpatients in NHS hospitals), no real comparisons can be made between the incidence of death and the use of health services by cause, because of the large number of ill-defined, intervening variables involved. Similarly the data here, on causes of death, are limited in regard to providing a view of the incidence of ill-health and disability. This is because many of the latter are rarely responsible for death. For example, arthritis affects 41 per cent of the population aged over 65 years (Dreghorn et al., 1986), yet together with related disorders is recorded as responsible for significantly less than one per cent of mortality of people of that age (Wells 1987).

Perhaps a more revealing set of data is contained in Table 3.13,

Table 3.13   Percentage[a] of deaths due to selected, grouped causes, by sex, England and Wales, 1985.

	Female	Male	All
Cancer	23	25	24
respiratory organs	3	9	6
digestive organs	7	7	7
breast/bone/skin	5	0.4	3
genitourinary organs	3	4	4
Mental disorders	3	1	2
Diseases of circulatory system	49	48	49
ischaemic heart disease[b]	24	31	28
cerebrovascular disease[c]	15	9	12
Diseases of respiratory system	10	12	11
pneumonia and influenza	6	4	5
pulmonary	3	7	5
Disease of digestive system	4	3	3
Injury and poisoning	3	4	3
motor vehicle accidents	0.5	1	0.8
suicide	0.5	1	0.8
accidental falls	0.8	0.5	0.7
Other causes	8	7	8
All causes	100	100	100

a. Percentages over 1 rounded to nearest whole number.
b. Inadequate supply of blood to an organ.
c. Relating to blood vessels and blood supply to brain [stroke].
Devised from Table 14, *Mortality Statistics 1985c* [1987].

which shows deaths in 1985 expressed as percentages of deaths in each sex and overall, by cause. It is very clear that circulatory diseases, particularly heart disease, and cancer are the major causes of death in our society, together accounting for some 73 per cent of all deaths. Comparing the percentages for each cause for the population and the sexes reveals some interesting differences. Diseases of the circulatory system are responsible for almost half of all deaths (49 per cent). However, males are more likely to die of ischaemic heart disease (31 per cent compared with 24) and less likely to die of cerebrovascular disease (9 per cent compared with 15), than are females. (For definitions of these conditions see footnotes to table.) While about 24 per cent of all deaths are from cancer (male 25 and female 23 per cent), there are sex differences in its siting. The percentage of males dying of cancer of the respiratory organs is three times higher than that for females. While the sexes do not differ in the percentage of deaths from

Table 3.14   Sex differences in the expectation of life at various ages

	Female	Male
Expectation of life in years, at age[a]		
0	77.0	71.0
10	68.0	62.2
20	58.1	52.5
30	48.3	42.9
40	38.7	33.3
50	29.4	24.3
60	20.9	16.4
65	17.0	13.0
70	13.4	10.1

a. In years of life from age specified (rounded to first decimal place) based on deaths and estimated population for 1980–82.
Derived from Table V, *English Life Tables* [1987].

cancer of the digestive organs, markedly higher percentages of females die from cancer of the breast (together with that of bone and skin) – 5 compared with 0.4 per cent. While cancer of the cervix is an important cause of female death (0.6 per cent), the overall figure for cancer of the genitourinary system displays a higher percentage of male than female deaths (4 compared with 3 per cent).

The higher percentage of female deaths from influenza and pneumonia probably reflects the differences in the age structure of the sexes, while higher male figures for pulmonary disease and other conditions, including cancer of the lungs, may well be related to sex differences in occupation and smoking habits. More males than females die through injury and poisoning – twice the percentage in motor vehicle accidents (related to their greater exposure to risk). On the other hand, more females die from accidental falls and accidents in the home, again related to level of risk and age. Suicide, while the cause of only 0.8 per cent of all deaths, is twice as high for men as for women, although women are more likely than men to be admitted to hospital for non-fatal deliberate self-harm (Wells, 1981).

Expectation of length of life
It is evident from the differences in the age structure and death rates of the sexes that they also enjoy different average lengths of life. The Registrar General, using the actual deaths and the estimated population for the years 1980–82 computed the life

expectancy figures displayed in Table 3.14. Somewhat similar figures are used by insurance companies for fixing the rates for life insurance. It should be appreciated however that the life expectancies given here do not refer directly to the lives of the current population, since they are based on previously recorded lives and deaths which have been affected by conditions that may now be changed. With this limitation, however, they remain as accurate a view of life expectancy as is available. The table shows that in our society a girl at birth would, on average, be expected to live some six years longer than a boy, the expectation of life being 71 for males and 77 for females. This difference remains at just over five years, though dropping marginally through the age groups to 60 years, where it is 4.5, and to 70, where it is only 3.3 years. Notice that the age given should be added to the expectancy, so that at the age of 70 men would, on average, expect to live to 80.1 and women to 83.4 years.

During the present century there has been a fairly dramatic increase in life expectancy, though with marked sex differences, women benefiting more than men. Between 1910–12 and 1980–2 expectation at birth increased by 19.5 years for boys and 22 years for girls. Much of this change is due to the reduction of infant mortality, though at the age of 20 years life expectancy over the period has increased by over 8 years for men and just over 11 for women. At older ages the proportional improvement in expectation is even greater for women; whose expectation at age 60 displays an increase over the period of 5.4 years compared with only 2.6 years for men. As a consequence of this and differing retirement ages, expectation of life in pensionable age is almost 21 years for women (from the age of 60) but only 13 years for men (from the age of 65). And, as we have seen, women are in any case more likely to survive to pensionable age than men. Expectation of life is clearly related to other aspects of life in our society, particularly social class. For example, *Occupational Mortality* (1978) showed that a male subject from birth to the mortality rates of the Registrar General's social class I (professional) was in 1970–2 expected to live 7.2 years longer than one subjected to those of class V (unskilled manual).

Marital condition

Except for the family and school, marriage is the commonest institution in our society, being experienced by all but a minority of people. By the age of 40 only about 5 per cent of women and 9 per cent of men in our society have not been married (*Marriage and Divorce Statistics 1985* [1987]). The overall incidence of

Table 3.15   Percentages[a] of those aged 16 years and over, by marital status and sex, England and Wales, 1985

	Women	Men	Both	Total (millions)
Single	24	29	26	10.1
Married	58	63	61	24.0
Widowed	14	4	9	3.6
Divorced	5	5	5	1.9
Total (millions)	20.6	19.1		39.7

a. Estimated and rounded.
Devised from Table 1.1a, *Marriage and Divorce Statistics 1985* [1987].

Table 3.16   Average and median[a] age at marriage, by sex and marital status, England and Wales, 1985

Women	All brides	Spinsters	Widows	Divorced
Average age	27.5	23.8	54.5	35.7
Median age	24.3	22.8	55.3	34.4
Men	All grooms	Bachelors	Widowers	Divorced
Average age	30.2	26.0	59.9	38.9
Median age	26.7	24.9	61.3	37.3

a. Age which divides all into two groups, one marrying younger the other older, than that age.
Derived from Tables 3.5a and 3.5b, *Marriage and Divorce Statistics 1985* [1987].

marriage in the population of England and Wales is shown in Table 3.15. Of each 100 persons over the age of 16 in 1985, 61 were married, 26 single, 9 widowed and 5 divorced. While the same percentage of each sex was divorced, men were more likely than women to be single (29 compared with 24 per cent) and married (63 per cent compared with 58) and much less likely to be widowed (4 per cent compared with 14). These sex differences are mainly accounted for by three facts: women tend to marry at an earlier age than men; men are somewhat less likely to marry at all (to some extent related to the fact that there are more men than women under the age of 50 and that people of that age currently account for around 9 in 10 of all marriages); and women, who live longer, are more likely to outlive their spouses.

Sex differences in age at marriage can be illustrated in a number of ways. For example, of those aged between 16 and 19 years in 1985 it is estimated that 36 in each 1000 women but only 7 per 1000 men were married – a dramatic change from 1975 when the corresponding figures were 101 and 22 respectively. Table 3.16

shows the differences between sexes and marital conditions in terms of their average age and their median age at marriage. Median age is the age that splits all brides and grooms into two equal groups, one of which married before the given age and the other after it. Both sets of figures show consistent and markedly lower ages for women than for men. Leete (1979a) identified a growing surplus of single men at the younger marriageable ages, due to the unequal sex birth ratio, as well as to the fact that men tend to marry women from younger age groups than their own, which have been affected by declining birthrates. In turn, this widens the gap between the marriage rates of the sexes and leads to more men marrying women older than themselves. In the long term, it seems likely that the proportion of men who never marry will be larger than the proportion of women, reversing the pattern established between the wars. The gap between the number of bachelors and spinsters has grown quite dramatically – from 107 bachelors per 100 spinsters in 1961 to 123 per 100 in 1985.

Marriages are formally broken either by divorce or by the death of one partner, and, obviously, those divorced and widowed are eligible for remarriage. Consequently, marriage opportunities and rates are related not only to the basic demographics of the sexes and to differences in their length of life, but also to the incidence of divorce and changing cultural factors surrounding marriage, divorce and second and subsequent marriages. In 1985 only 64 per cent of all marriages were the first for both parties; 20 per cent were the first for one party only (of the other parties 94 per cent were divorced and 6 per cent widowed); and 16 per cent were second marriages for both parties (of which 76 per cent were both divorced, 10 per cent were both widowed, and 15 per cent were mixed). The divorce rate in our society has risen from 3.7 per 1000 of the married population in 1968 to 13.4 per 1000 in 1985. Leete (1979a), in analysing divorce data, suggested that 1 in 5 of the marriages of the early 1970s would end in divorce within 15 years of the ceremony, and that the figure would increase with the length of marriage. Wives are more likely than husbands to be granted a divorce: of divorces in 1985, 72 per cent were granted to wives, 28 per cent to husbands and hardly any (0.4 per cent) to both (*Marriage and Divorce Statistics 1985* [1987]. There is a similar sexual bias in the petitions for divorce, though a majority were filed by husbands in the period 1901–5 and during and immediately following both world wars. Differences exist between the sexes over which of the five 'facts' for the 'irretrievable breakdown of marriage' (the sole grounds for divorce since the Divorce Reform Act 1969) were used in divorce proceedings.

While nearly half of the divorces granted to women cited husbands unreasonable behaviour, 44 per cent of those granted to men cited wife's adultery.

The main differences between the sexes in widowhood are accounted for by factors we have already viewed – the higher death rates and shorter lives of men and their older average age at marriage. In 1985 there were some 0.7 million widowed men compared with nearly 3 million widowed women in England and Wales. Differences in the expectation of life are clearly indicated by the fact that of these, 0.5 million of the men compared with 2.3 million of the women were aged over 65 years. However, widows outnumber widowers at all ages over 20, for example, there are some four times the number aged between 20 and 29 years.

The remarriage rate of divorced and widowed men is nearly three times higher than that for women. This is mainly due to differences in the sizes of the eligible populations. There are many more widows and divorced women, especially in the older sections of the population, than men (*Social Trends* No. 17). Overall, the ratio of divorced men to women in 1985 was 78 per 100, and was due almost entirely to higher remarriage rates for male divorcees aged over 25 (Sparks, 1986). Leete's (1979b) study of divorced couples suggested the fact that women generally have care of children after the divorce does not explain sex differences in remarriage.

Some broken marriages result in one-parent families, of which Haskey (1986) estimated there were some 940,000 in Great Britain in 1984. *GHS* data suggest that by 1982–4 one-parent families amounted to 13 per cent of all families with dependent children in our society – an increase from 8 per cent in 1971–3. Only one per cent of all families with dependent children were headed by a lone father (a figure that has been stable since 1971), while 12 per cent were headed by a lone mother (a rise from 7 per cent in 1971). Some 91 per cent of heads of one-parent families were women. Table 3.17 provides a breakdown of the marital status of lone parents by sex and compares the early 1970s with the early 1980s. During that period the proportion of one-parent families headed by men fell from around 1 in 7 to 1 in 11. Among lone mothers there has been a marked increase both in the proportion who were divorced (25 to 40 per cent) and single (15 to 21 per cent). The first rise is accounted for by the general increase in divorce over the period and the accompanying decline in remarriage rates. The second rise is due in part to an overall rise in the number of illegitimate births and to an increasing proportion of mothers bringing up children on their own. The decline in the percentage

Table 3.17   One-parent families by marital status and sex of head, Great
Britain, 1972*4 and 1982*4

	1972–4	1982–4	Percentage change
Mothers			
Single	15	21	+6
Widowed	21	12	−9
Divorced	25	40	+15
Separated	26	18	−8
Fathers			
Single	1	—	−1
Widowed	6	2	−4
Divorced	3	4	+1
Separated	4	3	−1
All mothers	86	91	+5
All fathers	14	9	−5
Both	100	100	−

Derived from Table 6, Haskey [1986]; source *GHS*.

of lone parents of both sexes who were widowed or separated is
largely due to increasing numbers in the other categories.

Overview

With the exception of the first and last sections, this chapter has been
concerned with sex differences in the vital aspects of life – birth,
health and death. The illustration of these differences, at least within
the limitations of the data, has been straightforward. Their
explanation is much more problematic, as are their implications.

Explanations for sex differences in health and survival are, and
have been, sought across a broad spectrum. At one end are biological
factors, such as reproduction, constitutional and hormonal
differences, at the other social factors, such as differences in social
environment, roles and behaviour. Many of these provide evidence of
association rather than causal relationship. What remains clear, then,
is that health and its lack is affected by a complex interrelationship of
factors which are also dynamic. Currently attention is focused on
lifestyle and behavioural habits as key factors to health and morbidity
(Wells, 1987). It is also obvious that our knowledge is at present
limited and requires a considerable amount of new research which
directly addresses sex differences in health. Hence it is still
appropriate to conclude with Morris (1975):

> Prenatally and during infancy major biological causes are postulated
> for feminine superiority. Thereafter ways of living may be very

different – in occupation, for example . . . in the behaviour that culture expects. How much is biological, what social, is a continuing debate.

To which it is necessary to add, as this chapter has done, only some elaboration of the concept of culture, particularly in respect of those aspects which bear upon the incidence of disease, sickness and injury, people's reaction to ill-health, and the operation and use of the health services.

The whole of this chapter has demonstrated the very real effects of demography on the sex differences observed. The age structure and proportional differences between the sexes, together with cultural and economic factors, must be taken into account when viewing empirical data on differences in vital statistics between the women and men. Demographic factors also affect, or are related to, almost all the substantive areas dealt with in the rest of this book. This chapter has identified one distinct advantage to being a woman in our society: having a longer expectation of life than men. In the face of the extensive illustration of disadvantage for women in the data surveyed throughout this book, and indeed in itself, longer life might well be recognized as a crucial and enviable advantage.

4 Women and welfare

Tony Kidd

It used to be conventional to assume that the aims of the welfare state were to resolve human crises like poverty, ill-health and homelessness, and to deliver its services in such a way as to allow equal access to them. Thus Richard Titmuss (1963) defined welfare policy as 'all collectively provided services . . . deliberately designed to meet certain socially recognized "needs"; they are manifestations, first, of society's will to survive as an organic whole and second, of the expressed wish of all the people to assist the survival of some people'; and went on a few years later, to comment that social policy in Britain was 'moving towards . . . services . . . of high quality for all citizens in all areas irrespective of means, social class, occupation or ethnic group' (Titmuss, 1968). Readers of this book will be sensitized to his omission of 'gender'. Indeed, his belief in general terms that equal access to welfare was achievable will need careful and critical scrutiny, and more particularly, in relation to gender.

There is now abundant evidence that socio-economic factors continue to result in welfare inequalities. Le Grande (1982), for instance, has documented the stark failure of the post-Beveridge welfare state in achieving equality, and draws on a number of welfare services for evidence. Others have focused on particular services: the Black Report (1980), Townsend and Davidson (1982), Walters (1980) and Whitehead (1987) have demonstrated the disadvantageous position of lower socio-economic groups in gaining access to the National Health Service.

This chapter however will be concerned with the disadvantage suffered by women as compared to men in respect of access to welfare support. The basis of this discrimination lies in the state's assumption that women's natural role is fundamentally a domestic and childcare one. We shall see this expressed in a number of welfare measures drawn contemporaneously and historically. While some advances in overcoming sex discrimination have been made recently by virtue of our membership of the European Economic Community, the evidence suggests that these gains are modest, for they have been contradicted by other, more recent policy changes which have reinforced the discriminatory posture of public services.

We shall see that women's access to particular welfare services is conditioned by the nature of their contact with the labour market, which, although considerable, is generally not identical to that of men. It is this which diminishes their eligibility for welfare benefit. All this, however, is embraced by a cultural expectation that women pursue a domestic and caring role. Both factors account for their differential experience of welfare.

The unconventional family

So far as the woman who lives in a conventional family is concerned, the welfare state has historically regarded her role as residual to that of the husband, for in treating her as a dependant of the husband it has enabled the state to discharge its services at considerably less cost than if she were treated as an individual. We can see this well illustrated by referring to the nineteenth-century Poor Law. In those days paupers could be removed to the parish of 'settlement', particularly if they were likely to be a long-term burden on the parish. Parishes were reluctant to bear the burden of relief where they could legitimately claim that that burden belonged elsewhere. So far as the woman was concerned, she acquired the settlement of her husband on marriage. However, women without husbands and therefore forming an unconventional family, posed a long-term problem of dependency:

> widows with dependent children or single women with illegitimate children were prominent amongst these. The 58 cases removed from Leeds in 1841 included 11 widows, 10 single women with a bastard child and another single woman who was pregnant. In 1878 in Birmingham 34 of the 118 paupers removed were single or widowed women and 30 more of them were women with dependent children. (Rose, 1976)

Responsibility for the lone woman and her plight was more easily transferred. Whilst the widow has been more favourably treated since, the lone mother has continued to experience discrimination.

Sir William Beveridge had a clear conception of the form of family which was to underpin his model of the welfare state. He was keen to do everything possible to restore the family's unity after the disruptions of wartime. He therefore considered the family to be a unit, husband and wife regarded as a team. He was aware, however, that women's new status on marriage brought with it new risks:

> all women by marriage acquire a new economic and social status, with risks and rights different from those of the unmarried. On marriage a woman gains a legal right to maintenance by her husband as a first line

of defence against risks which fall directly on the solitary woman; she undertakes at the same time to perform vital unpaid services and becomes exposed to new risks, including the risk that her married life may be ended prematurely by widowhood or separation. (Beveridge, 1942)

Beveridge proposed (para. 347) insurance for the woman to cover divorce, legal separation, desertion and voluntary separation, but added the condition that the break-up should not be her fault, and that the husband's liability for maintenance remained. He did, however, recognize the difficulty of determining responsibility for the break-up of the marriage. Widows were incorporated into the insurance scheme and treated comparatively favourably compared to the deserted, separated and divorced women. While he recognized the latter group were a product of a 'risk' of marriage, he was greatly concerned not to be seen to be contributing to family break-up, and a more generous scheme might, he reasoned, produce that result. Nevertheless, the Report did propose to meet the 'marriage needs of women' by a furnishing grant for setting up home, a maternity benefit, a separation allowance, provision of domestic help for sick housewives, and family allowances. In the event, family allowances and maternity benefit were the only two to be successfully implemented.

Beveridge's scheme therefore sought to encourage and reaffirm family unity: 'taken as a whole, the plan for social security puts a premium on marriage, in place of penalising it' (para. 117). One-parent families were not discussed as a group by Beveridge, and unmarried mothers were only mentioned briefly in respect of the needs of their children. Only with the publication of the Finer Report in 1974 were they recognized as a separate and significant group. Beveridge's recommendations, however, were based on the social conditions of the 1930s. Divorce was then relatively rare (0.4 per 1000 married people in 1931); now it is around 12 per 1000 married people, some 30 times higher than in 1931. This above everything helps explain the steady growth of one-parent families, particularly in the 1970s and 1980s.

We are unable to say for certain how many one-parent families there are – we cannot tell, for instance, how many separated men and women there are at any one moment. The Census measures the number of one-adult households but this excludes those one-parent families living with other adults, e.g. their parents. Since 1971 however the *GHS* has provided data on the subject and a certain amount can be gleaned from the administration of social security benefits, particularly child benefit.

What seems clear is that, overall, there are about one million

Table 4.1   Families by type and lone mothers by marital status, Great Britain, 1971–85 (percentages)

Family type	1971	1977	1981	1985
Married couple	92	90	87	86
Lone mother	7	9	11	12
Single	1	2	2	3
Widowed	2	2	2	1
Divorced	2	3	4	5
Separated	2	2	2	3
Lone father	1	1	2	2
All lone parents	8	10	13	14

Derived from Table 3, *GHS 1985* (1986).

such families in Great Britain caring for over 1.6 million children. They have grown from 1 in 12 in 1971 to about 1 in 8 in the 1980s. During this period those categories of one-parent family which have grown the most have been unmarried mothers – from 1 in 7 to 1 in 4 of lone mothers, and divorced women – now representing nearly a half of the total. The growth in one-parent numbers has been almost entirely accounted for by an increase in lone mothers (an increase of about two-thirds) – the proportion of families headed by a lone father has hardly changed. Table 4.1 provides the evidence for these conclusions.

Eleven out of twelve one-parent families are headed by a woman and about six out of ten of all one-parent families are living in or on the margins of poverty (this compares with about two out of ten two-parent families). To be the head of a one-parent family, then, means you are most likely to be a woman and dependent, partly or wholly, on state benefits. Over a half of one-parent families in 1983 were either receiving supplementary benefit or had incomes below this minimum level (see Table 4.2) and in 1985 42 per cent of families dependent on Family Income Supplement (a benefit paid to families who are working but on low incomes) were one-parent (see Table 4.3).

Of all the groups classified as one-parent families the single, divorced and separated women are the most in need. A survey conducted for the Royal Commission on the Distribution of Income and Wealth indicated the relatively disadvantaged position of one-parent families, and the large proportion of the single, divorced and separated living under the official poverty line.

The low figure for 'lone men' is because 86 per cent of them worked and so would not be eligible for supplementary benefit,

Table 4.2   *Low income families with children, Great Britain, 1983*

	Below supplementary benefit level	In receipt of supplementary benefit	Above but within 140% of supplementary benefit	Total on low incomes
Number of families				
One parent	30,000	460,000	80,000	570,000
Two parents	170,000	390,000	770,000	1,330,000
One & two parents	200,000	850,000	850,000	1,900,000
Number of children				
One parent	50,000	770,000	160,000	980,000
Two parents	350,000	860,000	1,690,000	2,900,000
One & two parents	400,000	1,630,000	1,850,000	3,880,000

Derived from DHSS, and Hansard Written Answers, 30 October 1986, unpublished statistics published in *One Parent Factsheet* (1986).

Table 4.3   *Families receiving Family Income Supplement (FIS), Great Britain, 1985/6*

	Numbers in receipt of FIS	Average Payment
Two-parent families	118,000	£12.60
One-parent	84,000	£14.20
Total	201,000	

Figures may not add up due to rounding.
Derived from Hansard Written Answers, 16 July 1986; and DHSS unpublished statistics published in *One Parent Factsheet* (1986).

and the position of widows is eased by the existence of an insurance benefit for them and the possibility of additional earnings without it affecting benefit. Thus, it seems fairly clear 'that the problem of poverty in one-parent families relates mainly to those where the parent is a woman' (Royal Commission on the Distribution of Income and Wealth, 1978a).

While most two-parent families rely predominantly on earnings derived from one or more of their members' membership of the labour market, one-parent families rely heavily on other sources, more particularly social security benefits. The lone mother's link with the labour market is less tenuous than even the married

Table 4.4   Family income relative to supplementary benefit by type of parent

Type of parent	Family income as % of supplementary benefit under 100%
Single woman	58
Widow	18
Separated woman	43
Divorced woman	51
Lone man	12
All one-parent families	38
All two-parent families	4

Derived from Table 8.1, Royal Commission on the Distribution of Income and Wealth (1978a).

mother. Indeed, there seems some evidence that the position of lone mothers has been worsening in recent years. In 1982–84 lone mothers were less likely to work than married mothers (39 as against 49 per cent). In 1973–75, on the other hand, they were *more* likely to be in work, and the proportion of each group in work continued at around 50 per cent until the early 1980s. Since 1980–82, however, declining proportions of lone mothers have been working full-time from 22 to 17 per cent and from 11 to 6 per cent for those with a child under five. Their involvement in economic activity is likely to be constrained by the availability of both work and childcare facilities, and both have suffered recently. It should be noted, however, that lone mothers were more commonly in full-time work in 1980–82 (17 as compared to 14 per cent) but less likely to be working part-time (22 as compared to 35 per cent).

Lone men seem less disadvantaged in this respect since their level of economic activity is higher, and they are less likely to experience what is the norm for the majority of one-parent families headed by a woman – poverty. Table 4.5 shows the higher level of dependency on state benefits for lone mothers, and Table 4.6 breaks down the level of economic activity for each type of lone parent, the single woman being shown with the lowest involvement, probably because of the likelihood of her having young children.

With the exception of widows, the social security system has not dealt with one-parent families as a special case. The main strategy has been to provide some additions to existing benefits. So, these families are entitled to a 'one-parent benefit' under the child benefit scheme, and they are treated relatively favourably (compared with two-parent families) for FIS and SB entitlement

Table 4.5 Main source of income for one- and two-parent families, Great Britain, 1981 (percentages)

Main source of income	One-parent families headed by:		Two-parent families
	Women	Men	
State benefits	55	27	8
Earnings from employment	34	73	92
Maintenance payments	10	—	—
Other items	1	—	0.2
All sources of income	100	100	100

The figures are based on estimates derived from Department of Health and Social Security analysis of the 1981 *Family Expenditure Survey*. Because of rounding figures may not add up to 100 per cent.
Derived from House of Commons Hansard Written Answers, 21 November 1984.
Published in *One Parent Families Factsheet* (1986)

Table 4.6 Economic activity in one-parent families by type of parent

Type of parent	% in paid work
Single woman	44
Widow	56
Separated woman	57
Divorced woman	50
Lone man	86

Derived from Table 8.8, Royal Commission on the Distribution of Income and Wealth, 5th Report (1978).

as regards income levels and qualification for benefit. Also, in the case of FIS, the definition of 'full-time work' is less in hours per week for one-parent families than is normally the case.

The changes introduced in 1988 as a result of the 1986 Social Security Act, has meant that 'Income Support' has replaced Supplementary Benefit, and the long-term rate, payable in the past to most groups (except the unemployed) who had been receiving benefit for 12 months, ceased. One-parent families however receive a 'lone parent premium', but the net effect of this, plus the abolition of the long-term rate, will result, it is estimated, in about 150,000 one-parent families losing and 190,000 gaining from these new arrangements with the short-term claimants being the gainers (Social Security Consortium, 1986).

If present trends continue to the end of the century, there are likely to be something between 1.5 million one-parent families in

2005 according to the Government (Fowler Report, 1985) and 2.8 million according to the National Council for One-Parent Families. It is clear that these families carry a heavy burden financially and that women shoulder this burden most heavily. The Social Security Act 1986 will ensure that large numbers of these families will continue to be part of the army of the poor, dependent on means-tested benefits, and therefore caring for their children under immense financial constraints.

Some of the difficulties faced by one-parent families stem from them not being the conventional family form recognized by the social security system. This system was built on the assumption that 'need' essentially resulted from an 'interruption of earnings', and that the typical insurance contributor was 'the adult male worker whose income was derived solely from earnings and who needed protection when such earnings were interrupted by unemployment, accident or disease' (Harris, 1977). So, the welfare state assumes a 'conventional' family and a typical recipient of benefit (i.e. the husband) as the assumed breadwinner. Two crucial assumptions are being made here: only the husband would control family finances, and that his distribution of it to his family would be equitable. We shall turn to these now.

The conventional family
When Beveridge outlined his proposals for the reconstruction of domestic life around the 'five giant evils' – want, disease, ignorance, squalor, and idleness – he had a clear idea of how women would fit into his scheme. He recognized three categories of women. The separated/divorced and widowed have already been discussed in this chapter. The single woman he expected to be a full member of the labour market and thus, as with men, make contributions and be eligible for benefits in accordance with the same criteria. He drew, however, a sharp distinction between them and the third group, the married woman: 'the attitude of the housewife to gainful employment outside the home is not and should not be the same as that of a single woman. She has other duties . . . in the next 30 years housewives as mothers have vital work to do in ensuring the adequate continuance of the British race and of British ideals in the world' (paras 114 and 117). 'Every woman on marriage will become a new person, acquiring new rights and not carrying on into marriage claims to unemployment or disability benefit in respect of contributions made before marriage' (para. 339). 'All women, by marriage, acquire a new economic and social status, with risks and rights different from those of the unmarried. On marriage a woman gains a legal right

Table 4.7 Economic activity rates of women, 1951–84 (percentage)

1951	1961	1966	1971	1976	1979	1984
31	33	36	44	47	47	48

The figures for 1951, 1961 and 1966 are based on females over the age of 15. All other figures are based on a female population of 16 years and over.
Derived from *Social Trends 1975* and *1986*.

to maintenance by her husband as a first line of defence against risks which fall directly on the solitary woman; she undertakes at the same time to perform vital unpaid services and becomes exposed to new risks, including the risks that her married life may be ended prematurely by widowhood or separation.'

In his concern to point up the unity of the conventional family, Beveridge made two fundamental assumptions about its operation, neither of which has since stood up well to empirical testing. First, he regarded the husband and wife to be a team. The insurance scheme, remarked Beveridge, 'treats a man's contribution as made on behalf of himself and his wife, as for a team, each of whose partners is equally essential, and it gives benefits as for a team'. The issue here is a distributional one: what happens to money once it has entered the family, who controls the family's finances, and is its distribution between family members, particularly in poor families, equitable?

The other assumption Beveridge made concerned the focal point of family unity. He assumed that this would be the woman since her role was to remain at home. The breadwinner was to be the man, and, accordingly, most of the wife's benefits would accrue to her through her husband as his dependant. Although women had been encouraged to join the labour market during the war, it was anticipated that these numbers would diminish to pre-war levels. The 1931 Census had found that seven-eighths of housewives 'made marriage their sole occupation'. However, since World War II women's level of economic activity has steadily increased. We shall consider the nature of their involvement in the labour market and the relationship between this and their right to be recipients of welfare services.

Women's economic activity
Married women's involvement in the labour market has grown steadily since World War II, although there has been a levelling-off in the 1980s. Table 4.7 demonstrates this where economic activity rates are expressed as a proportion of the total female

population (married and unmarried) over 15 or 16 years of age. Table 4.8 provides more detail on the nature of married women's economic activity in that they rely heavily on part-time work and that this reliance has grown during the 1970s.

Martin and Robert's (1984b) study, however, raises the question of how 'work' is defined. In their study women are defined as 'working' if, when interviewed, they said they had a job, or had a job but were absent from it because of sickness, holidays or maternity leave (but intended to return). The interviewees were also required to define part-time and full-time work. The results show 60 per cent economically active by the conventional definition and 5 per cent unemployed. The authors however sought to discover if there existed any 'subsidiary economic activity' of an occasional nature and which would normally not be included in the official statistics. Interviewees were asked if they engaged in any occasional paid work such as 'childminder, mail order agent, outworker or seasonal worker'. An extra 4 per cent responded positively. Students were also asked a similar question. The broader definition produced a total of 71 per cent of women who were 'economically active'. Table 4.9 summarizes this detail.

This overall picture, however, needs qualification in two respects. First, women's economic activity rates vary in accordance with the circumstances of their lifecycle. There is evidence that they are returning to work after childbirth more quickly. Daniel (1980), for instance, reports that in 1971 9 per cent of mothers were economically active 12 months after confinement, but in 1979 this had increased to 25 per cent returning after only 9 months. Nevertheless, generally women's membership of the labour market declines during the peak childbearing ages (see Table 4.10.)

The second qualification to add is that there is a tendency for women to work part-time when their children are young, to work full-time as the children grow up, and then return to part-time work in their fifties (Martin and Roberts, 1984b). Moreover, a greater proportion of women now work part-time than was the case in the 1970s – a third had part-time employment in 1971 and this steadily increased to around 42 per cent by 1981. Seven out of eight part-time workers are women.

So, the evidence suggests that women's commitment to economic activity is extensive, but their work pattern tends to be dissimilar to that of most men because of breaks for childbirth and their significant contribution to the part-time labour market. This has important implications for women when requiring access to benefits. We can illustrate this by referring to pensions.

Table 4.8 Economic activity of married women, of working age 1971–84: percentage working full-time, working part-time, and unemployed by marital status

	1971	1973	1975	1979	1980	1981	1982	1983	1984
Married women									
Working full-time	—	25	25	26	26	25	25	25	25
Working part-time	—	28	32	33	33	32	32	31	31
All working	48	54	58	60	60	57	57	57	57
Unemployed	2	1	2	2	3	4	4	4	4
(total)	50	55	59	62	62	61	61	60	61

Derived from Table 6.4, *GHS 1984* (1986).

Table 4.9 Proportion of women of working age in different economic activity groups

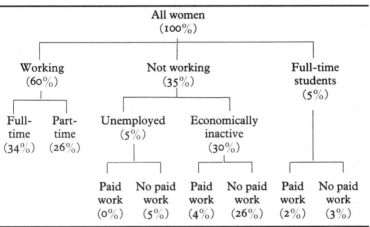

Derived from Martin and Roberts (1984b).

Land (1986) has pointed out that equality of access to benefit for women depends on them having an identical employment record to men, and this is mostly not the case. Moreover, in many cases women's pay is so low that they are not required to pay national insurance, thereby excluding them from statutory sick pay, unemployment, maternity and invalidity benefit. The basic state pension is the only benefit protected by a Home Responsibility Allowance, but the proposals contained in the 1986 Social Security Act for the State Earnings Related Pension

Table 4.10   Current economic activity by age: all women except full time students (percentages)

Economic activity	Age									All women except full time students
	16–19	20–24	25–29	30–34	35–39	40–44	45–49	50–54	55–59	
Working full-time	73	56	31	23	30	33	35	33	25	35
Working part-time	1	9	18	33	37	41	38	34	28	28
Total working	74	65	49	56	67	74	73	67	53	63
'Unemployed'	14	7	5	5	4	4	5	6	5	6
Total economically active	88	72	54	61	71	78	78	73	58	69
Economically inactive	12	28	46	39	29	22	22	27	42	31
	100	100	100	100	100	100	100	100	100	100
Base	346	565	683	762	643	584	554	566	592	5,295

Derived from Martin and Roberts (1984b).

(SERPS) will mean worse pensions, particularly for women, since the size of the pension will be calculated on the whole lifetime's earnings. The government has been encouraging occupational pension schemes but these discriminate against women also. McGoldrick (1984) has shown that despite their 'commitment to the labour force, women are still significantly under-represented in comparison to male employees in occupational pension schemes'. A significant cause of this is that many pension schemes exclude part-time employees.

Distribution of income within the family

While we know a considerable amount about the distribution of income in the country as a whole (see for instance the reports of the Royal Commission on the Distribution of Income and Wealth), we understand less about the process of income distribution within families. Since the family is a private and emotional unit, research into distributional issues within it is far from easy. Most studies, and official government statistics, adopt the family or the household as their smallest unit of analysis. As such, they can tell us nothing about experience within families.

Unit of analysis   It is important for us to understand the unit of analysis adopted in any particular piece of research because results can vary as the unit utilized changes. Table 4.11, drawn from a study undertaken by the Royal Commission on the Distribution of Income and Wealth, demonstrates some interesting variations. We should note that 'households' can contain more than one family. The table indicates the heavy relative burden of poverty carried by women, whichever unit of analysis is taken (household or family) – remember, of course, that most single-parent families are headed by a female. The existence of poverty appears less prevalent in certain family types when the household is taken as the unit of measure. This is because it is assumed that where for instance more than one family is in the same household their income is pooled. When however the incidence of poverty is measured according to family income, then we assume that 'each family is self-sufficient', and the results indicate greater poverty amongst those groups who are more likely to share houses with others, e.g. single man and woman, single elderly, and to some extent the single-parent family. Thus, to illustrate with an example, an elderly woman, whose income is 100 per cent or less than the supplementary benefit rates, may not necessarily appear in the above statistics if she is living with (say) her daughter and their combined income place them beyond the poverty line, and if the 'household' is used as the measuring rod. If the 'family' is used, then provided her income is insufficient to bring her above the poverty line she will appear in the statistics since now whom she is living with is immaterial. This is why those family types more likely to be living with other families show a greater incidence of poverty when each family unit is assumed to be a self-sufficient unit. Thus Table 4.11 indicates that 47 per cent of single elderly women and 35 per cent of single elderly men have an income of 100 per cent or less of supplementary benefit rates when 'family income' is assumed to be the unit of analysis, but these figures drop to 39 and 26 per cent respectively when 'household income' is used. The unit of analysis can obscure the nature and extent of poverty and this is the reason why some writers (e.g. see Glendinning, and Miller 1987) refer to the invisibility of women's poverty.

Mechanisms of income distribution Studies have indicated a number of typical arrangements for distributing income among family members. Zweig's (1961) early attempt to conceptualize these arrangements led to an eight-fold classification. His first three types (i.e. the fixed allowance system, the allowance which

Table 4.11   Percentage of family types with income of 100 per cent or less of supplementary benefit rates

Type of family	Elderly couple	Man	Woman	Couple no child	1	2	3	4	5+	Single parent	Single man	Single woman
Household income	16	26	39	2	2	3	5	11	20	35	5	7
Family income	18	35	47	2	2	3	5	10	20	38	9	16

Derived from Tables 3.2 and 3.4, Royal Commission on the Distribution of Income and Wealth, (1978a).

varies with income, and that which excludes the payment of bills dealt with by the husband) can be reclassified as allowance systems where the husband controls the amount of income being passed on to his wife. Zweig's fourth and fifth categories – whole wage and whole wage minus pocket money – represent whole wage systems where one partner, most usually the wife, manages all, or almost all, the family income; Zweig found some regional variations in this case but later research has found it to be particularly associated with low incomes. Zweig's sixth and seventh groups (where a fixed proportion of earnings is transferred, and 'in the drawer' where money is drawn from the drawer by both spouses) were found to be relatively rare, and have not been well documented since. His final category (the pooling system), where access to money is available to both partners, is more commonly found in higher income families, and particularly when the wife works. Pahl (1985) has added to Zweig's original formula the 'independent management system' where both partners control their own income separately.

Evidence suggests that the disposal arrangement is, to some extent, associated with income levels – see, for instance, Stamp (1985). Thus, Jowell et al. (1987) have shown that the 'allowance' arrangement varies by income in that it is more commonly found in lower income groups. Jowell found that 40 per cent of respondents whose income was less than £5,000 per annum reported that they practised an 'allowance' system, but only 25 per cent of those earning £18,000 or more per annum used this arrangement. Jowell's study also used this arrangement. Jowell's study also shows that the 'pooling system' is most common where the family earns between £12,000 and £17,999 per annum (60 per cent), whereas 50 per cent of those earning less than £5,000 per annum reported using the same system. It is interesting to note, however, that those falling in the top income category (£18,000 or more per annum) who reported using the pooling arrangement fell back to 48 per cent. The effect of the wife's earning on the housekeeping arrangement however appears not to be so clear-cut as has been suggested. Leonard (1980), in a study of young couples in South Wales, found that amongst those with the wife working about half operated an allowance system and a fifth a whole wage/pocket money system.

Gray's (1976) study of a sample of unskilled and skilled workers indicated two typical types of housekeeping arrangement:

1 A system where the husband keeps or has returned his own pocket money (similar to Zweig's 4th and 5th categories), but who pays for one or no major item for the household (e.g. rates, rent, coal, gas, etc.).
2 Where the wife is given an allowance but the husband pays for one, and usually several, major items of expenditure (similar to Zweig's 1st, 2nd and 3rd categories).

The two housekeeping systems appear related to certain 'social correlates'. For example, Gray found that the 'allowance' type was more commonly practised in homes where the husband had a skilled occupation, and where the oldest child was under eight years of age. The 'pocket-money' or 'whole wage' system was more common where parents had worked in a traditional primary sector occupation, and where the children of the marriage were over 14 years old. The 'allowance' system appeared to be associated with a greater flexibility in the housekeeping allowance and where the husbands were more prepared to work longer hours. It appears then that a housekeeping system which provides an expenditure stake for the husband leads to more frequent changes in the allowance the wife receives and may produce greater incentives at work.

There is some evidence that the type of arrangement may change where the main breadwinner is no longer employed. Both Land (1969) and Townsend (1963) have found that, when a family is dependent on social security benefits, the 'whole wage' system tended to be adopted. Townsend found that, prior to retirement, the husband was seen as the family banker who allocated a sum for housekeeping to his wife and held back sufficient for his personal pocket money and to pay for 'family entertainments, holidays, and some household goods, such as carpet, a new strip of lino, linen or a radio or television set'. On retirement however, 'his wife was no longer mainly dependent on him for her housekeeping money. Hers became the presiding financial influence in the household. His share of the total income was cut to a few shillings.'

Pahl (1980) has hypothesized that stages in the lifecycle may be associated with particular arrangements: that 'pooling' may be more common where couples are newly married and both working; the 'allowance' system more applicable to the period of childrearing; a return to 'pooling' once the children have grown up and the wife is more likely therefore to return to work, or a contribution to family income is being made by teenage children; and finally the exigencies of old age may lead to a 'whole-wage' system being adopted. These are, however, largely hypothetical thoughts at this stage. We need to know much more about the effects of the lifecycle on income allocation procedures within the family.

There is also some evidence that the major responsibility for household expenditure may be related to size of income. Land (1969), in her study of large families in London during 1965–6, found that the lower the income the more likely was responsibility for household expenditure to be the wife's. She suggests two reasons for this:

1 There was a tendency in all families for the mother to be responsible for the daily and weekly expenditure, and the father for the long-term payments, and since in low-income families most items of expenditure were of the regular sort then this would be normally discharged by the wife.
2 Low-income families usually had other sources of income (including social security benefits) in addition to the husband's. This meant that the wife often had other sources of income to rely on to partially meet household expenses.

Table 4.12 indicates the growing importance of the woman as family banker as the household income declines.

Pahl (1980) considers the possibility of constructing a typology which might classify the relationship between income level and allocation mechanism, and provides a suggestive scale which can be further tested empirically in the future. The whole wage system appears more likely to be related to low income levels, e.g. those families largely dependent on social security benefits, middle-income levels seem more associated with an allowance system of some kind, and high levels and a pooling system seem related. In an unpublished paper, Pahl (1984) later provided clear evidence that whole wage systems are overwhelmingly found among low-income families but the evidence for other allocative mechanisms is more equivocal.

Zweig (1961) had earlier noted that there were regional variations in the allocation mechanism commonly employed. Other studies confirm this. Todd and Jones (1972), for instance, found that the

Table 4.12 *Percentage of families with different income according to responsibility of mother or father for household expenditure*

Responsibility for household expenditure	Household income as % of national assistance scale[a]		
	Under 100	100–39	140+
Father and mother jointly	11	35	64
Mother with:			
a. part of father's earnings	28	44	19
b. all of father's earnings	61	19	16

a. National assistance is now known as income support.
Derived from Table 5.1, Land (1969).

proportion of wives who received their husband's whole wage was highest in the North (15 per cent), East Midlands, South-West and Wales (8 per cent each), and lowest in the South East and London (2 per cent). Why this relationship exists is difficult to ascertain. Pahl (1980) has suggested that one factor may be that where women are more commonly economically active then a whole wage or pooling mechanism may be preferred, and in the more traditional areas where fishing, mining or heavy industry predominate, and male solidarity is strong, an allowance system may more commonly apply. Again however we need to know much more about this relationship than presently we do.

The distinction between the 'whole wage' and 'allowance' systems can also be seen reflected in the contribution of young workers to the family budget. Millward (1968), in a study of working-class women between leaving school and getting married, has found two major types of family budget contribution:

1 'Giving-in', where the girl gives her total wage packet to her mother and receives a fixed amount of pocket money back.
2 'On-board', where the girl gives her mother an agreed sum of money and retains the remainder herself.

The two major types of arrangement however subdivide further into five stages which represent a path along which most girls in Millward's study travelled, although particular stages were sometimes missed.

1 The unopened wage packet is given straight to the parent (usually the mother), and a fixed amount of pocket money is returned. Some items of expenditure are paid for by the parent, e.g. clothes, lunches and fares.

2　As for 1 above but the girl opens her own wage packet.
3　As for 2 above, but keeps her own bonus and/or overtime earnings in place of pocket money from parents.
4　She pays an agreed fixed sum for board and lodging, and the parent continues to provide money for fares and lunch.
5　As for 4 except that the girl is now entirely self-supporting.

1, 2 and 3 represent the status of 'giving-in', while 4 and 5 represent 'on-board' arrangements. The transition from 'giving-in' to 'on-board' for marriage is commonly marked by a major event, e.g. engagement and the start of saving for marriage, 18th birthday, change in job, or increase in wages. This study confirms a finding of Gray's (1976) study above that the type of arrangement for handling and distributing income within the family may have an impact on incentives at work. Millward suggests that there was some evidence that those 'on-board' had a greater incentive to earn bonuses since they would keep the additional earnings themselves – 'girls "on-board" had a higher level of performance than those who were not.'

Process of income distribution　The mechanisms for distributing money within the family then vary considerably. The actual process of distributing that money however is also of considerable importance. It is, of course, difficult to assess the degree of equitability of a given distribution of funds. It may, on the subjective level, be difficult for some wives to make a judgement of this sort, since a number of women do not know what their husbands bring home in their wage packet. Oakley (1974b), for instance, found that 25 per cent of her working-class samples of wives did not know what their husbands earned. A government report (1976) found less than half the wives knew what their husbands earned, and in Townsend's (1963) study the figure was 27 out of 45 wives. In Gorer's (1973) study more than one wife in six, who received a housekeeping allowance, did not know what their husband's income was.

The most usual method of judging equitability, however, is to examine the wife's share of income over a period of time. Thus, Young (1952) concluded that 'there may be a tendency for wives to suffer, relatively to their husbands, in any period of inflation . . . like other unorganised workers, their money income may not advance as fast as prices.' Young and Syson (1974) confirmed this. They studied 50 households where the wife was not working, 20 had not received any increase in their allowance during the previous year, in four cases it had decreased, and in 26 it had

Table 4.13   Responsibility for items of household expenditure (percentages)

Who usually dealt with	Buying food	Pay for gas/ electricity	Pay for rent, rates and mortgage	Dealing with any surplus
Wife	89%	49%	45%	36%
Husband	3%	38%	45%	20%
Either or both	7%	10%	8%	43%
Other answer	1%	3%	2%	1%

Derived from Section 4.1, Todd and Jones (1971).

increased. In the course of that year the pound had fallen in value by at least 25 p over the previous year. In about 50 per cent of these cases then the housewives' and children's standard of living had declined while their husbands had improved.

Woman's Own (1975) and the National Consumer Council jointly conducted a survey from a representative sample of 4000 readers who had replied to a questionnaire. The average housekeeping allowance had increased between July 1974 and July 1975 by £2.40 when a rise of £3.63 (one third more) would have been necessary to keep pace with inflation. One in five received no increase in housekeeping allowance at all, and the worse off were the most likely to have had no increase.

Thus, it seems that income accruing to the wife decreases in value most in those families who are in any case most vulnerable to inflationary pressure. The amount of income allocated to the wife from husband and even working child may, in any case, be determined more by local tradition than according to the real needs of the family. Both Land (1969) and Millward (1968) have found evidence of this. Since the arrival of an extra child is likely to be an added drain on the wife's funds, pressure on her housekeeping is likely to be further exacerbated. Because the overwhelming responsibility of the wife's share of income is to cover expenditure on food (see Table 4.13), then it is reasonable to assume that economies may often be made in nutrition, particularly in poorer families. Land (1969), in her study of large families, found that the mother was the most likely to sacrifice food for herself, that over a half had no cooked meal in the middle of the day, a quarter had no breakfast and nothing more than a sandwich for lunch, and 1 in 12 never had a cooked meal. Her study indicated that the mother saw the needs of the father coming first, the children second, and herself third. Marsden's (1969) study of lone mothers showed that between a quarter and a third were missing meals every day or were regularly eating very little or the wrong sort of food. They were particularly concerned that their children be seen not to be unduly suffering, and were prepared to make sacrifices themselves to that end. Graham's study (1987) of one-parent families in a New Town confirm these sacrifices, as does Burghe's (1982) account of families living on supplementary benefit.

There is some evidence that financial difficulties which stem from inequitable income distribution may be a contributive factor in marriage breakdowns. In a study of 25 women whose marriages had broken down through violence, Pahl (1980) has found that 15 of the 25 had attributed their marital problems in part to financial difficulties. One half of the women whose husbands kept control of the money coming into the house either did not get any money for housekeeping or received irregular amounts.

The importance of appreciating the distinction between the control of family resources and their management is confirmed by findings which suggest that many women, on becoming the head of a one-parent family, recognize an improvement in their position even though they may be no better off financially. This is accounted for by their control of family resources. Graham's (1987a) account of a divorced mother with three children living on supplementary benefit was not untypical in her sample: 'Personally, I feel better off. Although we've got a lot less money in the family I feel better off because I can control it, you know.'

Parker's study (1987) of 30 families with two partners, and in circumstances of debt, found that women were frequently expected to manage finance without having control over the money entering the household. She found that nearly a half of her sample practised the allowance system, about a third the whole wage and a fifth pooling. This meant that in some households the husband was retaining for himself a disproportionate share of income for his spending money, thus placing his wife under severe pressure to manage the financial difficulties with the remainder.

The evidence suggests, therefore, that the use of the family as the unit of analysis has obscured inequalities within those families least able to cope with a relatively declining income. We need to know more about the mechanisms and the process of income distribution between members of the family, but the evidence thus far indicates that the assumption made of 'pooled income' by the social security system needs careful and critical examination.

Who controls the benefit?
Our discussion of income distribution within families and the control of family finances is important because, for the most part, benefits have been paid through the man. The payment of child benefit to the woman is an exception to this however, and many pressure groups, particularly those who represent women and children, have fought to retain this principle. In the 1986 Social Security Act the government had proposed paying the new Family Credit (replacement for FIS) through the pay packet – 'the new scheme should offer significant advantages for employers in ensuring that employees perceive more clearly the total net remuneration they receive rather than earnings net of tax and national insurance alone' (Fowler Report, 1985). The evidence discussed in the previous section showed that the employers' gain in limiting wage rates may be the loss of women and children in these families. In the event, the government were defeated on this issue by an alliance of the poverty, women's and small business lobbies. It is now envisaged 'that the woman will normally be the main payee, with the order book addressed to her, but that as in FIS the man would be shown as alternative payee.' (Lords Hansard, 14 July 1986, c. 742).

Our social security scheme contains numerous examples of the cultural expectation of male breadwinner and female dependant. The concept of 'insurance' in the Beveridge Report applied essentially to the adult male worker who needed protection when his earnings were interrupted by unemployment, accident or disease. His wife's share of support would accrue to her as his dependant and arrive through his hands. Moreover, on occasions when the wife qualified for insurance benefit in her own right she was required to meet extra conditions. Where she wished to claim for her husband as a dependant she had to demonstrate that he was not only unemployed but also infirm and incapable of supporting himself. On the other hand, for the woman to be treated as a dependant of her husband she had only to be not employed.

The assumption of domesticity also lay behind the denial to women of the right to claim supplementary benefit and family income supplement if they were living with or married to a man. More recently introduced benefits continued the pattern. The non-contributory invalidity pension was denied to around 240,000 women who had left paid work for reasons of sickness or invalidity because, while a man was subject to one condition, i.e. his incapacity to work, a married woman had additionally to prove that she was 'incapable of performing normal household duties'.

These duties included cooking, cleaning, shopping, washing and ironing. The recent replacement of this benefit with the severe disablement allowance has continued discrimination against women, though in an indirect form. The allowance is based on an 80 per cent loss of faculty requirement, a severe test which results in only 20,000 of the 240,000 women disbarred from claiming HNCIP being eligible for support. Discrimination continues therefore because women are more likely to be the claimant for it, most of them having an insufficient national insurance record for them to be eligible for contributory invalidity benefit.

Invalid care allowance was introduced to help those who have to cease paid work in order to care for a severely disabled relative. The married woman had hitherto been excluded from this benefit because she was a woman. The state had therefore expected the woman to fulfil her traditional role as carer of the sick and disabled, largely unaided. However, a private prosecution, brought by Ms Jackie Drake of Manchester with the support of the Child Poverty Action Group, and referred to the European Court of Justice, has led to the government conceding that the allowance is contrary to the EEC's equal treatment directive. Married women have since been able to claim the allowance and have it back-dated to 22 December 1984. By the end of 1986 more than 90,000 claims had been received, and others were being received at a rate of 2000 a week (*Welfare Rights Bulletin*, 1987).

The 1978 directive sought to undermine the discrimination referred to above by equalizing conditions on which benefits are claimed. In November 1983 the British government implemented the requirements of the directive by granting to women some rights to claim adult dependency additions to national insurance benefits, and to be the claimant for supplementary benefit and family income supplement. These rights, however, were constrained by certain conditions, to be discussed later as they apply to supplementary benefit. Changes to the housewives' non-contributory invalidity pension and the invalid care allowance were not originally incorporated into the 'equal treatment' package, although changes have taken place since.

In recent years women have won the right in law to be treated equally with men in a number of areas. The roots of much of this legislation lie in our membership of the European Economic Community. The EEC have issued a number of directives to member countries requiring them, within a given time period, to enact legislation on equal treatment for men and women in such matters as pay and social security. The reasons for the interest of the commission in the affairs of women are complex, but we may note, as Vallance and Davis (1985) has pointed out, that the number of women Euro MPs rose from 5 to 16 per cent in 1979, and that questions in parliament about equality and women's issues have also increased – on women from zero to over 2 per cent of the total, and on equality from 0.6 to 6 per cent. Women, moreover, are well represented on committees which specialize on social policy matters. In 1983 the Social Affairs Committee was 83 per cent female and Public Health 41 per cent – only 16 per cent of parliamentary members overall are women. The equal treatment directive has granted to women, in certain circumstances, the rights to control money entering the household in the form of benefit. A study on its implementation in the United Kingdom to supplementary benefits however indicates only moderate gains (Kidd, *Journal of Social Policy*, forthcoming).

The conditions of eligibility for supplementary benefit were altered when the British government implemented the directive in November 1983. The new conditions were that claimants had to demonstrate over a period of time an attachment to the labour market, or a specific reason for exclusion from it, e.g. unemployed and seeking work, sick and submitting medical certificates, studying in full-time education or on a training scheme. Whilst these conditions apply equally to men and women, they do however exclude domestic and childcare work as a valid criterion for eligibility. They thus continue to favour men.

The impact of this new regulation on supplementary benefits has been disappointing. The DHSS had expected around 17,000 successful and change of claimant cases in the first 12 months, but in the event received around 7000. Furthermore, there has been wide variation in take-up from local office to local office.

The reasons for this are complex. It is instructive however to contrast the heightened interest in Holland for equal treatment with the subdued atmosphere here (Sjerps, 1985). In Holland equal treatment was introduced alongside a fundamental reform of their social security scheme, and this appears to have heightened public sensitivity to it. In the UK it was introduced earlier as an isolated measure, and not part of the wider reforms which culminated in the 1986 Social Security Act. As such, it never achieved the political centre-stage. Put another way, its timing was such as to prevent the sensitization of extra-parliamentary activity.

We should also remember that the Thatcher government had successfully created a political climate not conducive to the principle of equality. This had particularly been the case in its perception of the role of family members: the man

> is said to complement the weaknesses of the female. The female sex-role is said to revolve around the privilege of gestation; that women are in the first place definable by the reproductive function. If the female is the biological mother, it follows that she is the natural social mother; thus 'her place of honour' is inside the household. (Fitzgerald, 1983)

In addition to the unfavourable political climate, the actions of DHSS headquarters in delaying the arrival of important documents in local offices and in withdrawing a central brief on staff training produced considerable confusion among local officials, and an understanding on their part that the new regulation did not share the importance of other regulations.

Where take-up of equal treatment has been above average, this appears to be associated with communities where women have been required to enter the labour market because of large scale redundancies among men (e.g. when a major employer has closed down), with the existence of ethnic minority groups where the husband periodically returns to his original homeland to attend to family responsibilities leaving the wife to become the claimant, and with the activities of welfare rights groups which, in some areas, have been quite successful at raising awareness among claimants e.g. Leicester, where a publicity campaign of leaflets, a 'Christmas party' demonstration featuring Mother Christmas and attracting local press and radio coverage, and a campaign to encourage women to register for work or sign on have persuaded a number of women to claim their legal rights and become the claimant.

Thus women continue to be disadvantaged, despite 'equal treatment', because the concept of work adopted for benefit eligibility, in that it excludes domestic work, favours men. They are further hindered from gaining ground by many women, and not a few officials, being unaware of the legal rights they have won in this respect. The successful prosecution of the British government by Ms Jackie Drake, with the support of the Child Poverty Action Group, over their refusal to include the Invalid Care Allowance in the equal treatment package, is an example of what can be achieved.

The government's original decision to continue to exclude women from a benefit designed to support those who have to leave work to care for a sick or disabled relative implies that such duties are expected of the woman. In other words, it is part of her 'natural' role to be a carer, and therefore she requires no 'compensation' for having had to forfeit her job. The political support for community care policies in recent years has reaffirmed this expectation.

Women as carers

Nobody knows precisely how many carers there are. The 1985 *GHS* included, for the first time, questions on caring but until its publication we have to rely on local surveys and other more dated material. However, the most conservative estimate suggests at least 1.3 million carers, whilst other estimates indicate 3.25 million (Family Policy Studies Centre Issue 3, 1987). One woman in eight is estimated to be caring for a dependent relative or friend (Family Policy Studies Centre: *Caring Costs Briefing*, 1988)

Community care policies have attracted increasing political support as an alternative to institutional care. Walker (1982) has defined community care as 'help and support given to individuals, including children, people with disabilities and elderly people, in non-institutional settings. Such care may be provided by formal, quasiformal or informal helpers or by a combination of all three.' The Short Report (1985) recognized that such policies, properly implemented, would be an expensive alternative. At the moment, however, adequate resources are not, for the most part, being made available. In practice, therefore, care by the community more properly means informal care by other members of the family.

Community care is a veil behind which predominantly women are expected to fulfil the caring role.

> An examination of the reality of community care, in a situation where there is minimal input of statutory resources, reveals that the provision of primary caring falls not upon 'the community' but upon identifiable groups and individuals, in a way which is not necessarily equitable. Indeed this can be best expressed in terms of a double equation – that in practice community care equals care by the family, and in practice care by the family equals care by women. (Finch and Groves, 1980)

The evidence for this statement is overwhelming:

1   The 1981 White Paper '*Growing Older*' stated that 'whatever level of public expenditure proves practicable, and however it is distributed, the primary sources of support and care for elderly people are informal and voluntary. These spring from the personal ties of kinship, friendship, and neighbourhood. They are irreplaceable.'
2   Women are not only the principal source of caring – in an EOC survey 75 per cent of carers were female – but they frequently operate as the sole carers with little or no support from other kin or professional staff. Table 4.14 shows the results of the EOC survey referred to above, and Table 4.15, with statistics from a local survey, shows an even larger

Table 4.14   Carers: by age and relationship to dependant

% of carers aged	16–24	25–34	35–44	45–54	55–64	65–74	75–84	Total %
Relationship of carer to dependant								
Mother	—	5	3	4	1	—	—	13
Wife	—	—	2	2	7	3	3	17
Daughter	—	3	5	14	4	1	—	27
Other female	1	3	3	6	3	2	—	18
Total female	1	11	13	26	15	6	3	75
Father	—	—	1	1	—	—	—	2
Husband	1	1	1	2	5	4	2	16
Son	—	1	—	3	2	—	—	6
Other male	—	—	—	2	—	1	—	3
Total male	1	2	2	8	7	5	2	29
Total	2	13	15	34	22	11	5	102[a]

[a]. Total = more than 100 per cent due to rounding up of figures.
Derived from EOC (1980c).

Table 4.15   Main and secondary carers of mentally handicapped adults living at home (percentages)

	Main carer	Secondary carer
Mother	80	3
Father	9	49
Sibling	6	4
Spouse	1	—
Other relative	4	8
No carer	—	36
Total (100%)	352	352

One male subject was not included in these figures as he was himself caring for his elderly, infirm mother.
Derived from City of Bradford MDC (1983).

proportion of women as carers with just over a third of them having no support from other members of the household or others.

3   Parker (1985) has reviewed major studies on informal care and concluded that 'to talk of "care by the community" or even "family care" is to disguise the reality ... care by family members almost always means care by female members with

little support from other relatives.' Thus studies on the elderly (Sheldon, 1948; Townsend, 1957; Hunt, 1978; Nissel and Bonnerjea, 1982; Gilhooly, 1982), on children with disabilities (Burton, 1975; Wilkin, 1979; Carey, 1982; Cooke, 1982; Glendinning, 1983), and on adults with disabilities (Sainsbury, 1970; Harris, 1971; Bayley, 1973; Cartwright, 1973; Blaxter, 1976; Seed, 1980; City of Bradford, 1983; Wright, 1983) confirm unequivocally that the burden of care falls disproportionately on women. Those burdens are emotional and financial in terms of lost or reduced employment prospects. The saving to the country is potentially enormous – Wicks (1987) has estimated that 1.3 million carers provide care each year worth between £5.1 and £7.3 billion.

The Social Security Act 1986

The plight of carers has been explicitly ignored in the Social Security Act 1986. Hitherto carers could receive the long-term rate of supplementary benefit because they were not expected to be available for work. Income Support, the replacement for supplementary benefit, is not available on a long-term rate, although there are premiums for various kinds of disability – not all disabled people however are entitled.

This Act represents the most radical statement on social security since Beveridge, and it will particularly disadvantage women in a number of respects. In future the basis of social security will be means-tested selective benefits aimed at particular groups and the insurance scheme will be correspondingly downgraded. This could well threaten child benefit which is paid directly to all women with children. The government have recently announced, for the second year running, that they intend allowing the real value of this benefit to fall, and this might well signal a threat to its existence in the future.

The marginal gain for women in entitlement to Invalid Care Allowance, introduced in the Lords the day before the European Court ruled that its exclusion was a contravention of the equal treatment directive, has been counterbalanced by significant losses elsewhere. Women, along with others who experience fluctuating earnings, long periods of unemployment or are disabled during their working life will find that their State Earnings Related Pension will be worse. The maternity grant, a payment of £25, was abolished as from 6 April 1987 (around 720,000 women received the grant in 1985/86). The present maternity allowance will be replaced by state Maternity Pay administered by employers or State Maternity Allowance for those who do not qualify for the former. It is estimated by the Social Security Consortium that up to 94,000 mothers will lose their right to this benefit because of the new qualification tests – about 70,000 will however gain. Most of the losers will be women who stopped work more than a year before their entitlement to benefit, or who were unemployed and seeking work during the qualifying period. Finally, section 42 of the Act abolishes reduced rates of unemployment and sickness benefit and maternity allowance for people who have paid some contributions although not at the full rate. Women again are likely to be among the losers.

Overview

Income is earned in the labour market and distributed within the family for consumption. To control both these processes enables power to be exercised. Men have traditionally wielded that power. The Social Security scheme has recognized and reinforced this by granting the husband breadwinner status. In doing so the welfare state has reflected the existing distribution of power, and done little to support its weakest members. Women have been disadvantaged by the welfare state because they were relatively powerless to begin with. The gains achieved for women by virtue of our membership of the EEC have been modest.

Acquiring an identical work record to that of men is crucial to women gaining full and equal membership of the social security scheme. This is why it is important to consider aspects of the welfare state in connection with economic activity. However, all this is contextualized by a powerful ideology which has ascribed to women a domesticated and caring role. In the 1987 election an unprecedented 42 women were elected to parliament. It remains to be seen whether an agenda for women will be established and the traditional cultural expectations of the woman overturned.

5 Gender differences in education

Beverley Skeggs

The present organization of education in this country has to be seen in the context of its development alongside both social welfare regulations and provisions, and the changing demands of the labour market. As an illustration of this, David (1980) documents how the introduction of compulsory education imposed financial and time restrictions upon parents, who had to ensure that their children regularly attended school, and that they also received certain standards of care at home (Poor Law Act 1899; Maternity and Child Welfare Act 1918).

It is also important to remember that the education system was established and developed for specific reasons – primarily to prepare young people for adult life (Johnson, 1970). This adult life was clearly segregated on the divisions of both class and gender. Thus Purvis (1981, 1984) notes that the earliest forms of education, provided for middle-class girls, were to confer social status rather than equip them with knowledge and skills for the labour market. Likewise Bryant (1979) and Burstyn (1980) illustrate that such education was an education for gaining husbands rather than paid employment. The belief that middle-class women were frail and possibly uneducable was substantially different from the robustness attributed to working-class women. The early provision of education for working-class women was often directly related to local labour market demands for domestic servants (Blunden, 1982, 1983) in which working-class girls were schooled in 'useful' domestic tasks; a direct contrast to the 'useless' ideal of lady-like accomplishments that was held for middle-class girls (Summers, 1979; Hall, 1979, Dyhouse, 1981). Moreover, an influential factor in the development of working-class girls' education was the notion that they could be the regenerators of a morally replete nation (Dyhouse, 1977; Skeggs, 1986). These concerns are substantially different from the origins of working-class boys' education which was vocational and directly related to the labour market (Marks, 1976). The belief that the purpose of schooling is to prepare and fit young people for their future has resulted in the incorporation of the established unequal sexual and class divisions of employment into the organization of education (David, 1981). Thus Arnot (1986) has pointed out that if adult life is sex-segregated, it would seem only natural to devise an education system that catered for a sex-segregated world.

Education reports

Major education reports, which have influenced the structure and development of education, all indicate how schooling is a gender-related experience in which a different form of social control and pedagogy operates for women and men based on the anticipation of their future primary positioning in the family household structure (Delamont and Duffin, 1978, David, 1980). For example, both the Hadow Reports (1923, 1926) suggest that provision should be made to fit young working-class girls to the duty of home life and motherhood, and the Norwood Report (1943) suggests domestic and housewifery subjects for non-academic girls. The Crowther (1960) and Newsom (1963) Reports have been well documented for their sexist assumptions about working-class girls' futures (Wolpe, 1975; Deem, 1978) in their emphasis on the importance of men, courtship and marriage and their suggestion that young working-class women's future was outside of the paid labour market. And although, in contrast, the Robbins Report (1963) acknowledged the depth of social inequality across different classes and sexes, it nevertheless failed to have any significant impact on the access available to higher education by working-class women (Kelsall, Poole and Kuhn, 1972).

Whereas Crowther and Newsom deliberated over the future positioning of working-class girls in the home, the Carr Report (1957) has a substantial impact on current thinking about women and the labour market (Wickham, 1986). It, however, excluded any consideration of women's training requirements. In addition, the TUCWA Report (1968) concluded that the improvements in women's training had been insignificant and in 'penny numbers' (ATTI, 1971: 376). Their conclusions were echoed by the Donovan Commission (1968) and the Industrial Training Boards, which did not consider it their role to encourage the training of girls (Wickham, 1982). Moreover, Gleeson and Mardle (1980) have documented how much educational debate stemming from the 1960s, together with the 'White Heat of Technology Debate' (Crosland, 1956), was concerned to link educational planning and development with the perceived 'needs' of technology (Baron et al., 1981). This synchronization between education and industrial development has influenced recent developments in education, with the Department of Employment (through the MSC) coming to exercise greater control in education, and also serving to push concerns about improvements in women's education off centre-stage. Arnot (1983) notes, for example, how, as in the past, 'the nation's interest' correlated with the educational needs of male children, so today 'industrial needs' correlate with technical training from which most women are still excluded. Wickham (1982) takes this argument further; she believes that the association between industry and education reinforces the sexual division of labour that already exists, and further separates women off as a distinct group with quite specific labour market roles, namely, those related to gendered definitions of femininity.

Legislation
Even legislation, such as the Sex Discrimination Act 1975 which prohibits preference being given to one sex at the expense of another, has not been effective in reforming educational practice (Wolpe, 1977; David, 1980). Weiner (1985) notes how in the first ten years of the Act not one complaint of educational discrimination had been upheld. The Equal Opportunities Commission, established to monitor the Sex Discrimination Act, has provided evidence of discriminatory practices, such as the unequal pupil access to subjects not traditionally associated with their sex, for example boys to domestic science, girls to technical drawing (1979, 1982). More generally, Cornbleet and Libovitch (1983) documented the gap between the rhetoric and reality revealed by the Sex Discrimination Act. Most schools, they argued, were actually ignoring the spirit of the Act. For as Blackstone (1976) has noted, 'the removal of formal barriers does not mean that barriers no longer exist . . . but can continue to exist in a number of hidden and subtle ways.'

Attempts to initiate educational reform, Arnot (1986) argues, have been limited to improving girls' education in scientific and technological subjects rather than tackling the problems of sexism or the restructuring of relations between the sexes.

Moreover, a social policy is, at present, being established (see David 1985; Kidd, this volume) which continues to reinforce the sexual division of labour in the family; reinforcing assumptions that it should be women who are the primary domestic workers and carers. Likewise, the increasing influence of unemployment further reinforces the sexual division of labour (West, 1982b; *Feminist Review*, 1986). Thus, whilst some small attempts at education reforms are being introduced, opportunities for breaking down traditional sexual divisions outside of education remain ignored.

In an analysis of the period 1940–80, Deem (1981) notes how

most advances that have been achieved by women, both inside and outside education, can be linked to periods of full employment, so that whenever educational reforms occur they are framed by the role of the education system *vis-à-vis* the labour market. Wolpe (1978) has pointed out that even if girls are provided with equality in education, they still have to enter a labour market divided by sex.

However, the fact that the labour market has developed and is organized on the basis of sexual divisions (see Webb, this volume) only partly explains the organization of the education system. It does not explain what actually happens to girls and boys within the education system. Do they automatically accept that they will only have access to future roles that sustain sex differences and in which boys predominantly have greater choice? Nor does it explain why, when girls appear to exhibit more learning-appropriate behaviour and attitudes in their early years (Barker Lunn, 1972; Ingleby and Cooper, 1974; Hartley, 1980) and show superiority in a number of educational skills, they, nevertheless, progressively withdraw from competitive participation in post-compulsory education. To understand such a phenomenon we need to examine what actually happens to girls and boys while at school; why girls, who display initial promise, fail to maintain their position *vis-à-vis* boys in terms of educational success, when most of the formal sex barriers in education no longer exist.

The sex-differentiated school experience

The evidence suggests that, in terms of ability, girls and boys may have an approximately equal start in the educational race, or even that girls may enjoy a slight advantage. An early survey by Douglas (1964) provided data from a large national sample on the academic attainment of children in Britain up to the age of 11 years. According to teachers' judgements of reading, more boys than girls were found to be outstandingly bad, and fewer outstandingly good. When tested at both 8 and 11 years, girls were the more advanced readers, although at 11 their superiority was less marked. The boys, however, had a larger vocabulary throughout. Fourteen years later, the survey *Primary Education in England* (DES 1978) echoed these findings, showing girls in a superior position initially, and the reading abilities of the sexes diverging less as age increased. Tests were administered to over 5000 children in more than 370 schools, and the conclusion reached was that, although at nine years of age girls obtained slightly higher scores on the reading test, at the age of eleven the difference was smaller. Further studies (Start and Wells, 1972;

Maxwell, 1977) have demonstrated similar results. Studies on the mathematical ability of eleven year olds have also shown similar levels of attainment as between girls and boys, with girls performing better at computation (Ward, 1979) and boys displaying general mathematical ability (APU Mathematical Development Primary Survey 1980).

One explanation offered for this initial success of girls has been the predominance of women teachers in primary schools (Acker, 1983). Arnot (1983) argues that in the 'feminine atmosphere' of the primary classroom female teachers may equate feminine behaviour such as being quiet, obedient and neat with the image of a 'good' pupil and thus encourage conformity to a feminine image. Lee (1973) argues that the school ethos in early years, when order and conformity are prized, favours girls. Later, he argues, girls lose out when achievement becomes based on autonomy and independence. Sutherland (1981) and Hartley (1980) suggest that girls may do better in primary schools because they identify more with women teachers than do boys.

However, a focus on classroom interaction suggests that such advantages are negligible. For instance French and French (1983), who studied British primary school classes of children aged 10 and 11, found boys dominating teachers' time in nearly all classroom situations. In one lesson, which comprised 66 pupil interactions, 50 of them were produced by boys who numbered less than half of the class. In addition, a good many of these interactions were not 'spontaneously' allocated to boy pupils by the teacher, but achieved through interactional techniques designed to gain the teacher's attention. Other studies (Brophy and Good, 1970; Galton, 1981; Stanworth, 1981; Spender, 1982) have all supported the evidence that boys take up most classroom time. Mahoney (1985) and Wood (1984) also illustrate how boys use their domination of the physical and linguistic space of the school to harass girls sexually. However, Wright (1987) argues that when we consider race (or ethnicity) as a variable in classroom interaction, the domination of teachers' time and space becomes more complex. In her study Afro-Caribbean girls and boys receive far more attention from teachers, but the attention was negative and confrontational and operated effectively to discourage pupils from school-based work.

Walkerdine (1981) has illustrated how boys learn at an early age (the study was based in a nursery school) to challenge the authority of female teachers by using sexist language and behaviour. It is in such aspects of classroom life, the 'hidden curriculum', where sex differences appear more frequently, but are less obvious than the overt forms of discrimination. It is the 'taken for grantedness' or the 'naturalness' of these sex differences, such as language and interaction, which make them not only 'invisible' to the general onlooker but also very difficult to challenge. King (1978) in a study of infants' classrooms, notes how most forms of classroom organization, such as seating and registers, were organized on the basis of sex and were completely taken for granted by teachers. Likewise Buswell (1981) notes how in one particular classroom pupils were classified by sex up to 20 times per day.

This 'natural' division between girls and boys has been a major focus of educational research, whereby stereotypical images are shown to invade most aspects of school life. Walker and Barton (1983) have described three main points of entry for the perpetration (and transformation) of gender stereotypes in school: first, through the communication of teacher expectations, second, through classroom practices, and third, through school rituals. Many studies have illustrated how teachers operate with assumptions about how girls and boys should behave in accordance with their sex. Claricoates (1980) for instance, found that the teachers she researched assumed boys to be 'livelier, adventurous ... independent, energetic' while the girls were assumed to be 'obedient, tidy, conscientious and gossipy'. Likewise Deem (1978), Delamont (1980), Ingleby and Cooper (1974) found girls were under more pressure to be quiet, studious, neat and careful. Boys, on the other hand, were expected to be more adventurous, noisy and inquisitive. Claricoates (1978) also reported that classroom projects were usually designed with boys' interests in mind. Such assumptions are not just characteristic of the British experience; Hamilton and Leo-Rhynie (1984) have demonstrated the persistence of familiar stereotypes in Jamaican schooling. Evans (1984) documents how stereotypes are transmitted through the unspoken assumptions which govern teachers' behaviour and transactions in the classroom. These gender assumptions also contain within them assumptions about social class. Thus Arnot (1983) shows how the model of femininity presented in girls' public schools is the opposite to the model of masculinity presented in boys' public schools, which has been interpreted as class and gender complementarity; boys as strong, independent leaders, and girls as obedient, dependent and supportive (Okely, 1978).

However, it is not just teachers' expectations in early schooling that are solely responsible for gender differentiation in young children. The books and materials that children encounter, and are encouraged to use, are clearly gender-differentiated. Lobban

(1978) examined reading schemes used in infant and primary schools in 1974 and 1975 (the 'Pirates' schemes and the 'Language in Action' schemes). From this analysis Lobban put forward the 'apron theory', namely the clear association between females and the performance of domestic roles. The two schemes showed 33 adult male occupations and only 8 female ones (shop assistant, teacher, witch, queen, princess, granny, handywoman, mum). On the basis of her evidence Lobban concludes that a female child who took her view of reality from the schemes could easily be led to believe that women in society are in a minority, and that those females that do exist are intrinsically inferior to and less worthy of mention than males. In similar research by Sharpe (1976) and the Sheffield Women and Education Group (1978) there was evidence of stereotypical representation. In a study of a selection of maths books used by teachers, Northam (1982) found that females and males are portrayed in stereotypical roles: in junior books women are under-represented (6 references to women compared to 40 references to men). When girls do appear their roles are strikingly different from the boys: they are featured as less likely to be involved in the identification, setting and solving of problems, less skilful and competitive, less likely to teach maths skills to others and to display less initiative and inventiveness. They are efficient record-keepers, they practise and modify already learned mathematical skills, develop themes suggested by others and set standards of behaviour. Northam (1982) concludes that there is a clear tendency in the books studied to define maths as the province of males, especially adult males. She draws an interesting parallel between the near oblivion of girls aged thirteen and over from maths books and the decline in girls' involvement in maths between 7 and 16 years. Although we cannot measure the impact of such schemes, McDonald (1981) argues that we must not underestimate their effect, especially as they reinforce many of the gender stereotypes presented elsewhere. Thus Delamont (1980), in an examination of toy catalogues, found that the toys and games available for girls offered a far more restrictive range of roles than for boys. Arnot (1986) notes that girls were encouraged to be passive, home-centred, non-scientific, non-technical and 'good'; whereas boys were offered the exciting roles of Robin Hood, a big-game hunter, spacemen, Dracula, cowboys and indians, girls by contrast were limited to Miss World and a ballerina. Moreover, as children grow up they continue to experience more reinforcement of these stereotypical images of masculinity and femininity through their contact with socializing agents such as the media, peer group and family. The next section will examine the attainment

Table 5.1 Percentage of school leavers with 'O' level GCE/CSE passes[a] in given subjects, England, by sex

| | 1975/6 | | 1984/5 | |
	Girls	Boys	Girls	Boys
English	39	31	46	34
Maths	19	26	28	33
Science	20	20	26	35
Modern Languages	17	12	21	13
Any subject	49	45	58	51

a. GCE 'O' level grades A–C; CSE grade 1.
Derived from Table CF, *Statistics of Education*, School Leavers, January 1986.

differences between the sexes and the differential experiences of the secondary school system by girls and boys.

Attainment at secondary level

By the time pupils sit their first public examination, differential subject specialization has become firmly established and gender differences more pronounced (Willms and Kerr, 1987). The subject choices for girls for 'O' level/CSE leans strongly towards the arts subjects (English, French, History, Music, Drama, Visual Arts and Social Science), whereas for boys the inclination is towards the Sciences (Physics, Chemistry and Geography). Both the particular subjects studied and the number of passes gained are important for securing entry to a labour market or for further study. Subject choice is an important factor in gaining entry into particular areas. Often qualifications in one area act as disqualification in another.

Table 5.1 indicates that in particular subjects such as English and Modern Languages, girls are more successful in gaining 'O' levels than boys. Likewise girls' increasing success in areas such as Maths (9 per cent increase in pass rate) and Science (6 per cent increase) suggests a trend towards diminishing differentials between girls and boys. It is clear that, overall, both girls and boys are increasing their pass rate in all subjects. Research in Scotland by McPherson and Willms (1987) also indicates that between 1976 and 1984 girls had increased their attainment by, on average, gaining one 'O' grade more than their male counterparts. At the lower end of the ability range, research indicates that boys with learning disabilities tend to outnumber girls (Bentzen, 1966).

However, when we examine the curriculum in general, the model that Harding (1982) devised for illustrating the sex

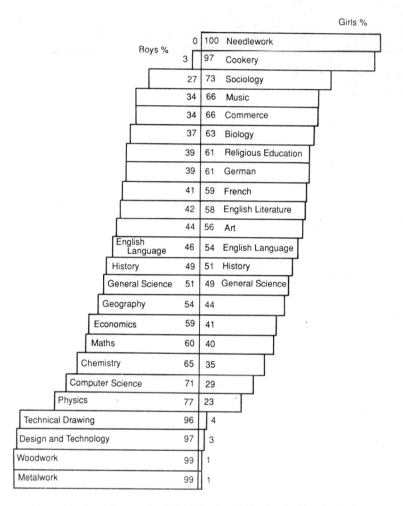

Boys %

Girls %

Boys %		Girls %	
	0	100	Needlework
	3	97	Cookery
	27	73	Sociology
	34	66	Music
	34	66	Commerce
	37	63	Biology
	39	61	Religious Education
	39	61	German
	41	59	French
	42	58	English Literature
	44	56	Art
English Language	46	54	English Language
History	49	51	History
General Science	51	49	General Science
Geography	54	44	
Economics	59	41	
Maths	60	40	
Chemistry	65	35	
Computer Science	71	29	
Physics	77	23	
Technical Drawing	96	4	
Design and Technology	97	3	
Woodwork	99	1	
Metalwork	99	1	

Derived from Harding, J. (1982) 'CDT What's Missing?', *Studies in Design, Education, Craft and Technology* 15 (1), Department of Education, University of Keele.
Figure 5.1   Sexual divisions of knowledge in school subjects

differences in relation to subject choice is still valid. Figure 5.1 illustrates that very specific gender divisions remain with regard to subject areas.

Thus, while girls have progressively increased their share of the pass rate and begun to succeed in non-traditional areas, their

Table 5.2   Percentage of school leavers in Great Britain with
GCE/SCE/CSE 'O' level passes[a] in given subjects, by sex

| | 1979/80 | | 1985 | |
	Girls	Boys	Girls	Boys
English	43	32	46	35
History	16	14	16	13
French	18	11	19	11
Music/Drama/Visual Arts	15	10	18	11
Mathematics	26	31	30	35
Physics	7	20	10	22
Chemistry	9	14	12	17
Biology	18	12	19	12
Vocational Subjects[b]	19	3	20	4
Any Subjects	55	50	58	52

a. Irrespective of any 'A' level passes.
b. Includes Business and Domestic Subjects.
Devised from Table 13 (1982 edition), Table 31 (1987 edition), *Education Statistics for the United Kingdom*.

success still remains in subject areas traditionally associated with females, areas such as English and Languages which arguably have less value in terms of specific employment outcomes or higher education demands. Mathematical skills are a 'critical filter' regulating entry into high-status occupations. Few universities, for instance, accept domestic science as an academic 'A' level. These gender divisions of knowledge within the education system highlight both the influence of history and the contemporary employment structure. The subjects in which girls predominate are those originally introduced into the curriculum to prepare them for either domestic service or home management (Blunden, 1983). They are also subjects in which girls often have previous experience and/or expertise; subjects in which they feel both confident and comfortable. By continuing to take these subjects girls contribute towards making themselves less available for employment in high-status occupations and thus reproduce the historical legacy of state education as a prerequisite for family life. Although the majority of girls follow a traditional 'female' curriculum, changes are being made. Table 5.2 attempts to locate these changes in more general education.

In general education, the differentials between the sexes remain similar. For instance, in 1985 girls still represented 91 per cent of domestic science students and 74 per cent of commercial subject students, while boys predominated in technical drawing (93 per cent), metalwork and woodwork (98 per cent). An important educational shift (*Social Trends* 1987) has occurred, however, as a consequence of an increase in the number of girls obtaining passes at CSE level in Maths, Physics and Chemistry with rises of 4, 3 and 3 per cent, respectively. However, boys have also increased their share of these subject passes by 4, 2 and 3 per cent.

When we examine the pass rate in groups of subjects at 'O' level or its equivalent, the percentage of girls achieving passes is increasing at a faster rate than boys (Table 5.3). Taking English and Maths together, it has increased by 4 per cent for girls compared with 3 per cent for boys between 1980 and 1986; with the same respective increases in English/Maths and Science taken together.

Studies of new developments in education such as the Technical and Vocational Educational Initiative (TVEI) suggest that similar changes are not occurring for pupils who are pursuing such innovatory courses. Thus Millman and Weiner (1987) argue that despite the positive effect which TVEI had in placing equal opportunities on the agenda, it has done little more than this. Equal Opportunities, they maintain, has all the appearances of another subject on the curriculum, whilst ignoring the underlying practices which characterize inequalities in the links between school and work. Berry et al. (1987) illustrate how, after two years on one TVEI project, boys appeared to be widening their interest while girls appeared to remain within the traditional 'female' subjects.

At 'A' level, an examination of the distribution of pupils by sex reveals that traditional differences remain. Table 5.4 shows that while young women have increased their share of the subject area Maths/Science and Other Subjects by 4 per cent, young men continue to dominate Maths and Maths/Science A level courses.

Table 5.4 suggests that when young women do pursue 'A' levels, the means of entry into forms of higher education and career grade levels of recruitment (such as banks), they pursue in far greater numbers than young men subjects not associated with Science and Maths, thereby excluding themselves from certain employers' entry requirements and perpetuating the sexual division of labour. However, Willms and Kerr (1987), in a study of Scottish examination results in 1976–84, illustrate that by 1980 a female advantage was beginning to appear in the proportions of pupils with one Higher. Likewise the Department of Education and Science (1986) statistics show that more girls than boys gained one 'A' level, whereas 2 per cent more boys than girls

Table 5.3   Percentage of school leavers in Great Britain with GCE/SCE/CSE 'O' level passes[a] in joint subject areas, by sex

| | 1979/80 | | 1985/86 | |
	Girls	Boys	Girls	Boys
English and Maths	23	24	27	27
English/Maths and Science	16	21	20	24
English/Maths/ Science and Foreign Language	12	10	14	11

a. Irrespective of any 'A' level passes.
Devised from Table 13 (1983 edition) and Table 31 (1987 edition), *Education Statistics for the United Kingdom.*

Table 5.4   Percentage of pupils in maintained secondary schools (England): by 'A' level course of study and sex

| | 1979 | | 1983 | | 1986 | |
	Female	Male	Female	Male	Female	Male
Courses involving 'A' level Maths	21	51	24	53	26	53
Maths/Science only	16	41	17	42	16	38
Maths/Science and Other Subjects	26	29	29	30	30	33
Other Subjects only	58	30	54	28	54	29

Derived from Table A27/86(I), *Statistics of Education, Schools*, 1986.

Table 5.5   Percentage[a] of school leavers with 'A' levels by sex, England and Wales, 1984/85

	One or More	One	Two	Three
Females	16.1	3.3	4.2	8.6
Males	16.8	2.6	3.6	10.5

a. Of total 17 year age group.
Derived from Table 33, *Education Statistics*, United Kingdom, 1987.

gained three 'A' levels (Table 5.5). Such trajectories influence the number of women able to enter higher education, which usually requires the possession of three 'A' levels.

The data so far show girls making significant advances in terms of

Table 5.6   *Percentage of pupils[a] staying on beyond the statutory leaving age,[b] England, by sex*

Age at 31 August of preceding year	Girls	Boys	Girls and boys
Aged 16			
1982	33.1	30.1	31.6
1986	30.8	29.1	29.9
Aged 17			
1982	19.7	19.5	19.6
1986	18.9	19.0	18.9
Aged 18			
1982	1.8	2.5	2.1
1986	2.1	2.7	2.4

a. Excluding special schools.
b. Pupils aged 16, 17, 18 remaining at school in January of each year expressed as a percentage of the relevant cohort aged 15, one, two, and three years earlier respectively.
Derived from Table A14/86 (A5/85), *Statistics of Education, Schools*, 1986.

Table 5.7   *Percentage of pupils staying on beyond the statutory leaving age at maintained and non-maintained schools, in England, 1986, by sex[a]*

	Maintained schools		Non-maintained schools	
	Girls	Boys	Girls	Boys
Age 16	28.3	25.5	67.8	75.8
Age 17	16.7	15.9	52.2	59.5
Age 18	1.9	2.3	6.5	7.9

a. See notes to Table 5.5.
Derived from Table A14/86 (A5/85), *Statistics of Education, Schools*, 1986.

'O' level/CSE success and increasing numbers achieving one pass at 'A' level. However Table 5.6 indicates that, despite these gains, the percentage of girls staying on beyond the compulsory leaving age has actually declined to a greater extent than boys since 1982.

Table 5.7 shows that as a much higher proportion of girls stay on in non-maintained schools, this is likely to affect female representation in further and higher education. Those least likely to stay on at school are boys aged 16 to 17 in maintained schools; however by the age of 18–19 girls in maintained schools represent the smallest group. Table 5.9 provides data on the way in which staying on figures impact upon courses followed. Recently Willms and Kerr (1987), on the basis of their research in Scotland, have argued that in areas of high female unemployment, such as rural

Table 5.8   *Intended destination of school[a] leavers in England, 1985/86, by sex (percentages)*

	Female	Male
Employment[b]	54.1	62.7
All degree courses	7	8.7
of which:		
Teaching Degrees	0.7	0.1
All other advanced and further education courses	25.8	15.4
of which:		
Secretarial courses	3.7	[c]
Nursing courses	1.7	[c]
Catering courses	1.5	0.7
Not known	12.7	13.2

a. Excluding special schools.
b. Including temporary employment pending entry to full-time further education and other destinations.
c. Extremely small numbers.
Derived from Tables CC and CII, *Statistics of Education, School Leavers*, 1986.

areas, girls tend to surpass their male peers in overall examination attainment, ensuring an escape-route into higher and further education. In this regard, it is interesting to note that female school leavers in Scotland do better overall than their male counterparts in the number of subjects gained at Higher level (*Education Statistics*, 1987).

When we examine the different destinations of school leavers quite specific gender differences emerge (Table 5.8).

Of those who pursue degree courses, girls are less likely to opt to go onto non-vocational degree courses, or enrol on science and engineering courses. They are, however, more likely to opt for a degree course related to teaching or to pursue further education courses, such as nursing, secretarial and catering; thus as students move up the education system the gender divisions between courses and subject of study would appear to become even more marked.

Again, however, significant differences exist as between maintained and non-maintained schools (Table 5.9). In round terms 30 per cent of girls and 36 per cent of boys from the non-maintained sector continue on into degree courses, as compared to 6 per cent of girls and 7 per cent of boys from the maintained sector. Entry into higher education would appear to be influenced by social class to a greater extent than being female or male.

Table 5.9   The intended destination of school leavers (England) by type of school (1984/85) (percentages)

	Maintained[a]		Non-maintained		All schools	
	Girls	Boys	Girls	Boys	Girls	Boys
BA/BSc degree courses	5.0	± 6.5	28.0	36.0	6.3	8.6
B.Ed degree courses	0.7	0.1	1.5	0.1	0.7	0.1
Other A/FE courses	24.8	14.8	42.5	24.4	0.7	15.4
Employment[b]	56.5	65.1	19.5	30.9	54.5	62.7
Not known	12.9	13.6	8.5	8.7	12.7	13.2
Total all leavers (000s)	342	349	19.7	25.6	361.7	374.6

a. Excluding special schools.
b. Including temporary employment pending entry to full-time education and other destinations.
Derived from Table CC, *Statistics of Education, School Leavers*, 1986.

Further education

Although more young women are now pursuing further education courses, they are more likely to be found on non-advanced courses. For example, 66 per cent of those on advanced courses are males, but only comprise 34 per cent of those on non-advanced courses. The situation is reversed for women who have higher non-advanced participation rates (DES 1985, Table F16).

The type of course studied in further education is clearly differentiated by gender. These divisions occur at the inception of provision, when assumptions are made about working-class boys' 'vocational' training, which is seen in terms of their employment needs, and working-class girls' 'vocational' training which is seen in terms of their futures as domestic servants and housewives (Blunden, 1983) or traditional roles such as hairdressing and secretarial (Gibb, 1983). Gender divisions can be found in departments such as engineering dominated by males, and food (Gleeson and Mardle, 1980), fashion and health departments, dominated by females. Moreover, sexual divisions can occur within similar subject areas. In a study of a Northern College of Further Education Skeggs (1986) found that in a Catering Department, where boys only represented 15 per cent of students, they were predominantly located in the prestigious 'Professional Chefs Course' (68 per cent) as opposed to 'General Catering' (33 per cent).

More recently the development of YTS courses by the

*Table 5.10   The sexual composition of UK university undergraduates
(percentages)*

	1971–2	1975–6	1980–1	1984–5
Women	32	35	40	42
Men	68	64	60	58

Derived from UGC *University Statistics*, vol. 1, *Students and Staff* (1981/82, 1984/85).

Manpower Services Commission, with a written commitment to both sexual and racial equality of opportunity, has done little to eradicate the already existing divisions of labour and knowledge; rather they continue to reproduce and perpetrate the existing differentiation in both paid work and education (Brelsford, Smith and Rix, 1982; Cohen, 1982, 1984; Dex, 1983a; Gleeson, 1983; Bates et al., 1984; Finn, 1984; Skeggs, 1986).

Higher education
Since 1978 the recruitment of men onto degree courses from the non-maintained sector has declined by 7 per cent; whilst the percentage from the maintained sector has remained constant. The recruitment of women onto degree courses from both sectors has remained the same. Women, particularly working-class women, are less likely than men to attend university, although they are more likely to pursue a teacher training degree. Kelsall, Poole and Kuhn (1972) and Edwards and Roberts (1980) found that overall women undergraduates are more likely than men to be from the middle classes. However, although there has been a change of around a third in the proportion of women to men university students, and the number of women entering higher education is increasing, they still only represent 42 per cent of the student population (AUT 1987), whilst the number of male undergraduates is decreasing (Table 5.10).

In the case of postgraduates these are decreasing overall; in 1984/85 women represented 24 per cent of those studying for higher degrees, other than PGCE's (13 per cent), a decrease from 38 per cent in 1977. Class differences, as well as sex differences, are influential in determining the destination of students going on to further and higher education as has been illustrated by Table 5.9.

In addition, Rendel (1975) noted the trend for women as a whole to attend degree-awarding institutions, which incorporate some element of training (such as teaching or nursing) but which are of lower status than universities. However, if one was to look at vocational courses which have been traditionally male-dominated, such as engineering and medicine, one would obviously find the female/male proportions reversed. This is a reflection of their occupational status in comparison to traditional female areas such as school teaching. Moreover, Roweth (1981) notes how the number of women qualified to participate in Higher Education, who do not follow that option, has increased more rapidly than that of men; 'out of those qualified to enter higher education, currently around one in nine men and one in four women . . . do not take up that option.' Moreover, this situation is likely to become more acute as a consequence of teacher training being subjected to a large amount of cutbacks (Bone, 1980). This tendency for women to be under-represented in the high-status areas of education, which operate as an entry ticket to a wider choice of occupations, also occurs when we examine the position of women who are employed in education. The lower the status of the educational sector, the higher the number of women who will be found working there!

Educational employment

As fewer women than men enter university as undergraduates, it is likely that fewer will take higher degrees. In fact, women represent just under a quarter of postgraduates and, as in the other educational sectors, a sexual division of labour/knowledge exists in the areas of study they pursue. Women are less likely to pursue a higher degree by research than men, but are more likely to pursue a postgraduate teaching qualification. This is another example of the process of 'filtering-out'; a higher degree by research (usually a PhD) is now a requirement for entry into Higher Education teaching. In 1984/85 women represented only 16 per cent of teaching and research staff in universities, and 17 per cent of polytechnic lecturers (1985). The recruitment of women as full-time employees in universities has been rising over the last 20 years – by 9 per cent between 1965 and 1975, and 16 per cent between 1976 and 1982. However, 60 per cent of the women recruited in 1985 were research staff, working largely on short-term contracts. In 1984 nearly half of women academic staff were employed on this basis, compared with only a quarter of the men. The positions women occupy in universities further illustrates a sexual division of labour (Table 5.11).

As Table 5.11 indicates, women working in universities occupy few of the positions of responsibility; they also comprise the majority of part-time teachers (94 per cent). A recent report by the

Table 5.11   University academic staff (full-time) United Kingdom, 1984–85, by sex

All departments	Women	Men	Women %	Men %
Professors	101	4049	2	98
Readers and senior lecturers	614	8300	7	93
Lecturers and assistant lecturers	4657	22,022	18	82
Other	1521	2928	34	6
All	6893	37,299	16	84

Derived from Table 25, *University Grants Committee*, 1984–85.

AUT Women's Committee found that while nearly 85 per cent of male academics had been promoted to senior lecturer or professor by the age of 60, nearly half the women remained unpromoted. In 1985, only seven women were promoted to the professorial grade compared to 237 men.

The under-representation of women in university posts is reversed, however, in other types of educational institution. Thus, in the case of schools catering for the infant age-range, 85 per cent of the full-time teachers are female, and in primary schools as a whole, almost three-quarters of the teachers are women (Table 5.12). Not surprisingly in the case of part-time teaching staff, women again predominate (84 per cent) compared with 16 per cent of men. Thus, despite the fact that a higher proportion of women than men opt to follow a degree course leading to a teaching qualification (Table 5.8), women continue to predominate in the relatively low-status and insecure teaching posts.

However, female over-representation in primary and middle schools does not mean that they 'dominate' (only in numbers, not power) these areas. Thus Acker (1983) found in 'junior with infant' schools, women are 74 per cent of the teachers, but only comprise 26 per cent of the heads. In 'Junior without infant schools' they are 65 per cent of the teachers but only 16 per cent of the heads. In the secondary sector, women hold 60 per cent of scale one posts but only 32 per cent of deputy headships and 16 per cent of headships. Scribbins and Edwards (1982) note a similar trend in further education, where females comprised 68 per cent of the L1 and L2 category (the lowest) compared to only 32 per cent of male lecturers.

Women's chances of promotion are also smaller in comparison

*Table 5.12   Full-time qualified teachers in maintained schools: England,
1986, by sex*

Type of institution	Women	Men
All primary	74	26
Infant	99	1
First	88	12
Junior and Infant	76	24
First and Middle	77	23
Junior	66	34
All Middle	59	41
Deemed Primary	64	36
Deemed Secondary	55	45
All Secondary[a]	45	55
Modern	46	54
Grammar	39	61
Comprehensive	44	56
Sixth Form College	36	64
All schools	60	40

a. Includes technical and 'other' secondary schools.
Derived from Table A1/86, *Statistics in Education*, 1986.

to men's. The National Union of Teachers and The Equal
Opportunities Commission (1985a) found that promotion chances
for women fell drastically between 1963 and 1983. They also
found that despite the fewer chances, 82 per cent of teachers in
their sample were pursuing a career and hoping for promotion.
How then do we explain the existing sexual divisions within
education? Are women underselling themselves? Are they taking
an instrumental view of education by, for example, pursuing
vocational courses? Do many consider education to be irrelevant to
their futures? Do they automatically conform to the nurturing role
of women?

So far we have illustrated a 'filtering-out' process, whereby the
higher the form of education, the fewer women represented in it.
However, in contradiction to this, girls appear to start out with an
equal, if not greater intellectual advantage. Bocock (1972) has
argued:

> In the light of social expectations about women, it is not surprising
> that women end up where society expects them to: the surprise is that
> little girls don't get the message that they are supposed to be stupid
> until they get into high school.

How and why this process occurs will now be examined by
analysing the many different theories which purport to explain
women's 'under-achievement' vis-à-vis men.

Competing explanations

Psychological/biological theories
Maccoby and Jacklin (1974), in their book *The Psychology of Sex Differences*, report an analysis carried out of over 1400 research studies concerned with examining the link between sex and mental differences. The study questioned some long-standing beliefs and on the basis of their analysis they conclude that there are no reliably established differences between women and men in social orientation, suggestibility, self-esteem, cognitive or analytic ability. They conclude that environmental differences play an overwhelmingly important role in the development of sex differences. Subsequent criticism of these claims resulted in the establishment of many research projects to 'prove' sex differences, especially girls' superiority in verbal areas, and boys in spatial and mechanical tasks. However, Megarry (1984) in a summary of more recent research points to many inadequacies in their conclusions. First, the differences identified have usually been very slight, with tremendous overlap between the sexes. The large numbers of subjects allowed these slight differences to achieve *statistical* significance, whereas their *educational* significance is far from clear. Secondly, we do not know how many studies found no significant differences as these were never published. Thirdly, no tests exist for 'pure' aptitude; we can only infer aptitude from performance. By the time girls are old enough to be tested, their lack of experience, for example with mechanical toys, may account for lower performance on tests which employ or portray such objects. In addition, Macaulay (1978) has exposed how many investigators appear to have been biased by their own prior convictions. Likewise, Sayers (1984) documents the great ingenuity and effort expended to trying to attribute gender differences to biological theories, theories which she argues remain at most merely speculative. If there are so few, if any, innate reasons for explaining sex differences in educational performance, why do girls progressively filter out of the education system? Some theorists have suggested that socialization is the important variable in determining sex differences within education.

Socialization theories
Gaskell (1977/8) has identified a 'sex-role ideology' in schools. The ideology, or belief system, assumes that natural differences exist between girls and boys and that, therefore, any inequalities that appear are the result of natural differences. It is important to note that 'sex-role ideology' is a social belief which confuses

biological differences (such as different anatomies) with social expectations. A distinction therefore needs to be made between sex and gender. Sex is related to biological characteristics, whereas gender is related to social expectations; to the way that people are expected to behave depending upon which particular sexual group they belong to. Eichler (1980), for instance, argues that gender roles are the kinds of role people play in accordance with social norms and beliefs. For example, girls are expected to be quiet, pretty, non-aggressive, gentle, caring, whereas boys are expected to be the opposite. The way these characteristics are attributed to a particular sex has come to be known as ideologies of femininity and masculinity. They are not constant, like our biological differences, and as Oakley (1972) has clearly shown, they can change across cultures, throughout history and within or between different social groups. However, many people operate with the assumption that feminine and masculine behaviour is somehow in-bred. Unfortunately, as we have seen from our examination of early educational experience, many schools reinforce these differences through either the organization of the curriculum, reproduction of stereotypes, or teacher expectations; just as other socializing agents, such as the family, media and peer group reinforce and reproduce assumptions and expectations about masculinity and femininity. Wolpe (1977) and Arnot (1981) argue that the development of the British education system has been characterized by a sex-role ideology which assumes that the education of girls should be influenced by their assumed future role of mother and wife. Scott (1980) outlines the following assumptions that are made in relation to the education of women:

1 The main priority in girls' lives (particularly of low ability) is to marry and raise a family.
2 Paid work will play a non-essential part in their adult lives.
3 They will enter paid work only in limited fields.
4 The work they perform in the labour force is not important to society and only necessary as 'pin money'.

The effects of sex-role ideology have been found to operate in many educational areas. Kelly (1981), examining the reasons why girls did not study scientific subjects, relates the image of the scientific subject and scientist to such variables as the sex of the science teacher, the type of teaching and assessment used, and the career prospects associated with science. In all she maps out the many ways in which the different images of what science should be, how it should be taught, and who pursues science, come to influence perceptions of who eventually studies science. In effect,

Kelly demonstrates how girls often do not take scientific subjects because they do not associate science with something girls do. Gaskell (1977/8) has taken this further by arguing that sex-role ideology affects the ambitions and perceptions of students' possible futures, which in turn limit the educational aspirations of girls. Licht and Dweck (1983) found that girls, relative to boys, have less confidence in their ability to succeed in challenging intellectual tasks, blaming themselves for failure rather than the external effects which boys refer to when explaining failure. So sex-role ideology, they argue, can influence one's self-perception.

Sex-role ideology can also influence the way the school is organized. Benn and Simon (1972) found, when researching 587 schools, that 50 per cent of their sample restricted some subjects to boys while 48 per cent restricted some subjects to girls. More recently Grafton et al. (1983) found that the practice of blocking off subjects on the timetable, which, for example, enables pupils exclusively to take all domestic subjects, or all science subjects, severely restricts those pupils at 13 who may want to choose subjects not traditionally associated with their gender. Likewise a report by the Department of Education and Science (1975) found that much curriculum organization was based on different gender assumptions, for teachers considered such differentiation to be part of a conventional long-standing organization.

Pupils may also experience problems if they choose 'gender untypical' subjects. Ling (1981) found that those wanting to do so had to be prepared to be the only one of their sex in a particular class. Brelsford, Smith and Rix (1982) noted how this fact has acted as a disincentive to those wanting to choose unconventional YOP programmes. Moreover, Byrne (1975) found that sex-role assumptions influenced the allocation of resources to particular areas. She identifies how the implicit assumptions about the future marriage/wife roles of girls were seen as subsidiary when compared to the importance of paid work; as a consequence girls were believed to require less financial support funding within education than boys. Thus, in her study of 133 schools (Byrne, 1975), almost all the girls' school were found to be deficient in scientific equipment.

An analysis, which takes sex-role ideology as the determinant of sex differences in education, might conclude that if attitudes were changed gender differences could be eradicated. However, there are several limitations to this conclusion, as Arnot (1986) points out: first, socialization theorists cannot explain why gender has developed in the way that it has; secondly, socialization theories are inadequate as explanations of the diversity of experience between girls of different classes or different races; thirdly, the analysis assumes that there is only one ideology of femininity and one ideology of masculinity; fourthly, it assumes that girls and boys always and inevitably take on intact ideologies of masculinity and femininity, but which Anyon (1983) and Skeggs (1986) have shown to be a complex and contradictory process, where many aspects of masculinity and femininity are reworked, reflected and challenged. Finally, theorists have assumed that each site of socialization, such as the school, the family, the media, transmits the same gender ideology.

However, these theories have been important in alerting us to what actually happens in schools and some useful lines of inquiry have been pursued as a result. Radical feminists, for instance, who locate unequal gender differentiation in the relationship between women and men, specifically the domination of women by men, have been able to document how women have been made invisible by the process of academic research (Spender, 1980) and also in classroom interaction (Spender and Sarah, 1981). Claricoates (1980), on the basis of research in several schools, concludes that all women suffer oppression:

> It is patriarchy in the male hierarchical ordering of society, preserved through marriage and the family via the sexual division of labour that is at the core of women's oppression; and it is schools, through their different symbolic separation of the sexes, that gives this oppression the seal of approval. (p. 40)

While identifying the disadvantages that are widespread in the education of girls, what this analysis fails to address is the source of sex-role ideology and how and why it is perpetrated. Thus Beechey (1979) and Walker and Barton (1983) outline the problems in this analysis of the notion of patriarchy to explain sex-role ideology in education. They point out that patriarchy theorists usually locate the sexual divisions of labour within the family and at work as being the central features of capitalist society. However, capitalism has no essential, inbuilt desire to have a sexual division between women and men. The force behind capitalism is the need to keep accumulating profits; capitalism would be better served if it could exploit everybody's labour to make even greater profits. Some feminists (Brenner and Ramas, 1983; Humphries, 1977) have argued that, historically, women have attempted to preserve the sexual division of labour in order to preserve the family as a 'haven in a heartless world'; in addition, patriarchal relations assume different characteristics at specific moments in history and therefore cannot be defined simply as a coherent operation, over time, of male power over women. Likewise, gender differentiation works both within and across class formations. Although women do generally receive a multitude of discriminations in education, these are not coherent, and are received differently by girls/women of different classes and races, as the 'resistance' theories of education suggest.

Resistance and accommodation theories
These theories turn the notion of sex-role ideology on its head. They argue that rather than a uniform sex-role ideology being imposed by the school, boys and girls bring to school their own constructions of what it is to be male and female; constructions learnt from their own complex culture. Willis's (1977) work, for instance, documents how a group of working-class 'lads' bring into school a definition of masculinity which is based on the practical, strong and hard characteristics of manual labour. Their definition of what it is to be masculine, a definition they work hard at achieving and proving, is in contradiction to that of the school which is based on competitive, individualistic, academic success. The 'lads' are not remotely interested in anything academic, which they consider to be sissy and wimpish, and want to leave school as early as possible to start earning a wage. Thus, their gendered definitions and assumptions differ greatly from those of the school as an institution. They also use their gender definitions to challenge authority and the ethos of the school. McRobbie (1978b) and Griffin (1985a) document a similar process whereby groups of working-class girls consider the school and its definitions of femininity to be in opposition to their own. The school's emphasis on neatness, passivity and plainness was challenged by the increased emphasis the young girls placed on their sexuality. The girls took great pleasure in wearing make-up to school, spent vast amounts of time discussing boyfriends in loud voices in class, and used these interests to disrupt the class. This emphasis, and the importance attached to the outward accoutrements of femininity, are important factors in the female response to schooling (Meyenn, 1980); unfortunately, they only tend to reconfirm and reproduce the inequalities girls endure as a result of gender stereotyping. Likewise, Sharpe (1976) found some girls feared doing well at school because they perceived that it involved losing an important ingredient of femininity. The majority of her sample from four schools in Ealing confirmed that boys feel threatened by girls who are too clever. Deem (1978) suggests that the way a girl resolves this tension depends largely on her social class expectations, while Fuller (1980), taking the

argument further, suggests that responses to the contradiction between femininity and academic achievement depend on both class and race. Her research on young Afro-Caribbean women illustrates how they refuse to take on the school's imposed definitions of what it is to be feminine and black. Thus, rather than emphasizing their femininity, they instrumentally conformed at school when they considered it necessary, so as to gain the qualifications needed to escape from their subordinate position of being black, female and working-class. Riley (1981), in a study of Afro-Caribbean sixth-formers, identified a similar attempt to organize and exert some control over their own lives. More recently Skeggs (1986), in a study of YTS students, found a strongly instrumental attitude towards definitions of femininity, in which the students used partial definitions, such as 'caring', to gain status and/or financial security. This evidence supports Anyon's argument (1983) that complete acceptance of sex-role ideology is actually rare. Rather, in attempting to construct some form of self-esteem for themselves, women both resist and accommodate aspects of femininity. All these studies focus on the ideology of femininity, and through examining responses and reactions, they emphasize the importance of factors outside of schooling, such as working-class culture and family ideology. Thus sex differences in education are not just an 'educational problem with an educational solution' (Arnot, 1981). They also indicate that in their responses to schooling pupils and students make 'realistic appraisals' of their own situation and perceived futures, and it is here that the analysis needs extending to include the conditions from which these 'realistic appraisals' emerge. These conditions do not just happen, nor are they the product of ideology, rather they are part and parcel of a specific form of historical, economic, social and political organization.

The political economy
The 'political economy' perspective attempts to explain the 'why' part in relation to gender differences. Rather than just describing inequality and the processes through which it is reproduced, this perspective attempts to locate the origins and reasons for the existence of gender differences. Arnot (1981) describes it as an external rather than an internal account, in which the issue of gender differentiation is relocated into the social and material conditions of its existence. Arnot (1981) identifies the advantages of this perspective as being the ability to view critically the development of state educational policy in relation to class and gender; to relate the structuring of the school and its products to

the structuring of the labour process and domestic life; and to identify the forces and structures outside of the school. This perspective has been applied by Marxist sociologists to explain social class divisions in education. Thus Althusser (1971) considers the school to be one of the important sites for the transmission of the ideology of the ruling class, and Bowles and Gintis (1976) argue that the education system inculcates students with the attitudes and dispositions necessary to accept the social and economic imperatives of a capitalist economy. Feminist versions of these theories actually locate and identify the source of sex-role ideology in capitalist social organization (Dyhouse, 1977, David, 1978; Davin, 1979). They, like the patriarchy theorists, assume that capitalism has 'needs' which depend upon a sexual division of labour; a position which Beechey (1977) argues reduces gender relations to an effect of the operation of capital. Coward (1983), Arnot (1986) and Adamson et al. (1976) point out the coincidences in such a theoretical position, whereby the 'needs' of capital somehow come to coincide with those of men, and result in what is essentially the 'conditions' of female oppression. However, one must not underestimate the value of the sexual division of labour as a concept, for it enables an examination of both class and gender divisions. One needs, however, to take account of a third variable, race, in order to understand how these three determinants of social divisions and experience operate together. But, as Anthias and Yuval-Davis (1983) point out, any 'triple oppression' analysis must seek to understand how each division affects the others, and what outcomes are produced. Also, we have to avoid over-prioritization, in which one variable is always considered to be the most important; in different circumstances, different priorities will occur. Carby (1982) and Parmar (1982) have argued that the prioritization of patriarchy, for example, has failed to account for how racism divides women and classes.

The political economy perspective has been developed most recently through specific historical studies which are able to locate the effects of gender and class divisions within specific social and economic settings. The studies (see Dyhouse, 1977; David, 1978; Delamont and Duffin, 1978; Davin, 1978; Purvis, 1981) have all examined the state's social policies. This examines the reasons for the development of these policies and women's 'dual' location in waged work and the family household structure (Arnot, 1981). It also examines the development of the economy, the consequent transformation of the labour force and its process, resulting from the changing nature of domestic life and the division of labour within it. By focusing on particular events, and then generalizing into wider economic and political processes, these theories enable the subtleties and complexities of gender, class and race reproduction to be examined.

All the theories discussed have particular value in explaining aspects of gender differentation in education. The 'micro' or 'internal' studies of schooling have provided a wealth of evidence to show how disadvantage and discrimination for girls and young women operates in education through language, classroom practice, school organization, curriculum, teacher expectations, stereotyping and the transmission and reproduction of traditional sexist beliefs inherent within sex-role ideologies. Other studies, by concentrating on reaction by pupils to schooling, have indicated the importance of the external cultural influences that pupils bring with them into schools and colleges. Likewise 'macro' or 'external' studies have indicated the importance of locating such responses and discriminations within a wider context, in order to understand why discrimination and disadvantage are perpetuated. By locating education as just one area of the state's social policies, in which employment practices and family responsibilities are also related, the whole complexity of sexual divisions can be seen as part of economic, social and political development.

Ways forward

However, whilst this analysis is taking place and whilst this chapter is being read, girls and young women are suffering from the inequalities of our educational system. What the studies of state educational policy have shown is that it has operated to maintain differences between the sexes and the sexual division of labour, both implicitly and explicitly (Arnot, 1986). The potential therefore exists for some restructuring. However, as noted previously, the education system is only one part of the state's social policy, and inequality in education is not just an educational problem with educational solutions. If girls were given an equal schooling, what would happen when they left and faced a rigid sexual division of labour, and a tax and social welfare system which assumed their primary responsibility was to the family? Moreover, how would they survive and resist the bombardment of feminine ideology from outside of schooling, where romance and relationships become *raison d'êtres*?

This is not to say that we should not try to improve the educational chances and conditions for girls. Recent initiatives in developing anti-sexist materials and curricula appear to have had very promising results (Cornbleet and Sanders, 1982; Chisholm and Holland, 1986). Groups, such as the 'Women in Education

Group', have also provided support and ideas for teachers who are attempting to challenge many of the inbuilt assumptions within the education system. Furthermore, challenging the sexist assumptions within books used in schools contributes towards challenging the massive wall of sexism. Likewise Stanworth (1981) argues that teachers' intervention to challenge the negative degrading of young women in the classroom could constitute a 'significant political act', for the cumulative degradation that young women receive in classroom interaction gives such negative beliefs a concrete foundation in personal experience. Specific action is being taken to encourage girls to develop confidence in areas not traditionally associated with them, such as CDT (the GTE, Girls and Technology education project) and science subjects (the GIST, Girls into Science and Technology). Cornbleet and Saunders (1982) argue that such schemes, however, are not enough:

> An equal opportunities programme is a superficial attempt to answer a complex problem. Such a programme does not intrinsically contain a challenge either to the culture which produces stereotypes or to the language in which the curriculum is taught.

Anti-sexism, which directly challenges the taken-for-granted assumptions of classroom practice, organization and interaction, presents a more positive way of giving girls confidence. They need to learn social skills, such as assertiveness, so they can challenge degrading sexist labels, such as 'slags or drags'; these are influential factors in the development of young girls' sexuality and self-confidence, and in their relationship to others (Lees, 1986). Cornbleet and Saunders initiated the project 'Developing Anti-Sexist Initiatives' in two London schools, whereby specific single-sex groups were organized so girls could be given space to develop their abilities. In addition, both boys and girls received courses on sex-stereotyping and girls had assertiveness training.

Other commentators such as Sarah, Scott and Spender (1980) have suggested that single-sex schools are an essential prerequisite to challenging sexism. The debate over single or mixed sex schools is, however, very complex, as Arnot (1983) demonstrates. She draws our attention to the fact that historically single-sex schools were developed, alongside other state social policies, to reproduce and reinforce particular forms of class and gender relations – relations which reproduced male hierarchy and female subordination. Arnot questions whether single-sex schools, which are part of a state educational system supporting sexual divisions, can be expected to challenge gender relations. A separate strategy for one sex alone will not challenge the overall reproduction of dominant relations – 'gender as a basis for allocating individuals will not disappear as an educational or social variable if schools or classes are allocated to one or other sex' (Arnot, 1983, p. 87). Steedman's (1983) and Bone's (1980) research suggests that it is the type and style of school, rather than the sex allocated to it, that is the important factor. In addition small, single-sex schools are likely to be under-resourced and not necessarily be able, or want to, challenge traditional sex-role assumptions.

Overview

This chapter began by illustrating how the education system in this country was established on the basis of a class-and-sex division of labour and knowledge, and prepared young people for sex-segregation in many aspects of adult life. It has demonstrated how, throughout the development of the education system, many factors contributed towards maintaining and reproducing these divisions. The most influential education reports closely identified a young woman's education to her future domestic role in the family and a young man's to his role as a paid worker. The establishment of links between education and industrial concerns did not result in the identification of women's full needs as part of the educational agenda.

Whilst all these sexist assumptions were being made outside of the educational system, inside education similar assumptions were being reproduced. The curriculum and the classroom were being organized on the basis of sexual divisions; teachers' expectations were influencing the interaction and expectations of girls and boys, and they in turn were bringing their own assumptions about femininity and masculinity into the classroom. And although sex-role ideology was not being taken on intact, but was mediated by both race and class, the frameworks of masculinity and femininity influenced the interactive responses of the classroom.

It has been argued that this continual process of the reproduction of sexual divisions, both within and outside of education, contributes towards the filtering-out of girls from the education system. Thus attempts to make education 'more equal' can have little impact on a system which originated to maintain inequalities, and is informed by the economic imperatives and organization of the gender-divided labour market. Even the inroads into non-traditional areas and the increasing success of girls and young women at 'O' and 'A' levels does not appear to be having any significant effect upon their final destinations. Not only does this suggest that the education system maintains gender inequalities, but also, contains a considerable amount of wastage, whereby the achievements of young women are being neglected. As such, the gender differences in education, the filtering-out process, and the under-representation of girls and young women in areas associated with economic security and social mobility should not be surprising. What is surprising is that girls have achieved so much when the odds are stacked so highly against them.

6 Sex and gender in the labour market

Michael Webb

Participation in paid work, full-time and part-time

During the late Victorian period, women were to a large degree excluded from paid work; however, the twentieth century has seen a return to the situation where women are engaged in large numbers in paid economic activity (Table 6.1). We count as 'economically active' not only those with a job, but also those who are officially unemployed, for both categories of people together

Table 6.1 *Economically active population, by sex and marital status, Great Britain, 1901–86*

	Economically active population (000s)		Women as % of total economically active population		Economically active as % of each group[a]		
	Women	Men	All women	Married women	All women	Married women	Men
	(1)	(2)	(3)	(4)	(5)	(6)	(7)
1901	4,732	11,548	29	na	32	na	84
1911	5,424	12,927	30	4	33	10	84
1921	5,701	13,656	30	4	32	9	87
1931	6,265	14,790	30	5	34	10	91
1951	7,419	16,007	31	12	35	22	88
1961	8,407	16,366	33	16	38	30	86
1971	8,708	15,837	36	23	44	42	81
1981	10,134	15,942	39	26	48	51	77
1986	11,130	15,997	41	28	49	53	74

na = not available.

a. 1901, 1911 aged 10 or over; 1921 aged 12 or over; 1931 aged 14 or over; 1951, 1961, 1971 aged 15 or over; 1981, 1986 aged 16 or over.
Columns 1–4 devised from *British Labour Statistics Historical Abstract* (1971) Tables 102, 109; *Annual Abstract of Statistics*, 1981 and 1987. Columns 5–7 from: Hakim (1978); *British Labour Statistics Historical Abstract* (1971) Table 109; *Social Trends, 1979*, No. 11, Table 5.1; *Social Trends 1987*, No. 17, Table 4.3; EOC (1987b).

are available as the country's workforce (also known as the 'labour force' or the 'working population').

The rise in the female labour force during recent decades was due not principally to 'demographic' effects, such as an increase in the numbers in the working age groups, but rather to an increase in the female 'activity rate' (or 'participation rate'). Women's participation rate is still below that of men (see Table 6.1), although the gap is narrower if we exclude the oldest age groups (see Tables 4.8 and 6.30).

By contrast, since World War II, male economic activity has tended to fall, particularly in the 1980s. The activity rate of younger males has decreased, partly with the tendency to stay longer in education. However there has also been a reduction in male participation among the older ages in the working age group (GHS 1985, 1987). One special 'sub-group' is men aged 60–65: by the mid-1980s, only about half of these men were still in work, even through the formal 'retirement age' for men is five years later than it is for women.

However, when examining women's participation rates, it is important to distinguish between women of different marital status.

In 1911, only just below 10 per cent of married women were in the workforce; today the figure is about 50 per cent. It used to be common for married women to leave the labour force permanently once they got married. Now it is usual to have a merely temporary break while looking after children. Therefore married women's participation rate now has two peaks, one between the ages of 20 and 24, and the second between the ages of 45 and 50 (Table 6.2). This pattern was established by the 1960s, but since then the height of the second peak and of the trough has continued to rise, and over recent decades the trough has moved to an earlier position in the age-span (Dex, 1985).

It is also important to distinguish between people working full-time and those working part-time. The traditional distinction is that part-time workers are those who perform 30 hours of work or less per week. Of course, some people doing such work may have more than one job (*Social Trends*, 1987). However, in most cases of part-time employment, only one job is involved.

Much of the increase in female employment in the 1970s was in the form of part-time work (Table 6.3). Indeed the 1980s saw full-time jobs for both women and men fall sharply, while the part-time employment of women continued to rise, until by 1987 part-time work constituted 23 per cent of all employment.

Among part-time employees there are relatively few men (only

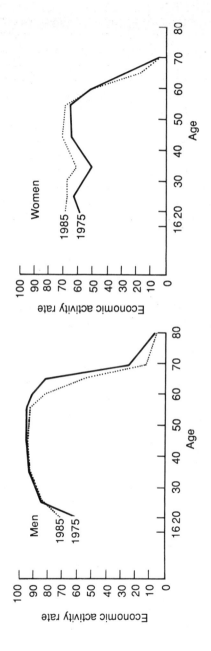

Table 6.2   *Economic activity rates by sex, Great Britain 1975 and 1985*
Derived from EOC (1987b), Figure 3.1

Table 6.3   Full-time and part-time employees, by sex, Great Britain, 1971, 1979 and 1987

	June 1971	June 1979	June 1987	1971–79	1979–87
	Numbers in 000s			% changes	
All employees	21,648	22,638	21,133	+5	−7
Female employees	8,224	9,455	9,516	+15	+1
Full-time	5,468	5,585	5,335	+2	−5
Part-time	2,757	3,870	4,181	+40	+8
Male employees	13,424	13,183	11,617	−2	−12
Full-time	12,840	na	10,748	na	na
Part-time	548	na	869	na	na
		Percentages			
Part-timers as % of all female employees	34	41	44		
Part-timers as % of all male workers	4	na	8		

Devised from *Employment Gazette*, Table 1.1 Vol. 80, No. 12; Vol. 87, No. 12, Vol. 95, No. 12.

one for every ten women part-timers). The few men who have part-time work mainly undertake it as they near retirement. However, for women part-time work is particularly associated with marriage and children.

It is married women who have taken up the new part-time jobs in large numbers (Table 4.8, this volume). Not only is most part-time work done by married women, but most married women workers work part-time (Table 6.4). Part-time employment is most common for women who are in the age-ranges where there are likely to be heavy demands on them at home (Table 4.10; Trades Union Congress, 1980).

Child-rearing also inhibits mothers' participation in full-time as well as part-time work. One estimate (quoted in Dex, 1985) calculated that child-rearing leads to a 30 per cent reduction in the overall participation of married women aged 16–34, and that if family sizes were to decrease by one child, the paid work hours of married women would increase by 12.5 per cent over their working life. None the less, the proportion of mothers and of married women who are in the workforce is much higher than many people realize.

We are now in a position to make a preliminary assessment of the causes of the overall rise in female employment in the postwar years. This increase in the 'supply' of women workers was partly

Table 6.4 *Mothers working part-time and full-time as percentage of all mothers,[a] by marital status, age, and age of youngest child, Great Britain, 1984*

	Working full-time	Working part-time	All economically active
Marital status			
Single	53	5	71
Widowed, divorced, or separated	32	23	63
All non-married	47	11	68
Married	25	31	61
All women	32	25	63
Age of youngest child			
0–2 years	4	19	28
3–4 years	8	28	41
5–9 years	12	41	60
10 years or over[b]	27	41	71
All ages[b]	15	33	53

a. Includes only women of working-age, 16–59.
b. Includes only dependent children.
Derived from *GHS 1984* (1986), Tables 6.4 and 6.14.

connected with changes in women's roles and the decision of women to remain in gainful employment for longer before having a child. However, the changes in the pattern of childbearing may merely have resulted from, rather than caused, the increase in women's labour market participation. Child-rearing patterns cannot be a complete explanation of the labour market changes, for the increase in paid work took place at all stages in the lifecycle including the period of child-rearing (Table 6.2).

A better explanation of the increase in the proportion of women in work lies not on the 'supply' side but involves looking at economic 'demand'. During the 1950s and 1960s the economy was booming, whereas there was a recession after the mid-1970s, and particularly after 1979. These periods match quite closely the periods of fastest and slowest rise in female employment. Therefore a key explanation for the rise in women's activity in the twentieth century lies in the increased demand in the economy for people to undertake paid work; in recent years this has mainly been in the form of part-time work.

Table 6.5   Average gross hourly earnings, manual and non-manual employees, full-time and part-time, by sex, Great Britain, 1986

	Manual occupations	Non-manual occupations	All (manual and non-manual) occupations
Earnings in pence per hour			
Women working part-time	239	308	279
Women working full-time	273	391	363
Men working full-time	393	627	489
As % of male full-time hourly earnings:			
Female part-time earnings	61	49	57
Female full-time earnings	70	62	74

Note: earnings include any overtime pay.
Derived from *New Earnings Survey 1986*, Parts A and F.

Inequalities in earnings, hours and conditions of service

Notwithstanding the increase in demand for women workers, women still earn substantially less than men (Table 6.5). The manual/non-manual comparison in this table is important for (as the next section will show) women disproportionately have non-manual jobs: it is in this category that the gap between the sexes is greatest. We have also previously noted that married women are concentrated in part-time work, and particularly non-manual occupations, once again, the very categories in which the gender pay-gap is greatest.

Differences in pay between the sexes – quite large in the case of hourly earnings – are greater in the case of weekly and annual earnings, because men tend to be the ones who work longer hours (Tables 6.6 and 6.7).. However, it should be noted that there have been changes over the years: the hours of work of male manual workers fell by almost one hour between 1980 and 1987, whereas there was almost no reduction for women, or indeed for non-manual male workers. The Royal Commission on the Distribution of Income and Wealth (1978a) showed that, among couples with children, mothers worked much shorter hours than fathers,

Table 6.6 *Normal hours of work and annual earnings, by sex and marital status, Great Britain, 1975*

	Wives	Husbands	Single Women	Single Men
Normal weekly hours	26.8	40.6	36.0	39.9
Overtime weekly hours	0.4	3.7	0.7	2.1
Weeks worked	47.7	50.8	50.4	49.8
Annual earnings (£)	1222.0	3193.0	2427.0	2685.0

Derived from Table 1, Greenhalgh (1980); based on data from the *GHS*.

Table 6.7 *Composition of earnings and hours worked, manual and non-manual full-time workers, by sex, Great Britain, 1987*

	Women (aged 18+)			Men (aged 21+)		
	Manual	Non-manual	All	Non-Manual	manual	All
As % of average gross weekly earnings						
Overtime payments	5.4	2.0	2.5	14.6	3.5	8.2
Payment by results, etc.	8.4	1.2	2.4	7.5	3.6	5.3
Shift premium payments, etc.	2.3	1.2	1.4	3.4	0.7	1.9
% of employees who receive						
Overtime payments	25.4	16.2	18.2	54.8	21.1	38.6
Payment by results, etc.	31.4	11.6	16.0	40.7	16.3	29.0
Shift premium payments, etc.	12.9	11.4	11.7	23.0	6.5	15.1
Average weekly hours worked						
Total hours	39.7	36.8	37.5	44.6	38.7	41.9
Overtime hours	1.6	0.6	0.8	5.5	1.5	3.7

Derived from Table 1. *New Earnings Survey* (1987), Part A.

although there was a tendency for women with more than four children to work longer than those with smaller families, presumably because of financial necessity. However, marital divisions of labour cannot explain all the differences in hours worked: for example, single men work longer hours than single women. Differences in hours arc probably mainly due to the different jobs done by these various groups of workers.

One important difference between jobs is the amount of overtime involved; this is a semi-permanent feature of many jobs, persisting even through periods of high unemployment. Overtime is usually paid at a higher rate, and Table 6.7 shows that the proportion of men who receive overtime payments is twice that of women. Although during the 1980s such payments have become more common than formerly for women, particularly women manual workers, women's opportunities for overtime as limited because they tend to do non-manual work where such work is rarer.

This same absence from manual work limits women's opportunity to improve their pay through payment-by-results, another feature of manual but not non-manual jobs. However, in the limited amount of women's manual work which does exist, payment-by-results is commonly used, often as a mechanism of controlling the workforce (Herzog, 1980). Women's absence from night-shifts (in many cases women are excluded from them by law) means they are unable to earn shift premium payments which are available to significant numbers of men (Wrench and Stanley, 1983).

Until the advent of the *New Earnings Survey* in 1968 and 1970, the only comprehensive data on earnings were for manual workers. Those data showed that the female/male earnings differential had remained remarkably constant over a very long period of time, female weekly earnings being 50.2 per cent of those of males in 1906 and 50 per cent in 1970, with only minor variations in between (Chiplin and Sloane, 1974). The stability in the earnings differential until 1970 is apparent from Table 6.8.

From 1970 onwards the data cover all full-time employees. It can be seen (Table 6.9) that women's relative pay rose significantly between 1970 and 1977, particularly in the two years after 1975 when the 1970 Equal Pay Act came into operation. However since then relative pay has settled at around the level reached in the mid-1970s. A new stable differential has emerged, with women's hourly earnings being just under three-quarters of men's, and women's weekly earnings being approximately two-thirds of men's.

So far, we have viewed earnings using arithmetic averages. An alternative view is given in Table 6.10, which gives an indication not just of an average figure (the median in this case), but of the top and bottom of the range of earnings. It is possible to calculate the 'real' increase in earnings between 1980 and 1987, which means that inflation has been allowed for before the increase was calculated. Full time women workers with higher earnings increased their pay faster than women with low earnings. None

Table 6.8   Hourly earnings of women as a percentage of hourly earnings of men, full-time employees, Great Britain, 1950–81

Derived from Zabalza and Tzannatos (1985a), p. 680.

Table 6.9   *Average earnings: women's as a percentage of men's; full-time*
            employees, manual and non-manual, weekly and hourly earnings,
            Great Britain, 1970–87

	1970	1975	1977	1979	1981	1983	1985	1987
Hourly earnings								
All employees	63	72	76	73	75	74	74	74
Weekly earnings								
All employees	55	62	65	64	65	65	66	66
Manual employees	50	58	61	59	61	61	61	62
Non-manual employees	50	58	61	58	59	59	59	59

Note: in any particular year the female:male ratios are higher for the total workforce than they are for either manual or non-manual work separately; this is because a much greater proportion of women's employment than of men's falls into the non-manual category, and thus into the category where earnings are higher. Devised from Table 5.6, *Employment Gazette* Vol. 87, No. 12, Vol. 95, No. 12.

Table 6.10   *Dispersion of gross weekly earnings, full-time adults in*
            employment, by sex, Great Britain, 1970 and 1987

	Lowest decile[a]	Median[b]	Highest decile[c]
1970 weekly earnings[d]			
Women	9.70	14.60	24.80
Men	17.80	27.20	43.70
1987 weekly earnings[d]			
Women	85.30	132.90	228.30
Men	117.90	198.40	349.50
1987 as ratio to 1970			
Women	8.8	9.1	9.2
Men	6.6	7.2	8.0
Women's earnings as % of men's earnings			
1970	55	54	57
1987	72	67	65

a. The lowest decile, i.e. 10 per cent of adults earn less than this figure.
b. The median, i.e. 50 per cent of adults earn more than this figure.
c. The highest decile, i.e. 10 per cent of adults earn more than this figure.
d. Earnings are in pounds and pence, rounded to nearest ten pence.
Derived from *Employment Gazette*, (1987), Vol. 95, No. 11, p. 569.

the less substantial rises were gained by men at the top end of the scale, thus ensuring a large female:male pay gap in this category.

A further view of the dispersion of earnings can be obtained by comparing the proportion of women earning less than any particular earnings figure chosen from the male spectrum. In April 1987, over four-fifths of women in full-time work earned less than the average (median) male earnings level (*Employment Gazette*, November 1987). Another significant figure is the lowest male decile (the amount earned by the top earner out of the lowest tenth of male workers), which is often the figures used to define low pay for either sex (Royal Commission on the Distribution of Income and Wealth, 1980). On this definition, nearly two-fifths of women in full-time work were low paid, as were nearly two-thirds of women manual workers.

At the other end of the scale, the Royal Commission on the Distribution of Income and Wealth (1976) was concerned about the small number of women in the higher-income tax ranges: in the 1973–4 tax year, women comprised only 2 per cent of people with employment incomes of at least £10,000. Because women tend not to figure in the higher earnings range, the spread of earnings is less wide for women than for men (Table 6.10; Chiplin, Curran and Parsley, 1980).

Our description of inequality in remuneration between the sexes is as yet incomplete, because we have ignored fringe benefits such as company pensions, sick pay, life assurance, cheap mortgages, school fees, company cars, and holiday entitlements. Fringe benefits are gained disproportionately by higher earners, and therefore widen the gap between women's and men's earnings (Royal Commission on the Distribution of Income and Wealth, 1978b; Low Pay Unit, 1984). Recently, there has been a narrowing of the female:male gap in terms of membership of an employer's pension scheme, although a smaller proportion of full-time women workers than of men are members of such a scheme (*GHS 1985*, 1987). There continues to be little difference between the sexes in entitlement to sick pay. However male employees are likely to do better than females when it comes to pensions, company cars and benefits in kind (Green, Hadjimatheou and Smail, 1985). They also get better redundancy payments (Callender, 1984, 1985).

These examples are based on full-time work, yet women suffer further because many of them work part-time, and are often excluded from the fringe benefits available to full-timers (McIntosh, 1980). Similarly, the exclusion of women is implicit in many fringe benefit schemes which are provided for the particular categories of employees in which men are concentrated. For example, although the same provisions for paid holidays apply to men and women, entitlements often increase with length of service and grade, so that the general level tends to be higher for men than for women. This exaggerates the tendency noted above for a relatively large gap to persist between the sexes in the highest earnings categories.

Moreover, part-time work has one other very important disadvantage compared with full-time work: much more of it is temporary. Although this is true to a greater extent for men, for whom in 1984 31 per cent of all part-time work was temporary, compared with 17 per cent of women's part-time work, the significance is much greater for women (and particularly married women), since larger absolute numbers are involved, and temporary work accounts for a larger proportion of women's total employment (11 per cent in 1984, compared with 6 per cent for men) (Manpower Services Commission, 1985).

One question of special interest is whether women who are married are at a particular disadvantage in matters of pay and remuneration. The limited data available have been subjected to statistical analysis. Main (1984) found that, after all other influences were taken into account, women's wages would be 20 per cent higher were it not for the effects of interruptions over childbirth. Stewart and Greenhalgh (1984) found that if married women had been able to pursue the same work pattern as single women, they would have earned at least 40 per cent more.

The Royal Commission on the Distribution of Income and Wealth (1978a) used 1975 data to calculate the typical earnings, by sex and marital status, of people with otherwise similar backgrounds. The findings were that among white people who left school at 15, after five years' work experience both single and married women would be earning only 90 per cent of the average age of similar men. Furthermore, the earnings of women (married or single) do not rise as fast as those of men as they get older: after ten years' work experience, single women would earn less than 80 per cent of male earnings, and married women less than 75 per cent.

The segmented labour market: occupations and grades

The occupational structure differentiates people according to their work task or trade. Joseph (1983) measures this by an index of segregation. Hakim (1979) has shown that over the twentieth century occupational segregation has not declined (Table 6.11). Only in a few fields (such as school teaching, nursing, or retail sales staff), is there actual competition for jobs between women and men, and in those few occupations where segregation is breaking down it is as likely to be a case of men infiltrating long-established women's areas (such as nursing) as vice versa.

Table 6.11   *Occupational segregation, 1901–71*

	% of women working in occupations which had:				% of men working in occupations which had:			
	100% female workers	90% female workers	70% female workers	50% female workers	100% male workers	90% male workers	70% male workers	50% male workers
1901	11	52	71	82	47	74	89	95
1911	3	45	64	78	44	70	86	93
1921	0	40	56	72	29	70	83	92
1931	0	41	62	73	35	69	84	94
1951	0	31	50	68	20	61	82	92
1961	0	21	53	79	22	62	77	85
1971	0	25	51	77	14	53	77	87

Derived from Table 12, Hakim (1979).

A not wholly inaccurate caricature of women's occupations is provided by the list of the 'ten deadly Cs'; catering, cleaning, clerking, cashiering, counter-minding, clothes-making, clothes-washing, coiffure, child-minding, and care of the sick. Some of these are trades which call upon the attributes, such as manual dexterity, supposedly fostered by traditional female upbringing. But many women's jobs involve the direct servicing of people's immediate needs, and are often extensions of the types of jobs associated with domestic tasks (Phillips and Taylor, 1980). An important sub-category of this is that highlighted by Hunt (1975): part-time work such as cleaning or catering which has little or no relationship with the main (usually full-time) work of the establishment.

Table 6.12 shows occupations which are effectively 'women's jobs' and those which are 'men's jobs'. Many of the former are jobs of low skill and status. It is, of course, important to be aware of the possibility that jobs are defined as skilled according to criteria that give extra weight to traditionally male skills (Finch and Groves, 1983). For example, many male jobs are defined as skilled even though they require little more skill than driving a car (Blackburn and Mann, 1979). None the less, there is an unmistakable pattern of work formally defined as less skilled being performed disproportionately by women.

A rather special class of work is homework (which should be distinguished from people working from home). Homework usually involves manufacturing, assembling or packaging small products or performing services such as typing. One survey (Crine, 1979) found that over half of homeworking involved knitting or machine-sewing, though the researchers deliberately excluded

Table 6.12   Occupations[a] Listed according to the degree to which they are dominated by one sex

Predominantly female occupations	Predominantly male occupations and groupings of occupations
90 per cent or over	*90 per cent or over*
Hand and machine sewers and embroiderers	Miners and quarrymen
Nurses	Furnace, forge, foundries etc.
Maids, valets, etc.	Electrical and electronic (excluding assemblers)
Canteen assistants	Engineering trades (excluding inspectors)
Typists, shorthand writers, secretaries	Woodworkers
	Butchers and meat cutters
75 and under 90 per cent	Construction workers
Shop salesmen and assistants	Painters and decorators
Charwomen, cleaners and sweepers	Drivers of stationary engines, cranes, etc.
Kitchen hands	Building and contracting labourers
Office machine operators	Drivers: road-passenger service and goods vehicles
Hairdressers, manicurists and beauticians	Postmen and mail sorters
Telephone operators	Commercial travellers, etc.
	Police
60 and under 75 per cent	Administrators and managers
Clerks and cashiers	Engineers
Waiters and waitresses	Technical and related workers
Primary and secondary schoolteachers	Armed forces
Packers, labellers and related workers	Groundsmen and gardeners
Cooks	
Bartenders	

a. The titles of occupations used in this table are taken from the Official Census; those with the suffix '-men' may include employees of both sexes.
Derived from *Social Trends* (1974), No. 5, p. 17.

childminding which could technically be considered as homework. Because the worker is often officially self-employed, there are no reliable statistics on this type of work. Townsend estimated that there were some 250,000 homeworkers, plus 130,000 childminders (Trades Union Congress, 1978), while the 1981 survey of home-based workers showed 100,000 homeworkers with a single employer, and 230,000 people working from home (Hakim, 1987a). Seventy-one per cent of homeworkers are women (Hakim 1987a).

The Low Pay Unit survey (Crine, 1979) found that most homeworkers were paid on a piecework basis, and a high

Table 6.13   Female percentage of employment, by social class, and by socio-
            economic group, Great Britain, 1911–81

	1911	1951	1961	1971	1981
Occupational groups[a]					
Employers and proprietors	18.8	20.0	20.4	24.9	25.3
White-collar workers	29.8	42.3	44.5	47.9	51.1
Managers and administrators	19.8	15.2	15.5	21.6	na
Higher professionals	6.0	8.3	9.7	9.9	na
Lower professionals and technicians	62.9	53.5	50.8	52.1	na
Foremen and inspectors	4.2	13.4	10.3	13.1	na
Clerks	21.4	60.2	65.2	73.2	na
Salesmen and shop assistants	35.2	51.6	54.9	59.8	na
All manual workers	30.5	26.1	26.0	29.4	28.6
Skilled	24.0	15.7	13.8	13.5	12.9
Semi-skilled	40.4	38.1	39.3	46.5	45.3
Unskilled	15.5	20.3	22.4	46.5	41.4
Total occupied population	29.6	30.8	32.4	36.5	38.9

a. The titles of socio-economic groups used in this table are taken from the Official
Census of Population; those with the suffix '-men' do include employees of both
sexes.
na = Data not available in the form specified in this table, owing to redefinition of
socio-economic groups.
1911–71 data derived from Hakim (1979), Table 16, from Census of Population;
1981 derived from 1981 Census of Population; definitions of social classes differ
slightly between 1981 and earlier years.

percentage work long hours for very little pay indeed. A survey of
people working from home for the toy industry found that only two
out of a sample of 178 got holiday pay, and none got sick pay
(Advisory, Conciliation and Arbitration Service, 1978). The
homeworkers have to accept poor remuneration because the women
involved have little alternative work. For this reason, Hakim (1984)
refers to homeworkers as a 'secondary labour force'. Because it is
an important category of low-pay work, homework is now receiving
much attention (see also Hakim, 1980, 1984a, 1984b, 1985, 1987a;
Cragg and Dawson, 1981; Trades Union Congress, 1985).

Table 6.13   shows the proportion of women in different
categories of occupations at different times this century. Although
women's employment has become concentrated into white-collar
occupations much more than has men's (Table 6.14), the position
of women in the occupational hierarchy has actually worsened in
the twentieth century.

Table 6.14   Numbers in particular occupational groups as a percentage of the workforce, by sex, 1961 and 1985

	Women in the occupational group as % of women in the workforce		Men in the occupational group as % of men in the workforce	
	1961	1985	1961	1985
Professional, employers, managers	na ⎫ 49	9 ⎫ 63	na ⎫ 30	26 ⎫ 43
Other non-manual	na ⎭	54 ⎭	na ⎭	17 ⎭
Skilled manual	12 ⎫ 51	8 ⎫ 37	36 ⎫ 70	37 ⎫ 57
Other manual	39 ⎭	29 ⎭	34 ⎭	20 ⎭
All occupational groups	100	100	100	100

Derived from Table 6.12, *Royal Commission on the Distribution of Income and Wealth* (1980) and Tables 6.29 and 6.30 *GHS 1985* (1987).

Handy (1984) points out that in 1881 44 per cent of working women were in domestic service, whereas in 1981 over half were in 'intermediate and junior non-manual jobs', mostly clerical and secretarial work. The post-war increase in the employment of women has been associated with increases in their share of the unskilled categories, including clerks and unskilled manual workers, and an actual fall in the share of some more skilled jobs, particularly skilled manual jobs (Crompton, 1984; Greenhalgh and Stewart, 1985). Indeed, Table 6.14 shows that only eight per cent of women now have a skilled manual occupation, whereas 37 per cent of men do. In recent decades, the emphasis in employment as a whole has shifted not just from manual to white-collar work (in which women do have a relatively large share), but also towards jobs of higher status and skill (in which men still predominate).

There is little sign that the occupational structure is becoming less sex-determined. The only high-status occupations previously the preserve of males, and into which women have made significant inroads, have been certain professions (Table 6.15). In many cases, the occupations that these middle-class or professional women are entering are ones such as accountancy which have a work-pattern and flexibility of hours that suit women with demanding domestic duties.

Of course, it is important not only to compare different occupational groups, but to look within each occupation. Women (both professional and working-class) do fare badly compared with men in terms of grades within an occupation. Even where a woman and a man are doing what is classified as the same job, the

Table 6.15   *Women as percentage of membership, selected professional bodies, 1971–2, 1980 and 1987*

	1971–72	1980	1987
Law Society	3	12	15
Institute of Bankers	1	13	18
Chartered Insurance Institute	4	10	15
Institute of Chartered Accountants (England and Wales)	2	4	8
Royal Institution of Chartered Surveyors	0.4	1	4
Royal Town Planning Institute	6	7	16
Institute of Building	0	0.4	0.7
British Medical Association	18	22	25
Institute of Health Services Management	na	14	27
Institute of Personnel Management	na	30	46
British Institute of Management	na	2	3
Institute of Mechanical Engineers	0.1	0.3	1

na = not available.
Derived from *Women and Work: A Review* (1975), Table 3.4, EOC *Annual Report 1980* (1981), and Table 6.5, EOC (1987b).

man is often on a higher rate of pay – for example, because he has typically been employed longer and so qualifies for a length-of-service award, or because he holds a position of seniority. Chiplin, Curran and Parsley (1980) found that only 7 per cent of the difference in pay between the sexes could be accounted for by the unequal distribution of the sexes among occupations, a further 13 per cent by differences in hours worked, and a total of almost 80 per cent by differences that occur within occupational groups.

It therefore seems that the key to understanding earnings inequality lies not simply in 'horizontal' segregation, which exists when different types of jobs are performed by women and men, but also in 'vertical' segregation, when both women and men work in the same general job categories, but within these men perform the work that is more skilled, responsible or better-paid (Hakim, 1979). For example, a much smaller percentage of women than men in clerical work can be classified as supervisors (*New Earnings Survey*). An example of the combined effect of horizontal and vertical distribution of women and men in a pay and grading structure is shown in Table 6.16. (The disproportionate representation of men in the upper reaches of career structures is also illustrated in Tables 3.10, 5.11, 5.12 and 8.5.)

*Table 6.16   Pay and grading structure for ancillary staff in a Regional
Health Authority, 1985*

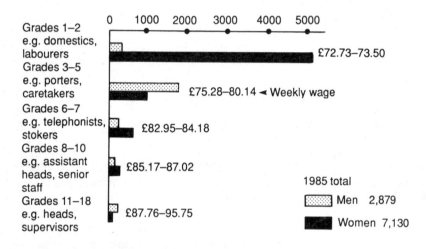

Number of employees (full-time equivalent)

Grades 1–2
e.g. domestics,
labourers
£72.73–73.50

Grades 3–5
e.g. porters,
caretakers
£75.28–80.14 ◄ Weekly wage

Grades 6–7
e.g. telephonists,
stokers
£82.95–84.18

Grades 8–10
e.g. assistant
heads, senior
staff
£85.17–87.02

Grades 11–18
e.g. heads,
supervisors
£87.76–95.75

1985 total

▒ Men   2,879

■ Women 7,130

Derived from NUPE (1986), p. 21.

To understand women's under-representation in the hierarchy
of a particular occupation, it is important to know its full
background. For example, the women may be unrepresentatively
young, particularly if women have only just begun to enter the
occupation (Jones, 1986). It is however true that women are
promoted in fewer numbers and less rapidly than men. For
example, in order to rise in the hierarchy of the medical profession,
women tend to have to be in less competitive fields to which men
do not aspire, such as specialities relating to children or mental
disorder (Oakley, 1981). Additionally, in many of the occupations
where women work in large numbers, there is simply little
opportunity for promotion or earnings enchancement, for example
in the case of clerical workers (McNally, 1979).

Whether analysed in terms of occupations or in terms of grades
within occupations, women are excluded from the positions of
power and influence at work. Women are remarkably absent from

management. In 1981 they accounted for only 21 per cent of managers (Census, 1981). In 1986 they accounted for only 3 per cent of the body to which many senior managers in large firms belong, the British Institute of Management (Table 6.15). There are however a few areas in which women have been increasing their share of positions of responsibility, though these are usually those associated with women's traditional interests, particularly personnel management (EOC, 1987b). However, even within personnel management, women are under-represented at middle and senior management levels (Long, 1984).

The 1981 Census showed that only 20 per cent of the self-employed were women. However, self-employment has been rising dramatically in the 1980s, particularly in the category of single-person businesses, that is individuals who have no employees (*Labour Force Survey*). In 1984 self-employment accounted for 11 per cent of jobs: however, for men the figure was 16 per cent, compared with 9 per cent for married women, and 5 per cent for other women (*GHS 1984*, 1986, Table 6.22). Although men still predominate in self-employment, particularly in large self-employed firms (Census, 1981), women have been prominent in setting up such businesses, and increased their share of self-employment as a result (Creigh et al., 1986). One reason for this is that women are concentrated in the occupations where the growth of self-employment was most marked: among professionals in education and health services, in clerical jobs, and in catering, cleaning and hairdressing (Manpower Services Commission, 1985). However it is also likely that married women (middle-class women in particular) become self-employed because of the restricted opportunities available to them as employees.

It should not be thought that it is only married women who are confined to jobs and positions of low status and skill. Greenhalgh (1980) shows how single women follow 'female career' patterns very similar to those of married women, despite having slightly higher qualifications: thus in 1975, whereas 60 per cent of married men with qualifications above 'A' level had a professional or managerial occupation, the proportion for single women of similar qualifications was only 16 per cent.

This pattern of inequality is reinforced by the fact that many women (particularly married women) work only part-time: outside the professions (and often within them as well) opportunities for part-time work usually occur in the lower-pay occupations, for example in semi-skilled or unskilled manual work rather than in its skilled counterpart (Ballard, 1984). Sloane and Siebert (1980) show that female part-time workers are unfavourably distributed by occupation, comprising a higher percentage of those occupations in which pay is low. Many married women who return to work after a period of childcare, particularly those who work part-time, experience 'downward occupational mobility' (Dex, 1984; Dex and Shaw, 1986).

To generalize about the trends summarized above, it would seem that there are still significant barriers between women and skilled, well-paid jobs. It is only middle-class women who are making any significant progress in entering previously male occupations, and even middle-class women are still failing to gain senior positions. Working-class women meanwhile remain in occupations of low skill, low status and low pay.

The segmented labour market: industry and workplace
After examining the position of the two sexes in terms of occupation and grade, it is important to analyse jobs in terms of the industries in which they take place. There are a number of industries whose business requires very few of the occupations in which women are found, and which therefore predominantly employ male workers, such as 'mining and quarrying', 'construction' or 'shipbuilding'. There are no industries with predominantly female labour forces, though there are several where women are in a majority such as clothing and footwear (73 per cent women in 1987) or education (68 per cent women). Women's work takes place disproportionately in service industries, whereas men's work is spread more evenly through service and manufacturing industry. Female part-time work is concentrated in the service sector even more than is full-time work (Ballard, 1984), notably in the distribution, education, catering and health industries. Much of this part-time work in service industries is manual work, such as cooking and cleaning.

The effect of recent changes has been to reinforce the extent to which women's employment is concentrated in the service sector; in 1980 76 per cent of women worked in this sector, but the proportion had risen to 82 per cent by 1987. This can partly be explained by the fact that, while employment in manufacturing has declined for both sexes in recent years, the reduction in employment of women has been more rapid than that of men, partly because semi-skilled manual jobs have been dispensed with, and partly because industries traditionally employing female labour (such as clothing and textiles) have been in decline. Meanwhile, the female labour force in service industries has grown more rapidly than the male, notably in the public sector.

The female:male earnings ratio is higher in service industries than it is in manufacturing industries. In the public sector too, the average female wage was almost 70 per cent of the male, compared with less than 60 per cent in the private sector (1980 figures). None the less, women are employed in the parts of these sectors where average pay is low and conditions of service are poor.

A particularly important long-established feature of women's employment is that it takes place disproportionately in smaller establishments (Bolton Committee of Enquiry into Small Firms, 1971). It is commonly argued that these firms are more likely to offer part-time work, have fewer positions of responsibility, and pay less: a complex question which is discussed by Craig, Garnsey and Rubery (1985).

Although it is true that the low pay of some industries may reflect the low pay of the occupations within them, there may be independent effects reducing the level of pay in each job. The nature and even direction of the causal link has been hotly debated using statistical analysis (e.g. Sloane and Siebert, 1980). Miller (1987), emphasizing the relative unimportance of occupation, purports to show that if occupational segregation was not a feature of the labour market, the gender wage gap would be narrowed by only 5 per cent. It is a powerful and plausible hypothesis that female earnings are depressed, not by the occupations they enter, but by the industries or establishments they work in. Some firms will inevitably be more prosperous, and perhaps offer better promotion and training prospects than others, even to people in the same occupation.

Promotion and training
This section shows how the employment potential of women is underutilized in comparison with that of men, and draws on our earlier discussion of women's relative exclusion from higher grades.

One indicator of potential for employment is a person's educational qualifications. Table 6.18 shows that women are likely to earn less than men with similar qualifications. For example, Williamson (1981) found in his 1977 survey of graduates that when other differences such as hours of work and length of work experience had been taken into account, female graduates' salaries were more than 10 per cent below those of men.

An alternative way of showing how the potential of women is not realized is to look at the profile of earnings of people of different ages, which should give an indication of whether or not people 'make progress' through a career structure (Table 6.19). Women's earnings peak much earlier than those of men, and

Table 6.17   Industrial distribution of employment, by sex, Great Britain,
1987, and changes 1974–80 and 1980–87

	1987 Women as a % of industrial group	1987 % of total of each sex in employment Women	Men	1974–80 % change in numbers in employment Women	Men	1980–87 % change in numbers in employment Women	Men
All manufacturing industries	30	16	31	− 22	− 14	− 14	− 18
All service industries	54	82	57	+ 8	+ 1	+ 12	+ 9
Agriculture, forestry, fishing	27	1	2	− 6	− 4	− 4	− 16
Mining and quarrying	4	—	3	+ 9	− 5	− 43	− 46
Construction	12	1	7	+ 9	− 7	+ 4	− 12
Totals	43	100	100	+ 6	− 3		

Derived from Table 1.2, *Employment Gazette*, No. 83, No. 12, Vol. 89, No. 12,
Vol. 96, No. 12.

Table 6.18   Highest earnings attained, by educational qualifications, by sex:
cumulative percentages of persons ages 20–69 in full-time
employment, Great Britain, 1985

	Degree or equivalent Women	Men	Higher education below degree Women	Men	GCE A level or equivalent Women	Men
Gross earnings (£)						
60 +	98	98	97	99	95	97
90 +	96	97	92	98	78	92
120 +	86	93	76	92	49	82
160 +	59	82	44	73	18	61
200 +	33	70	17	50	5	37
300 +	9	34	1	16	1	10
400 +	3	17	0	7	1	4

Derived from Table 7.12, *GHS 1985* (1987).

subsequently remain stable, whereas men's earnings rise faster and
peak much later (Royal Commission on the Distribution of
Income and Wealth 1980, Table 8.1). Of course, part of men's
greater earnings is accounted for by the overtime and bonus

Table 6.19   Age–earnings profile for full-time employees, by sex, 1978

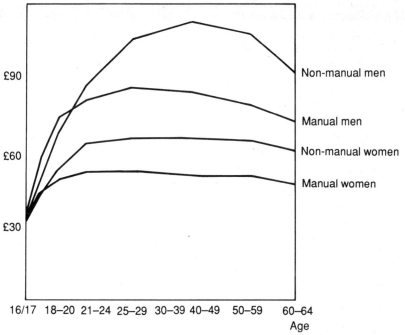

Note: The earnings figures relate to average gross weekly earnings.
Derived from *Royal Commission on the Distribution of Income and Wealth* (1980 p. 12).

payments mentioned earlier, and the decline in these accounts for the tailing off of men's earnings in later years. However the principal reason for the flat profile of women's earnings is that they either work in occupations where there are few promotion opportunities, or they simply do not get appointed to the senior positions which do exist. Many promotion structures are organized so that for women a break in employment for child-rearing acts as a significant handicap; however, it is also likely that women are excluded in other ways from opportunities for advancement (Greenhalgh, 1980).

Yet it is not that women cannot do higher paid jobs: Davidson and Cooper (1983b) showed that women managers used 'the efficient, sensitive/sympathetic and co-operative management styles' more frequently than men. To restrict women is to waste their potential.

Table 6.20   *YTS starters by occupational training family, percentages
female and male, Great Britain, 1985*

	Females	Males
Community and health services	86	14
Administration, clerical and office	76	24
Personal service and sales	72	28
Food preparation and service	55	45
Processing	26	74
Agricultural, horticultural	24	76
Manufacture and assembly	19	81
Technical and scientific	18	82
Craft and design	18	82
Transport	9	91
Installation, maintenance and repair	4	96

Derived from Cockburn (1987a), p. 9.

One major factor leading to failure to realize the potential of women
in the labour market is the way in which training schemes fit them for
certain limited roles. The number who are trained for 'gender-
atypical' jobs is small, although this training can be successful despite
the difficulties (Breakwell and Weinberger, 1985).

Cockburn (1987a) shows how 'the occupational segregation by
sex that characterises employment at large is faithfully reproduced
in the Youth Training Scheme.' Indeed, because the 'Occupational
Training Families' quoted in Table 6.20 are so broad, those
figures considerably understate the sex divisions on the YTS
scheme. For example, the Fawcett Society report that only one in
250 YTS trainees in construction was female (Fawcett Society,
1985).

Government training schemes for adults, including the
Community Programme, also replicate the sex-typing found on
the YTS (Dickens, 1983). TOPS courses reinforced the traditional
occupational patterns of the sexes; very few women train at skill
centres or employers' establishments, which is where the majority
of craft courses are taken (*EOC Annual Report 1979*, 1980, Figure
2.16) At the time of writing it is too early to tell how women will
fare under the new Job Training Scheme.

The pattern of training differs between women and men not
simply in the type of training but in its amount (Table 6.21; also
Greenhalgh and Stewart, 1982; Martin and Roberts, 1984b). In
the workforce as a whole, women do not receive a proportionate
share of training. Among young employees aged 16–18, four times
as many males as females are given day-release for training (Benett

Table 6.21   Percentage of employees taking advantage of types of in-service training, by sex, 1980

	Women	Men
On-site		
On the job	16	16
Off the job	2	5
Off-site		
Ad hoc	3	4
Day release	1	3
Block release	1	3
Other further education	*	2
Employees taking advantage of any type of training	23	33

* = Less than 0.5 per cent.
Derived from *Employment Gazette*, Vol. 88, No. 11, p. 1147.

and Carter, 1983). The 1981 Census of Population shows that there were over twice as many male apprentices as female (Census 1981, 1984, Table 2). The Institute of Employment Research (1982) reports that of full-time employees, 30 per cent of men but only 25 per cent of women have received some full-time, on-the-job training during paid time; the duration of the training was more than a year for half of these men, but training lasted this length of time for only one fifth of the women. Table 6.18 shows that women take part as much as men in training 'on the job', but receive much less training away from work; the latter is, of course, often crucial to promotion prospects.

Government-sponsored schemes for adults also provide for men more than for women. For example, the Enterprise Allowance, paid during the first year of self-employment, is only payable to those who have been receiving social security benefits; this stipulation excludes many married women.

Overall, we find that the inadequacy of provision for training of women is not a reflection of lack of demand by women (Women and Training Project Report, 1983). Rather, it reflects the undervaluation of much of women's work. The lack of training means that women are further confined to low-paid jobs, grades and industries.

Unemployment: its extent and its effect on the labour market

The failure of the economy to make full use of women's work potential can also be seen by examining trends in employment and

Table 6.22   Numbers officially unemployed, by sex, Great Britain, 1976–87

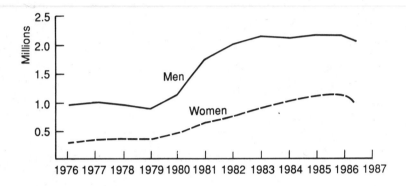

Derived from EOC (1987b), Table 3.3, from Department of Employment figures, updated from *Employment Gazette*, (1987), Table 2.2, Vol. 95, No. 12.

unemployment during periods of prosperity and periods of recession. Indeed unemployment has recently become an important focus of researchers interested in gender, (Cragg and Dawson, 1984; Marshall, 1984; Phillips, 1984; Callender, 1986; Purcell, 1986).

It is significant that the figures the state uses to indicate the level of unemployment fail to record fully the number who are out of work (Unemployment Unit, 1986). The official unemployment figures are now based on the numbers who are claiming social security benefits by reason of unemployment; the majority of the unemployed who are excluded from the statistics by this method of compilation are women. Many women are not entitled to unemployment benefit, either because they have not worked long enough to pay sufficient National Insurance contributions, or because they are married and exercised their former right to opt out of the full contributions. Women, married or not, who are living with a man, also lose the right to Income Support. Many women are thus excluded from the unemployment statistics even if they do not have a job and yet would like one.

The extent of this 'hidden unemployment' can be seen in various research findings. Joshi (1982) using National Insurance scheme records up to 1974, found that for every 100 extra people on the unemployment register, there were actually 214 in total

Table 6.23   Employment and unemployment, annual percentage changes; by sex and marital status, Great Britain, 1977–87

	Employed		Unemployed (official figures only)		
			All	Married	
	Women	Men	women	women	Men
1977–78	+1	+0.1	+13	+17	−0.8
1978–79	+2	+0.1	−6	+5	−8
1979–80	−2	−1	+22	+22	+10
1980–81	−5	−6	+53	+53	+73
1981–82	−1	−3	+19	+13	+16
1982–83	−0.9	−2	a	na	a
1983–84	+3	−0.4	+9	+18	−1
1984–85	+2	+0.5	+6	+7	+3
1985–86	+2	−0.5	+2	+7	0
1986–87	+3	+0.6	−13	−13	−9

a. 1982–83 percentage changes in unemployment are calculated from the Unemployment Unit Statistical Briefing, using the estimate of what the change would have been had there not been a revision to the official count in 1983.
na = not available.
Derived from Tables 1.1 and 2.2, *Employment Gazette*, various issues.

who had become unemployed, with women comprising over two-thirds of the 'missing' total. In 1985, when the official unemployment rates were 9 per cent for women and 13.5 per cent for men, the Department of Employment estimated that there were 580,000 women and 180,000 men unregistered, which would have brought the rates up to 14.5 per cent for both sexes.

Because registered unemployment is a misleading indicator, it would be preferable wherever possible to use 'true' or 'total' unemployment figures, although year-on-year changes in official figures may have some value, as long as corrections can be made for the changes in the methods of counting.

We are now in a position to examine whether recessions bring unemployment disproportionately to one sex. Data (see Tables 6.22 and 6.23) have been interpreted as showing that during periods of relative prosperity, such as the 1950s and early 1970s, men suffered more from unemployment (i.e. more than proportionate to their participation in the workforce), whereas during periods of recession, women bore the brunt of unemployment. This picture of women's employment being more volatile than that of men's has also been suggested by figures showing changes in employment (rather than unemployment) over a number of decades, particularly in the manufacturing sector

(Counter Information Services, 1981). It has also been argued that women suffer in recessions more than men in terms of reductions in hours worked. Such suggested volatility might be associated with the jobs women do, or may arise because more of them work part-time.

However there is no agreement about such results. Dex and Perry (1984) using data for the three decades to 1981 found that women did not suffer in recessions more than men even in manufacturing industry. Examination of official unemployment figures (Tables 6.22 and 6.23) for the recession in the early 1980s seems to bear out their conclusion, for between 1979 and 1983 male unemployment increased by 1.2 million and female unemployment by 500,000 – proportionately less. On the other hand, since 1983 male unemployment has remained relatively steady, with female unemployment showing a further increase until in 1986 it stood at one million.

Although the research on women and new technology has focused on women's role in technology-related occupations, it has also considered whether the sexes are affected differently by technology-related redundancies (Equal Pay and Opportunity Campaign, 1980; Huws, 1980; Simons, 1981; Arnold, 1982; Faulkner and Arnold, 1985; Mackenzie and Wajcman, 1985; Work Research Unit, 1985a). Despite the microelectronics revolution, men continue to be the technologists and women the low-paid operators (Cockburn, 1985a, 1985b). Five case studies in manufacturing suggested that women are not generally treated differently from men when redundancies are made (Martin, 1985). However, perhaps because of the specific jobs they do, female operators in the engineering industry lost jobs at a faster rate than their male counterparts in the 1978–83 recession (Fidgett, Laidlaw and McGuire, 1985). Indeed, it has been suggested that the majority of women work in jobs which are put at risk by microelectronics (Science Policy Research Unit, 1982). Women's weak position in the labour market puts them in a weak position when it comes to resisting technology-related redundancies (West, 1982a).

So far, this discussion has focused mainly on those in the workforce. However, researchers have also investigated the question of whether or not the general level of demand in an economy (of which unemployment is an indicator) influences the decision, particularly by married women, as to whether to enter the workforce at all. There is the possibility that a recession actually encourages married women to look for work if their husbands are laid off, thus increasing the female activity rate.

However, most research has found that this 'added worker effect' is swamped by the 'discouraged worker effect' in which the general difficulty of finding work discourages women from looking for it (Berg and Dalton, 1977; Greenhalgh, 1977; McNabb, 1977). This is the reverse side of the historical process by which women have been drawn into the labour market since the war; the government stimulated demand in the economy and, because labour was therefore in short supply, employers made every effort to attract women into the workforce.

If the willingness of women to do paid work is sensitive to the kind and amount of work available, this ought to be apparent in comparing data from different parts of the country with different job opportunities. This suggests that economic activity does vary with employment opportunities. For women, the variation in activity is more pronounced than it is for men, and female activity rates are lowest in the less urban areas such as Wales or the South-West where there is likely to be a more restricted range of jobs available (*Regional Trends*, 1987, Tables 8.5). None the less, high activity rates for women are also associated with a high share of total unemployment (*Employment Gazette*, Table 2.3) as in the case of Scotland (Breitenbach, 1982).

Marriage and childcare: their influence on choices about paid and unpaid work

Even if a woman marries and stays at home to look after children while they are young, she can still expect to spend the majority of her adult years in paid employment (Martin and Roberts, 1984a). However it is appropriate to examine the extent to which women's roles outside the labour market restrict their participation within it. Let us therefore look at the division of labour in the household, beginning with housework.

The vast majority of those for whom 'keeping house' is their major activity are women. However, even in 'dual-career' couples when both partners have paid jobs, survey and case-study evidence suggests that most men's involvement with housework is low or peripheral (Oakley, 1974b; Porter, 1982; Pahl, 1984; Sharpe, 1984; McNally and Shimmin, 1986). Ginsberg (1976) found that many husbands in her sample felt that wives worked principally for their own benefit and so should not expect help with domestic chores in consequence.

In 1984 27 per cent of unemployed men had a wife with a job (*GHS 1984*, 1986); approximately one third of a million households were in this situation. What effect has this unemployment-related swapping of work-roles had on gender-based division of roles in the home? Morris (1985) found that couples with unemployed husbands renegotiated the details rather than the fundamental principle of the domestic division of labour. McKee and Bell (1983, 1984) suggest that in their Kidderminster sample it actually hardened traditional patterns as attempts were made to preserve the husband's self-image. Wybrow (1987) finds husbands think they make an increased contribution, but the wives report that the actual increase in husbands' contribution to household tasks is much smaller than the men think it is. Anyway, it is not enough to show that tasks are divided between couples, for often the husband sees himself as merely 'helping' his wife, leaving her with the *responsibility* for organizing the household (Yeandle, 1985; Rapoport and Rapoport, 1976, 1983).

Such results contrast sharply with those of Young and Willmott (1973), who concluded on the basis of a survey of married couples in the London region that the family was becoming 'symmetrical', with men and women sharing household and childcare tasks. Young and Wilmott have been criticized (Bristol Women's Studies Group, 1979) for using a small sample of older and more settled families, and for being premised on the continuation of a substantial rise in the average standard of living.

What basis is there for the popular belief that partners in middle-class households share household duties more than in working-class households? Gavron (1966) suggested that working-class husbands were increasing their contribution to household tasks more than were middle-class husbands. Collins (1985) in a Middlesbrough survey found that it was right across the social spectrum that women were the ones most heavily involved in domestic labour, their involvement changing only marginally if they had paid employment as well. The study which most neatly highlighted the difficulties of the middle-class working wife was a survey of over 400 couples who were both doctors (Elston, 1980): this showed (Table 6.24) that male doctors received far more help from their spouse than did female doctors.

It has been argued that working wives effectively have two jobs, one paid and the other in the home, and that many accept this as 'their lot' (Shimmin, McNally and Liff, 1981). There is now extensive research to show how much time and effort is actually involved in both these aspects of women's work (Lewenhak, 1987). Housework is demanding, and can be thought of as an important component of the 'informal' or non-market economy. There have been attempts to make housework comparable with paid work by putting a monetary value on it (Goldshmidt-Clermont, 1983; Piachaud, 1984). Although this task is not easy, a

Table 6.24 *Percentage of each sex performing certain household tasks within married couples where both partners have medical careers*

| | Replies by female doctors Tasks undertaken by: | | | | Replies by male doctors Tasks undertaken by: | | | |
	Self	Spouse	Both	Hired help	Self	Spouse	Both	Hired help
Budgeting	27	23	50	0	39	16	45	0
Shopping	85	2	12	1	1	81	16	1
Arranging social activities	39	4	57	0	4	31	65	0
Household repairs	10	63	22	5	71	4	18	3
Cooking	81	1	12	6	1	84	14	2
House-cleaning	51	0	5	45	1	68	12	20
Looking after sick child	80	0	18	3	2	67	30	1
Major purchases	11	12	78	0	22	5	74	0

Derived from Table 5.2, Elston (1980).

figure of about 40 per cent of the value of the country's entire output is most widely quoted (Oakley, 1980). Legal and General Insurance estimated the commercial value of the work a wife does in the home as cook, laundress, childminder and nurse as £370 a week at 1987 prices (Legal and General, 1987).

It is commonly suggested that the availability of consumer durables such as washing-machines has reduced the housekeeping workload, yet American studies have shown that the spread of household appliances actually raised housework time by making possible tasks that were previously impossible. An apparently 'equal' division of roles, in which the husbands look after gardening, repairs and decorating, and their wives look after housework (Hunt, 1975), is clearly not equal in terms of time.

There is now a range of evidence showing how the two sexes, and women in particular, spend their non-work time (Deem, 1986). Table 6.25 shows that men have more free time or leisure time than women. Moreover, it seems likely that what is classed as 'leisure activities' in surveys may, for women in particular, contain an element of unpaid work, or social duty. *Social Trends*, No. 5 (1974) showed that, for women, crafts and hobbies (principally knitting) comprised 17 per cent of leisure time as against 4 per cent for men, and the 'social activities' category (9 per cent for women, 3 per cent for men) may well have involved helping relatives and others.

One survey of low-paid workers (National Board for Prices and

Table 6.25   Time use in a typical week: by economic status, and by sex, Great Britain, 1985

	Full-time employees[a]		Part-time employees[a]		House- wives	Retired people
	Females	Males	Females	Males		
Weekly hours spent on						
Employment and travel[b]	40.8	45.0	22.2	24.3		
Essential activities[c]	45.1	33.1	61.3	48.8	76.6	49.8
Sleep	57.5	56.4	57.0	56.6	59.2	60.2
Free time	24.6	33.5	27.5	38.5	32.2	58.0
Free time per weekday	2.1	2.6	3.1	4.5	4.2	7.9
Free time per weekend day	7.2	10.2	5.9	7.8	5.6	9.1

a. Excludes the self-employed.
b. Travel to and from place of work.
c. Essential domestic work and personal care. This includes cooking, essential shopping, child care, eating meals, washing and getting up and going to bed.
Derived from EOC (1987b), Table 5.6, using data from the Henley Centre for Forecasting.

Incomes, 1971) showed that, although journey-to-work distances were longer for most men, journey times were actually greater for most women because they tended not to have the use of the household's private transport.

Voluntary activities are another kind of work which is hidden from the 'formal' economy's employment statistics, because it is unpaid. To a large degree, helpers in such voluntary work are women (*Social Trends*, No. 5, 1974). Public-spending cuts affecting social services often lead to extra voluntary work (mainly by women), so that the same work is done, but it is no longer 'visible'. Similarly, the care of children and elderly relatives is a task which under a different social system could well be paid work, but which in Britain is mainly done unpaid by women. According to Mackie and Patullo (1977) there are an estimated 300,000 single women who care for elderly parents or relatives.

Probably the least well-known aspect of this unpaid work in the informal economy is the hidden employment of women within family enterprises. Official statistics do not count either domestic servants (including au pair girls) or family workers (such as wives working for husbands in a non-supervisory capacity) as employees; they are instead classed as economically inactive. Yet Scase and Goffee (1980) suggest that many small businessmen often prosper not just by their own efforts, but also by hidden and unpaid services of their wives. Buchanan, Giles and Errington (1982) showed the crucial but hidden role of the wife in the management and running of farms. Such help from wives is not confined to husbands in small businesses (Finch, 1983b; Callan and Ardener, 1984). An EEC (1979) survey showed that in the UK 22 per cent of wives helped in their husbands' work, 5 per cent of them giving help 'every day'.

While marriage can give a man an unpaid helpmate, the additional responsibilities it gives women probably restrict her in the labour market (Apter, 1985). The restrictions are more acute because of the absence of adequate childcare facilities in the community or attached to workplaces (EOC, 1986a). The 1980 Women and Employment survey showed that 23 per cent of full-time working women with pre-school children used childminders (Martin and Roberts, 1984a). However, it is probably only higher-paid women with professional occupations whose earnings are sufficient to pay for childcare or paid help in the home.

It has been shown that women in managerial positions were only a third as likely as their male counterparts to be married; married women managers have to cope with added stresses from career/home conflicts (Cooper and Davidson, 1982,1984a and b; Davidson and Cooper, 1983b 1984). To succeed, women with managerial or professional careers have to plan their lives much more than men, for example, delaying having children until their work success is well established (Moulsdale, 1987).

Although since 1975 it has been illegal to discriminate according to marital status, Turnbull and Williams (1974) showed that in schools the low proportion of married female headteachers was at least partly because school governors felt that family responsibilities would interfere with work. Although, typically, women seeking promotion do not involve the whole family in a move to another location, they themselves are often expected to move for their husband's career, which may harm their own pension rights and promotion prospects (Llewellyn, 1981).

Women's home duties may also restrict the hours which they can devote to work-related activities. For example, this may be the factor which prevents them from improving their position collectively via after-hours union activities (see below), or individually via overtime work (see above). And, most significant of all, domestic 'obligations' confine many women to part-time work with all its disadvantages (Beechey and Perkins, 1982), even when they would rather work full-time (Shimmin, McNally and Liff, 1981), and is a major factor in causing women to do very low paid home-work rather than work outside the home (Crine, 1979; Hope, Kennedy and De Winter, 1976). Another effect of having responsibility for children and domestic duties is that women have to work much nearer home than men (Mackay et al., 1971) and so to accept nearby jobs, however ill-paid.

This section would not be complete without examining the extent to which the tax and social security systems act as a further obstacle to married women entering employment, by perpetuating the assumption of the wife as dependent on a breadwinner husband (Kidd, this volume). There have been attempts to quantify the effects of taxation changes on women's work (Brown, 1983). Most discussion has centred on the structure of the tax system. At the time of writing, tax allowances differ between husband and wife. The wife's earned income allowance was introduced during World War II to encourage women to take up employment. It might therefore appear that the tax system positively encourages women to work, since, if there is a choice between the tax-paying husband working overtime and the wife taking up employment, their tax bill will be lower if the wife earns the additional money and takes advantage of her tax allowance. However, by comparison with a system where the current total of tax concessions was reallocated so that each individual within a marriage automatically received equal allowances, the present system where the married man receives a higher allowance makes it less imperative for the wife also to bring in an income. Indeed, the original idea of the married man's allowance was to help him 'keep' his wife at home by compensating him for the loss of her potential earnings.

Similarly, the social security system on balance discourages married women from undertaking paid work. Many women who marry, or cohabit with, a man lose their entitlement to benefits as a result, and thus become dependent on his earnings. However, if a husband is unemployed and drawing social security, then every pound his wife earns above a small amount reduces the dependants' portion of his benefit in proportion. Evidence that this may discourage women from working was found in a survey of the unemployed (Smith, 1981) and in a study of steelwork redundancies (Morris, 1985). The Royal Commission on the Distribution of Income and Wealth (1978a) showed that, after other influences were taken into account, the wives of unemployed husbands were 33 per cent more likely to be out of the labour force. Another way in which the social security system reduces the total of women's employment is that the statutory retirement age for women is 60, allowing income for retirement five years earlier than men.

What effect do the tax and social security systems taken together have on the likelihood of 'role-reversal' arrangements where the wife is the wage-earner and the husband the house-minder? Taken by itself, the income tax system appears to have given a positive impetus to such arrangements, since a working wife with an unemployed spouse has through an anomaly been able to claim more tax allowances (her own allowance plus her husband's) than a husband in the same position. However the social security system has tended to have the opposite influence. A man bringing up children has no right (unlike that of a woman) to be credited with National Insurance contributions; a woman has not been able to nominate her husband for pension rights; the couple could not always rely on her income, for if the woman lost her job she could not always claim benefit for her husband as a dependant unless he was actually incapable of self-support. It is therefore possible that the tax and social security systems taken together may have reduced the extent to which married women have participated in paid work, adding to the other obstacles described earlier.

Motivation, commitment and work satisfaction

Despite the handicaps and difficulties outlined in the previous section, there have been increases in the numbers of women working. This suggests that it is not just men, but women too, who have a strong desire to work (Apter, 1985; Goffee and Scase, 1985). It is now appropriate to examine whether there are differences between women and men in their reasons for working.

Oakley (1981) has criticized as sexist the question 'why do women work?', and yet in view of the constraints that society places on women's work, and the low earnings women can expect to get from work, people may be forgiven for asking.

At least in answering the question one can dispel the notion that for women pay is not important. Single women must earn to live, just as any man must. Lone mothers are responsible for both themselves and their children, and paid work is crucial to many of them (Kidd, this volume).

Within marriage, wives' earnings are in reality often crucial (see also Chapter 4). Table 6.26 shows that in the period 1968–77 there was a significant rise in the proportion of wives in full-time work who earned as much or more than their husbands. It seems unlikely that the change since 1980 will have been as great, since nationally the earnings differential between the sexes has stabilized.

The significance of wives' earnings in raising family living standards is well documented (Roberti, 1974; Hamill, 1978a;

Table 6.26   Earnings of full-time employee wives in relation to the earnings of their husbands. United Kingdom 1968, 1977 and 1980 (percentages)

Full-time employee wives with full-time employee husbands (all ages)	1968	1977	1980	Change 1968–80
Earning less than husband	95.0	85.5	85.5	−9.5
Earning same as husband	2.1	5.9	5.5	+3.4
Earning more than husband	2.9	8.6	9.0	+6.1

Derived from Elias, P., The changing pattern of employment and earnings among married couples 1968–1980, *EOC Research Bulletin* 8 (Winter 1983–84), 1–16.

Royal Commission on the Distribution of Income and Wealth, 1978a). Hamill has estimated that the number of families with incomes below the official poverty level would have been trebled if wives had not been in paid employment. Ironically, it is often the lowest incomes that are the most crucial to the family budget; almost all the well-known surveys of homeworkers found that the money earned was required for necessities and particularly for the needs of the children (whose presence was a major factor in forcing women to work from home in the first place) (Hope, Kennedy and De Winter, 1976; Advisory Conciliation and Arbitration Service, 1978; Crine, 1979; Hakim, 1980).

This is not to say that husbands always recognize the actual importance of their wives' earnings: a 1980 study of 36 women and men in Staffordshire found that women's earnings were often regarded by the partners as 'extras', thus maintaining the idea of the central importance of the man's wage. Even where women themselves share the perception of the husband as the breadwinner, they still think they have an equal right to work (Wood, 1982).

How important is the money motive in married women's decision to seek paid work? Its significance is suggested by the fact that a much higher percentage of housewives from lower-income households indicate that they intend to work in the future (*EOC Annual Report 1978*). One survey found that 50 per cent of the women questioned said that money was the overriding reason for working (Marsh, 1979). The Women and Employment Survey (Joshi, 1984; Dex, 1984; Martin and Roberts, 1984) found that 67 per cent of working married mothers worked to earn money for basic essentials or extras. In the 1985 *British Social Attitudes* survey (Table 6.27), over 80 per cent of women said they were

Table 6.27 Reasons for working, percentages of people in employment,ᵃ by sex, 1984

	Reasons for working		Main reason for working	
	Women	Men	Women	Men
Need money for basic essentials	58	81	50	71
To earn money to buy extras	43	32	15	2
To earn money of my own	38	21	8	4
Enjoy working	59	45	13	7
Working is the normal thing to do	21	46	2	9
To follow my career	26	30	8	5
For the company of other people	36	16	2	b
For a change from the children/housework	11	1	1	—

a. Employees working ten hours or more a week.
b. Very small percentage.
Derived from Jowell and Witherspoon (1985), pp. 68 and 70.

working to provide either essentials or extras, a striking confirmation of the financial importance of women's earnings.

Yet it is doubtful if anyone can completely disentangle their own complex motivations for working, and survey respondents may simply be giving the answer they believe to be expected or acceptable. Questions of a more definite nature are probably better; for example, Coote and Kellner (1980) asked workers how they would react to a choice between working shorter hours or having a substantial pay rise: the answers of men and women were very similar, with only 33 per cent of men and 34 per cent of women preferring shorter hours.

Despite the importance of earnings, work may be performed out of a mixture of motivations, such as the desire to escape domestic drudgery (McNally, 1979) and isolation (Hobson, 1978), and a desire for job satisfaction. In this respect, one survey suggested that women and men are equally committed to work for its own sake (EEC, 1979); 60 per cent of the women and 59 per cent of the men said they would continue working even if they had enough money to live comfortably.

Differences between the sexes in attitudes towards work have been a focus of studies over a number of years. Maizels (1970), in her study of workers under 18, found that girls rather less frequently than boys expressed the desire to earn money, and many fewer girls talked of promotion and advancement. Girls' attitudes may merely reflect the realities of the situation they find themselves in. The EEC survey (1979) found that many fewer women than men believed they had the chance of promotion. However, a survey of 3000 women teachers in England and Wales (National Union of Teachers, 1980b) showed that 77 per cent of married women teachers saw their careers as being as important as those of their husbands. In 1979 Smith and Langrish conducted a survey of female management in the textile industry (Guardian, 29 November 1979) and found that women were far more motivated to succeed than men. Finally, a 1977 survey of graduates who obtained their first degrees in 1970 (see Table 6.25) showed that, in choosing their latest job, women had given greater weight than men to the chance to use skill and to exercise initiative, but (again, perhaps reflecting the realities of the choices available) had given less weight to salary and promotion prospects. Once again, husbands showed up as a constraint on the career aspiration of wives, since more women than men were influenced by a desire to find work near that of their spouse.

It is also possible to get some insight into motivations to work (as well as the objective circumstances of the work involved) by examining differences between levels of job satisfaction reported by the two sexes (e.g. Shaffer, 1987). The *GHS* suggests that, while job dissatisfaction certainly increased among both sexes between 1971 and 1978, at the end of the period men were still more dissatisfied than women. Men's chief source of dissatisfaction was pay, whereas for women it was the kind of work they did (*GHS 1978*, 1980). Focusing specifically on earnings, a survey by Coote and Kellner (1980) found that approximately equal proportions of the sexes (women 73 per cent, men 71 per cent) thought they were fairly paid for their work. It has been suggested, though, that the relative satisfaction of women reported in response to questions on pay is because they only compare their pay to that of other women (Hakim, 1978); the Women and Employment Survey (Dex, 1984; Martin and Roberts, 1984a) which found satisfaction with hours and workmates, found women less satisfied with rates of pay and prospects.

In addition to the studies mentioned above, differences between women and men in terms of work motivation or orientation have been explored by a range of studies such as those of women and men in particular situations or industries (e.g. Cousins, Curran and Brown, 1982; Cavendish, 1982; West, 1982a; Coyle, 1984). One should not perhaps place too much reliance on studies which use methods such as questionnaires: reported levels of job satisfaction may be conditioned by a realism about the lack of better alternatives, and by people's reluctance to denigrate too strongly their own occupational circumstances. However, to generalize from the findings, it appers that there is relatively little difference between the sexes in terms of the intensity of motivation to work, and rather subtle differences in orientations to work. Sex differences in work-related behaviour tend to be a response to differences in the objective situation each faces.

Sex discrimination and sexism in the dual labour market
Segregation is established and maintained at least in part by discrimination and sexist attitudes on the part of employers and male employees. One survey of women employees (Marsh, 1979) showed that 62 per cent of working women believed that at work women were discriminated against. In a survey the previous year (EEC, 1979) far more men than women were shown to believe that their sex gave them an advantage at work. This EEC survey also gave an indication of the men's sexist attitudes: although 81 per cent of the women believed a man could do their job, only 55 per cent of the men believed a woman could do theirs. Men also have distinctive attitudes to women who are their managers or superiors at work (Long, 1984; Marshall, 1984; Gray, 1985).

One particular expression of sexism is sexual harassment, consisting of persistent and unwanted behaviour such as innuendo, leering, ridicule, verbal abuse, remarks or pin-ups intended to embarrass, unwanted physical contact, demands for sexual favours or physical assault (Read, 1982; Sedley and Benn, 1982; Hadjifotiou, 1983; TUC, 1983a, 1983c; Hearn and Parkin, 1987). The harasser is almost always male; it is common for harassers to be in a position of power over the victim, either as manager or supervisor, whereas women usually occupy subordinate places in the workplace hierarchy. The male harasser might even be in the role of client, and the Lamplugh Trust has emphasized the dangers experienced by women in occupations such as estate agency work where they will be alone with male clients.

The 1985 Gallup survey showed that a fifth of all women thought that sexual harassment put pressure on women at work, and a fifth thought that a patronizing attitude from male colleagues had the same effect (Table 8.26; Heald and Wybrow, 1986). Sexual harassment was prevalent in a Bristol tobacco factory (Pollert, 1981). In Liverpool, a NALGO questionnaire found that 98 employees had experienced sexual harassment yet only three had made complaints (NALGO, 1982). In response to a survey by teacher unions in Birmingham, 72 per cent of women secondary teachers revealed instances of harassment, which came mainly from male colleagues rather than pupils (unpublished; reported in the *Guardian*, 13 May 1987).

Sexual harasssment is particularly experienced from male 'colleagues' or subordinates who feel 'threatened' by women trying to break into areas of work traditionally undertaken by men, as a survey in Leeds found (Leeds TUCRIC, 1983). In Birmingham young women who joined a predominately male craft training scheme faced continual 'put-downs' and practical jokes (Griffin, 1982, 1984), while in British Rail women traction trainees and drivers face abusive graffiti and other harassment from the male workforce (EOC, 1986c). The purpose and effect of such harassment is to 'show' that women are unable to cope, and are unsuitable for promotion or positions of authority.

The process of discrimination also relies on the stereotyping of the sexes. There is every reason to believe that the US results of Heilman and Saruwatari (1979) apply to Britain as well: they arranged for subjects to participate in a simulation of employee selection, and found that for managerial positions there was no discrimination against women in general, but that attractive women were assessed as less suitable and recommended for much lower salaries than were unattractive ones. In Britain, the National Union of Teachers found in a survey that 60 per cent of women teachers had been asked at selection interviews about matters other than their professional life (NUT, 1980b), and the union felt obliged to produce literature (NUT, 1980a) to counteract the idea that the average woman teacher was married with young children and uncommitted to a career.

A seminal survey of employers (Hunt, 1975) found that men comprised 98 per cent of those responsible for the formulation of employment policies, and 88 per cent of those who implemented those policies. The survey established that the principal reasons for employers favouring men rather than women for particular jobs were that women were believed to have insufficient strength or stamina, and that the employer would get longer service from a man. The 1979 EOC survey was constructed to allow a comparison with some of Hunt's data, thus showing how employers' perceptions might have changed between 1973 and 1979, the period when the Sex Discrimination Act was introduced and widely discussed. Table 6.28 shows that for most measures of performance, the proportion of employers who perceived differences between men and women declined over this period. However, on absenteeism, the change was in the opposite direction: and more employers perceived a difference between the sexes on this one dimension than on any other.

Table 6.28   *Employers' perceptions of the performance of women and men at work*

| | % of all employers surveyed who believe: | | | | | |
| | Men better than women | | | Women better than men | | |
	1973	1979	Change	1973	1979	Change
Not taking days off for sickness	53	42	−11	5	6	+1
Not taking days off for other reasons	47	69	+22	10	2	−8
Staying with one firm	44	18	−26	15	23	+8
Being punctual	31	19	−12	15	12	−3
Working safely	22	5	−17	24	11	−13
Carrying out instructions	13	2	−11	18	12	−6
Working hard	12	3	−9	16	12	−4
Working conscientiously	11	4	−7	26	14	−12

Derived from Table 3, Coote and Kellner (1980).

The above comments prompt the question as to how far are these perceptions of employers based on reality.

It is, for example, common to believe that there are many jobs which women cannot do because (on average, at least) they lack the strength. Yet very few jobs nowadays require strength, because of the introduction of mechanization and power-assisted controls. Moreover, the physical strength that women are said to lack is often a prerequisite of some jobs that women regularly do, such as nursing.

It is, however, more complex to decide whether there is any basis in truth for female workers being stereotyped as having high absenteeism and turnover rates. Table 6.29 shows little difference between the sexes in the overall rate of absence from work. Within each age/reason category the differences are often so marginal that there is no consistency from year to year over which sex has the better absence record. The only clear pattern is that men are absent more often than women through strikes, layoffs and short-time work, and there is greater absence among women aged 25–34 (an age when one would expect mothers to have young children) than there is among men in the same age bracket.

Even if women had been shown to be absent more than men, it would be difficult to argue that this necessarily indicates less commitment to work on the part of women, since two other

Table 6.29   Percentage of people aged 16 years and over absent from work during one week, by reason for absence, sex and age, Great Britain, 1984

	Own illness or accident		Strike/short time/lay-off		Personal and other reasons[a]		Total reasons[a]	
	W	M	W	M	W	M	W	M
Age								
16–17	12	7	2	2	0	3	13	12
18–24	5	4	*	2	2	2	7	8
25–34	5	5	1	2	3	1	9	8
35–44	3	4	1	2	1	1	6	7
45–54	5	3	1	2	2	1	7	7
55–64	7	6	*	1	1	*	9	7
65 and over	0	2	0	1	0	2	0	5
Total	5	4	1	2	2	2	8	8

a. Excluding holidays.
* = less than 0.5%.
Derived from Table 6.31; GHS 1984 (1986).

factors are involved. First, employers may have neglected to adjust the hours of some jobs to suit the needs of married women, an idea supported by the lower rates of absenteeism among part-time and non-manual women workers, whose hours tend to be shorter or more flexible. Secondly, it is well established that low-paid and poorly-trained workers, and workers in certain industries, have higher rates of absenteeism; therefore differences between the sexes in absenteeism probably reflect the distribution of the sexes by grade, occupation and industry. Given this qualification of the figures shown in the table, it might be argued that women actually have a better record on absence than men.

Women do, however, change jobs more frequently than men (GHS 1984, 1986, Table 6.40). Most of the overall difference in turnover can be accounted for by the fact that women are concentrated into less skilled occupations, which have high turnover rates for both sexes. There is evidence too that women more than men leave jobs because of factors within the firm's control. In some cases the firm may deliberately be shedding labour to avoid having the obligations associated with established employees. However women may quit an employer because the work they are given is unsatisfying (GHS 1978, 1980), or because they are dissatisfied with the boring and repetitive tasks they are required to do (Cavendish, 1982; Charles, 1983), or because of low pay or unsuitable hours (Wild and Hill, 1970). Employers are then responsible for a vicious circle: they refuse to give women more interesting, demanding and skilful jobs; as a result the women show a greater propensity to quit; thus the employers come to believe that only men will give them the continuous work over a long period which will yield a return on the training investment involved; this in turn justifies the employers' policy of only recruiting or training men!

In doing this, it can be argued that employers are creating a 'dual labour market', in which women who are confined to less skilled jobs come to constitute a 'secondary workforce' (Bruegel, 1979). Gender-based segregation, which comes to be accepted, even if not liked, by most workers, is reinforced by organizing skilled work so that it is unsuitable for women, particularly those who can only work part-time. It is then not possible for these women to move to better-paid jobs; therefore there is no danger of the free play of market forces bidding up unskilled or semi-skilled wages, which has considerable advantages to employers. It is also less likely that women will compare their lot with male workers; potential dissatisfaction is defused.

Moreover, women in the secondary workforce could be displaced from the labour marked if not needed. Although then temporarily out of employment, they will be supported by the institution of the family, and so form a 'reserve army of labour', in that they can be drawn back into the labour market whenever necessary. This may happen either when male labour is in short supply (as in wartime, or during the expansion of the 1950s and 1960s) or when it is necessary for employers to seek an alternative source of labour to curb the rising demands of the male workforce (as in the 1970s).

This theory of the 'dual labour market' has gained some credence with studies which suggest that in recent years employers are reducing their 'core' workforce of full-time permanent employees, and expanding their flexible use of 'peripheral' workers (Atkinson, 1984a and b; Institute of Manpower Studies, 1984a, 1986; Atkinson and Meager, 1986; Curson, 1986; Hakim, 1987b). These peripheral workers include not just part-time employees, but people on short-term contracts, temporary workers obtained from agencies, homeworkers, and people on publicly-subsidized training schemes. It is likely that women will constitute a disproportionate number of most of these categories of the 'flexible' or peripheral workers (Yeandle, 1985).

If segregation is sufficiently complete, the dual labour market can persist without formal discrimination over pay. Indeed, McIntosh (1980) found that, in almost all jobs done by both sexes, scale rates of pay were the same for both sexes and, indeed, part-timers were usually paid the same hourly rates as full-timers. However, the dual labour market does depend on discrimination in recruitment and training.

There are several studies which summarize the evidence that sex discrimination by employers does exist (e.g. see EEC 1980, 1984a; Chiplin and Sloane, 1982; Wallace, 1984; Walczak, 1987). One survey of recruitment found that direct discrimination between women and men was 'widespread and blatant', particularly against mothers with small children (Curran, 1985). Discrimination is likely where recruitment takes place by informal methods (EOC 1986c, 1987a). Extensive discrimination by employers had been found on the former Youth Opportunities Programme (YOP) work experience schemes (Brelsford, 1982). In the case of the Youth Training Scheme (YTS), Cockburn (1987a) cites equally blatant examples of employers wishing to specify the sex of the trainees they would accept. The EOC has noted that women seeking to start a business sometimes have more onerous conditions imposed on them by financial backers than men do (EOC *Annual Report 1986*, 1987). Four out of five of Britain's top women directors thought that as a result of their sex women faced particular obstacles in their path to the top, most notably 'male prejudice' and 'the old boy network' (Institute of Directors, 1985).

Economists have attempted to determine how much of the female/male wage differential might be due to discrimination (Sloane, 1985). The approach is generally to try to measure the effect of all the other factors which might lower earnings for women, such as the discontinuous work experience as a result of child-rearing, and then the remaining female:male earnings differential might be the result of discrimination.

Such studies capture only the 'static' effects of discrimination and not the 'dynamic' effects which might be expected to reduce the drive to get 'qualifications' or to return to full-time work. Therefore one should treat with caution the general result of such studies that the 1970s legislation has removed most of the effect of discrimination on the female:male earnings gap (Zabalza and Arrufat, 1983; Zabalza and Tzannatos, 1985a and b). Siebert and Sloane (1981) examined data from five different establishments: in only one were single women paid substantially less than single men with similar characteristics. However, Greenhalgh (1980) found that, among people with similar educational and other backgrounds, in 1975 married men earned 10 per cent more than single men, single men received 10 per cent more than single women, and single women received 12 per cent more than married women. Although these differences had been reduced since 1971, they were still quite clear, and discrimination in its various forms might be one explanation for their continuation.

Ethnic minorities in the labour market

Some empirical overviews of gender and work fail to focus at any length on ethnicity as an influence on women's work experiences. Although this is an under-researched field, and although the 1981 Census of Population did not ask for information about ethnic origin, there are data from the *Labour Force Survey* and the *GHS*.

We need to examine gender as a variable in the labour market experiences of the various ethnic groups, not only because of concern for the individuals involved, but also because by doing so we can learn much about the labour market itself. One hypothesis is that ethnic minority women comprise one of a number of sub-groups in the 'secondary workforce' who when needed can be channelled into jobs of low status and pay. We therefore need to explore the extent to which ethnic minority women in the labour market have a double 'handicap' of gender and ethnicity, and form a very distinct segment in terms of levels of participation and types of occupation.

Participation rates are shown in Table 6.30. In the older age ranges, males of various ethnic groups tend to have economic activity rates that are very similar to each other; in the younger age ranges, males of minority ethnic origin have a markedly lower activity rate than the rest of the population, partly because of the large number who are students (Barber, 1980). By contrast, the activity rates for women of minority ethnic origin are generally lower than those of white women in every age range; however this generalization masks wide variations, for paid work is exceptionally common among West Indian women, but relatively rare among women from Pakistan or Bangladesh. Another point to notice is that black women who do have a job are far more likely than white women to work full-time.

This propensity for full-time work to be more common among black women than it is among white women is also true in the specific sub-group of mothers with children (Monck and Lomas, 1975). But in this, as in all the participation rates, there is wide variation between black women in different parts of Britain: work participation rates for black mothers with young children ranged in different towns from 13 to 33 per cent, whereas the range for white mothers was only from 20 to 23 per cent (Monck and Lomas, 1975). The variations in the case of black women partly reflects the balance of ethnic groups with the black population of each town.

Table 6.30 *Economic activity rates and economic status by sex and ethnic origin Great Britain, 1985*

	Females					Males				
	White	Ethnic minorities	of whom (selected examples) West Indian	Indian	Pakistani/ Bangladeshi	White	Ethnic Minorities	of whom (selected examples) West Indian	Indian	Pakistani/ Bangladeshi
Economically active as % of age group:										
All population of working age	67	52	72	52	16	88	80	84	84	79
Ages 16–24	71	48	64	44	21	84	62	78	60	51
Ages 25–44	67	55	75	58	17	96	88	92	95	90
Ages 45–59/64	64	53	80	42	4	81	84	84	83	82
Unemployed as % of economically active	10	20	21	17	31	11	21	23	18	28
Self-employed as % of employment	7	6	1	9	—	14	18	9	24	21

Derived from *Employment Gazette*, (1987), Vol. 95, No. 1, pp. 20, 22, 27.

The differences in participation between the different ethnic minority groups are partly a reflection of their different age structures: all 'New Commonwealth' ethnic groups are relatively young, but the proportion of women in the 'childcare' age ranges will vary. These ethnic minorities also have few persons over retirement age, particularly in the case of West Indians; as a result it is likely that a smaller proportion of women's time is spent in care of elderly relatives than is the case with the white population (although the latter are known to have a greater recourse to old people's homes).

The likelihood of women's participation in paid work may also be affected by the length of time individuals have spent in this country. Female immigrants may have followed husbands to the UK after a considerable time-lag, and so have had less opportunity to enter the employment networks, thus depressing their participation rate. The tendency for individuals to have a job may also increase as the ethnic group to which they belong becomes established. This is clearly relevant in the case of the West Indian community, and indeed the longstanding recruitment of West Indian women by one employer (the NHS) may have contributed to their above-average participation rate.

Variations in economic activity rates between different ethnic groups may also reflect relatively independent religious and cultural factors. For example, Muslim women (the majority of Pakistani and Bangladeshi women) are more likely to be confined to the home and effectively excluded from outside paid work. Smith (1976) found that Asian women who could speak English were more likely to go out to work than those who could not; employers often tend to recruit only those with some knowledge of English, and this severely restricted the job chances of Asian women, since 59 per cent of them, compared with only 30 per cent of Asian men, spoke English slightly or not at all.

The analysis above has explained variations in participation in terms of the individuals' own backgrounds. An important explanation which this omits, however, is racism within the labour market, either on the part of employers or of potential fellow employees. There is much evidence of the labour market discriminating against black people in general, black youngsters in particular (Dex, 1983b), and young women to an even greater degree (Lee, 1982). Griffin's (1986) study of young people in Leicester found that race barriers are added to those of gender for black girls. Because the occupational structure is so sex-stereotyped that young women tend not to compete with young men, within each sex black people do compete with white and racism is prevalent and visible. This tends to mean that black girls form a separate sub-group within a highly segregated labour market. Ironically, in Cockburn's study of the YTS in London, this segregation led to young black women finding a higher proportion of YTS places on employer-based schemes than did young black men because of differential availability of such places in the different occupational areas.

The analysis of participation so far developed relies on traditional definitions of economic activity. It is possible that a greater proportion of women of ethnic minorities work from home or work intermittently for relatives, particularly if excluded by language or racism from 'mainstream' cultures, and so are officially classified as not in work (Monck and Lomas 1975). This is suggested by the fact that self-employment, particularly in retailing and catering, is very common among Asian men, but less common among Asian women, suggesting that the women may be at work within family enterprises formally owned by their husbands (Brown, C., 1984a and b).

Another consequence of black women relying for jobs on their own ethnic community is that, when they do fail to find a job, they may not register as unemployed (Barber, 1980). It is important, therefore, to examine unemployment among ethnic minorities by looking at the real unemployment rate as well as the official rate (*Unemployment and Ethnic Origin*, 1984; *Ethnic Origin and Economic Status*, 1987). The *Labour Force Survey* shows that the real rate of unemployment for ethnic minorities is about double that for whites, and is broadly similar for women and men (Table 6.30). However, the unemployment problem is disproportionately acute among certain groups, particularly women from Pakistan and Bangladesh; the lack of employment opportunities for these groups which this indicates may in turn inhibit their participation rates mentioned above.

The employment of ethnic minority groups tends to be restricted to less skilled and manual work, partly reflecting their concentration into decaying urban centres. Both sexes are excluded from higher-status jobs, but minority female skilled workers are very few in number indeed. Ironically, the relative exclusion from employment of Pakistani or Bangladeshi women means that those who do have jobs tend to have work of comparatively high status. However, a very different picture emerges with those minority groups where participation is high: only 0.8 per cent of West Indian women in the labour market were employers or managers or professionals, as against 5.5 per cent for women as a whole. For them, ethnicity interacts with gender further to depress occupational status. This is true even after taking into account differences in educational attainment: in a survey of 1971 school leavers in Sheffield and Bradford (Allen and Smith, 1975), it was shown that half of West Indian girls with CSE or 'O' level qualifications were employed in routine jobs, whereas a much higher proportion of white girls with equivalent examination passes were in skilled jobs. Clarke (1980), summarizing statistical studies of all the factors which determine occupational choice, finds that ethnic background does limit that choice.

Minority group women are concentrated in particular occupations and industries. Asian women have a greater tendency than average to work in factories and laundries, and in the textiles industry; Afro-Caribbean women, to work in the lower ranks of the Health Service, public transport or public catering. In some of this work, women from the ethnic minorities face harsh conditions of employment (Hoel, 1982).

This segregation has important consequences for conditions of work and pay (Campbell and Jones, 1982; Phizacklea, 1982, 1983). Marsh (1979) found that whereas only 1 per cent of white women did night-shift work, 7 per cent of those of Caribbean origin did so. Minority women tend to work in smaller establishments (Smith, 1974), with all that this may imply in terms of lower unionization and lower remuneration. Layard, Piachaud and Stewart (1978) suggest that belonging to the West Indian ethnic group is more clearly associated with a lowering of income levels for women than it is for men. In short, women of ethnic minorities stand even less chance than do other women of gaining access to rewarding work.

Participation in trade union activity

In the field of industrial relations there is a dearth of information about the pattern of collective action on the basis of sex, although the number of studies is growing (Adams and Hunt, 1980; Coyle, 1982; Epstein et al., 1986; Hirsch and Addison, 1986; Clutterbuck and Devine, 1987). Even such basic data as the sex breakdown of trade union membership is unreliable, particularly since the phasing out of separate recordings or rates of women's subscriptions to the trade unions. Indeed it seems likely that female membership has been consistently understated (Bain and Elias, 1985). None the less, it is clear that men constitute a majority of the trade union movement (Table 6.31). This reflects men's greater share of employment, combined with the greater density of union membership by males.

Women tend to work in industries with a small firm-structure

Table 6.31   *Membership of trade unions, by sex, United Kingdom, 1911–81*

	Trade-union membership (millions)		Women as % of union membership	% of potential membership[a]	
	Women	Men		Women	Men
1911	0.3	2.8	10	6	23
1921	1.0	5.6	15	18	44
1951	1.8	7.7	19	25	56
1961	2.0	7.9	20	24	53
1971	2.8	8.4	25	33	58
1981	3.8	8.4	31	38	59

a. i.e. membership density: members of trade unions as a percentage of employees in employment.
Derived from Table 3.7, *EOC Annual Report 1980* (1981); Table 12.19, *Social Trends*, No. 11 1979 (1980); Table 11.10 *Social Trends, 1985* (1987).

where union activity is difficult to organize (*Employment Gazette*, January 1978). In small-scale establishments, there may be closer identification between worker and employer, and this is likely to be true in most offices – particularly between a secretary and the person she works for (Lumley, 1973). Women are also less likely to work in an establishment with a closed shop (Daniel and Millward, 1983).

There are particular barriers preventing part-time workers from joining and participating in trade unions. Coote and Kellner (1980) actually note a higher unionization of female than male part-timers; even so, in 1983 only 33 per cent of part-time women workers were members of a trade union (*GHS 1983*, 1985) and according to one survey, only 10 per cent of all low-paid part-time workers were members of trade unions (Low Pay Unit, 1978).

Generally, the very reasons why women work part-time (particularly domestic commitments) act as a barrier to their participation in union activity. However, this barrier may also exist for many married women workers, including those who work full time. Most working married women have two demanding activities – their job, and domestic or family responsibilities. To build an active participation in a trade union as a third sphere of activity requires a very high degree of commitment and organization (Middleton, 1977; Hammond, 1986). The problem is particularly acute for mothers of young children, which explains why the gap in union membership is greatest between the sexes in the 25–34 age group (Coote and Kellner, 1980). However, Bain and Elias (1985) argue by means of statistical evidence that married women and women with children are less likely to unionize than other women.

However, membership density has increased more rapidly among women than among men in the post-war decades. And in the 1980s, when trade unionism was in retreat, the share of women in the total membership has continued to expand. These trends partly reflect the general post-war rise in unionization in the types of industry in which women are concentrated, particularly white-collar work and the public sector: Coote and Kellner (1980) emphasize that the trade union membership density of women is almost as high as that of men in the white-collar socio-economic group C1 (Table 6.32), and it is actually higher than that of men among full-time employees in the public sector (*GHS 1983*, 1985, Table 7f). Women are now in a clear majority of many white-collar unions (Table 6.33), and in addition form sizeable minorities in some of the large general unions, including the largest, the Transport and General Workers.

However, women in trade unions are less likely to hold positions of responsibility than their male colleagues (Tables 6.33 and 6.34). In several industries where women work in large numbers (such as textiles, potteries or the retail trade) men retain a paternalistic control over a largely female trade union membership. It is a question of not only the number of posts but which posts are occupied by women. Surveys conducted by the National and Local Government Officers' Association (NALGO, 1980, 1984) found that women office-holders in trade union branches tended to occupy the more marginal posts, such as assistant secretary, and this is confirmed in a study of West Indian women (Phizacklea, 1982). The trade union posts held by women, such as education officer and welfare officer, tend to be extensions of the traditional female role. However, at least experience in such positions allows women a toehold in the power structure.

A common observation is that women are less willing than men to participate in industrial action (Table 6.34). Indeed, the proportion of females has been used, along with other variables, to predict the amount of strike activity in different establishments (*Strikes in Britain*, 1978). However, from the earliest history of the labour movement, there were examples of women engaging in industrial action – from the famous Matchgirls' strike of 1888, through the women's strike movement of 1911–13, to the equal-pay strike at Ford's, Dagenham, in 1968 (TUC, 1983c). Women were active in the miners' strike of the 1980s (Ridd and Callaway, 1986; Seddon 1986; Stead, 1987). These examples were not aberrations, and show that women cannot generally be thought of as unwilling to take collective action.

The Workplace Industrial Relations Survey found that there

Table 6.32   *Trade union membership as percentage of full-time employees,*
by sex, by size of establishment, by industrial sector, by socio-
economic group, Great Britain, 1983

		Women	Men
Establishment size:	1–24 employees:		
(total number of	All	33	67
employees)	Public sector	79	74
	Private sector	17	20
	25–99 employees:		
	All	33	67
	Public sector	82	84
	Private sector	26	37
	100–999 employees:		
	All	30	70
	Public sector	81	89
	Private sector	49	58
	1000 + employees:		
	All	25	75
	Public sector	72	87
	Private sector	58	73
	Total (all sizes):		
	All	50	57
	Public sector	78	85
	Private sector	34	43
Socio-economic group:	Professional	a	46
	Employers and managers	40	35
	Intermediate non-manual	65	69
	Junior non-manual	39	49
	Skilled manual (and own-account non-professional)	61	66
	Semi-skilled manual (and personal service)	53	63
	Unskilled manual	a	55
	TOTAL	50	58

a. The actual number is too small to permit calculation of a percentage in whole
numbers.
Derived from Tables 7.51, 7.52 and 7.E, *GHS 1983* (1985).

was no difference in the experience of industrial action between
establishments with a predominantly female workforce and those
with a predominantly male one in situations where there was low
trade union density; only at high levels of union density did the
proportion of female employees reduce the likelihood of industrial
action (Daniel and Millward, 1983). In a classic study of workers

Table 6.33 *Women as percentage of membership and offices, selected[a]*
unions, January 1987

	Member-ship	Executive members	Full-time officials	TUC delegates
Association of Professional, Executive, Clerical and Computer Staff (APEX)	54	31	5	36
Association of Scientific Technical and Managerial Staffs (ASTMS)	26	12	10	19
Banking, Insurance and Finance Union (BIFU)	53	12	22	27
Confederation of Health Service Employees (COHSE)	80	14	18	20
General, Municipal, Boilermakers and Allied Trades Union (GMBTU)	30	3	4	6
National Association of Local Government Officers (NALGO)	52	38	13	34
National Union of Public Employees (NUPE)	68	42	8	26
National Union of Teachers (NUT)	73	21	7	37
National Union of Tailoring and Garment Workers (NUTGW)	91	27	14	77
Transport and General Workers' Union (TGWU)	16	5	2	9
Union of Shop, Distributive and Allied Workers (USDAW)	61	19	13	31

a. The selection of unions comprises the unions with the largest numbers of members plus some additional unions with large numbers of women members.
Derived from Coote and Kellner (1980) and EOC (1987b), after EOC enquiries to individual unions.

in two industries, it was found that engineering workers operated collectively, while rainwear-makers operated individualistically, regardless of sex (Lupton, 1963). One study of the motor industry (Turner, Clack and Roberts, 1967) found no relationship between the proportion of women employed in car factories and relative strike-proneness. In a later study of two industries in Stockport (Purcell, 1979), it was found that men and women engaged in widespread action according to the tradition of the industry rather

Table 6.34   Percentage of trade union members who have participated in trade union activities, by sex, 1985

	Women	Men
Voted in a union election	43	66
Been to a union meeting	56	79
Put forward a proposal in a meeting	18	37
Gone on strike	24	51
Stood on a picket line	14	32
Been a shop steward	8	21

Derived from Table 7, Cockburn (1987b).

than according to sex: indeed, women in engineering had attitudes much closer to those of men in engineering than to those of women in the clothing industry. Recent manufacturing case studies (Martin, 1985) provided evidence to dispute an earlier suggestion by Wood (1981) that women were less committed than men to opposing redundancies.

It seems likely, then, that while statistics may suggest that women have a lower tendency to engage in strikes, this may be associated with the low strike-proneness of the places they work in and the work they do. The type of work affects not only membership, but also participation in union activities and industrial action. Low-paid and less-skilled workers are always more difficult to unionize, and show a reduced tendency to strike (*Strikes in Britain*, 1978). Women characteristically work in low-grade posts, where they are less likely to be allowed to leave their work-stations to discuss union business. Indeed, if some women employees in these circumstances assess the trade union as unimportant, they may actually be making an accurate assessment: establishments with a high proportion of women tend to have a less developed union represenative structure, and managers give the trade union less information (Daniel and Millward, 1983). Though Marsh (1979) showed that 'deliberate non-membership' of trade unions was not extensive, there is evidence that unions have often been seen as irrelevant to women's interests (Purcell, 1979). In the absence of a trade union dedicated to fighting for their interests, women may have to show resistance in other ways (McNally, 1979; Hoel, 1982) or simply leave to find other jobs.

Indeed far from fighting for women's interests, male-dominated trade unions may even fight against them – opposing the creation of part-time jobs lest it harm the position of full-timers, and jealously guarding male:female pay differentials (Boston, 1987).

Several pieces of research have established that male-dominated trade unions have kept women out of some areas of work work (Cockburn, 1983). Coyle's (1982) study of the clothing industry shows that men in craft unions have established and maintained skill divisions which served merely to preserve the relative position of men, and which bore no close relationship to an objective assessment of the skill-demands of the tasks involved. Cockburn (1987b) cites unions maintaining demarcation practices in the print industry which serve to exclude female YTS trainees from work experience and off-the-job training which is available to males. In 1986 the EOC had to issue non-discrimination notices against two branches of SOGAT '92 requiring them not to discriminate in the provision of information about job vacancies (EOC *Annual Report 1986*, 1987). The EOC further found that although women constituted 6 per cent of the National Union of Railwaymen, the union had no policy specifically for women (1986c).

It is not impossible for unions themselves to overcome the barriers which dissuade women from joining and participating in union activities (Beale, 1982). A survey by the shopworkers' union found that the main reason for not getting involved with the union was simply lack of confidence, cited by 69 per cent of women and 47 per cent of men (USDAW, 1987). When female trade unionists in Hull were asked what would encourage them to participate in union affairs, the factors mentioned most often were not reducing home responsibilities (important though this was), but rather the key factors were holding meetings in work time, and making available more information about how unions work (Stageman, 1980). In a NALGO (1980) survey, 85 per cent of branches were found to hold their meetings after working hours rather than at lunch-time. However, the data in Table 6.35 suggests that perceptions of female and male trade union members differed most not on organizational matters such as timing of meetings, but on whether the union was felt to be in touch with its members and responsive to their interests and political sympathies.

It could be argued that the reason why unions fail to respond to women's needs is because they are run mainly by men (Table 6.35). Even where women do gain positions of responsibility, however, their effectiveness may still be hampered. Fryer, Fairclough and Manson (1978) found that female shop stewards had poorer facilities and were able to have less time off work for union duties. Within trade union hierarchies, the representation of women has been increased through the practice of reserving some executive positions for women, but women are still under-represented.

Table 6.35   Trade union members' perceptions of their own union, by sex, 1980 (percentages)

	Women	Men
^o_o *agreeing that union:*		
Would fight hard to protect my job if it were threatened	48	52
Tried hard to keep its members in touch with what the union is doing	32	46
Good at looking after the interests of people like me	40	39
Usually holds meetings at times and places that are easy for me to attend	29	34
Fights hard for equality between men and women at work	33	30
Union meetings are usually boring	18	27
Encourages people like me to get involved	19	27
Too involved in politics and not enough in advancing its members' interests	12	25
Should do more to meet the needs of workers with young children	19	15
Controlled by extremists and militants	7	12

Derived from Table 3, Coote and Kellner (1980).

The picture may of course be changing, with perhaps a growing tendency among trade unions to respond to demands made on them by women members (Hunt, 1982; Cockburn, 1987b). In 1987, the TUC established a special women's affairs department. Participation is increasingly encouraged by the provision of crèche facilities. However, neither special representation for women nor the formation of special committees for women guarantees that the pay and employment problems of women will be dealt with by trade unions, as one study of ASTMS found (Harrison, 1979).

At the time of writing, trade unions are fighting sex discrimination cases in large numbers. None the less, they find it difficult to tackle the real problem, that the workforce is highly segregated, and the two sexes are therefore not found working side by side in one workplace, represented by one union (Ellis, 1981; EOC, 1986b). Moreoover, the passage of the Equal Pay and Sex Discrimination Acts, supported by the trade union hierarchies, was effectively an admission that collective bargaining as at present constituted would not give women equal opportunities. Trade unions are only slowly beginning to try to tackle the discriminatory attitudes and structures that perpetuate segregation and inequality in employment (Labour Research Department, 1986b).

Legislation: its impact on sex divisions in the labour market

A number of legal provisions have in theory restricted the ability of employers to determine the levels of structure of pay within their enterprises.

Wages Councils used to cover one tenth of the labour force and one quarter of all employed women, and fixed statutory minimum wages in the low-pay industries concerned (Neuberger, 1984). However, the Wages Inspectorate of the Department of Employment was too small to enforce the law, and the powers of Wages Councils were eroded almost to the point of abolition in 1987. Legal or voluntary 'incomes policies' constituted another means by which the government influenced pay rises for part of the 1960s and 1970s; from 1974 such a policy stipulated the maximum permissible pay increase as a flat-rate sum of money, which favoured the lower-paid, among whom women are concentrated. However, it is now generally agreed that the periods of free collective bargaining which followed the end of such policies usually reversed at least some of their effects.

The main legal weapon against the underpayment of women has been the Equal Pay Act 1970. Several early studies (Office of Manpower Economics, 1972; Snell, 1979) showed how employers minimized their obligations under the Act either by making it appear that women and men have non-comparable jobs (ordinary male shop assistants have been described in company books as 'management trainees'), or finding subtle ways of separating women and men into distinct categories of jobs, and ensuring that any women who are employed work on different contractual arrangements. Until the EEC-enforced Equal Pay Act amendment came into force at the start of 1984, women who worked only with other women had no legal basis for any claim that their low pay arose because of different treatment on the basis of sex. Potentially, then, the amended Act could be of some significance; however the job evaluation schemes upon which the new Act relies are in fact less common in establishments which employ a high percentage of women (Daniel and Millward, 1983). Moreover, because a woman can only compare her position with someone working for the same employer, it will do nothing to tackle the real problem outlined in this chapter, that women are segregated into the low-pay industries and workplace establishments.

The Labour government's Sex Discrimination Act 1975 made it illegal to discriminate in employment with regard to entry, training, conditions, promotion and redundancy. The Sex Discrimination Acts might in fact be the key to reducing pay inequalities even within an occupational category, since potentially it can guarantee women equal access to the higher-paid grades, and might prevent an employer selecting them for redundancy if they do succeed in closing the pay gap between women and men.

In practice, however, it has been as easy for employers to subvert the Sex Discrimination Act as it has been for them to undermine the Equal Pay Act. The number of legal cases brought under the former Act fell in number sharply after an initial burst, and many of the complaints about discrimination in recruitment came from men not women (EOC *Annual Reports*). Many women have felt that the male-dominated industrial tribunals are not always in sympathy with the spirit of the Act (Leonard, 1987). The passage of the Sex Discrimination Act 1986 widened the previous Act's scope (*Labour Research*, 1987b). However, it has been difficult for women to establish the existence of 'indirect discrimination', such as the age bars which preclude women from resuming a career after having children. It has been almost impossible to establish 'informal' discrimination, such as male colleagues excluding women from the workplace social life or fostering a general atmosphere hostile to their employment. The EOC survey of employers (McIntosh, 1980) found that a third of men, as opposed to only a fifth of women, had been recruited by 'informal' methods, such as private contacts or recruitment internal to the organization, and it is more difficult to find proof of discrimination if procedures are informal. To add to the category of failures, the Equal Opportunities Commission has been heavily criticized for failing to make effective use of its powers (Hewitt, 1980; Oakley, 1981). And since the armed forces are still (legally) segregated by sex, working-class men have more opportunity then working-class women to learn a trade.

There is, however, one kind of action by public bodies which has had more success shown in improving women's chances in the labour market: the 'contract compliance' policies of some local authorities, under which they award contracts only to companies with effective equal opportunities policies. Studies have shown that such action does improve women's chances in the labour market (*Contract Compliance and Equal Opportunities*, 1986; Trades Union Congress, 1986; Institute of Personnel Management, 1987). It is significant that (at the time of writing) the government is outlawing the practice of contract compliance. There is however still scope for public bodies to improve their own employment practices (Huws, 1987).

This points to the general conclusion that the law, framed as it is by a parliament in which the general interests of men and of employers are paramount, is unlikely to embody a serious attempt to erode the dual nature of the labour market. Women (and especially married women) are channelled into secondary jobs because the values of society then allow employers to deem those jobs worthy of lower rates of pay than would otherwise by the case. Legislative concessions to the needs of women are enacted in the knowlege that such provisions will not lead to significant costs to employers – that is, will not radically disturb the status quo.

Employers can be certain that women will not succeed to any large extent in using the law to improve their position, since women are hampered in their attempts to undertake more rewarding jobs by the domestic roles which they are expected to undertake. For example, business interests tolerated the passage of the Employment Protection Act granting some women the legal right to return to work after the birth of a child, because this right is useless in practice for many women, with the absence of significant support from husbands, and the failure of the state or employers to provide childcare facilities. Of course, workplace nursery provision might enable women to overcome some of the difficulties which face them, but nurseries do not relieve women of the ultimate responsibility for children nor for other domestic tasks.

7 Political participation

Laura Thomas and Eileen Wormald

In discussing sex differences in political participation, it is important to remember that women have had access to the nation's political system as persons rather than personalities for just over half a century; prior to 1918 they could make an impact directly only as monarchs or indirectly as influential political hostesses (Harrison, 1978), as the wives or mistresses of politicians, and in peripheral political groups, such as the Primrose League. It can therefore be assumed that men have an historical base for political activity that is lacking for women.

Political participation has primarily been analysed by political scientists within an empirical paradigm, and as such is confined to observable behaviour in the formal, 'public' political arenas. In this context, while women appear to participate at the basic level of voting in equal numbers with men, beyond that there is a pyramid of participation with fewer and fewer women to be found at each level. Explanations about the lower levels of women's participation are multifarious (see for example, Lovenduski and Hills, 1981) but broadly rest either with women not wanting or not being able to manage a political career, and/or with men erecting barriers to prevent their entry. In the former case, causes rest with the differential role requirements of family structure and domestic commitments or early socialization into an apolitical role. Alternatively, the political arena is regarded as a male preserve with members being reluctant to promote women. Vallance (1982b) notes that underpinning the theories of European and American commentators is the notion that a change of attitudes (of women and men) is needed before women can take their equal place in society. She suggests that as it is structures and institutions which reinforce and maintain attitudes, these therefore need to be modified to bring women in. How far this can be achieved depends on how society is analysed (see Chapter 2).

Clearly, the political position of women has been advanced since 1918 and a minority have reached the higher echelons of power. Studies of politically 'successful' women provide typologies, psychological explanations and the views of individuals on the reasons for their success (Currell, 1974; Vallance, 1979; Phillips,

1980; Wilson, 1983). They do not pose theories about the majority of women who are not active in the political structures. Furthermore, the views of 'unsuccessful' women remain untapped. Randall (1982) has argued that when the definition and arena of politics is broadened to include the private and informal aspects of social life, women's political participation is greater and more visible than the traditional paradigm allows for, e.g. pressure groups and single-issue platforms. However, the choice of areas examined here are, for the most part, conventional because the aim is primarily to examine women's penetration into social structures and that is where the data are available.

While this chapter looks at the extent of women's participation in a well-established male world, speculation about the reasons for women's political activity is left to Chapter 9. Quantitative and qualitative comparisons are made between men and women in politics and although consideration is given to variables of age, education, occupation and political party, the emphasis remains on sex differentials. Thus the sections on 'The government' and 'Local government' look at elected members in politics. 'Public bodies' and 'The civil service' give information on paid and some unpaid appointments to bodies that execute political decisions, while 'Party membership' and 'Pressure groups' examine voluntary participation in political activity. Other important influences on the political process, the judiciary, industry and trade unions are to be found in Chapters 8 and 6, while some, for example the media, are left out because they would have required a lengthy theoretical explanation of diverse forms of political communication, as well as information on the sex composition of the communicators, going beyond readily available sources (Hedblom, 1981). Finally, 'Voting behaviour' looks at the most generally exercised form of political participation and, together with the section on 'Political opinions', discusses the supposed conservatism of women, while 'Political socialization' examines some of the evidence about political learning.

Some of the facts are indisputable; the published numbers of women office-holders in European and central government are evidently small and cannot be argued out of existence. Data on other aspects of political behaviour are more difficult to obtain, and even more difficult to interpret. No 'official' figures are available on how women and men vote in elections, and none of the academic *Nuffield Elections Surveys* published relevant survey data on this until 1979. They then briefly examined the suggested 'conservatism' of women, a contentious issue in terms of both their stated voting habits and even more, their opinions. Myths once created, die hard, and certainly where opinions are concerned data could probably be produced that on specific issues supported either side of the debate. Again, detailed information is now annually published on the sex composition of the civil service, but statistics of women in local government are not well documented. Therefore, for the most part, it is necessary to rely on summation of data in the annual yearbooks, or on analyses by Royal Commissions or academic inquiries. Explanations regarding political activity vary from quantified views of participation (as in the Maud Committee on local government) to inside assessment of the situation (Brimelow, 1981, on the civil service).

Parliament: candidates and members

The vote was first given to women aged over 30 in 1918, and in the same year women aged 21 and over were allowed to stand as parliamentary candidates (Harrison, 1986). This was after a debate in which one of their supporters, Lord Robert Cecil, advocated their cause with the double-edged words: 'I think we should treat them as human beings with absolutely equal rights with men' (Brookes, 1967). During the same debate Herbert Samuel accurately prophesied that 'It is rather more probable that too few women will be elected rather than too many.'

Seventeen women stood for parliament in 1918 and one, Countess Markewicz, was elected. She was a Sinn Feiner, who compaigned from prison, and who refused to take her seat as a protest against British policy on Ireland. So the first woman to take her seat in the House of Commons was Lady Astor; she 'took up the mantle' from her husband on his succession to the peerage, and won for the Conservatives the Sutton division of Plymouth, at the by-election in 1919. Though a handful of women were elected in every succeeding election, there was no sharply rising curve or participation either as candidates or as elected members, and there have only been 139 individual women elected to parliament between 1918 and 1987.

Despite the changing electoral fortunes of the two major parties, there have always tended to be more women among the Labour MPs than the Conservatives. The exceptions being 1970, when fifteen Conservative as against ten Labour women were elected and in 1983, Conservative women outnumbered their Labour counterparts by thirteen to ten. It should be noted that the Labour Party field more women candidates than the Conservatives (see Table 7.2). Whilst female candidature has steadily risen over the years, with a much sharper increase in recent years, the number of women MPs more or less stabilized at around 4 per

Table 7.1   *Women candidates for, and elected Members of the British Parliament, 1918–87*

| | Women candidates | | Elected women members | | |
	Number	as % of all candidates	Number	as % female candidates	as % of all candidates
1918	17	1.0	1	6	0.1
1922	33	2.3	2	12	0.3
1923	34	2.4	8	21	1.3
1924	41	2.9	4	8	0.7
1929	69	4.0	14	20	2.3
1931	62	4.8	15	23	2.4
1935	67	5.0	9	13	1.5
1945	87	5.2	24	26	3.8
1950	126	6.8	21	17	3.4
1951	77	5.6	17	22	2.7
1955	92	6.5	24	26	3.8
1959	81	5.3	25	31	4.0
1964	90	5.1	29	32	4.6
1966	81	4.7	26	32	4.1
1970	99	5.4	26	26	4.1
1974[a]	143	6.7	23	16	3.6
1974[b]	161	7.2	27	17	4.3
1979	210	8.0	19	9	2.9
1983	280	10.9	23	8	3.5
1987	327	14.1	41	12	6.3

a. February
b. October
Note: Boundary changes after the 1979 election increased the number of seats from 635 to 650.
Derived from Appendix 2, Vallance (1979) and Conservative Women's National Advisory Council (1980, 1986).

cent. However, in June 1987, a record number of women MPs were returned, making up just over 6 per cent of the total (see Table 7.1).

One explanation for the discrepancy between candidature and election is the high proportion of women standing for the Liberal/SDP Alliance and other minor parties (see Table 7.2) which obviously lowers their electoral chances in a two-party, first-past-the-post electoral system.

The small number of women MPs does not seem to be a reflection of a significant bias against women candidates by the electorate. Work carried out between the two elections of 1974 showed that where a party put up a woman candidate at one election and a man at another, there was no sign that the sex of a candidate had any effect on voting, except perhaps marginally

Table 7.2   Party distribution of women candidates for the British Parliament 1983

	Number	as % of female candidates	as % of all candidates
Conservative	40	14	6
Labour	78	28	12
Liberal	32	11	10
SDP	43	15	14
Ecology	27	10	25
SNP	9	3	13
Plaid Cymru	6	2	16
Other	45	16	10
Total	280	—	11

Derived from Table 9, *Factsheet No. 22*, House of Commons Public Information Office.

among Liberals, who did not appear to find a woman candidate as acceptable as a man (Steed, 1975). The apparent prejudice against women among the Liberals is the more surprising, since it is among the minor parties that women have most chance of being both selected and elected proportionately to their male colleagues (Mellors, 1978). Other studies have also shown that the gender of a candidate makes only a small difference to voters (Hills, 1981a; Rasmussen, 1983) and this general finding endorses the view of candidates most succinctly expressed by the man who said: 'I'd vote for a pig if it wore a blue ribbon.'

Each of the main parties have made attempts to ensure that there should be more women candidates, and towards this end the percentage of women on the candidate approved lists has increased; prior to 1979, the Labour Party had the highest female representation at 10 per cent. By 1983, the figures of approved female candidature had risen to 15 per cent for Labour, Conservatives 10 per cent, Liberals 11 per cent and SDP 17 per cent (Vallance, 1984). Vallance makes the point that while the parties Central Offices are keen to increase female representation, they have no influence over constituencies where women continue to be underselected. One explanation for this is that local selectors (erroneously) believe women to be a bad electoral risk, and therefore do not select them as candidates in winnable seats (Vallance, 1981). This theory was not upheld by a survey of 487 Labour selectors' opinions but instead it was suggested that 'if more women with appropriate other qualities and characteristics were to put themselves forward they would stand every chance of being selected' (Denver, 1982). While it is true that women do not present themselves for selection in the same numbers as men, the theory of a proportional link between candidature and selection is as tenuous as that between selection and election.

Where women are selected, they tend to be adopted in marginal or 'unwinnable' seats which reduces their chances of being elected (see Table 7.3). Dr Edith Summerskill is quoted as saying that it was not until 1955 that two women contested seats with any certainty of success (Currell, 1974). Vallance (1984) estimates that in 1979, a man's chance of success was about one in four, whereas a woman's was less than one in ten, and by 1983, this figure had dropped to one in twelve. As can be seen from Table 7.4, the handicap ratio for women varies from one election year to the next. In 1964 and 1966, Labour women had a better chance of election than men when their party gained 56 and 48 seats respectively, and yet in 1979 the success rate for women from both parties had halved. The reason for the varying success rate seems to be a combination of party success, incumbency and the type of seats that women candidates are selected to contest (Hills, 1981b).

Further evidence of the fact that women have to work a harder passage than men in order to obtain a parliamentary seat is provided in Table 7.5 which shows the number of seats contested prior to election. Whilst it is true that 'attainment of a markedly different political status from one previously held is not an easy process' (Sapiro, 1983), it would seem that at all stages, this process is easier for men than for women.

Profile of elected members
Those women who both attempt and succeed in jumping the hurdles tend to be marginally older than men, having an average age of 43 compared to 41 for men, at the time of their first election (Mellors, 1978). The profile of women MPs differs from that of men in other demographic features. In educational background, the former are more likely to have a secondary school/university education as opposed to the public school and/or an 'Oxbridge' background of the men, whilst their occupations (Table 7.6) tend to be professional, particularly in the field of 'communication', like teaching and journalism (Mellors, 1978). This is not surprising given the overall sex differentials in education (see Chapter 5), and the sexual division of labour reflected in employment patterns detailed in Chapter 6. However, occupational sex differentials among MPs can also be attributed to the much greater trade union sponsorship of male MPs with working-class occupations. Furthermore, there is evidence to suggest that certain occupations

Table 7.3   *Percentage of women and men selected for 'good' and 'poor' seats in the 1974 and 1983 general elections*

	'Good' seats[a]			'Poor' seats[b]		
	Women	Men	Number	Women	Men	Number
1974 (Feb)						
Conservative	3.0	97.0	296	7.4	92.6	326
Labour	4.3	95.7	301	8.4	91.6	322
Liberal	3.8	96.2	159	9.5	90.5	358
1983						
Conservative	3.2	96.8	397	11.4	88.6	209
Labour	4.8	95.2	209	16.0	84.0	424
Liberal	10.6	89.4	180	9.2	90.8	142
SDP	13.4	86.6	112	14.0	86.0	199
L/All	11.6	88.4	292	12.0	88.0	341

a. 'Good' seats defined as seats won, or, for the Liberals and SDP, where candidates came either first or second.
b. 'Poor' seats are those contested without success.
Derived from Le Lohe (1976), and Craig (1984).

Table 7.4   *Sex differences in success rates for election to Parliament (1945–87) across the two main parties*

	Conservative			Labour		
	% of men elected	% women elected	women's handicap ratio	% of men elected	% women elected	women's handicap ratio
1945	35	7	0.2	66	51	0.8
1950	54	21	0.4	52	33	0.7
1951	53	24	0.4	49	27	0.5
1955	58	30	0.5	46	33	0.7
1959	59	43	0.7	42	36	0.9
1964	48	46	1.0	50	55	1.1
1966	40	33	0.8	59	63	1.1
1970	52	58	1.1	47	35	0.7
1974[a]	49	27	0.6	50	33	0.7
1974[b]	46	23	0.4	53	36	0.7
1979	53	26	0.5	45	21	0.5
1983	65	33	0.5	36	13	0.4
1987	61	37	0.6	38	23	0.6

a. February
b. October

Handicap ratio = $\dfrac{\text{percentage of women elected}}{\text{percentage of men elected}}$

Derived from Table 2.2, Hills (1981b).

Table 7.5   *Number of female MPs who contested parliamentary seats prior to their first election to parliament, 1918–74, by party*

Number of seats contested	Number of MPs Conserv-ative	Labour	Other	All parties	% of all MPs Women	Men
0	13	23	5	41	54	60
1	4	13	0	17	22	23
2	5	4	0	9	12	12
3	2	2	0	4	5	3
4	0	3	0	3	4	0.7
5	1	1	0	2	3	0.3
All women MPs	25	46	5	76	—	—

Derived from Table 7.8, Mellors (1978).

Table 7.6   *The occupations of Members of Parliament, 1945–74 (percentage[a])*

	Women	Men
The law	12	4
Teaching	27	10
Management	7	16
Journalism/writing	16	6
Housewife	15	0
Manual work	0	11

a. Percentages do not add to 100 because only the six most common categories of occupation are shown.
Derived from Table 7.12, Mellors (1978).

lend more readily to a political career because they provide readily transferable skills, i.e. 'brokerage' employment (Jacob, 1982). The lawyer is the classic example of this and women MPs are proportionately well represented in this category whilst being under-represented in other politically potential occupations, such as management (Mellors, 1978). Finally, their length of parliamentary service is normally shorter than that of men which probably results from a number of factors, not least that the preponderance of women MPs in marginal constituencies makes for a precarious political career.

The government

The first woman to take office, five years after Lady Astor entered the House of Commons, was Margaret Bondfield, a prominent

Table 7.7   *The numbers of women and men holding parlimanentary office during the years, 1950–87*

	Cabinet ministers		Ministers not in cabinet		Under secretaries		Parliamentary secretaries	
	Women	Men	Women	Men	Women	Men	Women	Men
1950	0	17	1	15	1	7	0	17
1960	0	19	0	20	0	11	1	16
1968	1	23	2	31	2	15	1	19
					Women		Men	
1970	1	17	1	20	0		30	
1974	2	19	1	26	2		30	
1975	2	21	1	27	3		35	
1979	1	21	2	27	1		36	
1987	0	22	3	26	4		31	

Derived from Table 2, Currell (1974) and *Dod's Parliamentary Companion* (various issues).

trade union organizer and Chair of the General Council of the Trades Union Congress. She was appointed in 1924 as the Parliamentary Under-Secretary of State at the Ministry of Labour in the first Labour government; in the same year Susan Lawrence, a middle-class intellectual who had taken the mathematics tripos at Cambridge, was appointed Parliamentary Private Secretary to the President of the Board of Education. In 1929 Bondfield became the first woman member of the cabinet as Minister of Labour, but it was not until 1945 that she was followed by another Labour cabinet minister, Ellen Wilkinson, and then in 1951 the first Conservative, Florence Horsburgh, was appointed Minister of Education but without a place in the cabinet.

From 1964 onwards, there has always been at least one female minister, though up until now there still have only been eight women cabinet ministers, and four of these were Ministers of Education. Hills (1981b) suggests that women MPs lack the length of service necessary for promotion to cabinet office because many of them represent marginal constituencies which results in a high turnover rate. Nevertheless, between 1974 and 1979, during the time in office of the Labour Party, nine out of nineteen women MPs were government ministers, with about one third of them in office at the same time, the same proportion as for Labour men (see Table 7.7). This evidence suggests that the major barrier against women's entry into high political office appears at the point of entry to, rather than during, their political career.

Although the Labour Party pioneered the entry of women into

high office and Harold Wilson is reported to have been instrumental in recognizing that women should be in the government as other than 'tokens' (Vallance, 1979), it was left to the Conservative Party to elect Margaret Thatcher as the first woman party leader. Four years later, in 1979, she became the first woman prime minister, ironically in an election where women had the lowest percentage of seats in parliament since 1945. Though her potential electoral support was seen as lying preponderantly with women (Vallance, 1979), her own election to leadership was purported to owe everything to the activities of her male sponsors, and the essential 'patronage' role of men, like Harold Wilson and Edward du Cann, for the advancement of politically successful women, has often been discussed in the literature (Currell, 1974). Shirley Williams, for example, joined the Labour Party at the age of 15 but had already been befriended by Herbert Morrison, then Home Secretary, who made a point of acting as political patron to young women. She is reported as saying:

> I met him in an air raid shelter when I was 13. I got to know him quite well and he half adopted me. He used to invite me to have dinner with him at the Home Office. He said to me, it takes a lot of courage for a man to encourage a young woman to go into politics because it could be misunderstood. Most men would not want the publicity. Even more than they are now, men were reluctant to put themselves into that position. (Phillips, 1980)

It is notable that women are advanced to high office in areas where they are concerned with matters thought to be of particular interest to women (for example, education and the social services); a woman has never held the major offices of Foreign Secretary or Chancellor of the Exchequer. The designation of certain subjects as the province of women has been interpreted as an example of the setting of the political agenda by men (Evans, 1980). In debates, the subject-balance of women MPs is influenced by factors other than their wishes, for example, on questions of education or social issues they are more likely to attract the Speaker's eye than during debates on the economy (Vallance, 1979). However, Vallance (1982a) has examined the extent that women MPs participate in 'feminine' areas through the construction of an Index of Specialization. She concluded that 'they do not do so to the exclusion of everything else, and indeed other areas would seem in most cases to preoccupy them a good deal more' (p. 409).

In general, women have been accepted into full executive membership of the House of Commons, becoming Whips and

Table 7.8   The sex composition of the House of Lords, 1987

	Women	Men	Women as % of total
Archbishops and bishops	0	26	0
Peers by succession	20	743	3
Hereditary peers of first creation	0	29	0
Life peers	47	323	15
All peers	67	1121	6

Derived from data supplied by the House of Lords Information Office, 1987.

Private Secretaries, playing a full part in, including chairing committees, and one, a Conservative, Betty Marie Anderson (later Baroness Skrimshire), has sat in the Speaker's chair as Deputy Chairman of Ways and Means (Vallance, 1979). Yet differences in political participation persist; despite the fact that women are full-time MPs while the majority of men pursue professional involvements and other interests, they are not summoned for committee work in the same numbers as men. Neither are they more diligent in attendance once summoned to committees (Vallance, 1982a).

The House of Lords
In the 'other' house women made an even later entry than into the Commons. Despite an early abortive attempt by Lady Rhonda to take her seat as a Viscountess in her own right in 1919, following the passage of the Sex Disqualification (Removal) Act, it was not until 1963 that women were admitted under the Peerage Act. Five years earlier the Life Peerages Act 1958 had enabled both men and women to be granted non-hereditary titles and between 1958 and 1970 25 women peers were created; their numbers have very gradually increased and now there are 64 women (5 per cent) out of 1171 members of the Lords (see Table 7.8). Life peers are appointed to membership of the Lords on the basis of distinguished service in politics or other fields of public life and as with other selection processes, the criteria mitigates against the majority of women who are 'hidden from power'. Their access to the Lords is lessened even further by the fact they are completely absent from other peerage promotional groups, such as the Church of England.

It could be argued that what women lack in terms of their numbers in the Lords is made up for by the extent of their political activity. Morgan (1975) reports that 35 out of 43 peeresses

Table 7.9   *The sex of candidates and those elected to the European Parliament in the United Kingdom, 1979, 1984*

	Women		Men		Women as % of total	
	1979	1984	1979	1984	1979	1984
Number of candidates	29	51	244	220	11	19
Number elected	11	12	70	69	14	15
% of candidates elected	38	24	29	31		

Derived from *Dod's Parliamentary Companion* (1980), Conservative National Women's Advisory Council (1985) and *The Times Guide to European Parliament* (1985).

attended more than one-third of the sitting days of the House compared with some 291 men out of 1062. It has been noted that they play a lively part in debates, and as in other spheres of political life, they appear to have a particular interest in matters of social concern so that, for example, they were active in pressing the Lords to amend a National Health Service Bill in order to provide free contraceptive services (Morgan, 1975). Moreover, some women peers have achieved high political office; in 1965, Lady Phillips was the first woman to be made government chief whip and in the same year Lady Wootton was made Deputy Chairman of Committees. The Rt Hon. Baroness Young became leader of the House of Lords in 1981, a post she served in until 1983 (Conservative Women's National Advisory Committee, 1986).

The European Parliament
In the first contest for the 81 United Kingdom seats in the European Parliament held in 1979, 11 per cent of candidates were women of whom 38 per cent were elected – six Conservatives, four Labour and one Scottish Nationalist. This figure was maintained in the 1984 election when 12 women were elected. The comparative success of women shown in Table 7.9 was heralded by the views expressed in a 1978 survey of opinions by nationals of nine member states of the European Community (EEC, 1979). In the United Kingdom a quoted sample of 1351 respondents showed that a small majority – 60 per cent of women and 45 per cent of men – thought it desirable that 'quite a lot of women should be elected to the European Parliament' as against 22 per cent of women and 36 per cent of men who thought it undesirable (the rest were 'don't knows'). Only in France was there a larger

majority of men (57 per cent) holding this favourable view and only in Ireland was the UK majority equalled among women.

The election of a high proportion of the women who did offer themselves as candidates endorsed the views expressed in the same survey about elections in general. Compared with other countries, where the main reason given why more women do not get elected to parliaments was that 'people prefer to vote for men', in the UK (and also Denmark) the most frequent reply among women (42 per cent) and men (37 per cent) was that too few women offer themselves as candidates.

It has been suggested that the European Assembly is not seen as a prestigious or influential body and therefore this accounts for the relative success of women in being elected (Stacey and Price, 1981). Lack of prestige may be reflected in the fact that in both elections, turnout amongst the British electorate was just over 32 per cent compared to 72 per cent at national elections. However, it is possible to surmise that women are both more willing to put themselves forward as candidates and more likely to be selected where there is not a well-established tradition of male dominance.

In 1984, there was a notable increase in the numbers of British women candidates particularly amongst the Liberals and other minor parties. This produced a smaller success rate for women than that which they held in 1979. Altogether, there are 76 women Euro MPs (17 per cent) of whom 16 per cent are from Britain. They take an active part in the Assembly, chairing six of the 18 committees. In addition, the European Parliament has its own committee on Women's Rights with 23 women sitting out of a total of 25 members.

Local government

'There we do things, here it seems all talk,' was the comment made by Ruth Dalton on leaving parliament to return to local politics (Vallance, 1979). She had in fact been 'keeping warm' a constituency for her husband, Hugh Dalton, yet the idea that women prefer local to national politics is a frequent suggestion. This has been argued both on pragmatic grounds, that it is easier for them to combine their supposedly primary role of wife and mother with the work of local government, as well as on the grounds that its concern with domestic and community matters is of immediate importance to them in that role. Chamberlain (1975) suggests that women on a parish council view their work as an extension of their interest and activity in village affairs, being about something concrete that they know and understand. It seems unlikely that this view could as readily be held by women on the powerful, but now defunct, Greater London Council, where they had constituted a relatively high proportion of the membership (20 per cent in 1975), and where it was noted that fears have been expressed about their impact (Sullerot, 1977).

In comparing the relatively greater participation of women in local than in national politics, it is important to remember that they gained entry to local government well before any of them were first granted the parliamentary suffrage: the 1831 Hobhouse Act gave the local vote to all ratepayers, male or female, while the Education Act 1870 permitted the election of school boards by ratepayers of either sex, and women were not barred from standing as candidates (Smellie, 1968). As a result, many years before 1918, women were active in local authorities (Middleton, 1977). Their contribution has been examined by two Royal Commissions: the Committee on the Management of Local Government (Maud Committee, 1966–9) and the Committee of Inquiry into the System of Remuneration of Members of Local Authorities (Robinson Committee, 1977). The Robinson Report was based on a sample of 6980 councillors out of a total of 25,741, and a 73 per cent response rate was achieved. This compares with a sample of 3721, for Maud and a response rate of 88 per cent.

Candidates and councillors

The Robinson Report used the Maud data as a baseline, so that comparisons could be made over the intervening decade. The Report noted an increase of female councillors from 12 to 17 per cent of the total but commented on the continued under-representation of a group that comprised over 52 per cent of the population. However, the numbers of women councillors varies with geographical location; 18 per cent of council members in English shire counties were women compared with 13 per cent in metropolitan counties and 11 per cent in Welsh counties (Bristow, 1978a). Since local government was reorganized in 1974, there has been an increase in the proportion of women councillors across all local authorities (Bristow, 1980) and in the 1985 county council elections they had just under 20 per cent representation (Karran and Bochel, 1986).

There is a much higher percentage of female candidates in local than in national elections and in contrast to parliamentary elections, the Conservative party nominates many more female candidates than does the Labour Party (Bristow, 1978a; Le Lohe, 1976), as shown in Table 7.10. Equally, it is in the Conservative-controlled districts, such as the counties of the south of England, that women's representation is highest. On this basis, Bristow

Table 7.10 Women candidates by party in English and Welsh shire counties, 1985

| | England | | Wales | |
	% female candidates	% all candidates	% female candidates	% all candidates
Labour	29	21	29	12
Conservative	32	24	24	23
Alliance	32	26	19	21
Plaid Cymru	—	—	10	14
Independent	3	16	14	10

Derived from Tables F and 6, Karran and Bochel (1986).

(1978a) concludes that the strength of the Conservative Party in county government (except for London) is the single best indicator of women's success. As an explanation of this, Bristow (1980) argues that there are more women eligible for candidacy amongst unemployed middle-class women active in local voluntary associations. However, Hills (1982) suggests that because Bristow utilizes data on elected women councillors, he is therefore measuring the activity of parties in the placement of candidates rather than recruitment to the pool or eligibility for local government candidacy.

As in national politics, women do not put themselves forward for selection at the same rate as men, and when they do they have slightly less chance of obtaining a winnable seat (Bristow, 1978b). In England in the 1985 county elections, 44 per cent of women elected were Conservative compared to 28 per cent for Labour, while in Wales, only 15 per cent of women councillors were Conservative as against 51 per cent for Labour (see Table 7.11). Compared to men, women had an equal or better chance of success in the minor parties, with the exception of the Alliance in Wales.

Profile of local councillors
The age distribution of the two sexes in local councils in 1976 was similar in that they are well represented in the 55–69 age group (Robinson Committee, 1977). There is a suggestion that politically active women are older than women in the population as a whole because that is when they are freed from the constraints of childrearing (Maud, 1967). However, in London boroughs 61 per cent of members were between 25 and 54 years of age (Robinson, 1977). Hills (1980) notes that women activists within the Labour

Table 7.11   Men and women councillors by party in English and Welsh shire counties, 1985

	England			Wales		
	% men elected	% women elected	women's handicap ratio	% men elected	% women elected	women's handicap ratio
Labour	36	31	0.8	72	55	0.8
Conservative	48	43	0.9	29	19	0.6
Alliance	24	25	1.0	28	6	0.2
Plaid, Cymru	—	—	—	15	22	1.4
Independent	28	39	1.4	63	44	0.7

Handicap ratio = $\dfrac{\text{number of women elected}}{\text{number of men elected}}$

Devised from Table 7, Karran and Bochel (1986).

Party tend to be those with young children whose community involvement is high. Some of these women may go on to become councillors despite the time-constraints of child-rearing. In other features of the councillor profile – education, income, occupation, dwelling tenure – the sexes were also not differentiated except in so far as 7 per cent of women classified themselves as housewives in 1976, as they had in 1964 (Robinson Committee, 1977).

The marital status of women and men is distinguished in the Robinson Report and shows that four times as many women (17 per cent) as men (4 per cent) are widowed, divorced or separated, and in this respect the sex differential accurately reflects the proportions in the total population. It is also possible that sex differentials on marital status reflect the fact that it is easier for those women without marital ties to be active in political life. Evidence from studies of Dutch local councillors (Van Arnhem and Leijenaar, 1981) showed that it is more important for women than for men, that the family, both spouse and children, should accept their political activities.

Local government activity

In examining the local government activity of councillors (see Table 7.12), the Robinson survey discovered that, while women spent slightly less time than men on council and committee meetings, they spent rather more time on dealing with electors' problems.

Women councillors also differ from men in the areas of council work they appear to find most attractive. Bristow (1978c) showed

Table 7.12   Percentage of total time spent on council duties given to various types of duty, by sex of councillor

	Women	Men
Council and committee meetings		
Attendance at	26	30
Preparation for	21	23
Travelling to and from	10	10
Other duties		
Party meetings	7	7
Dealing with electors problems	19	16
Meeting organizations on behalf of council	11	10
Other	5	5
Total	100	100

Derived from Table 23, Robinson Committee (1977).

that women most commonly chaired committees on the social services, education and amenities, and least often chaired policy, planning and transportation committees. An unpublished study by Bruce (Bristow, 1978c) of a sample of 646 district councillors in Greater Manchester found a similar sex differential in membership of committees, women being found preponderantly on education and social services committees. It is not known whether this is the result of women's choice or whether these are the committees they are most likely to be offered because they deal with matters believed to be their primary concern (Evans, 1980).

Local government offices
Just as fewer women candidates are elected than are nominated, so fewer of them become committee chairmen and fewer still attain the post of chairman, vice-chairman and leader of the council (Bristow, 1978c). This pattern of participation persists even ten years later (see Table 7.13). This was not so in 1964, when the Maud Report said of all types of local authority: 'Women are nearly as well represented (11 per cent) amongst the chairman [of authorities] as are men (12 per cent) ... and ... are just as likely as men to be chairmen of committees.' Bristow (1978c) shows that in 1977–78 only 7 per cent of women councillors held chairs as against 10 per cent of men, and these, as noted above, are predominantly in committees devoted to personal services (a pattern similar to one of ministerial offices held by women in national government). There had, however, been an improvement in the number of committee chairs held by women in county

Table 7.13   Chairmen/mayors and vice-chairmen/deputies of English county councils and metropolitan districts, 1987, by sex (percentages)

	Chairmen		Vice-Chairmen	
	Women	Men	Women	Men
English Non-Metropolitan (39)				
Party in Power				
Conservative (23)	4	96	17	83
Labour (12)	17	83	25	75
L/All (4)	0	100	0	100
All councils	8	92	18	82

	Mayor		Deputy Mayor	
	Women	Men	Women	Men
Metropolitan Districts (36)				
Party in power				
Conservative (4)	25	75	25	75
Labour (32)	21	79	19	81
All councils	19	81	17	83
London Districts (32)				
Party in power				
Conservative (13)	31	69	16	84
Labour (16)	25	75	6	94
L/All (3)	0	100	0	100
All councils	25	75	9	91

Derived from Municipal Year Book (1987).

councils between 1976 (9.8 per cent) and 1978 (11.2 per cent), and this may have been due to the swing to the Conservatives, since in local government this appears to be the party most favourable to the advancement of women.

Local government and parliamentary candidatures
Local government experience has often been considered an avenue to parliament for both men and women (Brown, 1980). In 1974 some 40 per cent of the Labour Members of Parliament and 30 per cent of the Conservatives had been local authority councillors (Mellors, 1978). Using data on all the 1758 MPs who have successfully contested one of more of the ten elections between 1945 and October 1974, Mellors produced a table showing their previous local government experience. A striking difference appears between women and men Conservatives, where almost 50 per cent of the women had served on a local authority compared

with 25 per cent of the men. He concurs with an earlier view (Currell, 1974) that, together with party activism and voluntary work, municipal experience ranks as 'probably the most significant pre-election experience' of MPs. For Conservative women, in particular, whose chances of success in local government appear greater than for Labour women, it may be an invaluable way of establishing credibility in the political arena.

Public bodies

In other areas of political life, information about sex differentials is difficult to obtain. Official data on the sex composition of the public boards has only recently become available, although since 1977 annual surveys of public bodies have been conducted by the Equal Opportunities Commission (EOC). At national level, public bodies are composed partly of people appointed by a minister, and partly appointed by outside bodies. Figures from the EOC surveys do not exactly verify the sex distribution as some of the departments surveyed only gave figures for ministerial appointments.

Over twenty years ago Maureen Colquhoun, speaking in the House of Commons on her Private Member's Bill on the Balance of the Sexes, estimated that there were 4500 jobs on 174 public bodies and corporations, councils and commissions and nearly all were occupied by men. The Bill, which sought to increase the number of women on such public bodies, was not passed into law. Since then, more women have been appointed as for example, efforts to involve them in industrial tribunals led to an increase of 75 women on the tribunals in two years, so that by 1974, of the 1200 members, 125 (11 per cent) were women (Milburn, 1976). In 1977, 18 per cent of appointments to the boards of nationalized industries and quasi-government agencies were women, and a third of those were appointed by the Scottish Office (Hills, 1981a). Between 1977 and 1981, there was a gradual increase in women's representation from 19.5 to 23.3 per cent (EOC, 1984); in 1986 the 'official' figure for female representation on public bodies was given as only 19 per cent (see Table 7.14).

Whilst the numbers of women on public bodies has increased, the pattern of representation has essentially remained unchanged because in many areas women continue to be unrepresented or under-represented. An investigation conducted by the EOC concluded that the low proportion of women in the public appointments field was a result of 'the use of particular channels through which names are sought' and 'most of the organisations from which it is customary – often legally necessary – to seek

Table 7.14   Sex composition of public bodies by department, 1986

Dept	Executive % women	Advisory % women	Tribunal % women	Total NDPBs Men	Total NDPBs Women	Women as % of all
MAFF	3.2	3.7	3.4	1601	57	3.4
OAL	12.6	10.0	—	297	41	12.1
Cab Off	—	46.0	—	68	58	46.0
COI	—	14.2	—	6	1	14.2
MOD	3.2	4.4	—	429	19	4.2
DES	11.0	13.6	—	507	71	12.3
DE	13.2	14.4	19.5	5066	986	16.3
DEn	0.0	0.0	—	97	0	0.0
DOE	6.6	12.4	16.5	3822	653	14.6
FCO/ODA	7.3	3.0	14.3	190	12	5.9
DHSS	32.8	22.3	26.3	7815	2691	25.6
HO	20.0	28.9	12.6	2296	1001	30.4
IR	—	—	7.0	4358	297	6.4
LCD	—	18.7	11.1	1797	396	18.1
NIO	14.6	17.8	19.3	2259	497	18.0
SCA	—	0.0	20.0	29	6	17.1
SO	14.5	15.2	50.9	3064	1279	29.4
OFTEL	—	18.2	—	18	4	18.2
TR & IND	30.6	1.9	0.0	1046	284	21.4
TRANSP.	1.4	6.0	0.0	176	6	3.3
HMT	3.3	11.5	—	75	7	8.5
WO	12.8	16.2	11.1	1074	163	13.2
Totals	15.1	16.8	20.8	36090	8529	19.1

Derived from *Cabinet Office* (1986), p. x

names are male-dominated, and are unlikely to volunteer many women's names' (EOC, 1984).

At local level there is also a lack of election or appointment of women to positions involving participation in public services, judging by a survey conducted by the British Federation of University Women (EOC, 1985b). In addition, patterns of participation reflect those at national level with women predominating on committees relating to health and family and being almost absent from others such as industrial tribunals. Organizations canvassed included local government, consumer councils, tribunals and judicial organizations, community relations councils and education and health services. Appointments to public life are made either from personal contact or sponsorship through membership of a prior organization and whilst the proportion of women is high in education services (47 per cent), they are lowest in local government (22 per cent) from which many local public bodies recruit. Although there are fewer women than men in public life, they hold proportionately more office and work longer hours (13.22 hours per month compared to 12.15 hours for men). Public service contribution was greatest among women in the 50–59 age range whereas men were older (60–69). Working women with full-time jobs contributed the highest number of hours which might suggest that women are most active when family responsibility lessens whilst men offer more time as work commitments decline.

The civil service
The civil service is the executive branch of the political system and is a career entered into by appointment or competitive examination. As the modern industrial state has become increasingly complex, so have the civil servants become increasingly involved in the management of that state. The extent of their political power is now frequently under discussion, but women are absent from the public debate, since they are mainly concentrated in the clerical group or in the junior grades of executive and administrative posts. In 1979, they constituted 39 per cent of civil servants and by 1982 their representation had risen to 48 per cent (Table 7.14). There are currently no female permanent secretaries (the top grade of the structure), although there have in the past been three: Evelyn Sharp in the Ministry of Housing and Local Government (1955–56), Mary Smieton at the Ministry of Education (1959–63) and Mildred Ridelsdall in the Department of Health and Social Security (1971–73). As such, the employment of women in the civil service reflects the patterns of employment of women in the labour market, and must be viewed within this context (see Chapter 6).

In 1970 a departmental committee was set up under Kemp-Jones to consider the employment of women in the civil service and to examine ways in which the opportunities for their employment might be improved. It discovered that, although there had been an increase between 1950 and 1970 in the percentage of women in all classes except the Science and Technical II, the numbers were still small. Only in the clerical group had there been a striking increase, to the point where there were then about equal numbers of men and women in that branch of the service. In monitoring the progress made in implementing the recommendations of that report, the department noted in 1975 that a third of all entrants as administrative trainees (previously Assistant Principal grade), who are usually graduates, were now women, a proportion approximately equal to the number of

*Table 7.15   Women as proportion of total staff^a in the various grades^b of
the civil service, 1979 and 1982*

	1979		1982	
	Women as % of total	Total Staff	Women as % of total	Total Staff
Permanent secretary	0	41	0	40
Deputy secretary	2	158	3	143
Under-secretary	4	615	5	554
Executive directing (middle)	4	52	2	97
Executive directing (lower)	0	18	3	152
Assistant secretary	5	1,155	4	4,000
Senior principal	3	710	8	4,200
Principal	8	4,456	7	13,900
Senior executive officer	8	8,060	6	22,900
Higher executive officer	16	22,382	12	50,900
Executive officer	37	47,395	27	132,100
Clerical officer	65	89,436	61	185,900
Clerical assistant	79	75,329	81	119,800

a. Part-time staff counted as half units (1979) and whole units (1982).
b. Staff's substantive grade at 1 January 1979 and 1 July 1982.
Derived from Table 4, *Civil Service Statistics* (1980); and Table 2, Joint Review
Group (1983).

women graduating, while women entrants to the executive office
and equivalent grades averaged 43 per cent in five years 1970–4
(*Civil Service Statistics*, 1975). As a result of the increase in the
number of women entrants in the decade since the Kemp-Jones
Report was published, there has been an increase in the proportion
of women in the administrative, executive and clerical grades (see
Table 7.15).

When women do succeed in entering the civil service, it appears
that they have less chance of promotion, as the report of the
Fulton Committee (1968) showed by comparing the 1967 positions
of women and men established before 1940; only 37 per cent of
women compared to 70 per cent of men were in the upper grades.
In their discussion of the reasons for the sex discrepancies in
employment, the Kemp-Jones Committee (*Civil Service* 1977)
found little discrimination against women but commented on the
expectation that there would be unbroken service for all entrants
until retirement – an expectation that militated against otherwise
good conditions of service for women – and they recommended
measures to help women combine family responsibilities with a
career. A slight improvement in promotion prospects for women,
particularly among those with between five and nine years'

Table 7.16   Women and men[a] promoted in the civil service by seniority band, 1981 (percentages)

| | | Seniority (years) | | | | | |
		Under 5	5–9	10–14	15–19	Over 20	Total
SEO to PRI							
	men	2.2	5.4	4.5	2.7	(4.6)	3.7
	women	2.9	4.4	(0.9)	—	(16.7)	3.2
HEO to SEO							
	men	2.1	4.8	4.7	2.8	3.7	3.4
	women	1.4	4.1	3.6	—	—	2.3
EO to HEO							
	men	1.8	4.0	2.5	1.9	0.7	2.7
	women	1.0	3.1	2.9	1.5	(0.5)	1.8
CO to EO							
	men	2.9	6.2	3.8	2.2	1.4	3.9
	women	1.3	4.6	2.1	1.2	0.6	2.4
CA to CO							
	men	10.8	5.2	2.5	(1.8)	(2.4)	9.3
	women	8.9	3.3	2.0	1.7	1.6	7.0

a. Part-timers counted as whole units.
Figures in brackets refer to rate where the number of promotions was less than ten.
Derived from Table 9, Joint Review Group (1983).

service, was also noted, but voluntary wastage among women (12 per cent) was still more than twice that of men (5 per cent) across all age groups. Brimelow (1981) suggests that any discrimination does not stem from promotion boards but from assessments of suitability for promotion, and that such prejudices may be most telling at the level of promotion to higher executive officer (see Table 7.16). She concluded that, while there may be bias in committees that select for promotion, the most obvious explanation for the exclusion of women from top positions lies in women leaving or interrupting their careers to have children.

Between 1980 and 1982, a Joint Review Group monitored the employment opportunities in the civil service for women. They concluded that despite the recommendations of the Kemp-Jones Report being accepted as policy, they have not always been applied and therefore the position of women had changed very little since 1975. In their recommendations, they reiterated many of the Kemp-Jones proposals such as the restructuring of work patterns, career development and the provision of childcare and maternity/paternity facilities.

Pressure groups

Another major avenue of political involvement is through activity in pressure groups. Apart from trade unions and the cooperative movement, most pressure groups are not affiliated to political parties although there is often a covert commitment to political causes. However, membership of such organizations provides a channel of communication to government for the purpose of protecting group interests and/or promoting causes. In addition, participation in such groups, particularly at the higher levels of organization, is an avenue for promotion into the formal, political structures. The most notable example is trade union membership; in general, there are fewer women than men in trade unions but even in unions with a substantial female membership, there are disproportionately low numbers of women executive council members (see Chapter 6).

It has been estimated (Shipley, 1979) that there are some 2000 pressure groups and representative associations, but the sex composition of their membership is not published. However, Shipley does include information obtained by questionnaire on 600 groups; in the twelve that were listed as Women's Organizations, where it might be expected that the majority of subscribers would be female, there were 22,100 members. These figures excluded the 417,000 members of the Women's Institutes and the 210,000 members of the Townswomen's Guild, which, while they are non-political, may lead to activity in local politics (Chamberlain, 1975). The most overtly political pressure group for women is perhaps The 300 Group which was established in 1979 in order to highlight the disproportionately low numbers of women in political office and to promote women to a political career.

It has been suggested (Evans, 1980) that phenomena such as the Women's Aid Movement and the National Abortion Campaign demonstrate that women's political interest and activity are high when focused on matters of intense political concern to them but which are often thought to be outside or above the customary political agenda of party politics. Campbell (1987a) notes that amongst the Conservative women she interviewed, there was a 'profound pessimism about all political parties' which probably reflects a feeling that the agenda of 'politics' is devised by men and tends to ignore matters of most concern to women (Goot and Reid, 1975). If so we might expect to find the major extent of women's political activity to be outside the 'public' political arena (Randall, 1982). In addition, given the constraints on women's participation in the public political forum, activity in pressure

Table 7.17   Female chairs of national political parties, 1926–1985

	Conservative	Labour	Liberal
Number	18	15	6
% of all chairmen	31	25	11

Derived from Conservative Women's National Advisory Council (1980, 1985).

groups provides an 'easier' outlet for political action. On collective action, gender differences have been recorded with young women (18–24) registering the highest scores whilst women over the age of 65 obtained the lowest scores, compared to men (Jowell and Witherspoon, 1985). This broadly linear relationship with age becomes curvilinear on individual action, where women in the 45–54 age group have the highest score (the same as men) whilst in all other age groups their personal efficacy score was lower than men's.

Party membership
Information on the sex composition of the general membership and of the local and regional executives of the national political parties is not readily available. The Maud Committee on Local Government Organization in 1967, investigating what they described as the 'community conscious elector', found in their sample of 989 men and 1195 women that 7 per cent of men and 8 per cent of women said they were paid-up members of political parties. It is estimated that overall only 10 per cent of the population belong to a political party (Crewe et al., 1976).

In 1971 the National Labour Women's Advisory Committee report on Women and the Labour Party said that 'although no analysis exists it appears that in the majority of constituencies, on the General Commitee and the executive Committee, there are more men than women', and went on:

> The imbalance in the power position of men and women can be clearly discerned in Labour youth organisations. The 1971 Young Socialists Conference had only 25 per cent girls as delegates and there are no girls at all out of a total membership of 11 on the National Committee of Young Socialists. On the National Organisation of Labour Students, there are three girls out of a membership of 22.

The existence of separate women's sections in the parties, while sometimes a cause of controversy, has at least ensured women's presence in the national party executives, and, as shown in Table 7.17,was fundamental to their appearance in the chair of the national party (Vallance, 1979). The NEC of the Labour Party has a 'closed' section for women, so that there are always at least five on that body; in 1986/7 there were eight women (28.5 per cent). While the Central Council of the Conservative Party may be composed of nearly 50 per cent women, the legal requirement is only that one third should be women, the other two thirds being represented by men and young people (Brown, 1980).

Data on the sex composition of selection boards is not provided by any of the political parties although from personal correspondence with the SDP Political Organizer, it was stated that 'selection committees are frequently chaired by women who act in this capacity according to their role as an Area Party Officer'. Rush (1969) found that in the selection committees he observed, only three out of nine members were women whilst he estimated that half the members of local Conservative associations were women. He concludes that 'Whatever their numerical strength, women do not dominate selection, nor would it seem that their influence is commensurate with their numbers.'

Voting behaviour
Women were granted equal suffrage with men in 1928; for the previous ten years, from 1918, while all men could vote at the age of 21, women had to wait until they were aged 30, in order that they might not outnumber men at the polls in the aftermath of the death toll of the Great War.

Voting is the most basic and freely accessible level of political activity, and over three-quarters of the population in Britain exercise their suffrage at general elections: 72.7 per cent in June 1983 and 75.3 per cent in June 1987. No 'official' information on voters other than turnout and votes cast for each party is published, and other information has to be obtained through opinion polls or academic surveys. There is little written about sex differential in turnout – which may be because it does not exist: an early analysis showed that, where non-voters and voters for other than the main parties were counted together, they constituted 16 per cent women and 17 per cent men (Blondel, 1966).

Women and Conservatism
The party preferences of men and women has been of great interest and concern and the idea that women are more Conservative than men appears in many texts (Pulzer, 1967). Using Gallup Poll data for 1970, Rose (1974) showed that a Conservative bias could be located among working-class women though he noted that there is a particular preponderance of

Table 7.18   Voting in the 1983 general election by class and sex (percentages)

	Conservative	Labour	Alliance	Other
Salariat:				
Women	54	14	30	2
Men	54	14	31	1
Routine non-manual				
Women	45	26	27	2
Men	48	23	27	2
Petty bourgeoise				
Women	72	11	17	0
Men	70	13	16	1
Foremen and technicians				
Women	48	30	21	0
Men	48	24	26	1
Working class				
Women	29	46	24	1
Men	30	51	17	2
All voters				
Women	44	28	27	1
Men	46	30	24	1

Working class combine VI and VII. Salariat combine Classes I & II.
Derived from Table 2.6, Heath, Jowell and Curtice (1985).

women of pensionable age among the working class and there is a tendency for older people to vote Conservative. Other opinion polls have reinforced this explanation (Evans, 1980) and though a National Opinion Poll in 1978 found women favouring Conservatives in each age group, by voting day in 1979 the Conservatives collected exactly the same percentage of women's and men's votes. Men's voting has swung proportionately more towards Conservatism since 1974, whilst in women the swing was towards the Liberals (Kellner, 1980). An analysis of the 1983 general election (see Table 7.18) finds no major differences in the voting behaviour of men and women within a class, with the exception that working-class women are more likely to vote for the Alliance than working-class men (Heath, Jowell and Curtice, 1985). A Mori Poll of 1985 showed that for the first time in many years, support for the Labour Party amongst women was greater than for either of the other two parties, although Tory preference continues to remain high among older women. Therefore, Campbell (1987a) concludes that, on present trends, 'men have been moving to the right and women have been moving away from the right'. Party allegiance is not determined by sex alone (and for men this has never been assumed) and changes in the composition of gender, age and occupational groups inevitably will produce changes in how the electorate votes. On this basis, the idea of a 'women's vote' and women's Conservatism must be regarded as mythical.

Political opinions
A related argument is that women hold more conservative views than men but there is some difficulty in defining such views, as well as locating either consistent or coherent opinions of individuals or groups (Evans, 1980).

Francis and Peele (1978) found a divergence along sex lines on most issues but a convergence of views among the younger age groups. Once again, the 'conservative' tendency was highest in the older age groups, so for example, more women preferred tax cuts to social services and this trend increased with age. However, an opinion poll carried out by Mori in February 1981 produced inconclusive evidence on sex differences in conservative views, while a national quota sample of 1911 respondents showed only marginal differences; for example, 2 per cent more women than men believed that more industries should be nationalized, and 5 per cent more men than women believed public schools should be abolished.

There is some evidence that women are more conservative than men in their views on parliamentary institutions: a Mori survey of July 1980 showed that 45 per cent of men but only 35 per cent of women favoured the abolition of the House of Lords. On the other hand, Campbell's review of opinion polls on nuclear issues found an enduring gender gap in which men could be labelled more 'conservative' (Campbell, 1987a). Norris (1986) has examined conservative attitudes in recent British elections with the aim of establishing whether America's gender gap and increase in men's conservatism is applicable to Britain. She concluded that, with a few notable exceptions, such as use of troops in Northern Ireland, nuclear issues and race relations, there is no ideological difference between sexes. Her evidence concurs with an analysis of a number of earlier NOP polls (Evans, 1980) and whilst women are not generally more right-wing than men, they cannot be labelled more left-wing (see Table 7.19).

Political socialization
The comparative lack of political participation by women has been generally acknowledged, and the argument, or myth, that women

Table 7.19   *Women's and men's attitudes towards tax reductions, social services, New Commonwealth immigrants and nuclear issues (percentages)*

	Women	Men
Would prefer		
Tax cuts	68	63
Increases in social services	24	31
'Don't know'	9	6
Would		
Assist sending immigrants home	20	
Allow to stay put but stop further immigration	50	48
Allow in immigrant families and skilled workers	21	21
Other or 'Don't know'	10	11
Nuclear issues		
against cruise	64	51
against Trident	60	53
because of cost	14	30
because it is nuclear	68	43

Derived from Tables 5 and 8, Francis and Peele (1978); and Campbell (1987a).

are less politically knowledgeable, interested and active than men has been described as the 'orthodoxy of women's lesser achievement' (Evans, 1980). The idea of apolitical women has a long history: the nineteenth-century prime minister, Gladstone, thought that granting women the suffrage would 'trespass upon their delicacy, their purity, their refinement, the elevation of their whole nature', and as recently as 1955 Duverger wrote:

> While women have legally ceased to be minors they still have the mentality of minors in many fields and, particularly in politics, they usually accept paternalism on the part of men. The man, husband, fiancé, lover or myth, is the mediator between them and the political world.

This has often been explained by early differential political socialization of boys and girls. Stradling (1978), in a nationwide survey of adolescents based on questionnaires administered to 4033 pupils in a stratified sample of 100 schools, located lower levels of political knowledge among girls than boys (Table 7.20). At an earlier date, however, Dowse and Hughes (1971) had not found significant sex differences in general political socialization.

Table 7.20   Percentage of girls and boys with high scores^a on aspects of political knowledge

	Girls (N = 1972)	Boys (N = 2061)
Political office holders	29	51
Local politics	15	21
Political institutions	8	15
Issue awareness	18	28
International affairs	8	19

a. Those obtaining high marks on a set of questions about politics.
Derived from Table 21a, Stradling (1978).

While finding that, controlling for education, girls tended to be less well informed politically than boys, there was no difference between them when asked to classify themselves as politically interested. A more recent inquiry using extensive interviews rather than questionnaires has disputed the existence of early political sex differences among working-class adolescents in Britain (Wormald, 1983). This would support the suggestion that questionnaires used in political knowledge surveys have a sex bias (Goot and Reid, 1975), and that this accounts in part for any perceived sex differentials. Further, it must be noted that the very concept of political socialization as the manner in which humans 'learn their political behaviour early and well and persist in it' (Hyman, 1959) has been under attack since its heyday in the 1960s (Marsh, 1971). Even if there was reliable evidence which showed girls to be more passive than boys, there is no evidence of a direct link between early political learning and later political behaviour. In short, political behaviour may be learnt but not persisted in and therefore adult experiences may be a more potent influence on patterns of political participation.

The notion that adult women are less politically active than men has been debated in many texts (Bourque and Grossholtz, 1974; Randall, 1982). The standard of political behaviour has been measured by political scientists as a set of roles although even using this criteria it seems that sex differences in political activity are decreasing except at the level of holding political office (Verba, Nie and Kim, 1978). Social changes effect change in the behaviour of groups so for example, the increasing employment of women outside the home has been noted in America to produce greater politicization of women (Andersen, 1975). Similarly, changes in policies relating to issues of home life for example, education and welfare has politicized some women into becoming involved in community action, although generally women's relative marginality persists (Mayo, 1977).

Overview

The overall picture of sex differences in political participation is one which is gradually narrowing in that women's political activity has increased where access if freely open to them. However, in any field where selection and competition is involved, women still lag behind men. This may be due to women's acceptance of a subordinate political role, what Lane (1961) has called the 'properly dependent role of her sex', although it seems more likely that they are held back by situational or institutional constraints and the demands of the dual role of mother and employee. In addition, there is the knowledge that politics is a man's game played according to the rules made by men for men as evidenced by Shirley Williams reportedly comparing the Commons to a public boys' school where the traditions, rules, uniform, language and non-work facilities are all masculine (*Observer*, 1987).

From the evidence given in this chapter, breaking into the male-dominated preserve is a slow and difficult process which is why Stacey and Price (1981) question not why so few women participate but why so many do. It seems likely that, if women are made aware of the possibilities of entry into political life, are sustained in that effort, and see increasing signs of success for the pioneers, they might obtain truly equal political participation in the nation's political system and no longer find that they have equal rights but apparently, unequal opportunities to participate in the public political forum.

8 Involvement in crime

Erica Stratta

An examination of the official statistics over the past fifty years underlines the fact that women, in contrast to men, form a very small proportion of the criminal population. The effect of this was that for many years research was mainly carried out into crimes committed by men, as they constituted the majority of those involved in criminal acts, and generalizations, if any, about female crime were derived from this research. Women's crime was seen to be a kind of appendage to that of men's.

Crime, however, is a social problem, unlike the other areas examined in this book. A continuing increase in crime, and of offences committed by women in particular, has not surprisingly spurred on the search for explanations and solutions to the problem. One result of this was the increasing recognition, since the 1960s, of the sex variable as a contributory factor to criminal behaviour. Early research into this focused at the level of the individual, and sought to isolate supposedly innate female characteristics, such as passivity, specific bodily processes and low intelligence, as reasons both for the involvement of women in crime and the kinds of crime carried out by them (Pollak, 1961; Cowie, Slater and Cowie, 1968). This was often considered in conjunction with an underlying assumption that for women, unlike men, criminal behaviour was contrary to normal gender roles, and therefore pathological.

However, relatively recently this emphasis on 'innate' characteristics has been challenged, resulting in a shift from intrinsic and biological explanations of women's crime to an emphasis on the effect of the social structure of the society, and of the social processes. Thus there has been a shift to a concern with sex-specific structural factors which might explain the extent and form of women's criminality as opposed to that of men; these factors include women's employment experience, their lack of power, the effect of gender stereotyping by male-dominated agencies of social control, and definitions of legality which reflect masculine values. This focus on a special theory to explain female as opposed to male criminality has been challenged, however, on the grounds that it is reductionist and ahistorical; the search for a

Table 8.1   *Percentage of persons found guilty of indictable offences, by sex*

	1930	1950	1960	1970	1975	1979	1985
Females	11	14	12	13	15	14	13
Males	89	86	88	87	85	86	87

Derived from Table 4, Smart (1979), and Table 5.8, *Criminal Statistics for England and Wales, 1985* (1986).

monocausal sex-specific explanation, it is argued, is as irrelevant to female crime as it is to male (Cousins, 1980; Carlen, 1985).

However, the effect of these changes in emphasis has been to challenge the validity of the official statistics and accepted definitions of illegal behaviour. These are now no longer considered as given, but have come to be considered as highly problematic, as much a reflection of the male-dominated processes of social control, and therefore of power relationships between the sexes, as they are an indication of crime in general, and sex differences in particular, within our society (Rosenblum, 1975; Smart, 1976).

This chapter traces the shifting debate and also considers other important factors relevant to a discussion of sex and gender differences in relation to crime. It begins with an examination of the criminal statistics (these, however, are recognized as being problematic), moves to a consideration of 'the dark figure' and its implications for the official data, analyses the statistical evidence related to the processes of social control as exemplified by sentencing policy and penal institutions, and finally examines sex differences in relation to the experience of victimization.

Thus the argument tries to suggest that explanations for the differential involvement of women and men in crime are more complex than the evidence presented either by the statistics or by any one theoretical perspective.

The following section demonstrates that the evidence is now considerable on the limitations of the official statistics, as sources of information on the extent and form of criminal behaviour in our society (Wiles, 1970; Box, 1971; Bottomley and Coleman, 1981).

Sex and crime: the official statistics

It has already been pointed out above that crime is very much a male-dominated activity. A scan through the official statistics and the volumes of research into deviance as a whole, and juvenile delinquency in particular, confirms this. Table 8.1 gives details, over a 55-year period, of the sex ratio of adult offenders.

While the proportion of women in comparison to men has risen slightly during this period, male offenders continue to account for approximately 85 per cent of all persons found guilty of indictable offences in England and Wales. Recent research in the USA has shown that the figure is over 90 per cent male, if the sample is limited to offenders who have experienced four or more previous arrests (Datesman and Scarpetti, 1980).

Traditionally, it has been argued that the low level of female involvement is one reason why they, unlike male offenders, have attracted very little attention until recently, either from researchers or from the public in general (Heidensohn, 1968; Walker, 1973). A further reason for this lack of attention may well be due to the fact that the kinds of crime with which women have been traditionally associated, such as prostitution, are often victimless. There is also considerable emphasis on the part of the police and courts in linking female juveniles to what are commonly termed juvenile-status offences, such as truancy, moral danger and illicit sexual activity (which are illegal only because the offender is under age) – which means that female delinquency has tended to be seen as a relatively minor problem. This is in contrast to the treatment of male offenders, whose behaviour is more frequently categorized as criminal offence (Ingleby, 1960; Richardson, 1969; Smart, 1976). This attitude has been reinforced by the fact that status offences are no longer considered criminal once women have reached the age of 18.

The last decade, however, has seen increasing recognition of the relevance of the sex variable in any general theories of deviance (Simon, 1975; Harris, 1977; Box, 1983). This is, in part, a reflection of the recent interest in women's studies in female emancipation; it could also be related to what is thought to be a dramatic rise in the female crime rate and to the subsequent speculation that, as women move into what has been traditionally a male-dominated activity, this reflects a break from gender-role behaviour. For example, between 1969 and 1978, in the category of violent offences against the person (excluding sexual offences), female crime rose by 192 per cent in comparison to 86 per cent in the case of male offences. Further, the dramatic presentation in the media of the activities of women as members of radical revolutionary groups, and as gun-carrying hijackers and bank robbers, has heightened the public awareness of female deviance, and has mirrored the evidence that female involvement in crime is increasing. Percentage increases, however, have to be measured against the actual figures on which they are based. The number of female criminals in any single category is so small that in

Table 8.2   Offenders found guilty of indictable offences, England and Wales 1969, 1977 and 1985

	1969 Females	Males	1977 Females	Males	1985 Females	Males
Number of offenders (000s)						
Violence against the person	1.1	19.7	3.5	39.1	3.6	43.8
Sexual offences	—[a]	6.5	—[a]	6.9	0.1	5.9
Burglary	1.8	65.1	2.4	67.7	2.1	67.4
Robbery	0.1	2.4	0.2	3.0	0.2	4.2
Theft and handling stolen goods	33.3	153.5	54.0	179.8	42.1[b]	173.0[b]
Fraud and forgery	2.5	12.1	4.5	16.4	5.4	20.0
Criminal damage	0.8	18.5	0.6	8.3	0.8	10.5
Other (excluding motoring offences)	0.7	3.8	1.7	13.6	3.6[b]	30.5[b]
Total	40.4	281.6	66.9	334.8	58.0	355.3
Percentage of offenders						
Violence against the person	2.7	7.0	5.2+	11.7+	6.2+	12.3+
Sexual offences	—[a]	2.3	—[a]	2.1−	0.2+	1.7−
Burglary	4.5	23.1	3.6−	20.2−	3.6	19.0−
Robbery	0.3	0.8	0.3	0.9+	0.3	1.2+
Theft and handling stolen goods	82.5	54.5	80.7−	53.7−	72.6−	48.7−
Fraud and forgery	6.2	4.3	6.7+	4.9+	9.3+	5.6+
Criminal damage	2.1	6.6	0.9−	2.5−	1.4+	3.0+
Other (excluding motor offences)	1.6	1.4	2.5+	4.1+	6.2+	8.6+

a. Less than 50 offenders.
b. The size of this figure is in part affected by the fact that, from 1978 onwards, offenders found guilty of 'abstracting electricity' were no longer categorized under 'Other offences' but under 'Theft and handling stolen goods'.
Derived from Table 5.8, *Criminal Statistics for England and Wales, 1985* (1986).

comparison to males (see Table 8.2) an increase of 1000 can represent a considerable increase when translated into percentage terms. By comparison, the number of male offenders has to increase by a much greater amount in order to make the same impact (Table 8.2).

A comparison of the total number of female offenders in 1969 with that of 1977 (Table 8.2) shows an increase of approximately 26,500 (66 per cent); in the case of males, the increase is approximately 53,200 (16 per cent). Comparison between 1977 and 1985 (Table 8.2) shows the total number of female offenders to have decreased by 13 per cent whereas that for males has increased by 6 per cent. What explanations might be offered for such shifts over a fifteen-year period, particularly in the case of females? Undoubtedly the figures are indicative of actual increases and decreases, but other important influences on how these overall totals are constituted are likely to be such factors as changes in public and police priorities as to the importance of particular groups of offenders (for example, women) and offences (for example domestic violence); an increase in police manpower and efficiency, resulting in more offenders being caught; the size of the base figure; new offence definitions (Criminal Law Act 1977) and counting procedures which affect particular offence categories (for example, Criminal Damage). It is for this reason that 1977 has been selected as the base line for comparison throughout this discussion of the official criminal statistics; earlier figures have not been adjusted to take account of changes introduced in 1977 (which have made comparisons difficult between pre-1977 and post-1977). What is apparent from Table 8.2 is that in relation to particular crime categories there is no difference in overall trends between females and males, apart from the categories of sexual offences and robbery, even if there has been an increase or a decrease in the number of offenders. Only a more detailed breakdown into specific offences, such as shoplifting or car theft, to be considered later, can reveal if there are sex differences which are masked by these general categories.

It is, however, evident from the discussion so far that the extent to which comparisons of crime figures over a relatively short period of time can be used to predict a trend is somewhat questionable (Smart, 1979). Table 8.3 indicates that the size of the increase in female offences since the mid-1960s is not unique, and that from time to time there have been considerable increases in these offences since the mid-1930s. This would seem to suggest that rises in the female crime rate cannot be attributed solely to the revival of the women's movement in Britain from the 1960s onwards, and to provide further evidence for the argument that a monocausal explanation for crime is as inappropriate to female crime as it is to male crime. An attempt will therefore be made to indicate some of the other variables that need to be taken into account in any consideration of the interrelationship between female and male crime rates as recorded in the official statistics.

Table 8.3   *Percentage increases and decreases in persons found guilty of indictable offences, over five decades*

	1935–46		1946–55		1955–65		1965–75		1975–85	
	Women	Men	Women	Men	Women	Men	Women	Men	Women	Men
Violence against the person	+94	+70	−30	+108	+111	+102	+225	+100	+33	+30
Offences against property with violence	+365	+199	+97	+74	+129	+176	+149	+55	−15	+2
Offences against property without violence	+68	+32	−5	−0.7	+127	+84	+66	+46	−7	+3
All indictable offences	+68	+46	−1.5	+14	+121	+103	+95	+83	−2	+12

Derived from Table 3, Smart (1979), and Table 5.8, *Criminal Statistics for England and Wales, 1985* (1986).

The figures given so far relate to offences known to the police which have subsequently been cleared up. They do not, therefore, include crimes that have not been reported or recorded by the police, or crimes that have not been traced to particular offenders. These crimes are classified by criminologists as 'the dark figure', since they are not recorded in the official statistics. The relationship between the official statistics and 'the dark figure' is unknown, and it is therefore open to speculation whether an increase in the official statistics merely represents a shift from 'the dark figure' into the recorded statistics or is, in fact, an actual increase. Thus any examination of sex and gender differences with regard to the committing of crime, or speculation about changes in that relationship, must clearly take into account the evidence related to 'the dark figure', as revealed by self-report studies. This is discussed in the following section.

The effect of 'the dark figure'
The existence and extent of unreported, unrecorded crime ('the dark figure') has been recognized for some time as being relevant to any consideration of sex differences in crime rates. For example, Pollak (1961) argued that the actual extent of female criminality is comparable to male, but this fact is masked in the official statistics because of women's traditional role within the home and family. He argues that as women spend more of their time than men in the private arena, much of their crime remains hidden.

Pollak's theorizing has been followed by several attempts to measure 'the dark figure' in relation to sex differences in criminal behaviour, particularly in the case of juveniles (Wise, 1967; Jensen and Eve, 1976; Campbell, 1977). The technique used is known as self-report, a method of questioning whereby respondents are asked to indicate which of a variety of activities, legal and illegal, they have been involved in. It thus seeks to eliminate bias and filtering, which occurs when police and welfare reports are the sole source of evidence concerning illegal behaviour. In this form of research, however, the effects of lying have to be taken into account, but the results suggest that only a small proportion of the responses are lies (approximately 11 per cent: Campbell, 1977), and that there is no sex difference in the extent of lying (Mawby, 1980). This is obviously relevant to any consideration of the extent of, and reasons for, sex differences in criminal behaviour which emerge from self-report studies.

The results of these anonymous, self-report studies have, however, confirmed that, while there is a difference between female and male involvement in crime, it is not as great as when the official statistics are the sole source of evidence. The latter indicate a ratio in the case of juvenile delinquents of between four and six boys committing an offence for every one girl, and for more serious crimes a ratio of 7:1 (Cowie, Slater and Cowie, 1968), whereas the results of the self-report studies show the ratio to be more even. Campbell (1977), for example, after averaging all the offences in her study, found that the boy to girl self-admission ratio was 1.12:1; and Wise (1967) concluded that boys and girls participated almost equally in sexual offences (50.1 per cent boys, 49.9 per cent girls) and alcohol offences (50.8 per cent boys, 49.2 per cent girls), and that, whereas there was not equal participation in other offences, differences were less than those reported in the official statistics. A recent study in Sheffield (Mawby, 1980), using the self-report method, found that on a checklist of 19 items there was a consistent difference between the sexes in the level of involvement, with a higher proportion of boys than girls committing the offence in 14 out of the 15 items listed (Table 8.4). However, an interesting point to emerge from the data below is the differences that exist within the broad categories. Thus under the heading 'vandalism', a relatively non-violent and victimless activity, graffiti, is an offence in which the sex differences are small. This is also evident in the case of stealing from school; this must reflect the compulsory characteristic of the institutional experience, which is not the case with access to a building site, where there is an element of choice.

In considering the evidence from self-report studies in relation to sex differences, it is obviously important to bear in mind the choice of incidents that respondents are asked to consider. In the

Table 8.4   *Percentage of each sex saying they had committed various offences*

	Girls (N = 266)	Boys (N = 340)
Corporate theft		
From building site	8	41
Shoplifting	39	54
From school	44	42
From kiosks, machines, etc.	4	10
Burglary		
Housebreaking	1	6
Burglary of shop, school, factory, etc.	1	12
Breaking into empty building	8	37
Attempted breaking offence	5	19
Vandalism		
Breaking window, property, etc.	18	53
Graffiti	46	49
Firework vandalism	5	33
Arson	5	14
Violence		
Hit or kicked causing bruising or bleeding	50	64
Robbery by threat	12	25
Violence using a weapon	8	19

Derived from Table VI, Mawby (1980).

Sheffield study (Mawby, 1980) the sample was not asked to record their participation in sexual offences or those involving alcohol. These are both categories in which female offenders have been shown to have a high level of involvement (Wise, 1967), and their omission must affect any conclusions as to the ratio between female and male.

The process of social control
The discrepancy between the official figures and self-report studies has led some researchers (Smart, 1976; Edwards, 1984; Morris, 1987) to suggest that there are double standards of morality operating in the courts, depending on the sex of the offender. This, it is argued, is the result of gender-role expectations on the part of the police, social workers and the judiciary, who have a tendency to see female deviance as being in the main related to sexual behaviour and male deviance to be concerned with a wider range of indictable offences (Smart, 1976). Research has consistently shown that girls are more likely than boys to come within the aegis of the juvenile justice system for status or moral danger offences (Chesney-Lind, 1973; Casburn, 1979; Sarri, 1983).

This is confirmed by the latest figures for Care Proceedings brought under section 1(2) of the Children and Young Persons Act 1986 (Home Office, private correspondence). These show that, in the 10–17 age group, 8 per cent of girls as compared to 2 per cent of boys were put into care for reasons of exposure to moral danger; whereas 3 per cent of boys were found guilty of a criminal offence, as compared to 0.5 per cent in the case of girls.

Further support for the argument that double standards of morality operate in the courts is also to be found in the research into juvenile delinquents in institutions. This has shown that concern about the sexual behaviour of female offenders results in a higher proportion than males being referred to the care of social workers, and being committed to institutional care, even though, by comparison with males, their records of delinquency are less extensive. A study by Terry (1970) revealed that girls committed only 18 per cent of all the offences in the police records but were responsible for nearly 50 per cent of all the charges related to sexual offences and being beyond parental care. Richardson (1969), in a study of girls in approved schools, pointed out that only 24 per cent of her female sample were admitted for criminal offences, the majority being admitted for reasons of moral danger or because they were in need of care and protection. In the case of boys, however, 95 per cent were sent to an approved school because they had committed a notifiable offence (Ingleby, 1960). Further, over one-third of Richardson's female sample were institutionalized after a single court appearance, whereas in the case of boys long-term institutionalization of a first offender was found to be a rare occurrence (Stratta, 1970). Further evidence of differential processing in a NACRO report (1977) showed that female juvenile first offenders were five times more likely to be sentenced to an institution than male juvenile first offenders.

On the basis of this evidence, therefore, it is suggested that the discrepancy between the official and self-report figures, in female and male criminal involvement, can be accounted for to some degree by the perception and processing of the deviant on the part of the agents of social control; a point confirmed by recent research (Hudson, 1983) into the relationships between girls and welfare service professionals. Hudson points out that whereas boys in trouble are likely to be referred to the social services 'by the formal agents of social control (predominantly the police) the behaviour of girls is often . . . the source of consternation for the families.' Thus for girls, the onus of control is put on the family. The evidence suggests a dual standard operating in relation to the response to female and male juvenile delinquency. In the case of

Table 8.5   Sex composition of agencies responsible for processing criminals

	Number		Percentage	
	Females	Males	Females	Males
High Court and circuit judges	19	450	4	96
Police	11,303	109,399	9	91
Barristers	713	5,192	12	88
Stipendiary magistrates	8	54	13	87
Solicitors	9,620	56,975	14	86
Probation officers	2,607	3,985	40	60
Lay magistrates	11,672	15,978	42	58

Derived from Table 4.2, *Annual Abstract of Statistics*, 1987; and from private contact with the Lord Chancellor's Office and Home Office.

boys, the methods of control are obvious and easily identified – the notifiable offence; whereas for girls, they 'are more subtle, hidden and diffuse' (Hudson, 1983).

The numbers of women and men in those agencies responsible for the processing of offenders would therefore seem relevant to the overall discussion. As can be seen from Table 8.5, apart from the voluntary, unpaid lay magistrates and probation officers, these agencies are dominated by men. This it is suggested, has certain implications for the processing of offenders, not least in the stereotyping of offenders on the basis of gender (Carlen, 1983). It will be argued in what follows that the proportion of women and men in the agencies of social control is relevant to any consideration of the relationship between female and male crime rates, and the relationship between the sex of the offender and the particular categories that are applied to certain forms of criminal behaviour.

It is interesting, for example, to speculate on what might be the effects of a continuing rise in the number of women police officers, 94 per cent since 1975, in comparison to male police officers, 8 per cent since 1975 (*Annual Abstract of Statistics*, 1987). In relation to prostitution, for example, women police officers have been observed to be much more scrupulous than men in following the letter of the law (Cunnington, 1980). This could in part explain why the number of women found guilty of this offence has increased so dramatically – 188 per cent between 1979 and 1985.

Female and male involvement in crime
Figures for offenders found guilty of a particular category of

Table 8.6   Female and male offenders found guilty, England and Wales 1977 and 1985

| | 1977 | | 1985 | |
	Women	Men	Women	Men
Number of offences (000s)				
Offences against the person (violence and sexual offences)	3.5	46.0	3.7	49.7
Offences against property with violence (burglary, robbery)	2.6	70.7	2.3	71.6
Offences against property without violence (theft, handling stolen goods, fraud and forgery)	58.5	196.2	47.5	193.0
Other (including criminal damage)	2.3	21.9	4.4	41.0
Motoring offences	91.0	1,031.6	105.5	978.6
Summary offences	49.5	377.8	84.8	328.6
Total	207.4	1,744.2	248.4	1,662.5
Percentage of offenders				
Offences against the person	1.7	2.6	1.5 −	3.0 +
Offences against property with violence	1.3	4.0	0.9 −	4.3 +
Offences against property without violence	28.2	11.2	19.1 −	11.6 +
Other	1.1	1.3	1.7 +	2.5 +
Motoring offences	43.9	59.2	42.5 −	58.9 −
Summary offences	23.8	21.6	34.1 +	19.8 −
Total	100	100	100	100

Derived from Table 5.8, *Criminal Statistics for England and Wales, 1985* (1986).

offence (Table 8.6) indicate that for both sexes the highest number of offences are concerned with motoring, although in 1985 in comparison with 1977 its proportion as part of the total number of offences shows a small decline. Examination in more detail of this global figure indicates, however, that the sex ratio is not evenly distributed: 99 per cent of the total number of persons (3004) found guilty of dangerous driving offences in 1985 were male as were 98 per cent of those found guilty of driving while disqualified. Table 8.6 also indicates that there has been a decline in the number of female offenders (9 per cent in the case of non-violent offences against property) in most of the major categories. The number of male offenders continues to rise, if rather less rapidly in the case of violent offences. The exception, however, is summary offences which are those offences regarded as less serious and where the defendant can only be tried in the magistrates' court. Here the number of female offenders has increased by 10 per cent in comparison to a decline of 2 per cent in the case of male offenders. Part of the explanation for this must be the large increase in the number of women found guilty of prostitution referred to above. The broad categories in Table 8.6 cover a number of more specific offences, and it is therefore necessary to look at the offences within each category to enable more precise sex differences to emerge. It is also argued that differences are also to be found at the level of criminal action. Thus Pollak (1961) concludes that 'women commit all types of crime, but their procedure is different to that used by men in their criminal pursuits'.

One reason why differences arise is the existence of crimes, which because of their legal definition, are sex-specific. Examples of these, within the overall category of sexual offences, are the crimes of rape and the new indictable offence, soliciting by a man (Sexual Offences Act 1985) which are solely male offences, and prostitution, which legally can only be committed by women. In relation to the latter, it is interesting to note that the English law clearly recognizes that both women and men can be prostitutes, as it is an offence for either sex to live off the earnings of a male or female prostitute. However, the single category 'offence by prostitute', in the official statistics, contains figures only in the column headed 'female', which in 1985 were shown as 8684, compared to a nil figure in the male column. Charges of male prostitution, however, are placed in a different legal category, described as 'indecency between males.' This use of a different category for the same offence, depending on the sex of the offender, would seem an obvious example of the differential processing of women and men by the police and other agents of social control.

It is also widely recognized that some crimes can be described as sex-related (Pollak, 1961; Smart, 1976; Caplan, 1980). In the case of these crimes the level of involvement of a particular sex is higher than their involvement in other offences. A comparison between female and male involvement in a group of sex-related offences is given in Table 8.7.

Figures for 1973 and 1985 show that in addition to the concentration by sex of offenders around certain offences, the sex-ratio has remained fairly constant. The one exception, offences

Table 8.7   Some examples of the statistical basis of sex-related offences, 1985[a]

Type of offence	Number of persons found guilty	Female offenders as % of all those found guilty	Male offenders as % of all those found guilty
Offence by prostitute[b] and related offences	8,684	99.7 (81.5)	0.2 (18.5)
Shoplifting	72,407	37.5 (50.2)	62.4 (49.8)
Larceny	219,174	19.5 (19.3)	80.4 (80.7)
Car theft	26,681	2.5 (2.3)	97.5 (97.7)
Burglary	72,735	3.0 (3.3)	96.9 (96.7)

a. Percentages in brackets are taken from Smart's original table calculated from the criminal statistics for 1973.
b. Includes 'aiding offence by prostitute', i.e. brothel-keeping.
Derived from Table 1.2(a) Smart (1976) and *Criminal Statistics England and Wales*, Supplementary tables, Vols 1 and 2, 1985, 1986.

associated with prostitution, cannot be said to reflect an actual decline in male offenders; rather it reflects the creation of a new offence category 'soliciting by a man' (Sexual Offences Act 1985) and the consequent shift of male offenders from the category, 'offence by prostitution and related offences'.

Further evidence of the sex-related nature of certain offences is revealed in the examination of statistics for shoplifting offences. These show that, unlike in the majority of criminal offences, the number of women found guilty has in one period between 1969 and 1971, exceeded that of men although later figures show the gap to be widening along traditional lines. Sex differences also emerge in relation to the kind of items stolen and their value; women tend to shoplift items of lower value (Gibbens and Prince, 1962). This suggests that female involvement may well be higher than that recorded in the official figures, since petty shoplifting is an offence where retailers have traditionally not brought charges against offenders because of the time-consuming prosecution procedures.

Table 8.8 gives further examples of crimes in which the official statistics indicate a high concentration of female offenders, such as theft at work, from machines or meters, forgery and violence against members of one's family (Wolfgang, 1958; Pollak, 1961; Smart, 1976). Crimes which are male sex-related are murder, burglary (which involves breaking into premises) and violent offences against persons unknown.

It could be argued that these differences would seem to reflect

Table 8.8   Sex composition of offenders by selected offences

	Number of persons found guilty	Female offenders as % if all those found guilty	Male offenders as % of all those found guilty
Indictable offences			
Murder	156	5.1	94.9
Other wounding	44,743	7.4	92.6
Theft by employee	6,555	20.4	79.6
Theft from an automatic machine or meter	6,012	19.5	80.5
Handling stolen goods	26,963	14.9	85.1
Forging of drug prescription	141	34.0	65.9
Other forgery	3,121	26.6	73.4
Cruelty to a child	104	50.9	49.0
Summary offences[a]			
Drunkenness	60,509	7.4	92.6
Social security offences	6,320	24.2	75.8
Motoring offences	1,058,274	9.6	90.4

a. Offences categorized thus are regarded as less serious and therefore must be tried in a magistrates court.
Derived from Table 1.4, Smart (1976); and data from *Criminal Statistics for England and Wales*, Supplementary tables, Vols 1 and 2, 1985, 1986.

traditional gender roles; 'female' crime involves those kinds of behaviour that do not require a great deal of strength, and also reflects women's concerns and their greater occupation of 'private space'; 'male' crime involves a greater emphasis on the use of force and occupation of 'public space' by men, as exemplified in male dominance in crimes such as car theft and burglary.

In the case of juveniles, sex differences relating to the charges brought have already been referred to (pp. 230–31). Further differences in the type of offence can also be seen in the results of large-scale Canadian research (Caplan, 1980). Here the proportion of boys (12 per cent) charged with some form of violent offence against property was much higher than the proportion of girls (3 per cent). The pattern was, however, reversed in the case of truancy, where the proportion of girls involved (20 per cent) was twice as high as the proportion of boys (10 per cent).

It should be remembered, however, that these figures are likely to be a reflection of the assumptions made by their compilers about appropriate gender-role behaviour, as well as the actual behaviour of offenders.

Sex and crime: theoretical explanations

Theoretical explanations for the differences between women and men in criminal behaviour, which have attempted to look behind the surface manifestations, have concentrated, first, on variables that can be said to operate with differential effects on women and men and, second, on the reaction to, and processing of, women and men whose deviance is similar. These theoretical attempts would seem to fall into five broad headings: biological and psychological; socialization; sub-cultural; social interaction; structural (Davies, 1980; Carlen, 1985).

Biological and psychological

Researchers concerned with biological and psychological explanations argue that the sex differences in criminal behaviour can be traced to basic biological differences between women and men, and the consequent adaptive learning (Pollak, 1961). Other researchers have sought to establish the particular variables that distinguish the deviant from the non-deviant, and in particular those characteristics which, it is argued, are sex-related. Thus Cowie, Slater and Cowie (1968) emphasize such variables as the below-average intelligence of their sample of delinquent girls and their widespread educational retardation; the higher incidence of broken homes than in a comparable group of delinquent boys; and the fact that a large proportion of their sample (52 per cent) were diagnosed as psychiatrically abnormal. This latter fact, they suggest, indicates that the behaviour of delinquent girls is likely to be affected by psychiatric abnormality, in contrast to social factors in the case of boys. This point is emphasized by Konopka (1966), who concludes that female delinquents are more abnormal than male delinquents in that delinquent behaviour for females is the result of a confused or masculine sex-role identity, thus it is a perversion of their natural role.

Socialization

Researchers concerned with socialization explanations argue that differences in criminal behaviour can be traced to the differential experience of women and men, which in turn reflects gender-role typifications and expectations. Thus the family is seen as having a major influence, for example, in its sex-related emphasis on aggressive or non-aggressive behaviour, the effects of which can be borne out in sex differences in criminal behaviour. This is offered as an explanation of why men predominate in crimes involving violence, physical strength and skill, whereas women are more involved in crimes requiring less physical strength, and are also to be found in secondary supportive roles in traditional male crime, such as robbery (Wolfgang, 1958; Hoffman-Bustamente, 1973). Further sex differences in criminal behaviour, it is argued, are the result of a greater emphasis on conformity in female socialization, and the fact that parents exercise more control over their daughters that their sons (Newson and Newson, 1976). Thus boys are not discouraged from delinquency-related, risk-taking behaviour in the same way as girls, since this is seen as much more appropriate to their sex and status (Hagan, Simpson and Gillis, 1979).

Subcultural
Subcultural explanations were a major research concern, particularly through the 1950s and 1960s, in the search for the causes of male juvenile delinquency; researchers emphasized the effects of a closely knit, single-sex, delinquency gang upon the behaviour of individual members (Downes, 1966; Gill, 1977). Some theorists hypothesized that gang membership was a consequence of the frustrations of male working-class adolescents at their lack of occupational mobility; the delinquent gang was postulated as an alternative means of achieving status (Cohen, 1955; Cloward and Ohlin, 1960). Empirical studies have not totally supported this hypothesis, but have put forward alternative explanations for the existence of the male delinquent gang. Downes (1966) stressed the influences of adolescent culture, while Gill (1977) emphasized the complex interrelationship of particular structural determinants, such as housing policy, low income and the effects of an inner-city social environment.

In the case of females, there is very little evidence to suggest that the single-sex gang is relevant to an explanation of juvenile delinquency. It is argued that it is the female concern for sexual relationships which attracts them to male-dominated groups (Shacklady-Smith, 1978). Here their role appears to take two main forms, which are not mutually exclusive (Campbell, 1984a). Research points to female gang members, either as sex objects or less frequently, as tomboys involved in fights with male members and also having strong friendships with members of the same sex. Both forms, however, involve sexual relationships with male members and consequent rivalry with other women, although female status in the gang is increasingly determined by female members. However, this focus on the sexual activity of female gang members is not matched by an equivalent focus in the case of male members, and could reflect the gender bias of the researchers. In addition, it is increasingly recognized that subcultural explanations have to be located firmly within the social structure and consequently can only reflect the relationships that exist within wider society (Campbell, 1984).

Social interaction
In this approach explanations are related to the social interaction between the deviant and non-deviant and are concerned with differences in the application of rules and the processing of deviants. Such studies have found considerable sex differences (whether informally as related to social interaction, or formally through the legal system), as this chapter has already indicated. This has been demonstrated in the discussion of sex differences revealed when comparing the official statistics with self-report studies, in the examination by sex of the proceedings brought under the Children and Young Persons Act 1969 (Smart, 1976; and see p 231 above), and in the research of Terry (1970), related to sexual offences and parental control, and Richardson (1969), who examined the criteria for sentencing female juveniles to institutions. Additional evidence of the processing of adult offenders is provided by research in the United States into court proceedings in New York State. It concluded that women were less likely than men to spend time in prison, either awaiting a sentence or after a conviction; and if convicted they were less likely than men to receive the more severe sentences (Nagel, 1981). In addition to the official agencies of social control, this chapter has also made reference to the different socialization process of women and men within the family (Newson and Newson, 1976; Hagan, Simpson and Gillis, 1979).

Structural
This explanation argues that a focus on sex and gender differences, either at the level of individual characteristics or resulting from social interaction at the micro-level, ignores the influence of a dominant ideology and the wider social structure. A focus on cultural and structural relationships at the macro-level leads to the conclusion that explanations for crime are not simply sex-specific, which is reductionist. They are to be sought in the analysis of a whole variety of complex, rational responses to a set of discriminatory and exploitative relations, based on race, class and gender, which affect both women and men (Carlen, 1985);

explanations for the differential criminal involvement of women and men should be sought, therefore, in the power of the state, which through its economic, political and legal institutions determines social and labour divisions, and as a consequence relationships between the sexes (Greenwood, 1981; Edwards, 1984; Carlen, 1985).

In conclusion, it would seem that on the basis of the research to date the most fruitful line of inquiry, in relation to explanations of criminal differences between women and men, is that which stresses, at the macro-level, the regulatory control on the relations between the sexes wielded by the institutions of a society, in conjunction with the process of socialization and interaction at the micro-level.

Sentencing policy

As is evident from the types of sentences shown in Table 8.9 the police and the courts have a wide range of responses from which they can select in dealing with individual offenders. These range from a caution (a non-custodial sentence) at one end of the spectrum to a youth custody or prison sentence (a custodial sentence) at the other end.

In arriving at a decision about the sentencing of a particular offender, the courts take into account easily quantified criteria, such as the type of crime committed, the existence and length of previous criminal records, and the experience (if any) of particular types of sentence. However, the additional use of medical and social workers' reports also indicate that less easily quantified criteria, such as the offender's family background and commitments, the availability of certain forms of treatment, and the sex of the offender, are also taken into account in determining sentence. Thus, in the case of women as compared to men, such factors as their often exclusive responsibility for running the home and caring for dependent children and others; the belief that the effects of removal from the home environment into an institution are more painful for women than for men (NACRO, 1980); the woman's marital status; the existence of a deviant family background; drugs and drink related problems; and the sexual composition of the bench – all have been shown to exert an independent influence on sentencing decisions (Eaton, 1983; Farrington and Morris, 1983; Dominelli, 1984).

Sentencing decisions by courts, summarized in Table 8.9, reflect the influences of both the criminal history and social characteristics of offenders. The biggest change to note in 1985, in comparison with 1979, is the large increase in the number of men

Table 8.9 Percentages^a of (a) non-custodial and (b) custodial sentences given to offenders by sex (1979^b) 1985

	Caution	Absolute/conditional discharge	Probation	Supervision order	Fine	Community service order	Attendance centre	All
Females	47(39)	13(14)	9(9)	1.1(2.6)	21(36)	1.6(1)	0.4(0.1)	93(93)
Males	9(17)	4(8)	1.7(4)	0.6(3.0)	75(42)	2(3)	0.8(2)	94(79)

	Care order	Detention centre	Youth custody	Fully suspended	Prison Partly suspended	Unsuspended	Otherwise dealt with	All
Females	0.2	c	0.8	2.7	0.4	2(2)	0.5	7(8)
Males	0.1	0.6	1.1	1.5	0.2	2(9)	0.6	6(22)

a. All percentages over 2 have been rounded.
b. 1979 Figures in brackets.
c. There are no detention centres for women.
N(ooos) = 111.6 women, 1829.2 men.
Devised from Tables 5.1 and 7.2, *Criminal Statistics for England and Wales, 1985* (1986).

Table 8.10   Average prison population: by sex, 1982–86

	1982	1983	1984	1985	1986	% change
Females	1,326	1,390	1,473	1,532	1,570	+18
Males	42,381	42,072	41,822	44,701	45,092	+6

Devised from Table 1.9, *Prison Statistics 1985* (1986); and Table 2, *Report on the Work of the Prison Department 1985/86* (1986).

receiving non-custodial sentences. This now slightly exceeds the number of women, whereas in 1979 the percentage of women exceeded men by 14 per cent. This shift could reflect a decline in sexual stereotyping and gender bias which does not, however, seem to have affected the use of cautions or fines, where the traditional sex differences have increased. A more likely explanation for the increase in non-custodial sentences for men is concern about the size of the prison population which rose by 2900 in 1985 'the rise occurring almost entirely amongst adult sentenced males' (*Prison Statistics*, 1985). In relation to the range of non-custodial sentences which courts have at their disposal, it would appear that women are treated more leniently than men, with 38 per cent more women than men receiving a caution, and a higher proportion than men receiving a discharge or a probation order. The fact that an increasing proportion of men, in comparison to women, are being given a fine probably reflects recognition of their superior earning power and ability to pay in comparison to women. Overall figures for custodial sentences indicate once again that the sex differences have narrowed considerably, particularly in relation to the receipt of an unsuspended/immediate prison sentence (Seear and Player, 1986). It is hard not to conclude, however, that these shifts reflect the numerical dominance of the male prison population (see Table 8.10), and consequent fears about the effects of overcrowding in male prisons, rather than greater sexual equality.

The custodial sentence

As is evident from Table 8.10, between 1982 and 1985 the number of females in custody rose by 18 per cent in comparison with a 6 per cent increase in the number of males, but despite this the ratio of female to male offenders in custody remains approximately 30:1. A detailed breakdown of the figures in Table 8.10 reveals that the number of women prisoners held on remand, awaiting trial, has risen by 72 per cent in comparison with 51 per cent for men over the four years, which has resulted in both sexes being held in overcrowded, and often airless prison cells.

Figures of the daily average prison population, in comparison with the accommodation provided (Table 8.11), indicate a problem of overcrowding in local prisons and remand centres for both sexes, but only for women in closed prisons.

Figures showing the distribution of type of offence among women and men given a custodial sentence (Table 8.12) show a similar sex distribution to that revealed by earlier tables (see Tables 8.6 and 8.8). In the case of women, the largest proportion have been sent to prison because of some form of non-violent offence against property (a sex-related crime category), whereas in the case of burglary, the proportion of men sent to prison is more than three times that of women. This again supports the conclusion that burglary is largely an activity carried out by males, as shown in an earlier section (See Table 8.7).

As noted in a recent report, drugs offences are now the second largest category for which women are sent to prison. However, only a minority are convicted for unlawful supply or illegal possession; the majority of women are sent to prison because they have acted as couriers, usually of cannabis, and been convicted of illegal importation (Seear and Player, 1986).

Table 8.13, giving details of the sentencing of women and men to different types of institution, also reveals some interesting differences in the treatment of the sexes. Thus, of the female population, the highest proportion (66 per cent) is concentrated in training prisons, in comparison to the male population (45 per cent). However, in the case of local prisons, which are characterized by severe overcrowding, lack of training facilities, and a high turnover in the population, the proportion of male prisoners detained in these establishments is more than three times that of female prisoners (Sparks, 1971). This, however, is counterbalanced to some extent by the proportion of women, as compared to men, who are detained in remand centres, which are essentially short-stay institutions intended for offenders awaiting trial, sentence, or transfer to another institution.

Details of the length of sentence handed out to offenders (Table 8.14) show that a higher proportion of females (84 per cent) than males (72 per cent) receive less than an 18 months sentence. This could be a reflection of a more lenient sentencing policy towards women, although evidence on the responses to women as prisoners, by the various agents of social control (police, courts, prison service), makes this unlikely (Carlen, 1983; Peckham, 1985). It could reflect the characteristics of female offending, mainly non-violent (theft, forgery) and victimless (prostitution, drugs), and the fact that women as a whole have shorter criminal records than

Table 8.11   Overcrowding in penal establishments – excess of population over accommodation (percentages)

	Local prisons	Training Prisons		Remand centres	Youth Custody centres		Detention centres		Over-all
		Open	Closed		Open	Closed	Senior	Junior	
Females	38	3	29	33	0	0	a	a	12
Males	48	0	0	41	0	0	0	0	13

a. There are no detention centres for women.
N = females 1570 population; 1401 accommodation; males 44,803 population; 39,805 accommodation.
Derived from Appendix 4, *Report on the Work of the Prison Department 1985* (1986).

Table 8.12   Population under sentence (June 1985) by type of offence (percentages)

	Females	Males
Violence against the person	15	19
Sexual offences	0.7	5
Burglary	8	28
Robbery	5	8
Theft, handling, fraud, forgery	44	21
Drugs offences	16	6
Other offences	10	11
Not recorded	1	1

N = 1157 females 36,187 males.
Derived from Table 1.5, *Prison Statistics 1985* (1986).

Table 8.13   Population under sentence, June 1985, by type of establishments (percentages)

	Remand centres	Local prisons	Training prisons		Youth custody centres		Detention centres		Number
			Open	Closed	Open	Closed	Senior	Junior	
Females	7	10	30	36	8	10	a	a	1,157
Males	1	30	9	36	4	15	3	2	36,187

a. There are no detention centres for women.
Derived from Table 1.5, *Prison Statistics 1985* (1986).

men; 55 per cent of men committed to prison have a record of six or more previous convictions compared to 26 per cent of women (Tables 4.3 and 5.3, *Prison Statistics 1985*).

Differences   in   female:male   institutional   experience   (a

Table 8.14   Length of sentence given to receptions (over 21) into prison (percentages)

	Up to 3 months	3–6 months	6–18 months	18 months	18 months– 4 years	4–10 years	10+ years	Life	Number
Females	37	23	24	5	11	1	—	0.3	2,467[a]
Males	26	21	25	6	18	4	0.2	0.4	43,467[a]

a. Number excludes fine defaulters committed to prison.
Derived from Tables 4.3 and 5.3, *Prison Statistics 1985* (1986).

male:female ratio of about 30:1) are also likely to be affected by the size of the respective populations. Thus there are 15 institutions for female offenders compared to 133 for men, and the former are widely dispersed around the country; in the case of particular types of institutions, the position is even further exacerbated, there being only one local prison for women (Holloway) compared to 26 for men, and 3 remand centres compared to 16 for men. The *Report of the Work of the Prison Department* (1979) noted that 'many women have to serve their sentences at long distances from their home areas making visiting difficult or impossible'. In addition, Home Office provisions to aid the rehabilitation of prisoners, such as temporary release to obtain a job, or interviews with a probation officer from their own area, often cannot take place in female institutions because of the travelling distances involved. Heidensohn (1981) concludes that, as a consequence of the population size, the visiting needs of female prisoners cannot be related to the geographical distribution of institutions, and specialist provisions, such as education or trade training, are not found to the same extent as in male institutions. It is further argued that the cumulative effect of these limitations on female institutions is to reinforce an environment which focuses on traditional female roles; and by considering women to be child-like, and treating them accordingly, attempts to reconstruct their identities so that they take on particular feminine and domestic values (Price, 1977; Carlen, 1983). It is unlikely that such stereotyped gender-roles need to be encouraged in male prisons, or if they were, that the population would be expected quietly to acquiesce.

The view that females who commit crime are 'abnormal', in that their behaviour indicates rejection of the 'normal' gender expectations, is not a perception that is applied to male offenders. Evidence of its effect may be seen in the provision for personality disorders and psychiatric care in women's prisons as compared to men's (Dobash and Dobash, 1986); in the level of violence recorded in women's establishments, where the incidence of assaults is three times that in men's (Report of the Work of the Prison Department, 1979); and in the fact that 9 per cent of female prisoners on remand were discharged to mental hospitals, as compared to 4 per cent of male remand prisoners (Table 2(g), *Prison Statistics 1985*).

It is suggested that the apparent gender differences in the incidence and related mental disorders is rooted in nineteenth-century attitudes towards women prisoners, who as a consequence have been regarded as more difficult and neurotic than men (Dobash and Dobash, 1986). The first official challenge to this point of view was to emerge in evidence to a Parliamentary Sub-committee examining women in prison (Heidensohn, 1981; Dobash and Dobash, 1986). It is now increasingly recognized that traditional beliefs about female prisoners have resulted in a heightened expectation of abnormality, which does not apply in the case of male offenders.

To sum up: It would seem that, in relation to sentencing decisions overall, a higher proportion of women are treated more leniently than men. However, it has been argued that, unlike men, women who are given custodial sentences are perceived as double failures; not only have they broken the law but in doing so they have failed as women in their clear rejection of feminine and domestic values. This belief is reflected in institutional regimes which focus on therapy and traditional female skills in an attempt to 'normalize' and 're-educate' women offenders; but such gender reconstruction does not inform the regime in male prisons.

Victims of crime
Table 8.15 provides evidence of sex differences concerning the experience of victimization. It supports the earlier conclusions of a national survey (*British Crime Survey*, 1983) that men are twice as likely as women to be the victims of a robbery, a crime which involves the threat or actual use of force, compared to non-violent theft, where the sex differences are reversed. The table also shows the predominance of male victims in crimes involving violence against the person; males are five times more likely than females to be the victims of a serious wounding and three times more likely to be the victims of a more minor assault. This again supports the findings of *The British Crime Survey* (Hough and Mayhew, 1983) which concluded that males living on their own were in the highest risk category for these offences.

What also emerges from these figures is further evidence of the

Table 8.15   Victims (by sex) of certain offences recorded by the police, 1984 (percentages)

	Serious[a] wounding	Other wounding, assault	Buggery, indecent assault on male	Indecent assault on female	Robbery	Theft from the person
Females	15.9	26.0	b	100	32.2	46.2
Males	78.5	69.8	100	b	63.1	15.0
Sex not known	5.6	4.2	—	—	4.6	38.8

a. Attempted murder and wounding endangering life.
b. Recorded as sex-specific offences.
Derived from Table 2A, *Criminal Statistics for England and Wales 1985* (1986).

problematic nature of criminal definitions and in particular the influence of gender bias. Thus the general term 'assault' subsumes the more specific offence of domestic violence, a crime where women are overwhelmingly the majority of victims. The lack of a separate legal category could be said to reflect the failure to recognize domestic violence as a specific offence and to add to the problems that victims experience in reporting such offences to the police. As a consequence, there is a high 'dark' figure for a crime in which the victims are almost exclusively female (Bowker, 1978; Stanko, 1985). Table 8.15 also shows that the police have chosen to record the offence of sexual assault as sex-specific, thus making any comparison of the female:male experience of victimization impossible, in a crime which has high risk for women.

The limitations of the official evidence relating to women's experience of sexual assaults, and as rape victims in particular, have been well documented (Hall, 1985; Stanko, 1985; Kelly, 1987). In national surveys of 11,000 households, *The British Crime Survey* (Hough and Mayhew, 1983, 1985) revealed only two victims of rape, which is in marked contrast with the evidence from a London study (1985). This, unlike the *British Crime Survey*, was a self-completion questionnaire given out at a variety of distribution points in 32 London boroughs by women to women, whose ages ranged from 10 to over 70. Two thousand copies were distributed, of which 1236 (62 per cent) were returned. Analysis of the results revealed that 17 per cent of respondents recorded that they had been rape victims, which included rape within marriage. Taking sexual assaults as a whole, two out of five respondents (481 women) said that they had been victims, at least

Table 8.16   Percentage of victims (by sex) who rate themselves or their household 'very much' affected over the first few days by a particular offence

Type of offence	Female	Male
Burglary/theft dwelling	40	27
Assault/wounding	39	17
Robbery/snatch	51	31
Threats	57	9
Vandalism	32	16
All other theft	12	13

Derived from Table 3.6, Maguire and Corbett (1987).

once, of rape, attempted rape, or other forms of sexual assault. Even more worrying than the number of assaults was the fact that of those who had been raped or sexually assaulted, 27 per cent said it had happened first when they were 12 or under and 43 per cent when they were 15 or under (Hall, 1985).

Explanations for the apparently wide differences in the two sets of data concerning female experience as rape victims are to be found in the legal definition of rape as compared to wider definitions of the term (e.g. Hall recognized that rape can occur within marriage); the selection of the sample, which in the London survey included a younger age group; and methods used for gathering data. Furthermore, it clearly demonstrates the influence of research methodology on the 'facts' to emerge.

Research which has shown sex differences in reaction to the experience of victimization has also noted significant differences (Table 8.16).

This summary of interview responses shows women as more affected by the experience of almost every category of offence than men, the main exceptions being vehicle theft and miscellaneous personal theft (Maguire and Corbett, 1987). Sex differences had also been found in earlier research by Maguire (1980) into the impact of burglary upon victims; the most frequent male response being one of anger (41 per cent) while a high proportion of women (40 per cent) were shocked or confused. The fact that these differences remain has been confirmed by research carried out in Toronto on the long-term effects of the experience of burglary. This found that a much higher proportion of women (42 per cent) in comparison to men (2 per cent) experienced fear of being alone; and that 36 per cent of women were afraid of going into their homes in comparison to 8 per cent of men (Waller and Okihiro, 1978).

Table 8.17   Avoidance behaviour (by sex) resulting from fear of victimization (percentages)

	Never		Occasionally		Often		Always	
	Female	Male	Female	Male	Female	Male	Female	Male
Avoid going out after dark	29.2	73.5	17.1	12.6	16.9	7.0	36.7	6.9
Avoid certain types of people	32.6	52.2	31.3	32.9	22.9	10.3	13.2	4.7
Avoid certain streets or areas	36.0	61.6	24.4	21.9	22.3	11.9	16.1	4.6
Go out with someone else instead of alone	27.3	73.4	20.3	13.5	29.1	9.2	23.3	3.9
Avoid using buses or trains	59.9	85.5	21.9	9.4	11.6	3.4	6.8	1.8
Use a car rather than walk	55.5	81.1	14.3	7.7	16.5	5.7	13.7	5.5

All respondents weighted; n = 9386.
Derived from Table 4.8, Jones et al. (1986).

More recently research has shown that fear of becoming a crime victim affects the behaviour of women and men in different degrees (Maxfield, 1984, Hough and Mayhew, 1985, Jones, 1986). Table 8.17 illustrates that there are substantial differences between women and men in the precautions they take to avoid the possibility of victimization; for example, 37 per cent of women said they never went out after dark as compared to 7 per cent of men.

To sum up: it would appear that women's experience of victimization is under-recorded in comparison to men's. This is in part a reflection of the type of offence in which women are the overwhelming majority of victims such as domestic violence and rape; the feelings of shame and personal degradation which victims of sexual attacks experience; of the victim's fear of reprisals if the crime is reported; and the traditional lack of institutional support towards victims of such offences (Jones et al., 1986). Clear differences emerge in relation to the experience of victimization of a range of offences and in the effects on behaviour of fear of crime.

It has been suggested in *The British Crime Survey* that women's fear of victimization is excessive in the light of the facts (see Table 8.15; and Hough and Mayhew, 1983). However, the largely unreported experience of female victimization, particularly in urban environments, would seem to contradict these official statistics (Jones et al., 1986).

Overview

In examining the relationship between sex and crime, this chapter has mainly confined itself to the evidence presented by the official statistics, supplemented by data from recent research where relevant, which is the major thrust of this book. It has not, therefore, examined in any great depth the considerable amount of theoretical speculation that has emerged in relation to crime generally and sex differences in particular, nor the research derived from this, but has concentrated on an examination of empirical evidence. In addition, it has made little reference to any legislative changes, for example the Sexual Offences Act 1985, which have implications for the official figures in relation to female/male involvement in crime and experience of victimization.

The examination of the official statistics has shown that since 1977, while overall crime has continued to rise, the number of female offenders found guilty has declined. This erodes the belief that female emancipation is causally linked to an increasing female crime rate. Further analysis has also shown that certain crimes are sex-specific, as in offences such as rape and prostitution, and sex-related, with female crime tending to cluster only in certain categories, such as non-violent offences against property.

The fact that criminal statistics cannot be regarded as unproblematic was confirmed by the evidence of self-report studies into juvenile delinquent populations. These showed that the overall ratio of female to male criminal involvement is less than that officially recorded, although differences are still significant in traditional 'male' crime, such as that involving violence against property. Examination of charges brought against juveniles provided evidence of sex stereotyping; thus females were, in the main, thought to be in moral danger because of behaviour such as sexual deviance or truancy, in contrast to males, who were found, in the main, to have committed indictable offences. It was argued that these differential attitudes were, in part, the result of the male domination of the agencies of social control, such as the courts and the police.

Theoretical explanations of the relationship between sex and crime revealed a number of different emphases, including biological and psychological explanations, socialization experience, subcultural explanations, social interaction and structural explanations. The argument that stressed the interrelationship between the institutions of a society, their influence on the socialization processes and hence gender differences in crime commission was felt to be the most powerful, thus locating the characteristics associated with crime and gender within an overall social framework.

Sentencing policy showed that in general women tended to be treated more sympathetically than men, with a higher proportion receiving a caution or non-custodial sentence. This was not shown to be the case in respect of institutional experience, however, where the effect of gender stereotyping in relation to female prisoners results in the provision of a narrow range of opportunities for rehabilitation in comparison to male prisoners.

In relation to victimization, a higher proportion of men were found to be victims of violent offences, but it was argued that women's experience of victimization, in the case of sexual assault and domestic violence, was very much under-recorded, and that this therefore distorted the official figures. Considerable sex differences exist in relation to reaction to crime victimization and in avoidance behaviour resulting from fear of crime.

Unlike other areas examined in this book, it would seem that in the case of crime, women are not always at a disadvantage in relation to men. The fact, however, that the political and legal institutions are dominated by men does mean that women enjoy that advantage only as a consequence of male discretion.

9 Sex and gender in Britain: continuity and change

Erica Stratta and *Ivan Reid*

Two clearly observable features can be seen to emerge from the examination of sex and gender differences in Chapters 3–8. First, where historical data are used to illuminate the current position, what is demonstrated is that, despite deliberate attempts in many areas to equalize opportunities for the sexes, women in general remain a relatively disadvantaged group. Second, there is a common assumption, or myth, that there has been a significant change in women's position in the twentieth century, both in relation to the equalizing of opportunities, and in women's ability to take advantage of the increased opportunities that have become available in all walks of life. As is evident from earlier discussion of ideology (Chapter 2), the creation of such a myth is not irrelevant to an examination of sex and gender differences. It promotes the question why should people believe despite the evidence to the contrary, that equality has been achieved. As has been suggested (Chapter 2) one explanation might be that this is an attempt on the part of men (and some women) to defuse the situation, to deflate the opposition and by so doing to retain the status quo; another that it reflects a belief in the inevitability of progress with regard to human relations.

Clearly, it would be grudging not to admit that we have moved a long way from the point of view of gender differences and of the relationship between women and men contained in the following extract from the fourth edition of the *Encyclopaedia Britannica* (1800–10):

> The man, more robust, is fitted for severe labour, and for field exercise; the woman, more delicate, is fitted for sedentary occupations, and particularly for nursing children. The man, bold and vigorous, is qualified for being a protector; the woman, delicate, and timid, requires protection. Hence it is that a man never admires a woman for possessing bodily strength or personal courage; women always despise men who are totally destitute of these qualities. The man, as a protector, is directed by nature to govern; the woman, conscious of inferiority, is disposed to obey. Their intellectual powers correspond to

the destination of nature. Men have penetration and solid judgement to fit them for governing, women have sufficient understanding to make a decent figure under a good government; a greater portion would excite dangerous rivalry between the sexes, which nature has avoided by giving them different talents. Women have more imagination and sensibility than men which makes all their enjoyments exquisite; at the same time that they are better qualified to communicate enjoyment. Add another capital difference of disposition: the gentle and insinuating manners of the female sex tend to soften the roughness of the other sex; and wherever women are indulged with any freedom, they polish sooner than men.

These are not the only particulars that distinguish the sexes. With respect to the ultimate end of love, it is the privilege of the male, as superior and protector, to make a choice; the female preferred has no privilege but barely to consent or refuse.

Although we have moved a long way from this view, this book bears witness to the extent of sex and gender differences and inequalities and how far our society has yet to go really to affect and change them.

Legislation for sex equality

The passing in Britain of legislation to end the disadvantages experienced by most women seemed to suggest that the general public was prepared to accept equality and that Acts of Parliament would ensure it. An Equal Pay Act was passed in 1970, and supplemented by the Sex Discrimination Act 1975 and the Employment Protection Act 1975. Broadly speaking the 1970 Act gives a woman the right to equal treatment with a man when she is employed in like work to that of a man or employed in a job which, even if different from that of a man, has been given the same value as a man's job under a job-evaluation scheme. While it clearly established the principle of equal pay for equal work for women and men and therefore might be said to have helped create a climate that militated against discrimination on the grounds of sex, it did not guarantee complete equality. Thus, as discussed in Chapter 6, it has been possible for employers to subvert their intentions through, for example, extra payments for unbroken service or shift work, which are of benefit by and large to male employees. However, in 1984, as a consequence of a ruling from the European Court of Justice, the Equal Pay Act amendment came onto the statute book removing a further inequality; and it is now possible to claim jobs are of 'equal value' in sex-segregated occupations. Thus female secretaries can claim that their work is of 'equal value' to that of the more highly paid, male clerical staff working for the same employers; or, as in a recent successful claim, female machinists in car factories were awarded the same pay as male workers doing a similar assembly job. However, this gain has to be set against the ineffectiveness of minimum-wage machinery, evident in the almost complete erosion of the powers of Wages Councils (1987), with the result that the position of the lowest-paid workers, the majority of whom are women (Chapter 6), has become increasingly vulnerable.

Further legislation, the Sex Discrimination Act 1975, was very comprehensive in its coverage, setting out penalties and compensation for infringement of its directives. It outlawed discrimination on the grounds of sex in employment, certain organizations (such as trade unions), education and professional training, public appointments, provision of goods, facilities and services, property disposal and certain related matters such as discriminatory advertisements. Concurrently there was established the Equal Opportunities Commission, which was empowered to work for the elimination of discrimination, to promote equality of opportunity generally between women and men, and to keep under review the Acts of 1970 and 1975. The Commission was empowered to support individual complainants in the industrial tribunals and the courts, and themselves initiate action.

And more recently, additional legislation (Sex Discrimination Act 1986) has been introduced to make the United Kingdom comply with EEC law. It removes the restrictions on women doing shift work and opens the way to higher earnings (Chapter 6); extends the law to cover employment in small business and private households; opens up the opportunities to take positive action on behalf of women, through the provision of single-sex training; and introduces a common retirement age regardless of sex.

However, evidence that the original legislation (Equal Pay 1970; Sex Discrimination 1975) was not fully effective, and that the British government was resistant to the idea of sexual equality, may be judged by the fact that subsequent amendments were introduced as a consequence of directives from the EEC. As has been noted in Chapter 4, the EEC has been in the vanguard of proclaiming the need for equality between the sexes and has issued several directives: on Equal Pay (1975, 1983), Equal Opportunities (1976), Equal Treatment in Social Security (1978, 1984) and Sex Discrimination (1983). Earlier discussion (Chapters 4 and 6) has shown how inequalities under British law have been taken to the European Court of Justice, sometimes by individual women, such as Jackie Drake (over payment of the invalid care allowance) and Helen Marshall (over a common retirement age). As a consequence of the Court's decisions, injustices in the treatment of thousands of other women have been remedied. In ratifying the Court's decisions, the British Court of Appeal has confirmed that the EEC legislation has priority over British law where there are ambiguities. So women now have recourse to legislation not only in Britain but also in the EEC, together with the Equal Opportunities Commission, in claiming their rights. However, there is clearly a need for more publicity and economic support to pursue matters through the courts if women are to be encouraged to take action. A recent survey revealed that 42 per cent of the British sample either did not know, or thought there were no laws regarding, equality of treatment at work, and 66 per cent did not know about, or were not concerned with, what the European Community might be doing in this respect (*Women of Europe*, Supplement 5, 1980). Perhaps this should not be too surprising in the light of the evidence on equal treatment in relation to supplementary benefits in the UK (Kidd, *Journal of Social Policy*, forthcoming; and Chapter 4, this volume) where ignorance of legal rights was the result of obfuscation by the DHSS. Welfare rights groups have shown that awareness can be heightened and take up appreciably improved.

A conclusion might therefore be drawn that women are not aware of their disadvantage, or if they are, are disinclined to do anything about it because it requires not only that they seek redress through the courts, but also that they challenge male hegemony. The effect of such hegemony is apparent in the pervasive belief that equal treatment opportunities exist regardless of sex; thus the chief officer of a public body offers the following explanation for the lack of women among appointments: 'I must state that invitations to join any of our committees are issued on the basis of the suitability of people to do the job and they do not take much account of other factors such as sex' (Kerr, 1979). As was elaborated in Chapter 2, such statements are derived from a gender blindness located in male dominance, both at the level of ideology and the social structure.

Sexism and statistics

If we look at any of the chapters in this book we can see that women as a group are frequently disadvantaged as a result of their gender. As has been argued in several chapters (Chapters 2, 4, 5 and 6), it appears that women's position in society is rooted in the sexual division of labour both within the family, and in a complex relationship with this within the labour market. It is not possible, however, to provide all the evidence for women's disadvantage in a book based on readily available statistical data about women and men. As is evident from earlier discussion on specific areas (Chapters 3, 6 and 8), the prevalence of sexism in the compiling of official statistics obscures some of the realities of sex differences in the social structure. This has been underlined by an EOC seminar 'Women and Government Statistics' (1980a) which together with an increasing general awareness of this issue has begun to have an impact on the processing of official statistics (Chapters 5 and 8).

In trying to identify more clearly sexism in official statistics, which constitute the major sources of data for this book, Oakley (1979) defines it as a type of discrimination between people based on their social classification as female or male where sex is not a relevant characteristic, as for instance it is with childbirth and lactation.

They suggest that sexism in statistics is found in *areas* chosen for statistical analysis, the *concepts* used to organize and present the statistics, the way the *collection* of data is organized, the *processing* of the statistics and the *presentation* of the data.

In applying these criteria to the data in this book we can see that the authors of each chapter have noted gaps in the areas chosen for statistical analysis. For example: the definition of the family and the fact that it did not include accurate information on the number of one-parent families (Chapter 4); 'official' definitions of crime influenced by prevailing attitudes towards domestic violence and sexual harassment (Chapter 8); research into health which ignores sex as a variable relevant to the analysis (Chapter 3); electoral statistics which are not broken down by sex (Chapter 7); unemployment statistics which do not include the many women who are ineligible for benefit (Chapter 6). In addition, the authors have drawn attention to the *concepts* or assumptions about the basic familial role of women as dependants upon men which underlie how work is defined as a criterion for claiming supplementary benefit (Chapter 4); to sentencing decisions which are influenced by underlying assumptions related to the sex of the offender (Chapter 8); to the assumptions behind definitions of social class, based on the occupational status of the male head of the household (Chapter 2); to the concepts of femininity and masculinity which underpin subject and career choice (Chapter 5). Equal dangers have been revealed in the *collection* of data on employment, where limited definitions hide important contributions to the economy such as domestic and childcare, voluntary work, unpaid secretarial or accounting assistance as part of the family business (Chapters 4 and 6); health conditions where the separate recording of reproduction and menstruation reduces their impact (Chapter 3); and criminal statistics which are limited because they fail to recognize gender as a relevant characteristic (Chapter 8). Finally, it has to be noted in this context that many data that are collected are not *processed* – for example, information about wives' earnings and dependants' allowances available in the Inland Revenue which could help to provide invaluable information on family finances (Nissel, 1980); or the data on crimes which are reported to the police but not subsequently recorded (Chapter 8).

Since this is not a book of original data but a review of other people's work, it has not been possible to change the sexism inherent in many statistics. In addition, while the data we have drawn upon have been categorized on the basis of sex, little reference has been made to the implications of this. Our concern throughout has been to scrutinize existing data from this point of view. Where data are available, processed and published, it is usual for men to be taken as the base against which women are compared, so in our presentation we reversed this process by making women the focus of our interest, and to this end women appear first in each table. By highlighting gaps in the data, we have also drawn attention to information that we feel is needed in order to inform discussion about sex and gender differences and about discrimination against either women or men.

Sex and gender – continuity and change

So what changes have occurred since the first edition of this book, or more specifically, what can we point to as evidence of some advance towards greater sexual equality in the past decade or so? Alternatively, what evidence is there that inequalities remain and are likely to continue? In order to arrive at some overall conclusions, a brief summary of what emerges from the previous chapters is presented below.

The examination of education (Chapter 5) revealed that despite gender-biased expectations and the resulting differential treatment, women have made some significant gains. Thus in ten years (1975–85) the number of girls who achieved an 'O' level or its equivalent in Mathematics increased by 4 per cent; and more significantly in five years (1980–85) the number of girls gaining either a CSE or GCE in Physics increased by 48 per cent. These are both high-status subjects which should potentially open up greater occupational choice for women. For example, these kinds of educational gain could, in part, explain the increasing proportion of women on hospital medical staff, which between 1977 and 1985 has increased by a third (from 18 to 24 per cent) and in dentistry by over a half (from 11 to 17 per cent; see Chapter 3). More generally, recent research in Scotland concluded that, between 1976 and 1984, girls increased their overall attainment in comparison to boys (Willms and Kerr, 1987). In the light of these advances, it is not surprising that the percentage of women undergraduates in 1984 (42 per cent) represented an increase of 7 per cent since 1975, whereas for men the figure of 58 per cent was a decline of 6 per cent.

However, the evidence within education points to a gap between the rhetoric of legislation and the reality of practice. Thus research by the EOC (1983) concluded that women teachers' chances of promotion fell rapidly between 1963 and 1983; and not a single complaint of educational discrimination has been upheld between 1975 and 1985 under the Sex Discrimination Act (Weiner, 1985). Perhaps more invidious, because of its wideranging consequences, is that in opposition to women's educational advances, the current concern with links between education and industry appears to reinforce the sexual division of labour (Wickham, 1985a and b; see also Chapter 5, this volume). This is in response to the restructuring of the labour market which is increasing areas designated as specifically female, namely part-time, low-paid, low-status work (Beechey, 1986).

Some clues as to the relationship between education and the labour market and the implications for women has been revealed in our discussion of gender and the operation of the labour market (Chapter 6). This discussion (Chapters 2 and 6) has shown that, numerically, women are playing an increasing role in the labour force and now constitute 40 per cent of Britain's workforce; 63 per cent of mothers and married women are economically active, although between 1982 and 1987 the number of single mothers working fell by 5 per cent (Chapter 4). Initiatives, such as contract-compliance policies, in which some local authorities have insisted that any contractors they employ must conform to certain conditions, are attempts to break down discrimination on the basis of sex and race (Chapter 6).

In the seven years since 1980, women have made significant inroads into certain high-status professions; insurance and banking has an increase of 5 per cent; town planning an increase of 9 per cent, and personnel an increase of 16 per cent. At the same time, whilst overall trade union membership has been declining, the share of women in the total membership continues to expand; women are now in a clear majority in many white collar unions.

All of this might be seen as positive indicators of women's impact on the labour market, which has been paralleled by a decline in employers' perceptions of differences in performance between women and men.

However, in general, women's increasing economic activity has been characterized by their entry into jobs which are low-status, low-paid, and the least secure. In 1987, 44 per cent of all female employees were in part-time work, with the inevitable loss of work-related benefits, compared to 8 per cent of male employees. Recent decline in manufacturing has affected women's employment opportunities even more than men's, with greater numbers having to move into lower-paid, service sector jobs; ethnicity, when combined with gender, results in further depression of occupational status. Official statistics show female unemployment to be lower than that of males. This fact may reflect the compilation of the statistics, however, rather than women's availability for employment (Chapter 6). Although women's pay, relative to men's, rose significantly between 1970 and 1977 (Equal Pay Act 1970), a new stable differential has now emerged, with women on average earning 66 per cent of male earnings (Chapter 6). It is difficult not to conclude that despite the advances made in educational qualifications, being a woman in the labour market is more likely to result in being used as a member of a reserve army of labour; a secondary sector of the labour force, characterized by short-term and insecure employment, which paradoxically facilitates a rapid response to technological change.

In social welfare, we have already noted that women have made some achievements as a consequence of EEC directives (such as invalid care allowance, and eligibility for supplementary benefits). However, recent policies for community care, whereby children, the disabled and the elderly are discharged from institutions into the community, have placed a disproportionate burden on women in their role as 'natural' carers; an EOC survey (1980) revealed that 75 per cent of carers were female. In addition, changes introduced under the Social Security Act 1986 are likely to disadvantage women more than men. Thus, fluctuating earnings and periods of unemployment leading to a reduction in the state pension, the loss of some maternity benefits, an increasing dependence on full National Insurance contributions to qualify for certain benefits are all changes in which women will be the losers rather than men (Chapter 4). It would increasingly appear that the state draws on the myth of women's primary role as wife and mother, both as instruments of social control and in support of an idealized notion of family life; one which can provide 'care in the community', without substantial financial outlay.

With regard to political participation, since 1982, the number of women elected or appointed to public office has increased; in 1987 a record number of women (6 per cent of all Members of Parliament) was elected (Chapter 7). However, there is increasing awareness by all political parties that women are under-represented in the political sphere. Thus, women's issues are now on the political agenda. Nevertheless, although legislation may have succeeded in removing overt discrimination, the more subtle, covert discrimination remains in, for example, the procedures by which prospective parliamentary candidates are actually selected (Chapter 7). Overall, there have not been significant gains over the past decade in women's political participation, which is indicative of the persistent nature of inequalities based on gender. Analysis of the sexual division of labour (Chapters 2 and 6), which locates women firmly in the private domain of the family, has indicated the formidable barriers to women's equal participation in the public sphere. This is compounded by the fact that women who are successful in entering the political arena tend to adopt the dominant male ideology (Phillips, 1980).

It is in relation to criminal behaviour that assumptions about women's familial role appears to be an advantage (Chapter 8). Women appear to gain from the view generated by male-dominated agencies of social control that their crimes are of a different order (not just a different type) from that of men's and that they should be allowed for as long as possible to continue their caring role in the family. Despite this, the number of women in prison continues to rise, as does the number of men, and the effect of an institutional sentence is to confirm women in a double bind – failures both as women and as lawbreakers. Women, however, are clearly advantaged when it comes to health and life expectancy; thus for example 26 per cent of men die before the age of 65 as compared to only 16 per cent of women (Chapter 3). A glance through the advances that have been outlined would indicate, however, that we are, in the main, talking about advances in the position of middle-class women, through their involvement in employment and politics. As is evident (Chapters 2, 5 and 6), the characteristics of class and race result in a differential experience of the social structure for working-class and black women.

Overview
Clearly, there is a need to examine the extent to which, in any of the areas examined in this book, the position of women could be

altered so as to confront the question of social determinism of the position of women, and to discover what are, in a given social structure, the parameters of possible change. In the areas of education and politics it would seem that women, though disadvantaged, need not be imprisoned by their gender. The most problematic area is clearly the occupational structure which is fundamental to the whole social structure. The persistence of inequalities between the sexes in access to paid work, to career opportunities, in promotion prospects and in pay, is basic to an understanding of the relative positions of women and men in Britain today.

If women are effectively to challenge the inequalities of the occupational structure, they must come increasingly to realize that their designated female role as dependent on men is very much to women's disadvantage; the relative poverty imposed on women as a consequence of their expected familial role must be articulated and challenged. Women need to become aware that their situation results from the way society is organized; they must therefore challenge the institutional structure which seeks to impose gender roles. To achieve this, their whole perception of the female role will need to change, and their understanding of the realities, rather than the myths, of female activity will need to be revised. (Equally important is a corresponding need for change in male perceptions.)

However, the above arguments should not blind us to the processes by which gender roles are constructed and maintained; and to perceiving their location at both an ideological and material level. As the evidence in this book indicates, this implies a challenge not only at the personal but also at the institutional level; a challenge to the legal system; to social policy; to the sexual division of labour in the family and in employment; and to the cultural construction of gender relations perpetrated through the media. The aim will be to create a society in which women and men can live and express themselves unencumbered by cultural prescriptions, social constraints and an institutional structure underpinned by sexist principles and assumptions. In such a situation the range of choice and diversity of behaviour and roles will be greatly heightened. Women and men will be able to negotiate their relationships as people, without the imprisonment of expectations on how they should behave in accordance with their sex.

Notes on the contributors

Andrew Cooper graduated from the University of Southampton and received his doctorate from the University of Bristol. He has lectured both for the Extramural Department of the University of Birmingham and for the Workers' Educational Association. He taught Sociology at Worcester College of Higher Education before moving to the University College of Wales, Aberystwyth. His research interests include theories of the state, gender relations and social theory.

Tony Kidd read for a first degree in Sociology and Economics at the University of Manchester, a PGCE at Exeter University and a M.Soc.Sc. in Social Policy at Birmingham University. He began his teaching career at Hull College of Education where he taught Sociology and Social Anthropology on teacher education courses. This was followed by 'O' and 'A' level sociology teaching in a further education college in Teesside. Since joining the Social Science Division of Worcester College of Higher Education he has taught on BA, B.Ed and PGCE courses but specializes in social welfare and the sociology of organizations. He became Head of the Social Science Division in 1982. He has published a number of articles and monographs, and regularly reviews books for the *Times Educational Supplement*.

Ivan Reid attended a technical school and trained for two years as a teacher at St John's College, York, before reading a first degree in sociology at the University of Leicester and part-time higher degrees at the Universities of Liverpool and Bradford. His educational career commenced with secondary school teaching, but has been mainly in teacher education and particularly in-service education. He taught main-course sociology at Edge Hill College of Education and the sociology of education at the University of Bradford, where he was Chairman of the School of Applied Educational Studies, before transferring to his present post at the School of Education, University of Leeds. He has written several books, including *Sociological Perspectives on School and Education* (Open Books, 1978), *Social Class Differences in Britain* 3rd edition (Fontana, 1989) and *The Sociology of School and Education* (Fontana, 1986); a number of monographs and articles and is joint editor of *Research in Education* and an executive editor of the *British Journal of Sociology of Education*.

Erica Stratta graduated from Bedford College, University of London, and studied for her doctorate at the London School of Economics. She has taught in both secondary schools and further education. Currently she is senior lecturer in the Social Science Division of Worcester College of Higher Education, specializing in the area of deviance and social control. She has written several articles on the teaching of sociology and is the author of *The Education of Borstal Boys* (Routledge and Kegan Paul, 1970). Currently she is researching into the implementation of police liaison with local communities.

Beverley Skeggs graduated in Sociology from York University. After completing a PGCE, she studied for her PhD at Keele University, researching into young women's experience of further education. She has taught in further and higher education and currently lectures in the Social Science Division at Worcester College of Higher Education. She has written several articles on young women and sexuality and is currently writing a book arising out of her doctoral research.

Laura Thomas graduated from Worcester College of Higher Education. She worked with Eileen Wormald researching into The 300 Group and is co-author of a paper presented to the conference of Women's Political Aspirations at Nottingham University. As a research associate at Birmingham University she has co-produced a study of Mother and Baby Psychiatric Facilities in England and Wales. A paper, arising from this research, was presented at a conference at Keele University.

Michael Webb graduated with a degree in PPE from Trinity College, Oxford, in 1974, and researched in Economics at Leeds University. He trained as a secondary teacher at Coventry College of Education, and subsequently taught Economics and Social Science. As a Senior Lecturer in Economics at Worcester College of Higher Education he teaches on economics and sociology courses and is in charge of PGCE Economics. For a number of years he was Co-Director of Hereford and Worcester Education and Industry Centre, where he developed initiatives to promote girls' industrial and economic awareness. His publications include several articles on the teaching of Economics and Social Science. He is an active member of the Labour Party and stood as Labour candidate for Worcester in the 1987 General Election.

Eileen Wormald graduated from the London School of Economics and has since had a varied career as a research officer, abstractor, social worker and teacher. She is joint editor (with Robin Alexander) of *Professional Studies for Teaching* (SHRE, 1979) and (with Ivan Reid) of *Sociology and Teacher Education* (ATCDE, 1974) and *Sex Differences in Britain* (Blackwell, 1982). She has also written a number of journal articles on political socialization and women's participation in politics. Formerly Dean of the Faculty of Arts and Sciences at Worcester College of Higher Education, she currently teaches in the Education Department, of the University of Papua New Guinea. Here she continues her research into socialization and women candidates in the national elections, giving papers at international conferences in Australia and Papua New Guinea.

Bibliography

The following abbreviations are used:

ACAS	Arbitration Conciliation and Advice Service;
BSA	British Sociological Association
CCCS	Centre for Contemporary Cultural Studies;
CSO	Central Statistical Office;
DES	Department of Education and Science;
DHSS	Department of Health and Social Security;
DoE	Department of Employment;
EEC	European Economic Community;
EOC	Equal Opportunities Commission;
GMBATU	General Municipal, Boilermakers and Allied Trades Union
HMSO	Her Majesty's Stationery Office;
HOC	House of Commons;
ILO	International Labour Organization;
MSC	Manpower Services Commission;
NACRO	National Association for the Care and Resettlement of Offenders;
NAFE	Non-Advanced Further Education;
NCCL	National Council for Civil Liberties;
NFER	National Foundation for Educational Research;
OECD	Organization for Economic Co-operation and Development;
OPCS	Office of Population Censuses and Surveys;
PEP	Political and Economic Planning;
PSI	Policy Studies Institute;
TUC	Trade Union Congress;
TVEI	Technical Vocational Educational Initiative;
YOP	Youth Opportunities Programme;
YTS	Youth Training Scheme;
WRRC	Women's Research and Resourses Centre.

Abrams, P. (1981) *Practice and Progress: British Sociology 1950–1980*. London: Allen & Unwin.

Acker, S. (1983) Women and Teaching: A Semi-Detached Sociology of a Semi-Procession. In Walker and Barton (1983).

Acker, S., Megarry, J., Nisbet, S. and Hoyle, E. (1984) *World Yearbook of Education: Women and Education*. London: Kogan Page.

Adams, S. and Hunt, J. (1980) *Women, Work and Trade Union Organisation*. London: Workers Educational Association.

Adamson, O. (1976) Women's Oppression Under Capitalism, Part II. *Revolutionary Communist* (5).

Advisory, Conciliation and Arbitration Service (1978) The Toy Manufacturing Wages Council Report No. 13. London: ACAS.

Alexander, S. and Taylor, B. (1981) In Defence of Patriarchy. In *Feminist Anthology Collective* (1981).

Allen, I., Wicks, M., Finch, J. and Leaf, D. (1987) *Informal Care Tomorrow*. London: Policy Studies Institute.

Allen, S. (1982) Gender Inequality and Class Formation. In Giddens and Mackenzie (1982).

Allen, S. and Smith, C. (1975) Minority Group Experience of the Transition from Education to Work. In Brannen (1975).

Allen, S. and Wolkowitz, C. (1986) Homeworking and the Control of Women's Work, *Feminist Review* (1986).

Althusser, L. (1971) *Lenin and Philosophy and Other Essays*. London: New Left Books.

Anderson, K. (1975) Working Women and Political Participation, *American Journal of Political Science* 19 (3).

Annual Abstract of Statistics (117) (1981) CSO. London: HMSO.

Annual Abstract of Statistics (122) (1986) CSO. London: HMSO.

Annual Abstract of Statistics (123) (1987) CSO. London: HMSO.

Anthias, F. and Youal-Davis, M. (1983) Contextualising Feminism–Gender, Ethnic and Class Divisions. *Feminist Review*, 15.

Anyon, J. (1983) Intersections of Gender and Class: Accommodation and Resistance by Working-Class and Affluent Females to Contradictory Sex-Role Ideologies. In Walker and Barton (1983).

Apter, T. (1985) *Why Women don't have Wives – Professional Success and Motherhood*. London: Macmillan

APU (1980) *Mathematical Development in Prmary Schools Survey*. London: Assessment of Performance Unit.

Ardener, S. (1978) *Defining Females*. London: Croom Helm.

Arnold, E. et al. (1982) Microelectronics and Women's Employment, *Employment Gazette* 90 (9).

Arnot, M. (1981) Culture and Political Economy: Dual Perspectives in the Sociology of Women's Education, *Education Analysis* 3 (1).

Arnot, M. (1983) A Cloud over Co-education: An Analysis of the Forms of Transmission of Class and Gender Relations. In Walker and Barton (1983).

Arnot, M. (1986) State Education Policy and Girls' Educational Experiences. In Beechey and Whitelegg.

ATTI (1973) *The Education, Training and Employment of Women and Girls*. London: Association of Teachers in Technical Institutes.

Atkinson, J. (1984) *Manning for Uncertainty: Some Emerging UK Work Patterns*. Brighton: University of Sussex Institute of Manpower Studies.

Atkinson, J. and Meager, N. (1986) Is Flexibility Just a Flash in the Pan? *Personnel Management*, September.

AUT (1987) *Women into Higher Education*. London Association of University Teachers.

Bain, G. and Elias, P. (1985) Trade Union Membership in Great Britain: an Individual Level Analysis, *British Journal of Industrial Relations* 23.

Ballard, B. (1984) Women Part-time Workers: Evidence from the 1980 Women and Employment Survey, *Employment Gazette*, September.

Barber, A. (1980) Ethnic Origin and the Labour Force, *Employment Gazette*, August.

Barker, D. L. and Allen, S. (1976) *Dependence and Exploitation in Work and Marriage*. London: Longman.

Barker Lunn, J. C. (1972) The Influence of Sex, Achievement and Social Class on Junior School Children's Attitudes, *British Journal of Educational Psychology* 42 (1).

Baron, S. et al. (1981) *Unpopular Education*. CCCS Education Group. London: Hutchinson.

Barrett, M. (1980) *Women's Oppression Today*. London: Verso.

Barrett, M. (1984) Rethinking Women's Oppression – A Reply to Brenner and Ramas, *New Left Review* (146).

Barrett, M. and McIntosh, M. (1982) *The Anti-Social Family*. London: Verso.

Barron, R. and Norris, G. (1976) Sexual Division and the Dual Labour Market. In Barker and Allen (1976).

Bartok, K. M. (1980) Female Managers and the Quality of Working Life: The Impact of Sex Role Stereotypes, *Journal of Occupational Behaviour* (1).

Bates, I. et al. (1984) *Schooling for the Dole: The New Vocationalism*. London: Macmillan.

Bayley, M. (1973) *Mental Handicap and Community Care*. London: Routledge & Kegan Paul.

Beale, J. (1982) *Getting it Together – Women as Trade Unionists*. London: Pluto.

Beechey, V. (1977a) Female Wage Labour in Capitalist Production, *Capital and Class* (3).

Beechey, V. (1977b) Some Notes on Female Wage Labour, *Capital and Class* (3).

Beechey, V. (1979) On Patriarchy, *Feminist Review* (3).

Beechey, V. and Perkins, T. (1982) *Women's Part-time Employment in Coventry: A Study in the the Sexual Division of Labour*. Report to Joint EOC/SSRC Panel.

Beechey, V. (1986) Women's Employment in Contemporary Britain. In Beechey and Whitelegg (1986).

Beechey, V. (1987) *Unequal Work*. London: Verso.

Beechey, V. and Whitelegg, E. (1986) *Women in Britain Today*. Milton Keynes: Open University Press.

Bennett, Y. and Carter, D. (1983) *Day Release for Girls*. Manchester: EOC.

Bentzen, F. (1966) Sex Ratios in Learning and Behaviour Disorders, *The National Elementary Principal* (46).

Beral, V. (1979) Reproductive Mortality, *British Medical Journal* (2), 362–4.

Beral, V. (1985) Long Term Effects of Childbearing on Health *Journal of Epidemiology and Community Health* 39 (4).

Berg, S. and Dalton, T. (1977) UK Labour Force Activity Rates: Unemployment and Real Wages, *Applied Economics* 9 (3).

Berk, S. (1980) *Women and Household Labour*. London: Sage.

Berry, K., Grogan, K. and Hudson, G. (1987) *Hereford TVE Evaluation Pilot Project Final Report* Worcester: Worcester College of Higher Education.

Beveridge, W. (1942) *Report of a Committee on Social Insurance and Allied Services*, Cmnd 6404. London: HMSO.

Birke, L. (1986) *Women, Feminism and Biology*. Brighton: Wheatsheaf Books.

Black, D. (1980) *Inequalities in Health*. Report of a Research Working Group London: DHSS.

Blackburn, R. M. and Mann, M. (1979) *The Working-Class in the Labour Market*. London: Macmillan.

Blackstone, T. (1976) The Education of Girls Today. In Mitchell and Oakley (1976).

Blaxter, M. (1976) *The Meaning of Disability*. London: Heinemann.

Blaxter, M. (1987) Self-Reported Health. In *The Health and Lifestyle Survey* (1987).

Blondel, J. (1966) *Voters, Parties and Leaders*. Harmondsworth: Penguin Books.

Blunden, G. (1982) *Women's Place in NAFE: The Early Development of Three Colleges in South West England.* Unpublished PhD thesis: University of Bristol.

Blunden, G (1983) Our Women are expected to Become ... Women and Girls in Further Education in England at the Turn of the Century. In London Feminist History Group.

Bocock, D. (1972) cited in Spender (1982)

Bolton Committee of Enquiry into Small Firms (1971). London: HMSO.

Bone, A. (1980) *The Effect on Women's Opportunities of Teacher Training Cuts* Manchester: EOC.

Bosanquet, N. and Townsend, P. (1980) *Labour and Equality: A Fabian Study of Labour in Power 1924–9.* London: Heinemann.

Boston, S. (1980) *Women Workers and the Trade Unions.* London: Davis-Poynter.

Boston, S. (1987) *Women Workers and Trade Unions.* London: Lawrence & Wishart.

Bottomley, A. K. and Coleman, C. A. (1981) *Understanding Crime Rates.* Farnborough: Saxon House.

Bourque, S. C. and Grossholtz, J. (1974) Politics an Unnatural Practice: Political Science looks at Female Participation, *Politics and Society* (4).

Bowker, L. H. (1978) *Women, Crime and the Criminal Justice System.* Lexington, Mass.: Lexington Books.

Bowles, S. and Gintis, H. (1976) *Schooling in Capitalist America.* London: Routledge & Kegan Paul.

Box, S. (1981) *Deviance, Reality and Society*, 2nd edition. London: Holt, Rinehart & Winston.

Box, S. (1983) *Power, Crime and Mystification*, London: Tavistock.

Brannen, J. and Wilson, G. (1987) *Give and Take in Families: Studies in Resource Distribution.* London: Allen & Unwin.

Brannen, P. (1975) *Entering the World of Work.* London: HMSO.

Breakwell, G. M. and Weinberger, B. (1985) *Young Women in 'Gender-Atypical' Jobs: The Case of Trainee Technicians in the Engineering Industry*, Department of Employment Research Paper (49). London: HMSO.

Breitenbach, E. (1982) *Women Workers in Scotland: A Study of Women's Employment and Trade Unionism*, Glasgow: Pressgang.

Brelsford, P., Smith, G. and Rix, A. (1982) *Give Us a Break: Widening Opportunities for Young Women within YOP/YTS*, Research and Development Series (11). London: MSC.

Brenner, J. and Ramas, M. (1984) Rethinking Women's Oppression, *New Left Review* (144).

Brenton, M. and Ungerson, C. (1986) *Yearbook of Social Policy 1985–86*. London: Routledge & Kegan Paul.

Brenton, M. and Ungerson, C. (1987) *Yearbook of Social Policy 1986–7*. Harlow: Longman.

Brimelow, E. (1981) *Women in the Civil Service*. London: HMSO.

Bristol Women's Studies Group (1979) *Half the Story: An Introduction to Women's Studies*. London: Virago.

Bristow, S. L. (1978a) Women Councillors, *County Councils Gazette*, May.

Bristow, S. L. (1978b) Women Councillors, *County Councils Gazette*, November.

Bristow, S. L. (1978c) Women Councillors, *County Councils Gazette*, December.

Bristow, S. L. (1980) Women Councillors: An Explanation of the Under-representation of Women in Local Government, *Local Government Studies*, May–June.

British Labour Statistics Historical Abstract 1886–1968 (1971), DoE. London: HMSO.

Brod, H. (1987) *The Making of Masculinities*. London: Allen & Unwin.

Brookes, P. (1967) *Women at Westminster*. London: Peter Davies.

Brophy, J. and Smart, C. (1985) *Women in Law: Explorations in Law, Family and Sexuality*. London: Routledge & Kegan Paul.

Brophy, J. E. and Goode, T. L. (1970) Teachers' Communication of Differential Expectations for Children's Classroom Performance: Some Behavioural Data, *Journal of Education Psychology* 61 (5).

Brown, C. (1983) *Taxation and the Incentive to Work*. Oxford: University Press.

Brown, C. (1984a) *Black and White in Britain – the third PSI Study*. Aldershot: Gower.

Brown, C. (1984b) Patterns of Employment among Black and White People in Britain, *Employment Gazette* 92 (7).

Brown, G. W. and Harris, T. (1979) *Social Origins of Depression*. London: Tavistock.

Brown, R. (1980) *Going Places: Women in the Conservative Party*. London: Conservative Political Centre.

Brownmiller, S. (1976) *Against Our Will: Men, Women and Rape*. Ealing: Bantam.

Bruegel, I. (1979) Women as a Reserve Army: A Note on Recent British Experience, *Feminist Review* (3).

Bryant, M. (1979) *The Unexpected Revolution: A Study in the History of Education of Women and Girls in the Nineteenth Century*. University of London: NFER.

Buchanan, W., Errington, A. and Giles, A. (1982) *The Farmer's Wife: Her Role in the Management of the Business.* University of Reading: Farm Management Unit Study (2).

Burghes, L. (1982) *Living from Hand to Mouth: A Study of Sixty-Five Families Living on Supplementary Benefit* Poverty Pamphlet (50). London: Family Services Units and Child Poverty Action Group.

Burman, S. (1979) *Fit Work for Women.* London: Croom Helm.

Burstyn, J. N. (1980) *Victorian Education and the Idea of Womanhood.* London: Croom Helm.

Burton, L. (1975) *The Family Life of Sick Children.* London: Routledge & Kegan Paul.

Buswell, C. (1981) Sexism in School Routines and Classroom Practices, *Durham and Newcastle Research Review* 9 (46).

Byrne, E. (1975) Inequality in Education: Discriminal Resource – Allocation in Schools. *Educational Review* 27 (3).

Cabinet Office (1986) *Public Bodies.* London: HMSO.

Callan, H. and Ardener, S. (1984) *The Incorporated Wife.* London: Croom Helm.

Callender, C. (1984) *Women and Redundancy Payments: Another Unequal Struggle.* Oxford: Ruskin College, Trades Union Research Unit, Occasional Paper (91).

Callender, C. (1985) Women and Redundancy Payments, *Journal of Social Policy* (1).

Callender, C. (1986) Women and the Redundancy Process: A Case Study. In Lee (1986).

Campbell, A. (1977) What Makes a Girl Turn to Crime? *New Society* January.

Campbell, A. (1984) *The Girls in the Gang: A Report from New York City.* Oxford: Basil Blackwell.

Campbell, B. (1984) *Wigan Pier Revisited: Poverty and Politics in the Eighties.* London: Virago.

Campbell, B. (1987a) *The Iron Ladies,* London: Virago.

Campbell, B. (1987b) The Skeleton in the Family's Cupboard. *New Statesman,* August.

Campbell, M. and Jones, D. (1982) *Asian Youth in the Labour Market.* Bradford: Bradford College.

Caplan, P. J. (1980) Sex Differences in a Delinquent Clinic Population, *British Journal of Criminology,* 20 (4).

Carby, H. (1982) White Woman Listen! Black Feminism and the Boundaries of Sisterhood. In CCCS (1982).

Carlen, P. (1983) *Women's Imprisonment: A Study in Social Control.* London: Routledge & Kegan Paul.

Carlen, P. (1985) *Criminal Women: Autobiographical Accounts.*

Cambridge: Polity Press

Carlen, P. and Collison, M. (1980) *Radical Issues in Criminology*. Oxford: Martin Robertson.

Carr Report (1957) *Recruitment and Training of Young Workers in Industry*. National Joint Advisory Council London: HMSO.

Casburn, M. (1979) *Girls will be Girls* London: Explorations in Feminism WRRC.

Causer, G. A. (1987) *Inside British Society*. Brighton: Wheatsheaf Books.

Cavendish, R. (1982) *Women On the Line*. London: Routledge & Kegan Paul.

CCCS (1978) *Women Take Issue: Aspects of Women's Subordination*. London: Hutchinson.

CCCS (1982) *The Empire Strikes Back*. London: Hutchinson.

Census 1981: Economic Activity in Great Britain (1984). London: HMSO.

Chamberlain, M. (1975) *Fenwomen: A Portrait of Women in an English Village*. London: Virago.

Chapman, R. and Rutherford, J. (eds) (1988) *Male Order: Unwrapping Masculinity*. London: Lawrence & Wishart.

Charles, N. (1983) Women and Trade Unions in the Workplace, *Feminist Review* (15).

Chesney-Lind, M. (1973) The Judicial Enforcement of the Female Sex-Role: The Family Court and the Delinquent, *Issues in Criminology* (8).

Chetwynd, J. and Hartnett, O (1978) *The Sex Role System*. London: Routledge & Kegan Paul.

Chiplin, B., Curran, M. and Parsley, C. (1980) Relative Female Earnings in Great Britain and the Impact of Legislation. In Sloane (1980).

Chiplin, B. and Sloane, P. (1974) Sexual Discrimination in the Labour Market, *British Journal of Industrial Relations*, 12 (3).

Chiplin, B. and Sloane, P. (1982) *Tackling Discrimination in the Workplace*. Cambridge: University Press.

Chisholm, L. A. and Holland, J. (1986) Girls and Occupational Choice: Anti-Sexism in Action in a Curriculum Development Project. In Weiner and Arnot (1987).

Chodorow, N. (1978) *The Reproduction of Mothering: Psychoanalysis and the Sociology of Gender*. California: University of California Press.

City of Bradford (1983) *The Disabled*. Bradford: Social Services Department.

Civil Service Statistics (1975 and 1980). London: HMSO.

Civil Service (1977) *The Employment of Women in the Civil*

Service, Kemp Jones Report CSD Management Studies 3. London: HMSO.

Clarke, L. (1980) *Occupational Choice: A Critical Review of Research in the United Kingdom*, DOE, Careers Service Branch. London: HMSO.

Clarricoates, K. (1978) Dinosaurs in the Classroom: A Re-examination of Some Aspects of the Hidden Curriculum in Primary Schools, *Women's Studies International Quarterly* (1).

Clarricoates, K. (1980) The Importance of Being Ernest ... Emma ... Tom ... Jane. In Deem (1980).

Close, P. and Collins, R. (1985) *Family and Economy in Modern Society*. London: Macmillan.

Cloward, R. A. and Ohlin, L. E. (1960) *Delinquency and Opportunity: a Theory of Delinquent Gangs*. New York: The Free Press.

Clutterbuck, B. and Devine, M. (1987) *Business Woman: Present and Future*. London: Macmillan.

Coats, D. (1984) *The Context of British Politics*. London: Hutchinson.

Cockburn, C. (1983) *Brothers: Male Dominance and Technological Change*. London: Pluto Press.

Cockburn, C. (1985a) *Machinery of Dominance: Women, Men and Technical Know-How*. London: Pluto Press.

Cockburn, C. (1985b) *Women and Technology*. London: Workers Education Association.

Cockburn, C. (1986) The Relations of Technology. In Crompton and Mann (1986).

Cockburn, C. (1987a) *Two-Track Training: Sex Inequalities and the YTS*. London: Macmillan.

Cockburn, C. (1987b) *Women, Trade Unions and Political Parties*. London: Fabian Society Tract (349).

Cohen, A. K. (1955) *Delinquent Boys: the Culture of the Gang*. New York: The Free Press.

Cohen, P. (1982) School for the Dole, *New Socialist*, January–February.

Cohen, P. (1984) Against the New Vocationalism. In Bates et al. (1984).

Collins, R. (1985) 'Horses for Courses': Ideology and the Division of Domestic Labour. In Close and Collins (1985).

Comer, L. (1972) *Wedlocked Women*. London: Feminist Books.

Congenital Malformation Statistics (1983) OPCS Series MB3 (1). London: HMSO.

Connell, R. W. (1987) *Gender and Power*. Cambridge: Polity Press.

Conservative Women's National Advisory Council (1980 and 1986) *Women in Politics*. London: Conservative Party.

Contract Compliance and Equal Opportunities (1986) *Industrial Relations Review and Report* (381).

Cooke, K. (1982) *1970 Birth Cohort – 10 Year Follow-up Study: Interim Report*. University of York, Department of Social Policy and Social Work, Social Policy Research Unit, Working Paper DHSS 108 6/82 KC.

Cooper, C. and Davidson, M. (1982) *High Pressure – Working Lives of Women Managers*. London: Fontana.

Cooper, C. and Davidson, M. (1984a) *She Needs a Wife: Problems of Women Managers*. MCB: University Press.

Cooper, C. and Davidson, M. (1984b) *Women in Management: Career Development for Managerial Success*. London: Heinemann.

Coote, A. and Kellner, P. (1980) *Hear This Brother: Women Workers and Union Power*. London: *New Statesman*.

Cornbleet, A. and Libovitch, S. (1983) Anti-Sexist Initiatives in a Mixed Comprehensive School: A Case Study. In Wolpe and Donald (1983).

Cornbleet, A. and Sanders, S. (1982) *Developing Anti-Sexist Initiatives* (DASI), Project Report. London: ILEA.

Counter Information Services (1981) *Women in the 80s*. London: CIS.

Cousin, J., Curran, M. and Brown, R. (1982) *Working in the Inner City: a Case Study*. Department of Environment. London: HMSO.

Cousins, M. (1980) Men's Rea: A Note on Sexual Difference, Criminology and the Law. In Carlen and Collison (1980).

Coward, R. (1983) *Patriarchal Precedents: Sexuality and Social Relations*. London: Routledge & Kegan Paul.

Coward, R. (1984) *Female Desire: Women's Sexuality Today*. London: Paladin.

Cowie, C. and Lees, S. (1981) Slags or Drags, *Feminist Review* (9).

Cowie, J., Slater, E. and Cowie, V. (1968) *Delinquency in Girls*. London: Heinemann.

Coyle, A. (1982) Sex and Skill in the Organisation of the Clothing Industry. In West, J (1982b).

Coyle, A. (1984) *Redundant Women*. London: Women's Press.

Coyle, A. (1985) Going Private: The Implications of Privatisation for Women's Work, *Feminist Review* (2).

Cox, B. D. (1987) Body Measurements (heights, weights, girth, etc.). In *The Health and Lifestyle Survey* (1987).

Cragg, A. and Dawson, T. (1981) *Qualitative Research Among*

Homeworkers, Department of Employment Research Paper (21). London: HMSO.

Cragg, A. and Dawson, T. (1984) *Unemployed Women: A Study of Attitudes and Experiences*, DoE Research Paper (47). London: HMSO.

Craig, C., Garnsey, E. and Rubery, J. (1985) *Payment Structures and Smaller Firms: Women's Employment in Segmented Labour Markets*, Department of Employment Research Paper (48). London: HMSO.

Craig, F. W. S. (1984) *Britain Votes 3*. London: Parliamentary Research Services.

Crewe, I. et. al. (1976) *Party Identification and Beyond: Representations of Voting and Party Competition*. London: John Wiley.

Criminal Statistics for England and Wales 1985 (1986). Cm 10. London: HMSO.

Criminal Statistics, England and Wales, Supplementary Tables 1985, Vol. 1. *Proceedings in Magistrates Courts* (1986). London: HMSO.

Criminal Statistics, England and Wales, Supplementary Tables 1985, Vol. 2. *Proceedings in The Crown Court* (1986). London: HMSO.

Crine, S. (1979) *The Hidden Army*. London: Low Pay Unit.

Crompton, R. and Jones, G. (1984) *White-Collar Proletariat, Deskilling and Gender in Clerical Work*. London: Macmillan.

Crompton, R. and Mann, M. (1986) *Gender and Stratification*. Cambridge: Polity Press.

Crosland, A. (1956) *The Future of Socialism*. London: Cape.

Crowther Report (1960) *'Fifteen to Eighteen' A Report of the Central Advisory Council*, Vols 1–3. London: HMSO.

Cunnington, S. (1980) Some Aspects of Prostitution in the West End of London. In West (1980).

Curran, M. (1985) *Stereotypes and Selection: Gender and Family in the Recruitment Process*. London: EOC, HMSO.

Currell, M. (1974) *Political Women*. London: Croom Helm.

Curson, C. (1986) *Flexible Patterns of Work*. London: Institute of Personnel Management.

Dale, J. and Foster, P. (1986) *Feminists and State Welfare*. London: Routledge & Kegan Paul.

Dale, R. (1981) *Education and the State: Politics, Patriarchy and Practice*. Brighton: Falmer Press.

Daly, M. (1979) *Gyn-Ecology: The Metaethics of Radical Feminism*. London: Women's Press.

Daniel, W. W. (1980) *Maternity Rights: The Experience of Women*.

London: PSI.

Daniel, W. W. and Millward, N. (1983) *Workplace Industrial Relations in Britain – the DE/PSI/ESRC Survey.* London: Heinemann.

Datesman, S. K. and Scarpetti, F. R. (1986) *Women, Crime and Justice.* Oxford: University Press.

David, M. E. (1978) The Family–Education Couple: Towards an Analysis of the William Tyndale Dispute. In Littlejohn et al. (1978).

David, M. E. (1980) *The State, Family and Education.* London: Routledge & Kegan Paul.

David, M. E. (1981) Social Policy and Education: Towards a Political Economy of Schooling and Sexual Divisions. *British Journal of Sociology of Education* 2 (1).

David, M. E. (1985) Motherhood and Social Policy – A Matter for Education?, *Critical Social Policy* (12).

Davidoff, L. (1973) *The Best of Circles.* London: Croom Helm.

Davidson, M. and Cooper, C. (1983a) *Women Managers: Their Problems and What Can Be Done to Help Them.* Sheffield: Manpower Services Commission, Training Division.

Davidson, M. and Cooper, C. (1984) She Needs a Wife: Problems of Women Managers, *Leadership and Organisation Development Journal* 5 (3).

Davies, L. (1980) Deviance and Sex Roles in School. Unpublished PhD thesis: University of Birmingham.

Davin, A. (1978) Imperialism and Motherhood, *History Workshop Journal* (5).

Davin, A. (1979) Mind You Do As You Are Told, Reading Books for Board School Girls 1870–1902, *Feminist Review* (3).

Deem, R. (1978) *Women and Schooling.* London: Routledge & Kegan Paul.

Deem, R. (1980) *Schooling for Women's Work.* London: Routledge & Kegan Paul.

Deem, R. (1981) State Policy and Ideology in the Education of Women 1944–1980, *British Journal of Sociology of Education* 12 (2).

Deem, R. (1986) *All Work and No Play? The Sociology of Women and Leisure.* Milton Keynes: Open University Press.

Delamont, S. (1980) *Sex Roles and the School.* London: Methuen.

Delamont, S. (1981) *The Sociology of Women.* London: Allen & Unwin.

Delamont, S. and Duffin, L. (1978) *The Nineteenth-Century Woman: Her Cultural and Physical World.* London: Croom Helm.

Delphy, C. (1984) *Close to Home*. London: Hutchinson.
Denver, D. T. (1982) Are Labour Electors Prejudiced Against Women Candidates?, *Politics* 2 (1).
DES (1975) *Education Survey 21: Curricular Differences for Boys and Girls*. London: HMSO.
DES (1978) *Primary Education in England*. London: HMSO.
DES (1985) *Statistics of Education*. London: HMSO.
DES (1986) *Statistics of Education*. London: HMSO.
DoE (1985) *New Earnings Survey*. London: HMSO.
Dex, S. (1983a) Second Chances? FE, Ethnic Minorities and Labour Markets. In Gleeson (1983).
Dex, S. (1983b) The Second Generation: West Indian Female School Leavers. In Phizacklea (1983).
Dex, S. (1984) Women's Occupational Profiles: Evidence from the 1980 Women and Employment Survey, *Employment Gazette* 92 (12).
Dex, S. (1985) *The Sexual Division of Work*. Brighton: Wheatsheaf Books.
Dex, S. and Perry, M. (1984) Women's Employment Changes in the 1970s, *Employment Gazette* 92 (4).
Dex, S. and Shaw, L. B. (1986) *British and American Women at Work: Do Equal Opportunities Matter?*. London: Macmillan.
Dickens, M. (1983) Women and the Adult Training Strategy, *Unemployment Unit Bulletin* (9).
Dobash, R. and Dobash, R. (1980) *Violence against Lives*. Wells: Open Books.
Dobash, R. P. and Dobash, R. (1986) *The Imprisonment of Women*. Oxford: Basil Blackwell.
Dod's Parliamentary Companion. Hailsham: Dod's.
Dominelli, L. (1984) Differential Justice: Domestic Labour, Community Service and Female Offenders, *Probation Journal* 31 (3).
Donovan Commission (1968) *Report of the Royal Commission on Trade Unions and Employers Associations*. London: HMSO.
Douglas, J. W. B. (1964) *The Home and the School*. London: MacGibbon and Kee.
Downes, D. (1966) *The Delinquent Solution: A Study in Subcultural Theory*. London: Routledge & Kegan Paul.
Dowse, R. E. and Hughes, J. A. (1971) Girls, Boys and Politics, *British Journal of Sociology* 22 (1).
Drake, B. (1984) *Women in Trade Unions*. London: Virago.
Dreghorn, C. R., Roughneen, P., Graham, J. and Hambleden, D. L. (1986) The Real Cost of Joint Replacement, *British Medical Journal* (1).

Duverger, M. (1955) *The Political Role of Women*. Paris: UNESCO.

Dyhouse, C. (1977) Good Wives and Little Mothers: Social Anxieties and the School Girls Curriculum 1890–1920, *Oxford Review of Education* 3 (2).

Dyhouse, C. (1981) *Girls Growing Up in Late Victorian and Edwardian England* London: Routledge & Kegan Paul.

Eaton, M. (1983) Mitigating Circumstances: Familiar Rhetoric, *International Journal of Sociology of Law* (11).

Eaton, M. (1986); *Justice for Women? Family, Court and Social Control*. Milton Keynes: Open University Press.

Education Statistics for the United Kingdom (1982, 1987) London: HMSO.

Edwards, E. G. and Roberts, I. J. (1980) British Higher Education: Long Term Trends in Student Enrolment, *Higher Education Review* (12).

Edwards, S. S. M. (1984) *Women on Trial*. Manchester: Manchester University Press.

Eichenbaum, L. and Orbach, S. (1982) *Outside In, Inside Out*. Harmondsworth: Penguin Books.

Eichler, M. (1980) *The Double Standard: A Feminist Critique of Feminist Social Science*. London: Croom Helm.

Ellis, V. (1981) *The Role of Trade Unions in the Promotion of Equal Opportunities*. Manchester: EOC.

Elston, M. A. (1980) Medicine: Half Our Future Doctors?. In Silverstone and Ward (1980).

Employment Gazette, DoE. London: HMSO.

English Life Tables (14) (1987) OPCS Series DS (7). London: HMSO.

EOC (1979) *Research Bulletin* (1). Manchester: EOC.

EOC (1979) *Third Annual Report*. Manchester: EOC.

EOC (1980a) *Women and Government Statistics* Research Bulletin (4). Manchester: EOC.

EOC (1980b) *The Experience of Caring for Elderly and Handicapped Dependants*. Manchester: EOC.

EOC (1981) *Annual Report 1980*, Manchester: EOC.

EOC (1982) *Gender and the Secondary School Curriculum*, Research Report (6). Manchester: EOC.

EOC (1984) *Women and Public Appointments: Report of an Investigation into Appointments to Public Bodies*. Manchester: EOC.

EOC (1985a) *Occupational Segregation by Sex*, Research Bulletin (9). Manchester: EOC.

EOC (1985b) Voluntary Bodies can be a Stepping Stone to Public Life for Women, *News Release* (14). Manchester: EOC.

EOC (1986a) *Childcare and Equal Opportunities: Some Policy Perspectives.* London: HMSO.

EOC (1986b) *Men's Jobs? Women's Jobs? Practical Guidance On Why Many Jobs Are Done Only By Men Or Only By Women.* London: HMSO.

EOC (1986c) *Wanted Railman: Report of an Investigation into Equal Opportunities for Women on British Rail.* London: HMSO.

EOC (1986d) *Tenth Annual Report 1985.* Manchester: EOC.

EOC (1987a) *The Impact of Selection Testing on Employment Opportunities of Men and Women.* Manchester: EOC.

EOC (1987b) *Sex Discrimination in the Recruitment Process: Final Report.* Manchester: EOC.

EOC (1987c) *Eleventh Annual Report.* Manchester: EOC.

Epstein, T. S., Crehan, K., Garter, A. and Sass, J. (1986) *Women, Work and Family in Britain and Germany.* London: Croom Helm.

Equal Pay and Opportunity Campaign (1980) *Women and Word Processors: An EPOC Survey.* London: EPOC.

Ethnic Origin and Economic Status (1987) *Employment Gazette*, January.

EEC (1979) *European Men and Women in 1978: A Comparative Study of Socio-Political Attitudes in the European Community.* Luxembourg: EEC.

EEC (1980) *European Women in Paid Employment: Their Perception of Discrimination at Work.* Brussels: EEC.

EEC (1984a) *European Women in Paid Employment*, Brussels: EEC.

EEC (1984b) *Men and Women of Europe in 1983.* Brussels: EEC.

Evans, J. (1980) Women and Politics: A Reappraisal. *Political Studies* 28 (2).

Evans, T. (1984) Gender Differentiation and Interaction in Australian Primary Schools. In Acker et al. (1984).

Family Policy Studies Centre (1988) *Caring Costs: The Social Security Implications*, Briefing Paper. London: Family Policy Studies Centre.

Family Policy Issue 3 (1987) London: Family Policy Studies Centre.

Farrington, D. and Morris, D. (1983) Sex, Sentencing and Reconvictions, *British Journal of Criminology* 23 (3).

Faulkner, W. and Arnold, E. (1985) *Smothered by Invention – Technology in Women's Lives.* London: Pluto.

Fawcett Society (1985) *The Class of 1984: A Study of Girls on the First Year of the Youth Training Scheme.* National Joint Committee of Working Women's Organisations.

Feminist Anthology Collective (1981) *No Turning Back: Writings from the Women's Movement 1975–1980*. London: Women's Press.

Feminist Review (1986) *Waged Work*. London: Virago.

Fenner, N. (1987) Leisure, Exercise and Work. In *The Health and Lifestyle Survey* (1987).

Ferguson, M. (1985) *Forever Feminine: Women's Magazines and the Cult of Femininity*. Aldershot: Gower.

Fidgett, T., Laidlaw, C. J. and McGuire, S. (1985) Female Operators in the Engineering Industry, *Women and Training News* (18).

Fildes, S. (1987) *Contemporary Feminist Theory*. Brighton: Wheatsheaf Books.

Finch, J. (1983) *Married to the Job – Wives' Incorporation into Men's Work*, London: Allen & Unwin.

Finch, J. and Groves, D. (1980) Community Care and the Family: A Case for Equal Opportunities?, *Journal of Social Policy* 9 (4).

Finch, J. and Groves, D. (1983) *A Labour of Love: Women, Work and Caring*. London: Routledge & Kegan Paul.

Finegan, B., Gallie, D. and Roberts, B. (1985) *New Approaches to Economic Life: Economic Restructuring and the Social Division of Labour*. Manchester: University Press.

Finer Report (1974) *Report of the Committee on One Parent Families*, Cmnd 5629. London: HMSO.

Finn, D. (1984) Britain's Misspent Youth, *Marxism Today*, February.

Firestone, S. (1980) *The Dialect of Sex: The Case for Feminist Revolution*. London: Women's Press.

Fitzgerald, T. (1983) The New Right and The Family. In Loney et al. (1983).

Flude, M. and Ahier, J. (1975) *Educability, Schools and Ideology*. London: Croom Helm.

Foggerty, M., Allen, I. and Walters, P. (1981) *Women in Top Jobs, 1968–1979*. London: Heinemann.

Fonda, N and Moss, P. (1976) *Mothers in Employment*. Uxbridge: Brunel University.

Fowler Report (1985) *Reform of Social Security: Programme for Change* Vol. 2, Cmnd 9518. London: HMSO.

Francis, J. G. and Peele, G. (1978) Reflections on Generational Analysis: Is there a Shared Political Perspective between Men and Women?, *Political Studies* 26 (3).

Fraser, D. (1976) *The New Poor Law in the Nineteenth Century*. London: Macmillan.

French, J. and French, P. (1984) Sociolinguistics and Gender Divisions. In Acker et al. (1984).

Friedl, E. (1975) *Women and Men: An Anthropologist's View.* Eastbourne: Holt, Rinehart & Winston.

Fryer, R. H., Fairclough, A. .H. and Manson, T. B. (1978) Facilities for Female Shop Stewards: The Employment Protection Act and Collective Agreements, *British Journal of Industrial Relations* 16.

Fulton Committee (1968) *The Civil Service*, London: HMSO.

Fuller, M. (1980) Black Girls in a London Comprehensive School. In Deem (1980).

Galton, M. (1981) Differential Treatment of Boys and Girls During Science Lessons. In Kelly (1981).

Gamanikov, E., Morgan, D., Purvis, J. and Taylorson, D. (1983) *The Public and the Private.* London: Heinemann.

Garabedian, P. G. and Gibbons, D. C. (1970) *Becoming Delinquent*, Chicago Ill.: Aldine Press.

Gardiner, J. (1975) Women's Domestic Role, *New Left Review* 89.

Garnsey, E. (1978) Women's Work and Theories of Class and Stratification, *Sociology* 12 (2).

Gaskell, J. (1977/8) Sex-Role Ideology and the Aspirations of High School Girls, *Interchange* 8 (3).

Gavron, H. (1966) *The Captive Wife.* Harmondsworth: Penguin Books.

General Household Survey 1975. (1977) OPCS GHS (5) London: HMSO.

General Household Survey 1978. (1980) OPCS GHS (8) London: HMSO.

General Household Survey 1979 (1981) OPCS Social Survey Division Series GHS (9). London: HMSO.

General Household Survey 1980 (1982) OPCS (10). London: HMSO.

General Household Survey 1981. (1983) OPCS GHS (11) London: HMSO.

General Household Survey 1982 (1984) OPCS (12). London: HMSO.

General Household Survey 1983 (1985) OPCS (13). London: HMSO.

General Household Survey 1984 (1986a) OPCS (14). London: HMSO.

General Household Survey 1985 (advance summary) (1986b). London: HMSO.

General Household Survey 1985. (1987) OPCS GHS (15) London: HMSO.

Gibb, V. (1983) The Recreation and Perpetuation of the Secretarial Myth. In Gleeson (1983).

Gibbens, T. C. N. and Prince, J. (1962) *Shoplifting*. London: Institute for the Study and Treatment of Delinquency.

Giddens, A. and MacKenzie,G. (1982) *Social Class and the Division of Labour*. Cambridge: University Press.

Gilhooly, M. (1982) Social Aspects of Senile Dementia. In Taylor and Gilmore (1982).

Gill, C. (1977) *Luke Street: Housing Policy Conflict and the Creation of the Delinquent Area*. London: Macmillan.

Ginsberg, S. (1976) Women, Work and Conflict. In Fonda and Moss (1976).

Gleeson, D. (1983) *Youth Training and the Search for Work*. London: Routledge and Kegan Paul.

Gleeson, D. (1987) *TVEI and Secondary Education: A Critical Appraisal*. Milton Keynes: Open University Press.

Gleeson, D. and Mardle, G. (1980) *FE or Training: A Case Study in the Theory and Practice of Day Release Education*. London: Routledge & Kegan Paul.

Glendinning, C. (1983) *Unshared Care*. London: Routledge & Kegan Paul.

Glendinning, C. and Millar, J. (1987) *Women and Poverty in Britain*. Brighton: Wheatsheaf Books.

Goffee R. and Scase, R. (1985) *Women in Charge – The Experiences of Female Entrepreneurs*. London: Allen and Unwin.

Goldberg, S. (1974) *The Inevitability of Patriarchy*. Aldershot: Temple Smith.

Golding, P. and Middleton, S. (1982) *Images of Welfare*. Oxford: Martin Robertson.

Goldshmidt-Clermont, L. (1983) *Unpaid Work in the Household – A Review of Economic Evaluation Methods*. Geneva: ILO.

Goldthorpe, J. (1983) Women and Class Analysis: In Defence of the Conventional View, *Sociology* 17 (4).

Goldthorpe, J. and Payne, C. (1986) Trends in Intergenerational Class Mobility in England and Wales 1972–1983, *Sociology* 20 (1).

Goodson, I. (1984) *Subjects for Study: Case Studies in Curriculum History*. Lewes: Falmer Press.

Goot, M. and Reid, E. (1975) *Women and Voting Studies: Mindless Matrons or Sexist Scientism*. London: Sage.

Gorer, G. (1973) *Sex and Marriage in England Today: A Study of the Views and Experiences of the Under 45s*. London: Panther.

Grafton, T. (1983) Gender and Curriculum Choice: A Case Study. In Hammersley and Hargreaves (1983).

Graham, H. (1987a) Being Poor: Perceptions and Coping Strategies of Lone Mothers. In Brannen and Wilson (1987).

Graham, H. (1987b) Women's Poverty and Caring. In Glendinning and Millar (1987).

Gray, A. (1976) Family Budgeting Systems: Some Findings From Studies in Edinburgh and Portsmouth. In Newman (1976).

Gray, H. L. (1985) Men with Women Bosses: Some Gender Issues, *Management Education and Development* 16.

Gray, P. G., Todd, J. E., Slack, G. L. and Bulman, J. S. (1970) *Adult Dental Health in England and Wales in 1968*, OPCS Social Survey Division for DHSS. London: HMSO.

Green, F., Hadjimath, E. O. C. and Smail, R. (1985) Fringe Benefit Distribution in Britain, *British Journal of Industrial Relations* 23.

Greenhalgh, C. (1977) A Labour Supply Function for Married Women, *Economica* 44.

Greenhalgh, C. A. (1980) Male–Female Wage Differentials in Great Britain: Is Marriage an Equal Opportunity?, *Economic Journal* 90.

Greenhalgh, C. A. and Stewart, M. B. (1982) The Effects and Determinants of Training. Coventry: University of Warwick, *Warwick Economic Research Papers* (213).

Greenhalgh, C. A. and Stewart, M. B. (1985) The Occupational Status and Mobility of British Men and Women, *Oxford Economic Papers* (37).

Greenwood, V. (1981) The Myth of Female Crime. In Morris (1981).

Griffin, C. (1982) *The Good, the Bad and the Ugly – Images of Young Women in the Labour Market*, Birmingham: CCCS.

Griffin, C. (1984) Birmingham Girls: From School to Work. DoE: Careers Service Branch, *Careers Bulletin*, Spring.

Griffin, C (1985) *Typical Girls*. London: Routledge & Kegan Paul.

Griffin, C. (1986) *Black and White Youth in a Declining Job Market: Unemployment amongst Asian, Afro-Caribbean and White Young People in Leicester*. Leicester University: Centre for Mass Communication Research.

Grimes, J. A. (1978) The Probability of Admission to a Mental Hospital or Unit. In *In-Patient Statistics from the Mental Health Enquiry for England 1975* (1978).

Growing Older. (1981) DHSS, London: HMSO.

Hadjifotiou, N. (1983) *Women and Harassment at Work*. London: Pluto Press.

Hadow Report (1923) Differentiation of the Curricula between the sexes in Secondary Schools. Board of Education. London: HMSO.

Hadow Report (1926) The Education of the Adolescent. Board of Education. London: HMSO.

Hagan, J., Simpson, J. H. and Gillis, A. R. (1979) The Sexual Stratification of Social Control: A Gender-Based Perspective on Crime and Delinqency. *British Journal of Sociology* 30 (1).

Hakim, C. (1978) Sexual Divisions within the Labour Force: Occupational Segmentation, *Employment Gazette* 86 (ii).

Hakim, C. (1979) *Occupational Segregation*, London: DOE Research Paper (9.).

Hakim, C. (1980) Homeworking: Some New Evidence, *Employment Gazette* 88 (10).

Hakim, C. (1984a) Employers' Use of Homework, Outwork and Freelances, *Employment Gazette* 92 (4).

Hakim, C. (1984b) Homework and Outwork – National Estimates from Two Surveys, *Employment Gazette*. 92 (1).

Hakim, C. (1985) *Employers' Use of Outwork: A Study using the 1980 Workplace Industrial Relations Survey and the 1981 National Survey of Homeworking*. London: DoE Research Paper (44).

Hakim, C. (1987a) Homeworking in Britain: Key Findings from the National Survey of Home-Based Workers, *Employment Gazette* 95 (2).

Hakim, C. (1987b) Trends in the Flexible Workforce, *Employment Gazette*, November.

Hall, C. (1979) The Early Formation of Victorian Domestic Ideology. In Burman (1979).

Hall R. E. (1985) *Ask Any Woman: A London Inquiry into Rape and Sexual Assault*. Bristol: Falling Wall Press.

Halsey, A. H. (1982) *Trends in British Society Since 1900*. London: Macmillan.

Halsey, A. H. (1987) *Social Trends* (17). London: CSO.

Hamill, L. (1978) *Wives as Sole and Joint Breadwinners*. The Government Economic Service Working Paper No. 13. DHSS. London: HMSO.

Hamilton, M. and Leo-Rhynie, A. E. (1984) Sex Roles and Secondary Education in Jamaica. In Acker et al. (1984).

Hammersley, M. and Hargreaves, A. (1983) *Curriculum Practice: Some Ideological Case Studies*. Barcombe: Falmer Press.

Hammond, R. (1986) The Trade Union and the Conflict between Work and Home. In Epstein, et al. (1986).

Handy, C. (1984) *The Future of Work*. Oxford: Basil Blackwell.

Harding, J. (1982) CDT What's Missing?, *Studies in Design Education, Craft and Technology* 15 (1).

Harris, A. (1971) *Handicapped and Impaired in Great Britain*. London: HMSO.

Harris, C. (1979) The Sociology of the Family, *Sociological Review Monograph* (28).

Harris, J. (1977) *William Beveridge: A Biography*. Oxford: Clarendon Press.

Harrison, B. (1978) *Separate Spheres*. London: Croom Helm.

Harrison, B. (1986) Women in a Men's House, *Historical Journal* 29 (3).

Harrison, G. A. and Boyce, A. J. (1972) *The Structure of Human Populations*. Oxford: Clarendon Press,

Harrison, M. (1979) Participation of Women in Trade Union Activities, *Industrial Relations Journal*, Summer.

Hartley, D. (1980) Sex Differences in the Infant School: Definitions and Theories, *British Journal of Sociology of Education* (1).

Hartmann, H. (1982) Capitalism, Patriarchy and Job Segregation. In Held and Giddens (1982)

Haskey, J (1986) One-parent Families in Great Britain, *Population Trends* 45.

Heald, G. and Wybrow, R. (1986) *The Gallup Survey of Britain 1985*. London: Croom Helm.

Health and Personal Social Services Statistics for England 1986 (1986) DHSS. London: HMSO.

The Health and Lifestyle Survey (1987). London: Health Promotion Research Trust.

Hearn, J. (1987) *The Gender of Oppression*. Brighton: Wheatsheaf Books.

Hearn, J. and Parkin, W. (1987) *Sex at Work – the Power and Paradox of Organisation Sexuality*. Brighton: Wheatsheaf Books.

Heath, A., Jowell, R. and Curtice, J. (1985) *How Britain Votes*. Oxford: Pergamon Press.

Hedblom, M. (1981) *Women and Mass Media*. European Consortium for Political Research Workshop, University of Lancaster.

Heidensohn, F. (1986) The Deviance of Women: A Critique and an Enquiry, *British Journal of Sociology* 19 (2).

Heidensohn, F. (1981) Women and the Penal System. In Morris (1981).

Heilman, M. and Saruwatari, L. (1979) When Beauty is Beastly: Effects of Appearance and Sex on Evaluations of Job Applicants for Managerial and Non-Managerial Jobs, *Organisational Behaviour and Human Performance* 23 (3).

Held, D. and Giddens, A. (1982) *Classes, Power and Conflict* London: Macmillan.

Herzog, M. (1980) *From Hand to Mouth – Women and Piecework*. Harmondsworth: Penguin Books.

Hewitt, P. (1980) Sex Equality. In Bosanquet and Townsend (1980).

Hills, J. (1981a) Candidates: The Impact of Gender, *Parliamentary Affairs* 34 (2).

Hills, J. (1981b) Britain: In Lovenduski and Hills (1981).

Hills, J. (1982) Women Local Councillors – A Reply to Bristow, *Journal of Local Government Studies*, January–February.

Hirsche, B. T. and Addison, J. T. (1986) *The Economic Analysis of Unions: New Approaches and Evidence*. Boston: Allen & Unwin.

History Workshop (1985) Editorial, *History Workshop* (19), Spring.

Hobson, D. (1978) Housewives: Isolation as Oppression. In Women's Study Group: CCCS (1978).

Hoel, B. (1982) Contemporary Clothing 'Sweatshops', Asian Female Labour and Collective Organisation. In West (1982b).

Hoffman-Bustamente, D. (1973) The Nature of Female Criminality, *Issues in Criminology* 8 (2).

Hope, E., Kennedy, M. and De Winter, A. (1976) Homeworkers in North London. In Barker and Allen (1976).

Hospital In-Patient Enquiry 1985 (1987) Summary Tables, Series MB 4 (26), DHSS/OPCS. London: HMSO

Hough, M. and Mayhew, P. (1983) *The British Crime Survey*, Home Office Research Study (76). London: HMSO.

Hough, M. and Mayhew, P. (1985) *Taking Account of Crime: Key Findings from the 1984 British Crime Survey*, Home Office Research Study (85). London: HMSO.

House of Commons Social Services Committee (Short Report) (1985) *Community Care*. London: HMSO.

Hudson, A. (1983) The Welfare State and Adolescent Femininity, *Youth and Policy* 2 (1).

Humphries, J. (1977) Class Struggle and the Persistence of the Working Class Family, *Cambridge Journal of Economics* (1).

Hunt, A. (1975) *Management Attitudes and Practices Women at Work*, OPCS Social Survey Division. London: HMSO.

Hunt, A. (1978) *The Elderly at Home*, OPCS Social Survey Division. London: HMSO.

Hunt, J. (1982) A Woman's Place is in her Union. In West (1982b).

Hutter, B. and Williams, G, (1981) *Controlling Women: The Normal and the Deviant*. London: Methuen.

Huws, U. (1980) *Your Job in the 80s – A Woman's Guide to New Technology*. London: Pluto Press.

Huws, U. (1987) Bargaining for Equality, *Labour Research* 76 (4).

Hyman, H. H. (1959) *Political Socialisation*. New York: Free Press.

Ingleby, J. D. (1960) *Report of the Committee on Children and Young Persons* (Ingleby Report). London: HMSO.

Ingleby, J. D. and Cooper, E. (1974) How Teachers Perceive First Year School Children, *Sociology* 8 (3).

In-Patient Statistics from the Mental Health Enquiry for England 1975 (1978) DHSS. London: HMSO.

In-Patient Statistics from the Mental Health Enquiry for England 1982 (1985) DHSS. London: HMSO.

Institute of Directors (1983) *Survey on Women at the Top*. London: Institute of Directors.

Institute for Employment Research (1982) *Women's Working Lives: Evidence from the National Training Survey*. Warwick: University of Warwick.

Institute of Manpower Studies (1984) *Flexibility, Uncertainty and Manpower Management*. Brighton: University of Sussex Institute of Manpower Studies, Report CN526.

Institute of Personnel Management (1987) *Contract Experience – The UK Experience*. London: IPM.

Jacob, H. (1982) Initial Recruitment of Elected Officials, *Journal of Politics* 28.

Jaggar, A. (1983) *Feminist Politics and Human Nature*. Ottawa: Rowman & Allanheld.

James, S. and Costa, M. D. (1973) *The Power of Women and the Subversion of the Community*. Bristol: Falling Wall Press.

James, W. P. T. (1979) *Research on Obesity*, DHSS Series 23. London: HMSO.

Jenkins, R. (1985) Sex Differences in Minor Psychiatric Morbidity, *Psychological Medicine*, Monograph Supplement (7).

Jenkins, R. and Clare, A. W. (1985) Women and Mental Illness, *British Medical Journal* (1).

Jensen, G. and Eve, R. (1976) Sex Differences in Delinquency: An Examination of Popular Sociological Explanations, *Criminology: an Interdisciplinary Journal* 13.

Johnson, R. (1970) Education and Social Control in Early Victorian England, *Past and Present* 49.

Joint Review Group on Employment (1983) *Opportunities for Women in the Civil Service*. London: HMSO.

Joll, C. (1986) *Women in Britain*. London: Pluto Press.

Jones, S. (1986) *Policewomen and Equality*. London: Macmillan.

Jones, T., Maclean, B. D. and Young, J. (1986) *The Islington Crime Survey: Crime, Victimisation and Policing in Inner-City London*. Aldershot: Gower.

Joseph, G. (1983) *Women at Work: The British Experience.* Oxford: Philip Allan.

Joshi, H. E. (1982) Secondary Workers in the Cycle, *Economics* 48.

Joshi, H. E. (1984) *Women's Participation in Paid Work: Further Analysis of the Women and Employment Survey*, DoE Research Paper (45). London: HMSO.

Jowell, R. and Witherspoon, S. (1985) *British Social Attitudes: The 1985 Report.* Aldershot: Gower.

Jowell, R., Witherspoon, S. and Brook, L. (1987) *British Social Attitudes: The 1987 Report.* Aldershot: Gower.

Karran, T. J. and Bochel, H. M. (1986) *The English County Elections 1985.* Dundee: University of Dundee Election Studies.

Kellner, P. (1980) Not a Defeat, a Disaster. *New Statesmen* 18 May.

Kelly, A. (1981) *The Missing Half: Girls and Science Education.* Manchester: University Press.

Kelly, L. (1987) The Continuum of Sexual Violence. In Hanmer and Maynard (1987).

Kelsall, R., Poole, A. and Kuhn, A. (1972) *Graduates: The Sociology of an Elite.* London: Methuen.

Kerr, E. (1979) Letter from the Chief Officer of the Council for National Academic Awards, London, to one of the contributors.

King, R. (1978) *All Things Bright and Beautiful.* Chichester: John Wiley.

Knight, I. (1984) *The Heights and Weights of Adults in Great Britain*, OPCS. London: HMSO.

Konopka, G. (1966) *The Adolescent Girl in Conflict.* Englewood Cliffs, NJ: Prentice Hall.

Kuhn, A. and Wolpe, A. M. (1978) *Feminism and Materialism: Women and Modes of Production.* London: Routledge & Kegan Paul.

Labour Force Survey for 1985: Preliminary Results (1986) *Employment Gazette*, May.

Labour Research Department (1987b) *EEC Equality Law Brings UK into Line, Labour Research* 76 (10).

La Fontaine, J. S. (1978) *Sex and Age as Principles of Social Differentiation.* London: Academic Press.

Land, H. (1969) *Large Families in London.* London: Bell & Sons.

Land, H. (1975) The Myth of the Male Breadwinner, *New Society*, October.

Land, H. (1976) Women: Supporters or Supported. In Barker and Allen (1976).

Land, H. (1986) Women and Children Last: Reform of Social Security. In Brenton and Ungerson (1986).

Lane, R. (1961) *Political Life*. New York: Free Press.

Layard, R., Piachaud, D. and Stewart, M. (1978) The Causes of Poverty. In Royal Commission on the Distribution of Wealth and Income (1978a).

Lee, G. et al. (1982) Jobs for White Girls; Jobs for Black Girls?. Unpublished Paper, BSA: Manchester University.

Lee, P. (1973) Male and Female Teachers in Elementary Schools: an Ecological Analysis, *Teachers College Record* 75 (1).

Leeds Trade Union and Community Resource and Information Centre (1983) *Sexual Harassment of Women at Work – A Study from West Yorkshire*. Leeds: TUCRIC.

Lees, S. (1986) *Losing Out: Sexuality and Adolescent Girls*. London: Hutchinson.

Leete, R. (1979a) Changing Marital Composition, OPCS, *Population Trends* (10). London: HMSO.

Leete, R. (1979b) Divorce and Remarriage: A Record Lineage Study, OPCS, *Population Trends* (16). London: HMSO.

Legal and General (1987) *The Price of a Wife*. London: Legal and General Press Office.

Le Grande, J. (1982) *The Strategy of Equality*. London: Allen and Unwin.

Le Lohe, M. J. (1976) Sex Discrimination and Under-representation of Women in Politics, *New Community*, Summer.

Leonard, A. (1987) *Judging Inequality – the Effectiveness of the Industrial Tribunal System in Sex Discrimination and Equal Pay Cases*. London: Cobden Trust.

Leonard, D. (1980) *Sex and Generation: a Study of Courtship and Weddings*. London.

Leonard, D. and Speakman, M. (1986) Women in the Family: Companions or Caretakers. In Beechey and Whitelegg (1986).

Lerner, G. (1986) *The Creation of Patriarchy*. Oxford: University Press.

Lewenhak, S. (1987) *The Revaluation of Women's Work*. London: Croom Helm.

Lewis, J. (1985) The Debate on Sex and Class, *New Left Review* (149).

Licht, B. G. and Dweck, C. S. (1983) Sex Differences in Achievement Orientations. In Marland (1983).

Ling, V. (1981) *Option Choices and Sex Stereotyping*. Unpublished Paper, Department of Social Science London: Polytechnic of the South Bank.

Littlejohn, G., Smart, B., Wakeford, J. and Yuval-Davis, N. (1978) *Power and the State*. London: Croom Helm.

Llewellyn, C. (1981) Occupational Mobility and the Use of the Comparative Method. In Roberts (1981).

Lobban, G. M. (1978) The Influence of the School on Sex Role Stereotyping. In Chetwynd and Harnett (1978).

Lockwood, D. (1986) Class, Status and Gender. In Crompton and Mann (1986).

London Feminist History Group (1983) *The Sexual Dynamics of History*. London: Pluto Press.

Loney, M., Boswell, D. and Clarke, J. (1983) *Social Policy and Social Welfare*. Milton Keynes: Open University Press.

Loney, M. et al. (1987) *The State or the Market*. London: Sage.

Long, P. (1984) *The Personnel Professionals: A Comparative Study of Male and Female Careers*. Institute of Personnel Management. London: IPM.

Lonsdale, S. (1985) *Work and Inequality*. London: Longman.

Lovenduski, J. and Hills, J. (1981) *The Politics of the Second Electorate: Women and Public Participation*. London: Routledge & Kegan Paul.

Low Pay Unit (1978) *The Part-time Trap*. London: LPU.

Low Pay Unit (1984) *Unequal Fringe Benefits*. London: LPU.

Lumley, R. (1973) *White-Collar Unionism in Britain*. London: Methuen.

Lupton, T. (1963) *On the Shop Floor*. Oxford: Pergamon Press.

Macaulay, R. K. S. (1978) The Myth of Female Superiority in Language, *Journal of Child Language* (5).

Maccoby, E. and Jacklin, C. (1974) *The Psychology of Sex Differences*, Vol. 1. Stanford, Cal.: University Press.

MacDonald, M. (1981) Schooling and the Reproduction of Class and Gender Relations. In Dale (1981).

MacFarlane, A. (1979) Child Deaths from Accidents: Place of Accident. *Population Trends*, 15.

MacFarlane, A. (1980) Official Statistics and Women's Health and Illness. In EOC (1980).

MacFarlane, A. and Mugford, M. (1984a) *Birth Counts: Statistics of Pregnancy and Childbirth Tables (a) Birth Counts*. National Perinatal Epidemiology Unit and OPCS London: HMSO.

MacKay, D. et al. (1971) *Labour Market under Different Employment Conditions*. London: Allen and Unwin.

McGoldrick, A. (1984) *Equal Treatment in Occupational Pension Schemes*. Manchester: EOC.

McIntosh, M. (1978) The State and the Oppression of Women. In Kuhn and Wolpe (1978).

McIntosh, A. (1980) Women at Work: A Survey of Employers, *Employment Gazette*, November.

McIntosh, M. (1984) The Family, Regulation and the Public Sphere. In McLennan, Held and Hall. (1984).

McKee, L. and Bell, C. (1983) Marital and Family Relations in Times of Male Unemployment. In Finegan, Gallie and Roberts (1983).

McKee, L. and Bell, C. (1984) His Unemployment: Her Problem – *The Domestic and Marital Consequences of Male Unemployment. Unpublished Paper BSA.*

Mackenzie, D. and Wajcman, J. (1985) *The Social Shaping of Technology.* Milton Keynes: Open University Press.

Mackie, L. and Pattullo, P. (1977) *Women at Work.* London: Tavistock.

McLennan, G., Held, D. and Hall, S. (1984) *State and Society in Contemporary Britain.* Cambridge: Polity Press.

MacLeod, M. and Saraga, E. (1987) How Men Are, *New Statesmen,* 13 July.

McNally, F. (1979) *Women for Hire: A Study of the Female Office Worker.* London: Macmillan.

McNally, J. and Shimmin, S. (1986) *Working for Men – Female Labour in Factories and the Home.* Brighton: Wheatsheaf Books.

MacPherson, A. and Willms, J. D. (1987) Equalisation and Improvement: Some Effects of Comprehensive Reorganisation in Scotland, *Sociology* 21 (4).

McRobbie, A. (1978a) *Jackie: An Ideology of Adolescent Femininity.* Paper Birmingham: CCCS.

McRobbie, A. (1978b) Working Class Girls and the Culture of Femininity. In CCCS (1978).

McRobbie, A. and Nava, M. (1984) *Gender and Generation.* London: Macmillan.

Maguire, M. (1980) The Impact of Burglary upon Victims, *British Journal of Criminology* 20 (3).

Maguire, M. and Corbett, C. (1987) *The Effects of Crime and the Work of Victims' Support Schemes.* London: Gower.

Mahoney, P. (1985) *Schools for the Boys: Co-Education Reassessed.* London: Routledge & Kegan Paul.

Main, B. (1984) *Women's Earnings: The Influence of Work Histories on Rates of Pay.* Edinburgh: University mimeo.

Maizels, J. (1970) *Adolescent Needs and the Transition from School to Work.* London: Athlone Press.

Mann, M. (1986) A Crisis in Stratification Theory? In Crompton and Mann (1986).

Manpower Services Commission (1985) *MSC Labour Quarterly Report,* November. Sheffield: MSC.

Marks, P. (1976) Femininity in the classroom. In Oakley and Mitchell (1976).

Marland, M. (1983) *Sex Differentiation in Schooling*. London: Heinemann.

Marriage and Divorce Statistics 1985 (1987) OPCS Series FM2 (12). London: HMSO.

Marsden, D. (1969) *Mothers Alone*. London: Allen Lane.

Marsh, A. (1979) *Women and Shiftwork: the Protective Legislation Survey Carried Out for the EOC*, OPCS. London: HMSO.

Marsh, D. (1971) Political Socialisation: The Implicit Assumptions Questioned, *British Journal of Political Science* 1.

Marshall, G. (1984) On the Sociology of Women's Unemployment, Its Neglect and Significance, *Sociological Review* 32 (2).

Martin, J. and Roberts, C. (1948a) Non-Working Women: Evidence from the 1980 Women and Employment Survey, *Employment Gazette* 92 (6).

Martin, J. and Roberts, C. (1984b) *Women and Employment: A Lifetime Perspective*. DoE/OPCS: HMSO.

Martin, R. (1985) Women and Redundancy: Some Case Studies in Manufacturing Industries, *Employment Gazette* 93 (5).

Maud Committee (1966–9) *Royal Commission on Local Government*. London: HMSO.

Mawby, R. (1980) Sex and Crime: The Results of a Self-Report Study, *British Journal of Sociology* 31 (4).

Maxfield, M. G. (1984) *Fear of Crime in England and Wales*. London: HMSO.

Maxwell, J. (1977) *Reading Progress from 8–15*. Slough: NFER.

Mayo, M. (1977) *Women in the Community*. London: Routledge & Kegan Paul.

Megarry, J. (1984) Introduction: Sex, Gender and Education. In Acker et al. (1984).

Mellors, C. (1978) *The British MP*. London: Saxon House.

Metcalf, A. and Humphries, M. (1985) *The Sexuality of Men*. London: Pluto Press.

Metcalf, B. A. (1985) *The Effects of Socialisation on Women's Management Careers*. Bradford: MCB University Press.

Meyenn, R. G. (1980) School Girl's Peer Groups. In Woods (1980).

Middleton, L. (1977) *Women in the Labour Market*. London: Croom Helm.

Milburn, J. F. (1976) *Women as Citizen: A Comparative View*. London: Sage.

Miliband, R., Panitch, L. and Saville, J. (1987) *The Socialist Register*. London: Merlin.

Miller, P. W. (1987) The Wage Effect of the Occupational Segregation of Women in Britain, *Economic Journal* 97.

Millett, K. (1969) *Sexual Politics*. New York: Doubleday.

Millman, V. and Weiner, G. (1987) Engendering Equal Opportunities: The Case of TVEI. In Gleeson (1987).

Millward, N. (1968) Family Status and Behaviour at Work, *Sociological Review* 16 (2).

Mitchell, J. (1971) *Women's Estate*. Harmondsworth: Penguin.

Mitchell, J. (1974) *Psychoanalysis and Feminism*. London: Allen & Unwin.

Monck, E. and Lomas, G. B. (1975) *The Employment and Socio-Economic Conditions of the Coloured Population*. London: Centre for Environmental Studies.

Morbidity Statistics from General Practice 1981–1982 (1986) OPCS Series MB5 (1). London: HMSO.

Morgan, J. P. (1975) *The House of Lords and the Labour Government 1964–70*. Oxford: Clarendon Press.

Morley, R. (1987) *Violence Against Women: Male Power and Social Control*. Brighton: Wheatsheaf Books.

Morris, A. (1981) *Women and Crime*, Cropwood Conference Series (18). Cambridge: Institute of Criminology.

Morris, J. N. (1975) *The Uses of Epidemiology*, 3rd edition. London: HMSO.

Morris, L. (1985) Renegotiation of the Domestic Division of Labour in the Context of Male Redundancy. In Newby et al. (1985).

Mort, F. (1987) *Dangerous Sexualities: Medico-Moral Politics in England since 1830*. London: Routledge & Kegan Paul.

Mortality Statistics 1984 (1985) OPCS Series DH2 (11). London: HMSO.

Mortality Statistics 1985a (1987) OPCS Series DH1 (17). London: HMSO.

Mortality Statistics 1985b (1987) OPCS Series DH3 (19). London: HMSO.

Mortality Statistics 1985c (1987) OPCS Series DH2 (12). London: HMSO.

Moulsdale, S. (1987) She Who Waits, Wins, *Times*, 31 August.

NACRO (1977) *Children and Young Persons in Custody: Report of a Working Party*. Chichester: Barry Rose.

NACRO (1980) *Women in the Penal System*. London: NACRO.

Nagel, I. (1981) Sex Differences in the Processing of Criminal Dependants. In Morris (1981).

NALGO (1980) *Equal Rights Survey*. London: NALGO.

NALGO (1982) *Report on Sexual Harassment*. Liverpool: NALGO, Equal Opportunities Working Party.

NALGO (1984) *Equal Rights Survey*. London: NALGO.

National Board for Prices and Incomes (1971) *The General*

Problems of Low Pay. London: HMSO.

National Labour Women's Advisory Committee (1971) *Women Candidates in the Labour Party*. London: Labour Party.

National Union of Teachers (1980a) *Once Upon a Myth*. London: NUT.

National Union of Teachers (1980b) *Promotion and the Woman Teacher*. London: NUT.

Neuberger, H. (1984) *From the Dole Queue to the Sweat Shop: Minimum Wages and Government Policy*. London: Low Pay Unit.

Newby, H. et al. (1985) *Restructuring Capital: Recession and Reorganisation in Industrial Society*. London: Macmillan.

New Earnings Survey 1986 (1986) DOE London: HMSO.

New Earnings Survey 1987 [1987] *DOE London: HMSO.*

Newman, N. (1976) *In Cash or Kind: The Place of Financial Assistance in Social Work*. Edinburgh: Edinburgh University.

Newson, J. and Newson, E. (1976) *Seven Years Old in the Home Environment*. London: Allen & Unwin.

Newsom Report (1963) *Report of the Central Advisory Council for Education (England) Half Our Future*, DES. London: HMSO.

Nicholson, J. (1984) *Men and Women: How Different Are They?*. Oxford: University Press.

Nissell, M. (1980) Women in Government Statistics: Basic Concepts and Assumptions. In EOC (1980a).

Nissell, M. and Bonnerjea, L. (1982) *Family Care of the Handicapped Elderly: Who Pays?*. London: PSI.

Norris, P. (1986) Conservative Attitudes in Recent British Elections, *Political Studies* 34.

Northam, J. (1982) Girls and Boys in Primary Maths. *Books in Education*.

Norwood Report (1943) *Curriculum and Examinations in the Secondary School*, Report of the Committee of the Secondary School Examinations Council. London: HMSO.

Novitski, E. (1977) *Human Genetics*. London: Collier-Macmillan.

NUPE (1986) *Equal Value – Equal Pay*. London: NUPE.

Oakley, A. (1972) *Sex, Gender and Society*. London: Temple Smith.

Oakley, A. (1974a) *Housewife*. Harmondsworth: Penguin Books.

Oakley, A. (1974b) *The Sociology of Housework*. Oxford: Martin Robertson.

Oakley, A. (1979) *From Here to Maternity: Becoming a Mother*. Harmondsworth: Penguin Books.

Oakley, A. (1980) *Women Confined: Towards a Sociology of Childbirth*. Oxford: Martin Robertson.

Oakley, A. (1981) *Subject Women*. Oxford: Martin Robertson.

Oakley, A. and Mitchell, J. (1976) *The Rights and Wrongs of Women*. Harmondsworth: Penguin Books.

O'Brien, M. (1981) *The Politics of Reproduction*. London: Routledge & Kegan Paul.

Occupational Mortality (1978) The Registrar General's Decennial Supplement for England and Wales 1970–2, Series DS1. London: HMSO.

Office of Manpower Economics (1972) *Report on the Equal Pay Act*. London: HMSO.

Okely, J. (1978) Privileged, Schooled and Finished, in Ardener (1978).

One Parent Family Factsheet. (1986) London: Family Policy Studies Centre.

Ormerord, P., Farmflo, C. and Rigg, J. (1983) *Time-Series Analysis of Female Labour Supply in the UK 1973–82*. London: HMSO.

Pahl, J. (1980) Patterns of Money Management within Marriage, *Journal of Social Policy* 9 (3).

Pahl, J. (1985) *Private Violence and Public Policy*. London: Routledge and Kegan Paul.

Pahl, R. (1984) *The Divisions of Labour*. Oxford: Basil Blackwell.

Parker, G. (1985) *With Due Care and Attention: A Review of Research on Informal Care*. London: Family Policy Studies Centre.

Parker, G. (1987) Making Ends Meet: Women, Credit and Debt. In Glendinning and Millar (1987).

Parkin, F. (1972) *Class Inequality and Political Order*. London: Paladin.

Parmar, P. (1982) Young Asian Women: A Critique of the Pathological Approach, *Multiracial Education* 9 (3).

Parsons, T. (1951) *The Social System*. New York: Free Press.

Peckham, A. (1985) *A Woman in Custody*. London: Fontana.

Penrose, L. S. (1973) *Outline of Human Genetics*, 3rd edition. London: Hutchinson.

People in Britain (1980) Census Research Unit, Dept of Geography University of Durham, OPCS and General Registry Office (Scotland). London: HMSO.

Phillips, A. and Taylor, B. (1980) Sex and Skill: Notes Towards a Feminist Economics, *Feminist Review*.

Phillips, A. (1984) *Hidden Hands – Women and Economic Policies*. London: Pluto Press.

Phillips, M. (1980) *The Divided House: Women at Westminster*. London: Sidgwick & Jackson.

Phizacklea, A. (1982) Migrant Workers and Wage Labour: The Case of West Indian Women in Britain. In West (1982b).

Phizacklea, A. (1983) *One-Way Ticket: Migration and Female*

Labour. London: Routledge & Kegan Paul.

Piachaud, D. (1984) *Round About Fifty Pounds a Week – The Time Costs of Children* London: Child Poverty Action Group.

Pollak, O. (1961) *The Criminality of Women*. New York: A. S. Barnes.

Pollert, A. (1981) *Girls, Wives and Factory Lives*. London: Macmillan.

Porter, M. (1982) Standing on the Edge: Working Class Housewives and the World of Work. In West (1982b).

Price, R. R. (1977) The Forgotten Female Offender, *Crime and Delinquency* 23.

Prison Statistics England and Wales 1985 (1986) Cmnd 9903. London: HMSO.

Pulzer, P. G. J. (1967) *Political Representation and Elections in Britain*. London: Allen & Unwin.

Purcell, K. (1979) Militancy and Acquiescence Amongst Women Workers. In Burman (1979).

Purcell, K. (1986) *The Changing Experience of Employment – Restructuring and Recession*. London: Macmillan.

Purvis, J. (1981) Women's life is essentially domestic; public life being confined to men. *History of Education*.

Purvis, J. (1984) The History of Domestic Subjects. In Goodson (1984).

Randall, V. (1982) *Women and Politics*. London: Macmillan.

Rapoport, R. and Rapoport, R. (1976) Dual Career Families Re-examined. London: Martin Robertson.

Rasmussen, J. S. (1983) Women's Role in Contemporary British Politics, *Parliamentary Affairs* 36.

Read, S. (1982) *Sexual Harassment at Work*. Feltham: Hamlyn.

Regional Trends. (1987) CSO, London: HMSO.

Registered Blind and Partially Sighted Persons at 31 March 1986 England (1987) DHSS A/F 86/7 GSS. London: HMSO.

Reid, I. (1981) *Social Class Differences in Britain*, 2nd edition. Oxford: Basil Blackwell.

Reid, I. (1986) *The Sociology of School and Education*. London: Fontana.

Reid, I. (1989) *Social Class Differences in Britain*, 3rd edition. London: Fontana.

Reid, I. and Wormald, E. (1982) *Sex Differences in Britain*. Oxford: Basil Blackwell.

Reiter, R. R. (1975) *Towards an Anthropology of Women*. London: Monthly Review Press.

Rendel, M. (1975) Men and Women in Higher Education, *Educational Review* 27 (3).

Report on the Work of the Prison Department (1986) Cm 11.

London: HMSO.

Richardson, H. J. (1969) *Adolescent Girls in Approved Schools.* London: Routledge & Kegan Paul.

Ridd, R. and Callaway, H. (1986) *Caught Up in Conflict – Women's Responses to Political Strife.* London: Macmillan.

Riley, K. (1981) Black Girls Speak Out for Themselves. *Multiracial Education* 10 (3).

Robbins Report (1963) *Higher Education.* Cmnd 2154. London: HMSO.

Roberti, P. (1974) The distribution of household income in the UK 1957–72, cited p. 40 *Royal Commission on the Distribution of Income and Wealth.* (1978a).

Roberts, H. (1981) *Doing Feminist Research.* London: Routledge & Kegan Paul.

Robinson Committee (1977) *Committee of Inquiry with the System of Remuneration of Members of Local Authorities.* London: HMSO.

Rose, M. (1976) Settlement, Removal and the Poor Law. In Fraser (1976).

Rose, R. (1974) *Electoral Behaviour: A Comparative Handbook.* New York: Free Press.

Rosenblum, K. (1975) Female Deviance and the Female Sex Role: A Preliminary Investigation, *British Journal of Sociology* 26 (2).

Rowbotham, S. (1979) The Trouble With Patriarchy, *New Statesman* 98.

Roweth, B. (1981) Enigma APR = QLR GPR, *The Guardian* 9 January.

Royal College of Psychiatrists (1986) *Alcohol: Our Favourite Drug.* London: RCP.

Royal Commission on the Distribution of Income and Wealth (1976) Report No 3: *Higher Incomes from Employment.* London: HMSO.
(1978a) Report No. 5, *The Causes of Poverty.*
(1978b) Report No. 6, *Lower Incomes.*
(1980) Report No. 8, *Fifth Report on the Standing Reference.*

Rubenstein, M. (1982) *Wage Discrimination – The Sex Discrimination Issue of the 1980s.* London: Francis Pinter.

Rubery, J. and Tarling, R. V. (1983) *Women in the Recession.* Cambridge: University Department of Applied Economics, Economic Reprint no. 68.

Rush, M. (1969) *The Selection of Parliamentary Candidates.* London: Nelson.

Sainsbury, S. (1970) *Registered as Disabled*, Occasional Papers on Social Administration (35). London: Bell.

Sapiro, V. (1983) *The Political Integration of Women*. Illinois: University Press.

Sarah, E., Scott, M. and Spender, D. (1980) The Education of Feminists: The Case for Single Sex Schools. In Spender and Sarah (1980).

Sarri, R. (1983) Gender Issues in Juvenile Justice, *Crime and Delinquency* 29 (3).

Sayers, J. (1984) Psychology and Gender Divisions. In Acker et al. (1984).

Sayers, J. (1985) *Sexual Contradictions: Psychology, Psychoanalysis and Feminism*. London: Tavistock.

Scase, R. and Goffee, R. (1980) *The Real World of the Small Business Owner*. London: Croom Helm.

Scase, R. and Goffee, R. (1982) *The Entrepreneurial Middle Class*. London: Croom Helm.

Science Policy Research Unit (1982) *Microelectronics and Women's Employment in Bitain*. Brighton: University of Sussex.

Scott A. (1986) Industrialisation, Gender, Segregation and Stratification Theory. In Crompton and Mann (1986).

Scott, H. (1984) *Working Your Way to the Bottom: The Feminisation of Poverty*. London: Pandora Press.

Scott, M. (1980) Teach Her a Lesson: Sexist Curriculum in Patriarchal Education. In Spender and Sarah (1980).

Scribbens, K. and Edwards, S. (1982) Women in Further Education. *Journal of National Association of Teachers in Further and Higher Education*. June.

Scruton, R. (1980) *The Meaning of Conservatism*. London: Macmillan.

Scruton, R. (1986) *Sexual Desire: A Philosophical Exploration*. London: Weidenfeld & Nicolson.

Secombe, W. (1974) The Housewife and her Labour under Capitalism, *New Left Review* (83).

Seddon, V. (1986) *The Cutting Edge – Women and the Pit Strike*. London: Lawrence & Wishart.

Sedley, A. and Benn, M. (1982) *Sexual Harassment at Work*. London: NCCL.

Seear, N. and Player, E. (1986) *Women in the Penal System*. London: Howard League.

Segal, L. (1983) *What is to be done about the Family?*. Harmondsworth: Penguin Books.

Segal, L. (1987) *Is the Future Female?*. London: Virago.

Shacklady-Smith, L. (1978) Sexist Assumptions and Female Delinquency. In Smart and Smart (1978).

Shaffer, G. (1987) Patterns of Work and Non Work Satisfaction,

Personnel Management 19 (7).

Sharpe, S. (1976) *Just Like a Girl*. Harmondsworth: Penguin Books.

Sharpe, S. (1984) *Double Identity – the Lives of Working Mothers*. Harmondsworth: Penguin Books.

Sheffield Women and Education Group (1978) *Sexism in Schools*. Sheffield: Sheffield Women and Education Group.

Sheldon, J. H. (1948) *The Social Medicine of Old Age*. Nuffield Foundation Oxford: Oxford Unversity Press.

Sherman, J. A. and Beck, E. T. (1979) *The Prism of Sex*. Wisconsin: University Press.

Shimmin, S., McNally, J. and Liff, S. (1981) Pressures on Women Engaged in Factory Work, *Employment Gazette* 89 (8).

Shipley, P. (1979) *Directory of Pressure Groups and Representative Associations*. Cambridge: Bowker.

Short Report (1985) *Community Care*. Report of the House of Commons Social Services Committee. London: HMSO.

Siebert, W. S. and Sloane, P. J. (1981) The Measurement of Sex and Marital Status: Discrimination at the Workplace, *Economica* 48 (1980).

Simon, G. (1981) *Women in Computing*. Manchester: National Computing Centre.

Simon, R. (1975) *Women and Crime*. Lexington, Mass.: Lexington Books.

Sjerps, M. (1985) *Scylla and Charibdis: The EEC Directive on Equal Treatment of Women and Men in Matters of Social Security* (directive 79/7/EEC). Unpublished Paper.

Skeggs, B. (1986) *Young Women and Further Education: A Case Study of Young Women's Experience of Caring Courses in a Local College*. Unpublished PhD thesis: University of Keele.

Sloane, P. J. and Siebert, W. S. (1980) Low Pay Amongst Women. In Sloane (1980).

Sloane, P. (1980) *Women and Low Pay*. London: Macmillan.

Sloane, P. (1985) Discrimination in the Labour Market: A Survey of Theory and Evidence. In Summer et al. (1985).

Smart, C. (1976) *Women, Crime and Criminology: A Feminist Critique*. London: Routledge & Kegan Paul.

Smart, B. and Smart, C. (1978) *Women, Sexuality and Social Control*. London: Routledge & Kegan Paul.

Smart, C. (1979) The New Female Criminal: Reality or Myth, *British Journal of Crimonology* 19 (1).

Smart, C. (1984) *The Ties that Bind: Law, Marriage and the Reproduction of Patriarchal Relations*. London: Routlege & Kegan Paul.

Smart, C. (1987a) Law and the Problem of Paternity. In Stanworth (1987).

Smart, C. (1987b) Securing the Family: Rhetoric and Policy in the Field of Social Security. In Loney (1987).

Smellie, K. B. (1968) *A History of Local Government*, 4th edition. London: Unwin.

Smith, D. (1979) A Sociology for Women. In Sherman and Beck (1979).

Smith, D. J. (1974) *Racial Disadvantage in Employment*. London: PEP.

Smith, D. J. (1976) *The Facts of Racial Disadvantage: A National Survey*. London: PEP.

Smith, D. J. (1981) *Unemployment and Racial Minorities*. London: PSI.

Social Security Consortium (1986) *Of Little Benefit: A Critical Guide to the Social Security Act 1986*. London: Social Security Consortium.

Social Security Statistics 1986 (1986), DHSS. London: HMSO.

Social Trends (4) (1974) Central Statistical Service. London: HMSO.

Social Trends (5) (1975) Central Statistical Service. London: HMSO.

Social Trends (15) (1985) Central Statistical Service. London: HMSO.

Social Trends (16) (1986) Central Statistical Service. London: HMSO.

Social Trends (17) (1987) Central Statistical Service. London: HMSO.

Sparks, J. (1986) Marital Condition Estimates 1971–85: A New Series, *Population Trends* (45). London: HMSO.

Sparks, R. F. (1971) *Local Prisons: The Crisis in the English Penal System*. London: Heinemann.

Spender, D. (1980) *Man Made Language*. London: Routledge & Kegan Paul.

Spender, D. (1982) *Invisible Women: The Schooling Standard*. London: Writers and Readers Co-operative.

Spender, D. and Sarah, E. (1981) *Learning to Lose: Sexism and Education*. London: The Women's Press.

Stacey, M. (1981) The Division of Labour Revisited, or Overcoming the Two Adams. In Abrams (1981).

Stacey, M. and Price, M. (1981) *Women, Power and Politics*. London: Tavistock.

Stageman, J. (1980) *Women in Trade Unions*. Hull: University of Hull, Adult Education Department Paper (6).

Stamp, P. (1985) Balance of Financial Power in Marriage: An Explanatory Study of Breadwinning Wives. *Sociological Review*, (33).

Stanley, L. and Wise, S. (1983) *Breaking Out: Feminist Consciousness and Feminist Research*. London: Routledge & Kegan Paul.

Stanko, E. (1985) *Intimate Intrusions: Women's Experience of Male Violence*. London: Routledge & Kegan Paul.

Stanworth, M. (1981) *Gender and Schooling: A Study of Sexual Divisions in the Classroom*, Pamphlet (7). London: WRRC.

Stanworth, M. (1983) *Gender and Schooling*. London: Hutchinson.

Stanworth, M. (1984) Women and Class Analysis: A Reply to John Goldthorpe, *Sociology* 18 (2).

Stanworth, M. (1987) *Reproductive Technologies*. Cambridge: Polity Press.

Stark, J. (1987) Health and Social Contacts, *The Health and Lifestyle Survey* (1987).

Start, K. B. and Wells, B. K. (1972) *The Trend of Reading Standards*. Slough: NFER.

Statistics of Education, School Leavers, England 1986 (1987) DES. London: HMSO.

Statistics of Education, Schools 1986 (1987) DES. London: HMSO.

Stead, J. (1987) *Never the Same Again – Women and the Miners' Strike*. London: The Women's Press.

Steed, M. (1975) Analysis of the Results. In Butler and Kavanagh (1975).

Steedman, J. (1983) *Examination Results in Mixed and Single Sex Schools: Findings from the National Child Development Study*. Manchester: EOC.

Stewart, M. B. and Greenhalgh, C. A. (1984) Work History Patterns and the Occupational Attainment of Women, *Economic Journal* 94.

Stradling, R. (1978) *The Political Awareness of the School Leaver*. London: Hansard Society.

Stratta, E. W. (1970) *The Education of Borstal Boys*. London: Routledge & Kegan Paul.

Strauss, M. (1981) *Behind Closed Doors: Violence in the American Family*. New York: Doubleday.

Strikes in Britain (1978) London: DoE Manpower Paper (15).

Sullerot, E. (1977) The Changing Roles of Men and Women in Europe. In *The Changing Roles of Men and Women in Modern Society: Functions, Rights and Responsibilities*, Vol. 2. New York: United Nations.

Summer, M. (1985) *Surveys of Economic Theory – Labour Economics*. London: Longman.

Summers, A. (1979) A Home from Home – Women's Philanthropic Work in the Nineteenth Century. In Burman (1979).

Summerfield, P. (1984) *Women Workers and the Second World War: Production and Patriarchy in Conflict*. London: Croom Helm.

Sutherland, M. B. (1981) *Sex Bias in Education*. Oxford: Basil Blackwell.

Szyszczak, E. (1987) The Future of Women's Rights: The Role of European Community Law. In Brenton and Ungerson (1987).

Taylor, N. (1986) *All in a Day's Work*. London: Lesbian Employment Rights.

Taylor, R. and Gilmore, A. (1982) *Current Trends in Gerontology*. Aldershot: Gower.

Teitelbaum, M. S. (1972) Factors Associated with the Sex Ratio in Human Populations. In Harrison and Boyce (1972).

Terry, R. M. (1970) Discrimination in the Handling of Juvenile Offenders by Social Control Agencies. In Garabedian and Gibbons (1970).

Thorne, B. (1982) *Rethinking the Family: Some Feminist Questions*. London: Longman.

Times Guide to the European Parliament (1984). London: Times Books.

Titmuss, R. M. (1963) *Essays on the Welfare State*. London: Allen & Unwin.

Titmuss, R. M. (1968) *Commitment to Welfare*. London: Allen & Unwin.

Todd, J. E. and Jones, L. N. (1972) *Matrimonial Property*. London: HMSO.

Townsend, P. (1963) *The Family Life of Old People*. Harmondsworth: Penguin Books.

Townsend, P. (1979) *Poverty in the United Kingdom*. Harmondsworth: Penguin Books.

Townsend, P. and Davidson, N. (1982) *Inequalities in Britain*. Harmondsworth: Penguin Books.

TUC (1978) *Homeworking*. London: TUC.

TUC (1980) *Women Workers 1980*. London: TUC.

TUC (1983) *Sexual Harassment at Work*. London: TUC.

TUC (1983c) *Working Women*. London: TUC.

TUC (1984) *Equality for Women Within Trade Unions*. London: TUC.

TUC (1985) *Homeworking: A TUC Statement*. London: TUC.

TUC (1986) *Contract Compliance and Equal Opportunities*. London: TUC.

TUCWA Report. Women and Training. London: TUC.

Turnbull, P. and Williams, G. (1974) Sex Differentials in Teachers' Pay, *Journal of the Royal Statistical Society* 137 (2).

Turner, B. S. (1986) *Citizenship and Capitalism*. London: Allen & Unwin.

Turner, H., Clack, G. and Roberts, G. (1967) *Labour Relations in the Motor Industry*. London: Allen & Unwin.

Unemployment and Ethnic Origin (1984) *Employment Gazette* 92 (6).

Unemployment Unit (1986) *Unemployment Unit Bulletin* (20).

Ungerson, C. (1983) Women and Caring: Skills, Tasks and Taboos. In Gamarnikov et al. (1983).

Ungerson, C. (1985) *Women and Social Policy*. London: Macmillan.

University Grants Committee, *University Statistics Vol. 1* (Students and Staff) 1981/82 1984/85. Cheltenham: Universities' Statistical Record.

USDAW (1987) *Women in USDAW Survey*. Manchester: Union of Shop, Distributive, and Allied Workers.

Vallance, E. (1979) *Women in the House*. London: Athlone Press.

Vallance, E. (1981) Women Candidates and Electoral Preference, *Politics* 1 (2).

Vallance, E. (1982a) Women in the House of Commons, *Political Studies* 29 (3).

Vallance, E. (1982b) Writing Women Back, *Political Studies* 30 (4).

Vallance, E. (1984) Women and Candidates in the 1983 General Election, *Parliamentary Affairs* 37 (3).

Vallance, E. and Davis, E. (1985) *Women of Europe*. Cambridge: University Press.

Vaz, E. W. (1967) *Middle Class Juvenile Delinquency*. New York: Harper Adamson.

Verba, S., Nie, N. H. and Kim, J. O. (1978) *Participation and Political Equality*. Cambridge: University Press.

Wainwright, H. (1978) Women and the Division of Labour. In Abrams (1978).

Walby, S. (1983) Patriarchal Structures: The Case of Unemployment. In Gamarnikov (1983).

Walby, S. (1985) *Patriarchy at Work*. Cambridge: Polity Press.

Walby, S. (1986) Gender, Class and Stratification. In Crompton and Mann (1986).

Walczak, Y. (1987) *He and She: Men in the Eighties*. London: Croom Helm.

Walker, A. (1982) *Community Care*. Oxford: Basil Blackwell and Martin Robertson.

Walker, N. (1973) *Crime and Punishment in Britain*. Edinburgh: University of Edinburgh Press.

Walker, S. and Barton, L. (1983) *Gender, Class and Education.* New York: The Falmer Press.

Walkedine, V. (1981) Sex, Power and Pedagogy, *Screen Education* (38).

Wallace, J. (1984) *Part-Time Employment and Sex Discrimination in Great Britain.* London: DoE.

Waller, I. and Okihiro, N. (1978) *Burglary: The Victim and the Crime.* Toronto: University of Toronto Press.

Walters, V. (1980) *Class Inequality and Health Care.* London: Croom Helm.

Ward, M. (1979) *Mathematics and the Ten Year Old,* Schools Council Working Paper (61). London: Evans/Methuen.

Webb, D. (1984) More on Gender and Justice, *Sociology* 18 (3).

Weeks, J. (1981) *Sex, Politics and Society.* London: Longman, p. 10.

Weeks, J. (1986) *Sexuality.* London: Ellis Horwood and Tavistock.

Weiner, G. (1985) *Just a Bunch of Girls.* Milton Keynes: Open University Press.

Weiner, G. and Arnot, M. (1987) *Gender Under Scrutiny: New Enquiries in Education.* Milton Keynes: Open University Press.

Weitz, S. (1977) *Sex Roles.* Oxford: University Press.

Welfare Rights Bulletin. (1987) London: Child Poverty Action group.

Wells, N. (1981) *Suicide and Deliberate Self-Harm.* London: Office of Health Economics.

Wells, N. (1987) *Women's Health Today.* London: Office of Health Economics.

West, D. J. (1980) *Sex Offenders in the Criminal Justice System.* Cambridge: University Press.

West, J. (1982a) New Technology and Women's Office Work. In West (1982b).

West, J. (1982b) *Work, Women and the Labour Market.* London: Routledge & Kegan Paul.

Whitehead, M. (1987) *The Health Divide: Inequalities in Health in the 1980's.* London: Health Education Council.

Whitelegg, E. (1982) *The Changing Experience of Women.* Oxford: Martin Robertson.

Wickham, A. (1982) The State and Training Programmes for Women. In Whitelegg et al. (1982).

Wickham, A. (1986) *Women and Training.* Milton Keynes: Open University Press.

Wicks, M. (1987) *Social Change and the Family: Capacity to Care.* In Allen et al. (1987).

Wild, R. and Hill, A. (1970) *Women in the Factory*. London: Institute of Personnel Management.

Wiles, P. (1970) Criminal Statistics and Sociological Explanations of Crime. In Wiles and Carson (1970).

Wiles, P. and Carson W. (1970) *Crime and Delinquency in Britain*. London: Martin Robertson.

Wilkin, D. (1979) *Caring for the Mentally Handicapped Child*. London: Croom Helm.

Williamson, P. (1981) Careers of Graduates, *Employment Gazette* 89 (5).

Willis, P. (1977) *Learning to Labour: How Working Class Kids get Working Class Jobs*. Farnborough: Saxon House.

Willms, J. D. and Kerr, P. (1987) Changes in Sex Differences in Scottish Examination Results, *Journal of Early Adolescence*, June.

Wilson, D. (1978) Sexual Codes and Conduct. In Smart and Smart (1978).

Wilson, E. (1977) *Women and the Welfare State*. London: Tavistock.

Wilson, E. (1983) *What is to be Done about Violence Against Women?*. Harmondsworth: Penguin Books.

Wilson, E. (1987) Thatcherism and Women. In Miliband, Panitch and Saville (1987).

Wilson, J. (1983) The Professionals: A Study of Women in Parliament, *Political Science* 35 (2).

Winship, J. (1978) A Woman's World: 'Woman' – an Ideology of Femininity. In CCCS (1978).

Wise, N. B. (1967) Juvenile Delinquency among Middle-Class Girls. In Vaz (1967).

Wolfgang, M. E. (1958) *Patterns in Criminal Homicide* Philadelphia: University of Pennsylvania Press.

Wolpe, A. M. (1975) The Official Ideology of Girl's Education. In Flude and Ahier (1975).

Wolpe, A. M. (1977) *Some Processes in Sexist Education*. London: WRRC.

Wolpe, A. M. (1978) Education and the Sexual Division of Labour. In Kuhn and Wolpe (1978).

Wolpe, A. M. (1987) Sex in Schools, *Feminist Review* 27.

Wolpe, A. M. and Donald, J. (1983) *Is There Anyone Here From Education?*. London: Pluto Press.

Women and Training Project Report (1983). Cambridge: Cambridge Research Cooperative Ltd.

Women and Work: A Review (1975) DOE. London: HMSO.

Women of Europe: Supplement 5 (1980). Brussels: Commission of the European Communities.

Women's Own (1975) How Inflation Is Hitting Our Homes. London: IPC.

Women's Study Group – CCCS (1978) *Women Take Issue.* London: Hutchinson.

Wood, J. (1984) Groping Towards Sexism: Boys' Sex Talk. In McRobbie and Nava (1984).

Wood, S. (1981) Redundancy and Female Employment, *Sociological Review* 29 (4).

Wood, S. (1982) *The Degradation of Work? Skill, Deskilling and the Labour Process.* London: Hutchinson.

Woods, P. (1980) *Pupil Strategies: Explorations in the Sociology of the School.* London: Croom Helm.

Work Research Unit (1985) *Women and Quality of Working Life,* WRU Information Service (34). London: ACAS.

Wormald, E. (1983) Apolitical Women: The Myth of Early Socialisation, *International Journal of Political Education* 6.

Wrench, J. and Stanley, N. (1983) *Intrusion into the Night: A Trend towards Nightwork?.* Unpublished paper, BSA Conference.

Wright, C. (1987) The Relations Between Teachers and Afro-Caribbean Pupils. In Weiner and Arnot (1987).

Wright, F. (1983) Single Careers: Employment, Housework and Caring. In Finch and Groves (1983a).

Wybrow, P. (1987) Teeside Polytechnic: Unpublished research conducted for Thames Television; news item *News on Sunday* 19 July.

Yeandle, S. (1984) *Women's Working Lives: Patterns and Strategies.* London: Tavistock.

Young, M. (1952) Distribution of Income within the Family, *British Journal of Sociology* 3.

Young, M. (1974) *Poverty Report.* London: Temple Smith.

Young, M. and Willmott, P. (1973) *The Symmetrical Family.* London: Routledge & Kegan Paul.

Young, M. and Syson, L. (1974) Bethnal Green. In Young (1974).

Zabalza, A. and Arrufat, J. (1983) *Wage Differentials between Married Men and Married Women in Great Britain: The Depreciation Effect of Non-Participation.* London: London School of Economics Discussion Paper (151).

Zabalza, A. and Tzannatos, Z. (1985a) The Effects of Britain's Anti-Discriminatory Legislation on Relative Pay and Employment, *Economic Journal* 95.

Zabalza, A. and Tzannatos, Z. (1985b) *Women and Equal Pay: The Effects of Legislation on Female Employment and Wages.*

Cambridge: University Press.

Zweig, F. (1961) *The Worker in an Affluent Society*. London: Heinemann.

Subject index

Author index

313